THE ENDS OF THE EARTH

Robert D. Kaplan is a contributing editor of the *Atlantic Monthly* and the author of four previous books on travel and foreign affairs, including *Balkan Ghosts: A Journey Through History*, chosen by the *New York Times Book Review* as one of the best books of 1993. His articles of the 1980s and early 1990s were the first by an American writer to warn of the coming cataclysm in the Balkans. His most recent book, *The Arabists*, was chosen by the *New York Times* as a 'notable book' of 1993. His two previous books were set in Afghanistan and the Horn of Africa. He has travelled in nearly seventy countries and now lives outside Washington DC.

THE
ENDS
OF THE
EARTH

◙ ◙ ◙

*A Journey at the Dawn
of the 21st Century*

ROBERT D. KAPLAN

PAPERMAC

First published 1996 by Random House, Inc., New York

First published in Great Britain 1997 by Papermac

This edition published in Great Britain 1997 by Papermac
an imprint of Macmillan Publishers Ltd
25 Eccleston Place, London SW1W 9NF
and Basingstoke

Associated companies throughout the world

ISBN 0 333 64255 4

Grateful acknowledgement is made to the following for permission to reprint previously
published material: DOVER PUBLICATIONS, INC.: Excerpts from *Wanderings in West Africa* by
Richard Burton. Reprinted by permission of Dover Publications, Inc. HARCOURT BRACE &
COMPANY: Excerpt from *Shah of Shahs* by Ryszard Kapuscinski. Copyright © 1982 by Ryszard
Kapuscinski. English translation copyright © 1985 by Harcourt Brace & Company. Reprinted
by permission of the publisher. HARPERCOLLINS PUBLISHERS: Excerpt from *Ecocide in the USSR*
by Murray Feshbach. Copyright © 1982 by Murray Feshbach and Alfred Friendly, Jr.
Reprinted by permission of HarperCollins Publishers. LITTLE, BROWN AND COMPANY: Excerpt
from *Journeying* by Nikos Kazantzakis, published by Little, Brown and Company. Reprinted
by permission. THE OCTAGON PRESS LTD.: Excerpt from *The Teachings of Hafiz*. Reprinted by
permission of The Octagon Press Ltd., London. PRINCETON UNIVERSITY PRESS: Ten lines from
"Growing in Spirit" from *Collected Poems: C. P. Cavafy* edited by Edmund Keeley and Philip
Sherrard (Princeton University Press, 1975; revised edition, 1992). Copyright © 1975
by Edmund Keeley and Philip Sherrard. Reprinted by permission of Princeton University
Press. YALE UNIVERSITY PRESS: Excerpt from *Roots of Revolution* by Nikki R. Keddie and Richard
Yann (Yale University Press, 1981). Copyright © 1981 Yale University. Reprinted by
permission of Yale University Press.

1 3 5 7 9 8 6 4 2

A CIP catalogue record for this book is available from
the British Library.

Printed and bound in Great Britain by
Mackays of Chatham plc, Chatham, Kent

To Dick Hoagland, Ernest Latham, Kiki Munshi
and Graham Miller:
three diplomats and a relief worker

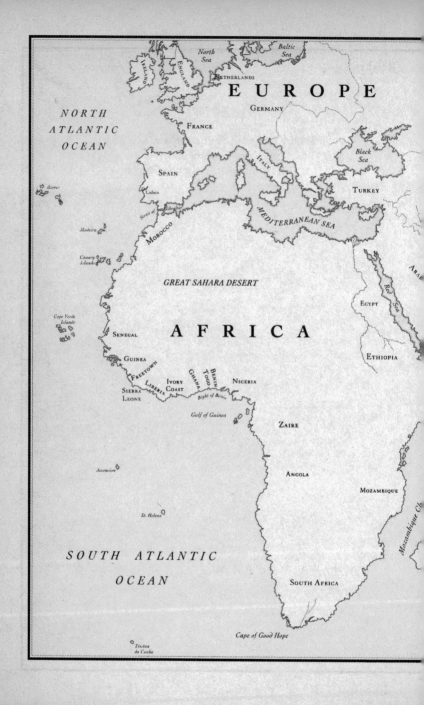

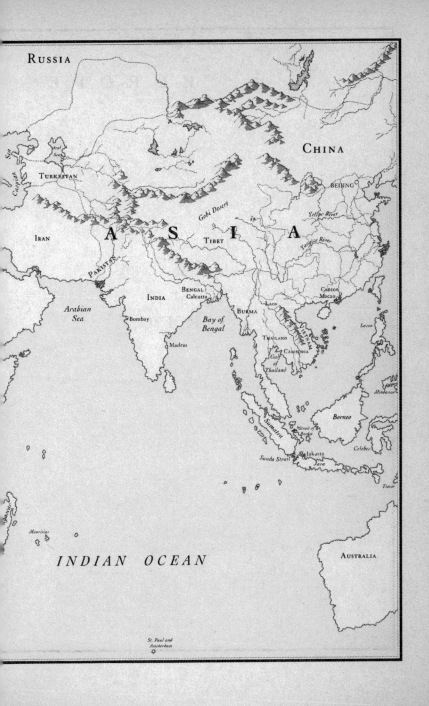

His face is turned towards the past. Where we perceive a chain of events, he sees one single catastrophe which keeps piling wreckage upon wreckage and hurls it in front of his feet. The angel would like to stay, awaken the dead, and make whole what has been smashed. But a storm is blowing from Paradise; it has got caught in his wings with such violence that the angel can no longer close them. This storm irresistibly propels him into the future to which his back is turned, while the pile of debris before him grows skyward. This storm is what we call progress.

—WALTER BENJAMIN, in *Illuminations*
writing about the Angel of History

The good geographer is a philosopher.

—CARLETON S. COON, SR.,
Caravan: The Story of the Middle East

Strife is the origin of everything.

—HERACLITUS

We all dwell in one country, O stranger, the world.

—MELEAGER

PREFACE

JACK LONDON WRITES in *Martin Eden* that "a reporter's work is all hack from morning till night . . . it is a whirlwind life, the life of the moment, with neither past nor future . . ." I have attempted to escape this restriction. In *Balkan Ghosts*, an earlier book of mine, completed before the outbreak of the war in Yugoslavia, I tried to see the present in terms of a difficult and bloody past. In *The Ends of the Earth*, I have tried to see the present in terms of the future, on the whole an ominous one for a significant part of the third world.

This is a travel book in the style of John Gunther, not Paul Theroux. It is a premodern generalist's book that mixes history and other subjects in with travel. It is concrete to the extent that my ideas arise from personal experience. It is subjective, given that no two travelers interpret a people and landscape in the same way. It is idiosyncratic: I spent relatively more time in Iran than in other places, and the text reflects that. Nor—as a record of one person's travels—is it comprehensive: India and China receive less coverage than they deserve, South America is missing, and so on. From the standpoint of many backpackers and relief workers, my journey was not arduous. Think of it as a brief romp through a swath of the globe, in which I try to give personal meaning to the kinds of issues raised in Paul Kennedy's *Preparing for the Twenty-first Century*.

Though many landscapes are increasingly sullied, that need not spell the decline of travel writing. It does mean that travel writing must confront the real world, slums and all, rather than escape into an airbrushed version of a more rustic past. This book, which folds international studies into a travelogue, is an attempt at that.

CONTENTS

PART I

◎ ◎ ◎

West Africa

Back to the Dawn?

Fraudulent identity cards; fake policemen dressed in official uniform; army troops complicit with gangs of thieves and bandits; forged enrollment for exams; illegal withdrawal of money orders; fake banknotes; the circulation and sale of falsified school reports, medical certificates and damaged commodities: all of this is not only an expression of frenetic trafficking and "arranging." It is also a manifestation of the fact that, here, things no longer exist without their parallel.

—ACHILLE MBEMBE AND JANET ROITMAN,
writing about 1990s Cameroon

Africa makes the last circle, navel of the world . . .

—JEAN-PAUL SARTRE

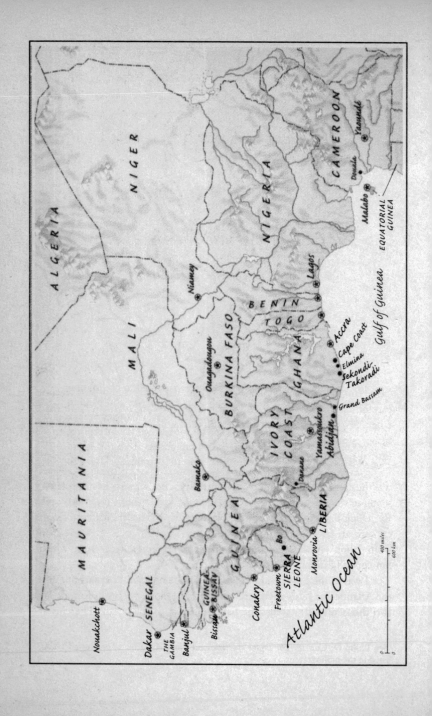

I

◎ ◎ ◎

An Unsentimental Journey

"THE THIEVES ARE very violent here. They will cut you up if you are not careful," warned the Liberian woman in fine, lilting English. Night had fallen. My protectress gripped my arm, then walked me to the hotel. I felt her eyes on me—two welcoming planets appearing out of the void. The little feet of a baby, wrapped snugly around her back, bobbed at her sides.

Here, on this road of decayed and oxidized red rock called laterite, was the earth without subtlety: an oppressively hot, in ways hostile, planet; seething with fecundity and—it seemed to a Northerner—too much of it. But tropical abundance is not the blessing many travelers believe: Tropical soils are not that fertile, and quick growth by no means releases man from labor.[1] At the equator nature is a terrifying face from which humankind cannot separate itself.

I was in the lower end of that great bulge of Africa that juts out into the Atlantic, far from anywhere familiar. The closest point in Europe lay two thousand miles across the Sahara Desert to the north. The closest

---

[1] See Philip D. Curtin's *The Image of Africa* and Pierre Gourou's *The Tropical World*, listed in the bibliography.

point in South America lay almost twenty-five hundred miles across the ocean to the southwest. North America was five thousand miles to the northwest. The town of Danane, in the western Ivory Coast, near the borders of Liberia and Guinea, is a good place from which to begin a tour of the earth at the end of the twentieth century, a time when politics are increasingly shaped by the physical environment. A brief moment marked by the Industrial Revolution, which gave humankind a chance to defend itself somewhat from nature, may be closing.[2] Population growth, along with migration that is tied to soil degradation, means we won't hereafter be able to control the spread of disease as we have been doing for the past 150 years. Viruses luxuriating in Africa may constitute a basic risk to humanity.[3] In the twenty-first century, Africa, like Europe in the twentieth, will have to be confronted. In my rucksack I carried a letter from a friend, a U.S. diplomat in the region. He writes:

"The greatest threat to our value system comes from Africa. Can we continue to believe in universal principles as Africa declines to levels better described by Dante than by development economists? Our domestic attitudes on race and ethnicity suffer as Africa becomes a continent-wide 'Wreck of the Medusa.' "[4]

◎　　　◎　　　◎

FROM THE PERSPECTIVE of space, where there is no gravity, there is also no up or down. The maps of the world that show north as up are not necessarily objective. Scan the map with the South Pole on top and you see the world entirely differently. The Mediterranean basin is no longer the focal point, lost, as it is, near the bottom of the globe. North America loses its continental width—and thus its majesty—as it narrows northward into the atrophied limb of Central America toward the center of your field of vision. South America and Africa stand out. But South America keeps narrowing toward the Antarctic nothingness at the top, insufficiently connected to other continental bodies.

[2] See Deudney's "Bringing Nature Back In," a University of Pennsylvania monograph, listed in the bibliography.
[3] I thank Dr. Martin Keller, of Ohio State University, an epidemiologist and specialist on tropical disease, for his insights.
[4] The diplomat was referring to an early-nineteenth-century French shipwreck, whose survivors were ravaged by starvation. The wreck was immortalized by the macabre painting of Jean-Louis-André-Théodore Géricault, *The Raft of the Medusa*, completed in 1819.

Africa, alas, is the inescapable center: Equidistant between the South and North poles, lying flat across the equator, with the earth's warmest climate, hospitable to the emergence of life in countless forms—three quarters of its surface lies within the tropics. Africa looms large in the middle of the vision field, connected to Eurasia through the Middle East. This map, with south at the top, shows why humankind emerged in Africa, why it was from Africa that our species may have begun the settlement of the planet.[5] Africa is the mother continent to which we all ultimately belong, from where human beings acquired their deepest genetic traits.[6] "We are all Africans under the skin," says anthropologist Christopher Stringer.[7] Africa is nature writ large. As Ben Okri, a Nigerian novelist and poet, writes:

> We are the miracles that God made
> To taste the bitter fruit of Time.[8]

"This hotel is good," the Liberian woman told me. "They lock the gate at night."

◎   ◎   ◎

"CARTOGRAPHY DEPLOYS ITS vocabulary . . . so that it embodies a systematic social inequality. The distinctions of class and power are engineered, reified and legitimated in the map. . . . The rule seems to be 'the more powerful, the more prominent.' To those who have strength in the world shall be added the strength of the map," writes the late University of Chicago geographer J. Brian Harley.[9] Maps, so seemingly objective, are actually propaganda. They represent the lowest common denominator of the conventional wisdom.

But what if the conventional wisdom is wrong?

What if the Mediterranean basin is no longer the center of civilization?

What if there are really not fifty-odd nations in Africa as the maps suggest—

[5]The story of our ancestors' migration is constantly being challenged by new discoveries. See Michael D. Lemonick's "How Man Began," listed in the bibliography.
[6]See *The African Experience*, by Roland Oliver, listed in the bibliography.
[7]This quote is taken from Stringer's interview with author Pat Shipman for her book *The Evolution of Racism*.
[8]From "An African Elegy." See Okri in the bibliography.
[9]This quote is taken from an editorial in the journal *Political Geography*. See the bibliography.

what if there are only six, or seven, or eight real nations on that continent? Or, instead of nations, several hundred tribal entities? What if the distance between the hotel in Danane to which I had just been directed and a town over the border in Guinea or Liberia, though only forty miles on the map, was really greater in terms of time than the distance between New York and St. Louis? What if the shantytowns and bidonvilles sprouting up around the globe that do not appear on any maps are far more important to the future of civilization than many of the downtowns and prosperous suburbs that do appear on maps? What if the territory held by guerrilla armies and urban mafias—territory that is never shown on maps—is more significant than the territory claimed by many recognized states? What if Africa is even farther away from North America and Europe than the maps indicate, but more important to our past and future than Europe or North America?

The first act of geography is measurement.[10] I have tried to learn by actual travel and experience just how far places are from each other, where the borders really are and where they aren't, where the real terra incognita is. It was Claudius Ptolemy, the second century A.D. Greek geographer, who first cautioned against exaggerating the importance of Europe and the West on the map. Thus, to map the earth as the twenty-first century approaches, I would begin in Africa, the birthplace of humankind. I would, more or less, trace our species' likely trajectory of planetary settlement from Africa across the Near East into the Indian subcontinent and, ultimately, Southeast Asia.[11]

I thought of my wanderings in almost geological terms. As John McPhee set out to do in *Basin and Range*—mapping "deep time" in a journey that mocked the "unnatural subdivision[s] of the globe . . . framed in straight lines"—I wanted to map the future, perhaps the "deep future," by ignoring what was legally and officially there and, instead, touching, feeling, and smelling what was really *there*.

I had many questions in my head, and many plans. The nineteenth-century French geographer Élisée Reclus writes: "Each period in the life of mankind corresponds to a change in its environment. It is the inequal-

[10]See *Mapping the Next Millennium*, by Stephen S. Hall, listed in the bibliography.
[11]I skipped East Africa—the specific birthplace of human beings—though I traveled through that region on previous reporting assignments. East Africa's situation is, in many places, no better than West Africa's. Birthrates there, while they have come down, are among the highest in the world, even as the squeeze on agricultural land continues apace. Tribal conflict in Kenya, resulting in thousands of internal refugees, has been the upshot. Rwanda and Burundi have been racked by violence between the Hutu and Tutsi ethnic groups.

ity of planetary traits that created the diversity of human history." My goal was to see humanity in each locale as literally an outgrowth of the terrain and climate in which it was fated to live.

For instance, even as Africa's geography was conducive to humanity's emergence, it may not have been conducive to its further development. Though Africa is the second largest continent, with an area five times that of Europe, its coastline is little more than a quarter as long. Moreover, this coastline, south of the Sahara, lacks many good natural harbors.[12] Few of tropical Africa's rivers are navigable from the sea, while the Sahara hindered human contact from the north. Thus Africa has been relatively isolated from the rest of the world.

Moreover, many of the most debilitating diseases flourish mainly in tropical climates. Some 10 million square miles of Africa (an area larger than the United States) are infested with tsetse-fly diseases. It is almost certainly not accidental that Africa is both the poorest and hottest region of the world.[13]

The ancient Greek historians asked: Why the differences between peoples?[14] It is still a fair question. On the other hand, so as not to exaggerate those differences, I had to bear in mind that it was Terence, an African who lived in ancient Rome, who said, "I am a man. I regard nothing that is human as alien to me."

◎   ◎   ◎

LIZARDS CRAWLED UNDER the door of my room in my hotel in Danane, and up the scabby walls. Mosquitoes circled the lightbulb and buzzed around my neck. I looked at the floor. Missing tiles exposed the red laterite earth.

The room had no windows. The air conditioner made a loud humming noise, with a background rattle like pouring rain. I couldn't sleep. What was I doing here?

I thought I was here for answers.

◎   ◎   ◎

AT THE BEGINNING of my journey, I was naive. I didn't yet know that answers vanish as one continues to travel, that there is only further complexity, that there are still more interrelationships, and more questions.

[12]The East African ports that traded vigorously with Arabia and India are an exception.
[13]See Deudney, as well as Andrew M. Kamarck's *The Tropics and Economic Development*, listed in the bibliography.
[14]See *Geography and the Human Spirit*, by Anne Buttimer, listed in the bibliography.

I had more than fifteen years as a foreign correspondent behind me, and had learned that when you write a magazine article, you try to fit observations into a theory, or "paradigm," so that each article will make sense. Without such paradigms or theories—however imperfect—debate is impossible. As Francis Bacon writes, "Truth emerges more readily from error than from confusion." This is why most of science is a mop-up operation: A paradigm is investigated until it is found to be so riddled with imperfections that it is discounted and another paradigm emerges, to undergo similar scrutiny.[15]

My initial goal was to find a paradigm for understanding the world in the early decades of the twenty-first century. Scholars have been writing more and more about the corrosive effects of overpopulation and environmental degradation in the third world, while journalists cover an increasing array of ethnic conflicts that don't configure with state borders. Of the eighty wars since 1945, only twenty-eight have taken the traditional form of fighting between regular armies of two or more states. Forty-six were civil wars or guerrilla insurgencies. Former UN secretary-general Perez de Cuellar called this the "new anarchy."[16]

The fighting in the Balkans, in the Caucasus, and elsewhere suggested that this anarchic trend was proliferating. In 1993, forty-two countries were immersed in major conflicts and thirty-seven others experienced lesser forms of political violence: Sixty-five of these seventy-nine countries were in the developing world.[17] In addition, improved global communications were bringing different cultures into closer contact, making us uncomfortably aware that we were anything but equal regarding the production of exportable, material wealth. If someone could write openly about culture, I thought, and interlock it with those other issues, a general state-of-the-world might emerge.

Africa was potent terrain for my enterprise. It was without a convincing paradigm. For decades, those sympathetic to Africa had been providing

[15]See Thomas S. Kuhn's *The Structure of Scientific Revolutions*, listed in the bibliography.
[16]See Georgie Anne Geyer's article "Our Disintegrating World: The Menace of Global Anarchy," in the *1985 Encyclopædia Britannica Book of the Year*. Geyer saw this trend despite the fog of the Cold War. Her piece was forgotten, as are many that report a trend too early. I first heard of her article after my own article appeared in *The Atlantic Monthly*.
[17]Though these statistics come from the 1994 UN Human Development Report, I thank Jonathan Moore for first pointing them out in his monograph *Morality and Interdependence*.

rationalizations for material poverty and hopeful scenarios for the future while living standards continued to plummet and wars proliferated. The reasons provided for this mess—"colonialism," "the evil international economic system," Africa's "corrupt elites," its "patriarchal society," and so on—could also apply to other third world regions that were daily pulling ahead of Africa economically: Africa's vital statistics concerning population increase, living standards, and violence were the worst on the planet.

An editor appropriately titled an article I wrote on West Africa and the third world "The Coming Anarchy." It ran in *The Atlantic Monthly* in February 1994. The ethnic genocide in Rwanda, in east-central Africa, coming as it did a few months later, gave the article a gruesome currency.

My problem, though, was that I kept traveling, an activity that inevitably complicated my paradigm. In 1994, immediately after this article was published, I began a journey by land—roughly speaking—from Egypt to Cambodia: through the Near East, Central Asia, the Indian subcontinent, and Southeast Asia. While "The Coming Anarchy" was being debated at home, I was already engaged in the mop-up operation. This mop-up operation did not so much disprove "The Coming Anarchy" as it showed me how culture, politics, geography, history, and economics were inextricable. Rather than a grand theory, the best I could now hope for was a better appreciation of these interrelationships.

At the end of my journey I still had a theory, but it was more refined. And I was less dogmatic about it. For instance, I had originally thought of population in neo-Malthusian terms, according to which state failure might be a direct result of overpopulation. By the end of my journey I understand that rapid population growth was just one of several agitating forces—a force that cultural ingenuity might sidestep. By the time I reached Cambodia, I realized that while I could still identify the destructive powers that I had seen in Africa, I understood their root causes less than I thought I did.

Writing these words now, I am sure of one thing: that even as some nations, including the United States, may be retreating into a fortresslike nationalism, this is only a temporary stage before the world tide of population and poverty forces us all to realize that we inhabit one increasingly small and crowded earth. The benighted part of the planet near the Liberian border where I, an American citizen, had found myself on that lonely night would, ultimately—on some not so distant morrow—become part of my planetary *home*.

◎   ◎   ◎

I DID NOT choose the path of my wanderings by accident. I recalled a vision propounded to me by Thomas F. Homer-Dixon, head of the Peace and Conflict Studies Program at the University of Toronto. "Think of a stretch limo in the potholed streets of New York City, where homeless beggars live. Inside the limo are the air-conditioned postindustrial regions of North America, Europe, the Pacific Rim, parts of Latin America, and a few other spots, with their trade summitry and computer-information highways. Outside is the rest of mankind, going in a completely different direction."

I wanted to wander outside the stretch limo, particularly in cities and large towns. According to the National Academy of Sciences, as much as 95 percent of all the new births in our world occur in the poorest countries, while more than half of those occur in urban and urbanizing areas.[18] Before independence, the average capital in Africa had about fifty thousand inhabitants. But during the first thirty years of independence, when overall population more than doubled in Africa, that of most capital cities multiplied by ten. By the early 1980s, Lagos and Kinshasa each had populations of around 3 million, while Addis Ababa, Abidjan, Accra, Ibadan, Khartoum, and Johannesburg all had over 1 million. Dakar, Nairobi, Dar es Salaam, Harare, and Luanda were not far behind. By 1990 one quarter of all Africans lived in towns; by the end of the century the proportion will have risen to one half.[19]

To me, economic success stories like Japan and Singapore seemed secondary. Most of the new children being born in the world are growing up in places like West Africa, not in Japan or Singapore. Even with declining fertility rates, sub-Saharan Africa's population will likely double in less than three decades: Japan's population won't double in two centuries.

Lying in bed in that hotel in Danane, I even considered the possibility that a second Cold War might be upon us—a protracted struggle between ourselves and the demons of crime, population pressure, environmental degradation, disease, and culture conflict. For those who still didn't believe that we live in revolutionary times, I had in mind a travel document that would serve as shock therapy.

[18]See Cheryl Simon Silver's *One Earth One Future*, listed in the bibliography.
[19]See Roland Oliver's *The African Experience*, listed in the bibliography.

◎　　　◎　　　◎

IN 1768, LAURENCE Sterne, an English parson, published *A Sentimental Journey: Through France and Italy*. The opposite sex uppermost in his mind, Sterne described his trip thus: "Tis a quiet journey of the heart in pursuit of NATURE, and those affections which arise out of her." Sterne's sentimental preference for French women caused him to be charitable concerning the national character: "The Bourbon is by no means a cruel race: they may be misled like other people; but there is a mildness in their blood." In 1789, twenty-one years after he published those words, came the horrific violence of the French Revolution. I would not be so naive, I told myself. Mine would be an unsentimental journey. My impressions might be the "wrong" ones to have, but they would be based on what I saw. And what I saw turned out to be consistent with what the statistics reveal.

◎　　　◎　　　◎

FOR INSTANCE, AFRICA is falling off the world economic map:

With 719,202,000 inhabitants out of a world population of 5,692,210,000 in 1995, Africans represented nearly 13 percent of humanity. But this 13 percent contributed only 1.2 percent of the world's gross domestic product, down from 1.8 percent in the 1980s. Thus, as Africa's population relative to the rest of the world has continued to soar, its contribution to world wealth has dropped by a third in the past decade. Meanwhile, Africa's share of world trade has fallen from 4 percent to near 2 percent. As per capita food production in the rest of the developing world rose by 9 percent in the 1980s, it decreased by 6 percent in Africa.[20]

When one looks at sub-Saharan Africa rather than at Africa as a whole, the situation becomes bleaker.[21] Sub-Saharan Africa's population is growing at over 3 percent per year. That is nearly double the planet's mean growth rate of 1.6 percent.[22] No other large region of the globe comes close. For example, North Africa's population, with the second highest rate of natural increase, grows at 2.6 percent. Southern Asia,

[20]See Per Pinstrup-Andersen's study for the International Food Policy Research Institute in the bibliography. Since African countries gained independence in the early 1960s, their total food production has dropped by 30 percent.
[21]These figures come from a variety of published sources, including the World Bank, *The Washington Post*, *The New York Times*, etc.
[22]See the Population Reference Bureau in the bibliography.

including such poverty-racked countries as Bangladesh, India, Pakistan, and Afghanistan, is growing at 2.2 percent annually. China's growth rate is lower. Moreover, while the growth of populations in the Indian subcontinent and China are supported by industrial development in those regions, sub-Saharan Africa's higher rate of natural increase occurs with generally no industrial growth to back it up.

In the 1980s, twenty-eight of the forty-six countries in sub-Saharan African had declining per capita gross domestic products, while in 1994 tropical African economies declined by 2 percent relative to population growth. Even if sub-Saharan African economies were to start growing at the "overoptimistic" rates predicted by the World Bank, Africans will have to wait forty years to reach the incomes they enjoyed in the 1970s.[23]

With little economic growth, sub-Saharan Africa's exploding population is sustained by slash-and-burn agriculture and the creation of shantytowns that erode the continent's environmental base. To wit, in an age of decaying cities, sub-Saharan Africa has the highest urban growth rate of any region on the planet: 5.8 percent from 1965 to 1980, and 5.9 percent from 1980–1990, according to the World Bank. (The second highest was the Arab world, with a 4.5 percent urban growth rate since 1965.) In Lagos, 61.1 percent of this population growth has resulted from migration from rural areas, which suffer, in many cases, from degraded soil that can no longer sustain agriculture. Africa shows how the urban environment may come to represent the locus of future conflict in the developing world. The perpetrators of future violence will likely be urban born, with no rural experience from which to draw.[24]

According to the United Nations Human Development Report of 1994, which rated 173 countries on the basis of literacy, schooling, population growth, per capita gross domestic product, and life expectancy,

[23]If you exclude Nigeria, that wait would last a century. These statistics are supplied by the World Bank, Oxford Analytica, *The Economist* magazine, and an article by Yale University scholars Matthew Connelly and Paul Kennedy. See Connelly in the bibliography.

[24]See Peter Gizewski's paper on urbanization and violence for the Pew Global Stewardship Initiative in the bibliography. Though it is difficult to find causal links between high population growth and specific eruptions of violence, Jack Goldstone of the University of California points out that "almost *all* of the major sites of recent civil wars, revolutions, and violent demonstrations"—Ethiopia, Rwanda, Nicaragua, Yemen, Tajikistan, etc.—have had population growth rates of 3 percent or above between 1980 and 1991. See the bibliography.

twenty-two of the bottom twenty-four countries are in sub-Saharan Africa.[25]

◎   ◎   ◎

THESE STATISTICS SHOW themselves in Africa through images of "abandonment and general decomposition," where "traffic circles are nothing more than a heap of old tires or empty, rusted barrels," and where "very few neighborhoods . . . have electricity," write University of Pennsylvania scholars Achille Mbembe and Janet Roitman.[26] Their model is Yaoundé, the capital of Cameroon, one of mainland Africa's few countries that rank higher than India and Pakistan on the UN's Human Development chart. Many Cameroonians blame their new "democracy" for the "confusion," "chaos," and "decline of public authority" that has overtaken their country. It is becoming clear that political freedom will not address Africa's steady deterioration. The civil disorder that often accompanies political reform has reduced foreign investment in many places.[27] Despite elections, real civil societies are a long way off and per capita economic growth rates continue to fall or stagnate. (South Africa may be somewhat of an exception. But the future will be driven by that new democracy's ability, or inability, to impede the demons of rising crime, diminishing resources, and soaring population growth.[28])

Sub-Saharan Africa's relative failure was apparent at New York's Kennedy Airport even before I left on my Air Afrique flight to the Ivory Coast. Adjacent to the Air Afrique departure gate were flights leaving for Seoul and Tokyo. When those were announced, all of the businessmen (and women) were expensively dressed and carrying laptop computers and leather attaché cases as they headed for their planes. I was left alone with

[25]Only fourteen of forty-six sub-Saharan African states rate higher in human development than India and Pakistan. And of these fourteen states, five are islands off the African coast, in four cases with small populations. According to the UN, of the fifteen countries with the world's lowest literacy rates, twelve are in sub-Saharan Africa. Of the twelve countries with the lowest per capita gross domestic product, all twelve are in sub-Saharan Africa.
[26]Mbembe and Roitman's article, appearing in the University of Chicago's journal *Public Culture*, is a searing eyewitness rebuke to the dangerously optimistic accounts regarding democratic elections in Africa. See the bibliography.
[27]See the article by Marguerite Michaels, *Time*'s Nairobi bureau chief, listed in the bibliography.
[28]At the end of 1993, South Africa's population was growing fast enough to double in twenty-seven years, according to the Central Intelligence Agency.

a throng of Africans bearing cheap luggage held together by rope, and a few missionaries and charity workers wearing wooden crosses, T-shirts, and khakis. Africa seemed further away than ever from the postindustrial developed world.

◎　　　◎　　　◎

IN MANY WEST African urban areas, streets are unlit, police lack gas for their vehicles, and armed burglars and carjackers are increasingly numerous. In Nigeria's largest city, Lagos, armed gangs attack people caught in the nonstop traffic jams. Direct flights between the United States and the city's airport were suspended by the U.S. secretary of transportation because of violent crime at the terminal and its environs, and extortion by law enforcement and immigration officials—one of the few times the U.S. government embargoed a foreign airport purely for safety reasons, and having nothing to do with politics or terrorism. (Though recently the situation at Lagos airport has improved somewhat.)

In Abidjan, effectively the capital of the Ivory Coast,[29] jewelry stores employ armed sentries even by day and customers often have to be "buzzed" inside (as they do on 47th Street in Manhattan). At night, by the early 1990s, several restaurants had hired club- and gun-wielding guardsmen, contracted by private firms, who walk you the fifteen feet or so between your car and the entrance, giving you an eerie taste of what American cities may someday be like. An Italian ambassador was killed by gunfire when robbers shot up an Abidjan restaurant in 1993, and the family of the Nigerian ambassador was robbed and bound at gunpoint in his residence. After university students caught bandits who had been plaguing their dorms, they murdered them by burning tires around their necks. Ivorian police stood by and watched the "necklacings," too afraid to intercede.

Crime, too, made West Africa a natural departure point for my journey. As crime becomes, perhaps, the greatest danger of the next century and national defense increasingly becomes a local issue, how could I avoid the issue of crime in West Africa?

Yet even the fascist writer Louis-Ferdinand Céline admits that the issue of violence has nothing to do with race. In *Journey to the End of the Night*, he says Africa is "a biological confession. Once work and cold weather cease to constrain us . . . the white man shows you the same spec-

[29]The Ivory Coast's official name is its French equivalent, Côte d'Ivoire.

tacle as a beautiful beach when the tide goes out: the truth, fetid pools, crabs, carrion, and turds." Beware of such determinism, I had to remind myself. Isn't violence pervasive in many cold regions, too?

◎ ◎ ◎

I HAD ARRIVED in Danane by bus from Abidjan. My last night in Abidjan before my bus left the next morning, I attended a dinner party at the home of a diplomat. The very luxury of the surroundings—imported wine, fine cutlery, ice cubes made from filtered water, armed guards at the gate—further emphasized the poverty I would encounter upon my departure. There were the stories that were told around the table: cautionary tales whose very telling, and the nervous silences that followed, constituted evidence of a tense divide—racial and economic—between us and *them*. One story was of an American embassy communications technician who, upon leaving a restaurant in the early evening in downtown Conakry, the Guinean capital, was bludgeoned over the head by robbers. Another was about the demand for bribes by Guinean soldiers at the checkpoints inside Guinea.

The next morning found me staring through my taxi window at Ajame-Bramakote, the section of Abidjan near the bus station. *Bramakote* means "I have no choice [but to live here]." I observed the rotting market stalls of blackened bile-green: rusted metal poles festooned with black plastic sheeting held down by rocks and old tires. In front of a mosque whose walls seemed almost to be melting in the rain, I spotted several women with bare breasts feeding their infants, and another woman urinating, oblivious of the crowd. Inadequate housing and the tropical heat had, perhaps, helped defeat attempts at decorum. The immodesty might also have indicated how Islam had been weakened in the course of its arduous journey across the Sahara. The mortar with which Islam had strengthened Arab civilization had loosened by the time Islam reached West Africa. Cairo, one of the poorest and most overcrowded cities in the world had, for example, an infinitesimal level of common crime—with no daytime locks on jewelry stores. Yet how much more violent would a city in the West be, faced with the same conditions as Ajame-Bramakote? It was my shock that had robbed this woman who was urinating of the privacy that others on the street gave her.

Young men scanning the street suddenly covered the windows of my taxi with their palms and fingers, blotting out my view from the backseat. They yanked open the door and demanded money for carrying my luggage a few feet to the bus, even though I had only a light rucksack. I was to find youths like these throughout urban West Africa: out of school, unemployed, loose molecules in an unstable social fluid that threatened to ignite. Their robust health and good looks made their predicament sadder.

The bus trip to Danane, in the northwest of the country, was scheduled to take nine hours. Clouds of a tropical rainy season raced across the sky. My last image of Abidjan was of a naked boy scavenging through a garbage receptacle at the edge of the sprawling bus terminal and of a woman, in nothing but pink underwear, combing her hair with a rusted nail. The graceful curves of her arm suggested the struggle to preserve dignity in the face of squalor.

Three hours later the bus approached Yamassoukro, the official capital of the Ivory Coast. The gargantuan Catholic basilica of Our Lady of Peace, which cost close to half a billion dollars and is as big as St. Peter's in Rome, loomed from miles away across an undulating sea of coconut palms. The basilica is so vast that the closer you get to it, the farther away it seems. It boasts the largest Corinthian and Doric columns in the world. Next to the air-conditioned monster that can accommodate seven thousand worshipers (not to mention three hundred thousand in the columned plaza) was a lonely row of rotting fruit stands, and then simply nothing: just the bush—palm trees, banana groves, and high grass, which until this century had been high-canopy tropical rain forest. The Ivorian president Félix Houphouet-Boigny built the Catholic basilica as his personal mausoleum. A mile away was his palace, guarded by a moat stocked with three hundred crocodiles—an animist symbol of royalty and warrior power.

◎　　　◎　　　◎

ONE'S FIRST MEMORABLE experience of West Africa, as with so many new places, is through smell. I remember noticing it in the Treichville market, which I visited the very day I got off the plane in Abidjan—an odor of sour sweat, rotting fruit, hot iron and dust, urine drying on sun-warmed stone, feces, and fly-infested meat in an immovable field of damp heat. It was a smell that I immediately became accustomed to: Once I had passed that barrier, I was free to appreciate the musky casket of the market defiles, boiling under corrugated zinc and sheet iron, packed tightly with the swirling motion of the women traders, each with one shoulder exposed and a baby wrapped in loud, colorful cloth around her back, offering me sardines, bats' wings, a slice of raw pork glistening on a hook. By the time I arrived in Danane after a few days in Abidjan, this smell was something I could no longer experience as a novelty. So, too, with the flowers and other delightful fragrances of West Africa.

◎ ◎ ◎

I COULDN'T SLEEP that night in Danane. I looked at my watch. Three A.M. Because of the air conditioner, I still thought it was raining outside. It was as though I had awakened from a dream. Dreams were another thing that we had discussed at the dinner party the night before in Abidjan, what the Peace Corps volunteer at the table had called those "mefloquine dreams, full of blood and violent sex." My dreams while I was taking mefloquine, a malaria prophylactic, were not nearly that bad. But they were vivid and turbulent.

Mefloquine is the most effective antimalaria drug commonly available. An analogue of quinine itself, mefloquine is more powerful than tetracycline or chloroquine. Even mefloquine, however, with all its toxicity, is losing the battle against the ingenious mutations of the malaria parasite, carried by the Anopheles mosquito, which in turn transmits the parasite to man. A strain of cerebral malaria resistant to mefloquine is on the offensive, crossing Asia toward Africa. In Asia, humanity first encountered malaria a million years ago after its arrival there from its African birthplace.[30] In the twenty-first century, malaria, the original "mother of fevers," is, after a fashion, reversing man's conquest of his environment and of the planet. In one year alone, 1990, perhaps 100 or 200 million people were expected to contract some form of malaria—many times the number who have ever been infected with HIV—and 2.5 million were expected to die from the mosquito-borne disease.[31] Since then the numbers have risen. Nearly every inhabitant of Danane in the western section of the Ivory Coast, of the whole African interior in fact, has had some form of malaria, and it is spreading through the coastal cities.[32] When primary rain forest covered Africa, the mosquito had no need to adapt to

[30]See *The Malaria Capers*, by Robert S. Desowitz, listed in the bibliography.
[31]*Ibid.*
[32]In *The Image of Africa*, Curtin wrote, "The chance of an individual living there [in West Africa] as long as a year with out receiving an infective [malarial] mosquito bite is negligible." Three decades after that book was published, the situation is, if anything, worse.

urban environments, and thus city dwellers were more protected from the disease. However, in the postcolonial era, as hardwood logging and population growth have attained critical mass, with bush replacing forest and concrete replacing bush, the malaria-bearing mosquito did not die off, but evolved. It can now thrive anywhere, especially since the forest's destruction led to soil erosion and subsequent flooding, which further encouraged the mosquito's proliferation.

It was because of malaria that the white slave traders on Bunce Island, near Freetown, Sierra Leone, had an average life expectancy of nine months after their arrival from Europe in the second half of the eighteenth century. A hundred years later, in 1862, the British explorer Sir Richard Francis Burton wrote that "the great gift of Malaria is utter apathy," which describes the condition for many of the earth's inhabitants in the late twentieth century.

Defending oneself against malaria in Africa has come to be like defending oneself against crime. You engage in "behavior modification": you don't go out at dusk; you wear mosquito repellent; you put screens equipped with a mosquito-killing agent on your house windows.

Because malaria can cause anemia, which necessitates blood transfusions, malaria is intensifying the spread of AIDS in Africa at the same time that AIDS and tuberculosis are intensifying each other's spread. Of three thousand new cases of tuberculosis in Côte d'Ivoire, 45 percent are accompanied by HIV. Of the 15 million people worldwide whose blood is HIV-positive, 10 million are in Africa.[33] In Abidjan, in the Ivory Coast, whose modern road system encourages the spread of the disease, 10 percent of the population is HIV-positive, even as war, famine, and refugee movements help the virus break through to more remote areas of Africa where AIDS is still scarce. The paved route along which my bus from Abidjan to Danane had been traveling, covering over four hundred miles in nine hours—an impressive feat for sub-Saharan Africa—is a principal "vector" for the HIV virus as Liberian war refugees and migrant laborers travel to and from Abidjan.

Besides malaria, there is hepatitis B, ten times easier to contract in Africa than in the United States. Then there are leprosy, polio, typhoid, spinal meningitis, schistosomiasis, river blindness, sleeping sickness, and other illnesses rampaging throughout Africa and other parts of the underdeveloped world. I spent several hundred dollars for disease prophylactics

[33]See Susan Okie's *Washington Post* article, listed in the bibliography.

merely to visit the places where I intended to travel.[34] A seemingly contradictory pattern had emerged: Rising life expectancy had led to more crowded living conditions, which now contributed to the spread of disease. A wall of disease is thus hardening around Africa and other tropical areas, a membrane more real than the frontiers I would explore when the sun came up.

◎　　　◎　　　◎

IN MY BED in Danane, my thoughts drifted to foot-long lizards with orange heads and tails, the kind that always stopped in their tracks, moving their bodies up and down as if doing push-ups. The crumbly laterite of "Chicago" had been crawling with them.

I don't mean Chicago, Illinois. I refer to a neighborhood of Abidjan that young men in the area had named after the American city, just as another poor section of Abidjan is called Washington. Chicago is not on tourist maps. It is a slum in the bush—a patchwork of corrugated-zinc roofs and walls made of cardboard, cigarette cartons, and black plastic wrap (the kind we use for trash bags), located in a gully choked with coconut and oil palms ravaged by flooding. There is no electricity, sewage system, or clean water supply. Children defecate in a stream, filled with garbage and grazing pigs, droning with mosquitoes, where women do the washing. In Chicago I was thankful for cigarette smoke since it helped keep the flies away. Babies were everywhere, as intrepid as the palm trunks sprouting out of the sand or the orange lizards. You couldn't help noticing the number of pregnant women.

After the rain there are frequent mud slides. Geology, like the birthrate in Chicago, appeared to be unduly accelerating. Here, young unemployed men passed the time drinking beer, palm wine, and medicinally strengthened gin while gambling on pinball games, constructed out of rotting wood and patterns of rusted nails arranged to steer the ball. These are the same youths who rob houses at night in more prosperous Ivorian neighborhoods. "The West can't make gin the way we do," one of the young men told me. The decaying, vegetal odor (it was then only my second day in Abidjan) was intense. Nature appeared far too prolific in this heat, and much of what she created spoiled quickly.

[34]A large part of this amount, though, would be for the series of expensive injections against hepatitis B.

Damba Tesele had come to Chicago from Burkina Faso in 1963. A cook by profession, he told me he had four wives and thirty-two children, not one of whom had made it to high school. He had seen his shanty community destroyed seven times by municipal authorities since coming here. Each time, he and his neighbors rebuilt. Chicago was the latest incarnation.

Zida Simande was another *Burkinabe*, with two children. He sat on a bench, beside a pile of garbage, a pair of makeshift crutches at his feet. He had been a security guard for a private firm in Yamassoukro when thieves broke in at night, crippling him with gunfire. "I migrated to the Ivory Coast to make money. Now I am stuck without a job and without a pension." Bernard Massu, also from Burkina Faso, worked as a tailor a few feet away from where I encountered Simande. One of seven children, he had one child himself but was unmarried. When I asked him how old he was, he took out his identity card, looked at it for a moment, and told me he was nineteen. "What do you do at night?" I asked him. He smiled. "I go with my friends to the bus station at Ajame and look for fun."

Chicago is bordered by the wealthy Abidjan quarter of Cocody, where diplomats live in spacious, jungly compounds near the five-star deluxe Hotel Ivoire. Cocody appears in the guidebooks, but not Chicago. Yet Chicago's population could one day overrun Cocody, and even now Cocody is increasingly dangerous at night. If a servant at one of the foreign embassies finishes work after dark, he is driven home for reasons of his security.

Next, I had gone to "Washington," another festering bush-slum that appears on few maps, bordered on all sides by buckling highways. Washington's mayor, Bamba Singo, a sixty-five-year-old man from the mountainous "Man" region of the Ivory Coast, asked me if Washington could become a sister community of Washington, D.C., in order to get some aid. I had no luck explaining to him the District of Columbia's own financial crisis. The mayor, who had "two wives and many, many children," showed me a picture of his father and father-in-law, in flowing white Moslem robes. Here in Abidjan, however, after twenty years in tropical shack towns like Washington, the mayor had literally shed his clothes. He now wore nothing in this heat except his shorts. In his zinc-roofed shack, whose walls were built of cigarette cartons, there was no real furniture, no sign, in fact, of a stable existence. There was only a gas lamp and a traditional African cloth decorated with fishes, a symbol of fertility. The mayor seemed caught in an upheaval that was tearing away at his culture without replacing it with anything equally substantial, leaving him and the other inhabitants of these shantytowns mercilessly exposed. But this drama goes largely unnoticed. The mayor's eyes told the story: bloodshot and yellow, like broken chicken embryos. I thought of a poem by the Nigerian poet Ben Okri:

> We rush through heated garbage days
> With fear in morbid blood-raw eyes:
>
> Mobs in cancerous slums . . .
> At noon. Angled faces in twisted
> Patterns of survival . . . [35]

Chicago and Washington are a microcosm of West Africa. Behind the huts occupied by migrants from Burkina Faso were huts of migrants from the Sahelian regions of Mali and Niger, with courtyards and wall enclosures built of zinc and cardboard, reminiscent of mudbrick abodes in the Sahara. For many of these immigrants, the Ivory Coast had not turned out to be the land of plenty, or even of relative plenty, but a slum-magnet for an emptying countryside. Now 50 percent of the country's population is non-Ivorian, and 75 percent of Abidjan's population originates from neighboring countries. According to current projections, the 1993 population of 13.5 million will grow to 39 million in 2025. As this occurs, the borders of this former French colony will be increasingly irrelevant.

◎   ◎   ◎

IN DANANE, SHORTLY after dawn I got up, unable to sleep, and opened the door. A blast of heat and dust. No rain after all—only the the rattling air conditioner. The hotel lobby functioned as a bar, stocked with a great variety of spirits. Behind the counter was a big, muscular man wearing a baseball hat and a traditional tribal robe, drinking a Flag beer. Several other Africans were sleeping on the chairs. I asked the bartender if someone could make me breakfast. He nodded, pointing me to the adjoining room, where a few tables and chairs were arranged. Everything was quiet, peaceful.

[35]"Darkening City: Lagos, 83." See Okri in the bibliography.

The butter on the table was rancid, the bread spotted with charcoal-black mold. I ordered two hard-boiled eggs and a pot of tea. It was while I waited for the eggs that Robert Johnson Semoka stalked into the room, sat down at my table, and proceeded to stare at me from a few inches away.

At 7 A.M. I was already in a sweat. There was no air-conditioning in the restaurant. A television set in the corner was playing a video of a professional wrestling match. Robert Johnson Semoka—he had shown me his expired California driver's license with his name spelled on it—talked loud over the wrestling commentary. He smelled of cologne and had a grizzled beard. "You're a writer, I see you have a notebook?" he asked in a booming baritone. Then, not waiting for my response: "Me, I'm a writer, too." I warmed to his eyes. Their aspect was Western—just barely, though. Like many people's here, they were yellow from sickness. At certain moments they lost their domesticated glow and became void of urbanity, untamed; as though they had been defiled by what they had seen, and by what they had been forced to decipher to stay alive through indescribable horrors.

Robert Johnson Semoka had a wife and two children in California: He took family pictures out of his wallet to show me. But he had left his wife and children in 1989—he didn't explain exactly why—to return to Liberia. That, he said, had been his big mistake, for it was then that Liberia ignited into civil war.

About 1 percent of Liberia's population of 2.5 million had been brutally murdered—not by armies, but mainly by illiterate thugs with uniforms, guns, and machetes. Officially, it was a war between the government of Master Sergeant Samuel K. Doe and the National Patriotic Front of Liberia (NPLF), led by Charles McArthur Taylor. In truth, President Doe was a semiliterate backwoodsman who began his presidency in 1980 by breaking into the suite of the former leader, William R. Tolbert, Jr., and disemboweling him and gouging out his right eye. Taylor, for his part, is an Americo-Liberian, a descendant of the freed American slaves who founded Liberia in 1847. Having escaped from a Massachusetts correctional facility while awaiting trial for embezzlement, Taylor fled to Liberia, then exploited the genocidal rage of armed teenagers. Prince Johnson, who led a breakaway faction of Taylor's NPLF, was also involved. Described by many as an "alcoholic psychopath," Prince Johnson is responsible for mutilating and killing President Doe. Johnson's soldiers ambushed Doe and his presidential bodyguard in September 1990 in the capital, Monrovia. They then cut off Doe's ears and inflicted further tortures on the captured despot. Johnson recorded the execution on video, copies of which are available throughout West Africa.

On the night of June 5/6, 1993, just three months before my journey to West Africa, when the Liberian war was supposed to have been long over, armed soldiers "systematically massacred and mutilated" six hundred refugees who were "mainly women, children, and elderly persons" at a camp not far from Monrovia.[36] It was assumed that the soldiers were from one of the various rebel armies. However, as a United Nations report later showed, the crime was perpetrated by the regular army, the Armed Forces of Liberia, on which Western donors had placed their hopes for national reconciliation. The motive for the attack: "45 bags of rice and beans and other loot . . . carried by 100 or more survivors abducted by the attackers."[37]

" 'What tribe are you?' " shouted Robert Johnson Semoka at me, mimicking the question that both government and rebel soldiers were always asking him and his fellow Liberians. " 'Are you Vai? Gio? Mano? Krahn' " he mimicked loudly.

" 'I am Vai.' 'You lie!' the soldier would say. 'If you Vai, speak Vai to me!' You see, that is how the soldiers would know if you were telling the truth. If you spoke Vai with an accent, they would push you into the jeep and drive you off to the beach and kill you. I saw the war. I saw a soldier point a bayonet at a pregnant woman and cut out her baby. I tell you, it's a tribal war. There are no ideas, no politics, just tribe. Doe is Krahn, so the Gios and Manos support Taylor. Vehicles in the streets had signs saying 'Death to Krahns' or 'Mandingos Should Be Exterminated.' " Robert went on:

"Prince Johnson's men had *juju*[38] sutures on their backs. Taylor's soldiers had scorpions on their arms. These marks gave them spirit power, so that bullets could not hurt them. The people really believe these things. I have written a book about it. I will give you my manuscript."

"Where do you live?" I asked him.

"In the refugee camp. I will show you."

I finished my breakfast and we left. The Liberian refugee camp, it turned out, was only a hundred yards away from my hotel. Robert and

[36]These quotes are taken from the United Nations' report on the incident. See United Nations Secretariat listed in the bibliography.
[37]*Ibid.*
[38]*Juju* is West African magic, akin to voodoo, and involves the use of fetishes.

about twenty other refugees, both men and women, plus a host of children, occupied an airless, dungeonlike shed lined with rows of wooden benches that served as beds. Outside in the steaming sun, one rotund lady was cooking peanut sauce in a jerrican while feeding her baby. "Hi," she said in the exquisite lilting English that Liberians speak. Many Liberians seemed so nice—just as many of the Ugandans I had met following the downfall of Idi Amin seemed so very nice. Where did all the violence come from? I would always ask myself. Despite the objective factors of ethnic politics, population growth, and the environment, whenever I encountered these people in the flesh I was puzzled.

The woman complained to me about how the Ivorian authorities had reduced the refugees' rice ration from nine to six kilos, and about how the Ivorians charged the refugees the equivalent of ten cents just for a bucket of water. There were no medicines. Her child had diarrhea. "Nobody helps us," Robert chimed in. "But you wait. Liberia was as peaceful during the decades of [William] Tubman's rule as the Ivory Coast is now. There will be Ivorian refugees like us in Liberia in a few years."

It was still early morning, yet the heat and humidity were already overpowering. Lizards and flies were everywhere. Women were feeding babies and men were dozing on the benches. Teenagers and younger children were playing, or just hanging out. Nothing suggested that Ivorian authorities were providing help. In Pakistan, I had watched the most destitute Afghan refugees organize Koranic schools with no outside help. In Eritrea, I had observed refugees that the rest of the world had forgotten making sandals out of plastic scraps, and war amputees manipulating their metal limbs to make tables and chairs out of captured ammunition boxes. But here I saw only passivity, fatalistic and defeated in the oppressive heat. The stillness presaged, it seemed to me, cataclysms to come.

Robert promised to come back later to the hotel with his manuscript. Though I waited for him, he never came.

"Liberia . . . is pretty far gone in the way of despotism. . . . [The country] is at present in trouble," wrote Richard Burton in mid-September 1862. According to a specialist on African history, Basil Davidson, Burton has "the hectoring tone of a man who has travelled much but understood little . . ." That may be too easy an opinion. Burton spoke twenty-nine languages and operated in native disguise in Mecca. Nevertheless, Burton's racism is evident in his description of some Liberians in *Wanderings in West Africa:*

Their appearance struck me as grotesque. Conceive the head of a Socrates or a Silenus upon the body of the Antinous or Apollo Belvedere. A more magnificent development of muscle . . . my eyes had never yet looked upon. But the faces! except when lighted up by smiles and good humour—expression to an African face is all in all—nothing could be more unprepossessing. The flat nose, the high cheek-bones, the yellow eyes, the chalky-white teeth pointed like the shark's, the muzzle projecting as that of a dog-monkey, combine to form an unusual amount of ugliness.

Keep in mind, though, that whatever Burton's limitations as revealed by a passage like this, Liberia is no better off—is perhaps worse off—than it was in Burton's day. Burton's depictions of other places in West Africa, to say nothing of his account of disease, are germane to present circumstances, given the region's economic decline. Africa, as I've said, has to be confronted. Whatever the wickedness of Burton and other colonialists, 70 percent of all Africans alive in 1993 were born since African states acquired their independence. True, they were born into a world made worse by the colonial experience, to say nothing of slavery. Nevertheless, the time for blaming Africa's dilemma on the likes of Burton may be past.

◎　　　◎　　　◎

IN AN AIR-CONDITIONED four-wheel-drive Toyota Land Cruiser—the medium through which senior diplomats and top Western relief officials often encounter Africa—suspended high above the road and looking out through closed windows, your forehead and underarms comfortably dry, you may learn something about Africa. Traveling in a crowded public bus, flesh pressed upon wet, sour flesh, you learn more; and in a "bush taxi," or "mammy wagon," where there are not even windows, you learn more still. But it is on foot that you learn the most. You are on the ground, on the same level with Africans rather than looking down at them. You are no longer protected by speed or air-conditioning or thick glass. The sweat pours from you, and your shirt sticks to your body. This is how you learn.

I left the refugee camp to walk around Danane. The laterite road had turned to mud and dust, a landscape of bruised and leaden skies, drenching sunlight, and hot Day-Glo colors where earth, water, and flesh soak up, rather than reflect, light. I saw a few circular wattle huts, but many more scrap-iron storefronts with roofs held down by rocks and old tires (the architecture of the future), plus giant banana leaves, majestic coconut palms, and the shorter, scruffier oil palms. Dark greenery, lush, knobby hills, and red dirt dominated. There was nothing sharp or focused about this landscape. Instead of crisp borders there were merging rhythms. Rather than a particular country, the writhing, bumpy green carpet stretching to the horizon was merely a particular place on the planet. It seemed to me that the myths which might emerge from such a landscape were either too local (connected with tribe) or too general (connected with the earth) to sustain nationhood.

Throngs of human beings ambled past, a cadence of limbs clogging the road and adjacent labyrinthine pathways. Women and little girls balanced round metal trays atop their heads, stacked with heavy loads of everything from papayas to detergent. The men carried nothing. They wore rock-poster-like T-shirts under tribal robes, and baseball caps and pump sneakers without laces. Poor men have no power except the power to oppress women, I thought. Working longer hours to make ends meet lowers women's status and keeps birth rates high, writes Jodi L. Jacobson of the Worldwatch Institute.[39] Regarding Africa, United Nations official Phoebe Asiyo states that "more and more girls are dropping out of both primary and secondary school or just missing school altogether due to increasing poverty."

On the road, a man came up to me and said, "Hello, don't you recognize me?" For a moment I thought it might be a scam. Then I remembered. I had met him on the road the day before, when the bus stopped at a string of huts. Eyeing a cooler of Coca-Colas, I asked for one but realized I had only a big bill and the vendor was without change. This fellow suddenly approached and bought me the Coke with his own money. Though I had thanked him profusely only yesterday, today he was at first glance just another black face, another one of my statistics. To see individuals, I realized, was to see possibilities and, thus, more hopeful scenarios.

◎   ◎   ◎

THE SAME DAY I hired a taxi to take me to the Liberian border, fifteen miles to the west. Just outside Danane, the bush became a nearly impenetrable mass of mangrove and palm trunks. Then, here and there, I began to see authentic rain forest: majestically tall black hardwoods forming a high

---

[39] See Lester Brown's *State of the World*, in which Jacobson's essay is included.

canopy of leaves blocking the sun. The road, a rich ocher laterite, arced broadly, but the enveloping darkness and the overgrown mangrove mass created a narrowing effect. The road became like an alley at night—especially as I knew how close I was to a porous border, through which both refugees and renegade Liberian soldiers easily slipped. A snake slithered across the road. We crossed a small river, the dark water absorbing every point of light. Suddenly, a cluster of wattle huts appeared, and then, after another mile or two, came a second settlement. Each settlement seemed partially deserted. A few old people sat around amid the flies. A girl was trying unsuccessfully to sell a few mandarins. A young, muscular man stood stoically by the side of the road, wearing an Elvis T-shirt. His eyes were terrifyingly vacant. There was no economy here, nothing: Innumerable settlements such as these throughout West Africa were emptying out so that slums like Chicago and Washington could expand, like pure air pouring out of lungs to emerge as carbon monoxide. Though I had seen no soldiers, let alone any atrocities or *juju* spirits, an indefinable wildness had set in. It occurred to me that, perhaps, the forest had made the war in Liberia. I have no factual basis for this, merely traveler's intuition. Here is a record of my thoughts at that moment, jotted in shorthand in the taxi, interspersed with some quotes from books.

◎ ◎ ◎

THE FOREST WAS partly to blame for the iniquities of humankind here—for President Doe disemboweling the previous president, Tolbert, and for Prince Johnson, in turn, cutting off Doe's ears; for Charles Taylor's teenage soldiers breaking into the bridal shops of Monrovia, dressing up like women-*cum-juju* spirits, and going on boozy rampages that ended in ritual killings.

Africanists occasionally find significance in the fact that Liberia, founded by ex-American slaves, was the only fledgling nation in the region that had not been colonized by the Europeans. American political and financial interests, which dominated Liberia for so long, had apparently been more harmful than those of the British or French. President Reagan's tolerance of the Doe thugocracy (a Voice of America relay station and a Firestone rubber plantation were located in Liberia, making President Doe a "bulwark against communism") was cited as proof of how America was to blame for Liberia's failure. That was certainly true, in part. At the moment, though, it was the forest that intrigued me.

From Alex Newton's *West Africa: A Travel Survival Kit*, I read a startling passage as the taxi continued to the Liberian border: "Liberia is one of the last West African countries with significant rain forests. They are everywhere and cover an estimated 44% of the total land area."

A forest reflects no light. In the forest there are no horizons. You cannot see more than a few feet ahead, so you are in fear of surprise. You are prone to excitable rumors. The slightest pinprick or jab may lead to panic. In other words, in the forest, where one's view is blotted out by every manner of tree and creeper (each containing its own "spirit"), men tend to depend less on reason and more on superstition.[40] The extraordinary profusion of carved masks in West Africa, which a visitor cannot help but notice, suggests the role of the forest (and of the savannah) in the regional psychology. The forest, a green prison with iron rain clouds draped low overhead, may have helped weaken Islam and Christianity. The staying power of animism, in competition with these two major world religions, might be traced to the survival of large tracts of forest here into the twentieth century. (Of course, the watering down of Islam or Christianity by paganism isn't unique to Africa. Mexico, for example, also features a baroque Christianity heavily influenced by pagan traditions.)

The tropical forests of West Africa, because they constituted their own environment, were also a factor in West Africa's relative isolation. The contrast with the Sahara to the north and northeast could not have been greater. Labelle Prussin, a specialist on the relationship between Islam and indigenous West African culture, points out that the Sahara first became a real desert around 3000 B.C.; therefore, "the desert effectively severed communication between West Africa and the Mediterranean world precisely when the latter was embarking on a course of nascent urbanization." The Sahara largely cut off West Africa from the traffic of peoples, technology, and ideas moving not just about the Mediterranean, but also into Eurasia. And whereas Islam, according to the scholar I. M. Lewis, spread quickly and directly along the coast of North Africa from Arabia, it spread only gradually and indirectly by partly Arabized peoples from North Africa across the desert to West Africa. Then the forest further interfered. The tradition of Islamic marabouts (and Christian saints) was infiltrated by spirit-possession cults.

[40]See Chapter IX, "The Worship of Trees," in Sir James Frazer's *The Golden Bough: A Study in Magic and Religion*, for a fuller discussion of tree spirits.

It is near the equator, says the Nobel laureate and analyst of human crowd behavior Elias Canetti, that the effect of the forest is most extreme: "In tropical forests the eye loses itself in the foreground; there is a chaotic and unarticulated mass of growth, full of colour and life, which effectively precludes any sensation of order . . ."

Liberia, with the wettest, densest forest in tropical West Africa, was, as the quality and scope of its violence indicated, still a forest culture: a land of spirits. Sustained population growth rates of over 3 percent and the importation of large quantities of automatic weapons were dominant factors in the initial implosion. Nevertheless, much of the violence was ritualistic in nature, amplified by drugs and alcohol, and carried out with machetes and other sharp implements. It made for an awful revelation: of how unprecedented birthrates, alcohol, mass-produced weaponry, and other artifacts of modern times could, under circumstances that are increasingly common in the third world, make for a new-age primitivism, far more deadly than the benign warrior cultures of old, characterized by ritualized—rather than real—combat.[41]

Whatever the drawbacks of forest culture, at least it *is* a culture. As it decays and people pour into coastal shanty-magnets, West Africa is left with high-density concentrations of human beings who have been divested of certain stabilizing cultural models, with no strong governmental institutions or communities to compensate for the loss. Liberia ignited at the start of this process: a forest culture still, yet undermined by overpopulation, a drift of people to the cities, and the attendant erosion of customs and values. I'm not saying that these factors, and these factors alone, caused the bloodbath of the 1980s and early 1990s, but they may have been some of the unseen, less discussed background elements.

◎   ◎   ◎

THE TAXI REACHED the border—a low, easily climbable fence with a gate, by a guardhouse. I went inside the guardhouse but found no one. I yelled. A few moments later an Ivorian soldier hobbled in, his eyes droopy. He was not interested in talking except to ask me for a *pourboire* ("tip"). I guessed that I had interrupted his nap.

[41]See John Keegan's *A History of Warfare* for a description of such ancient warrior cultures.

In the entrance hall at Thomas Jefferson's home, Monticello, there is an 1802 map of Africa that Jefferson bought from the London mapmaker Aaron Arrowsmith, showing West Africa without the country borders later created by colonialism. Instead, there are only indistinct regions: the Grain Coast, the Ivory Coast, the Coast of Guinea . . .[42] Would that 1802 map at Monticello someday turn out to be more useful than the present ones? I wondered.

---

[42]The Coast of Guinea refers not to the country of Guinea but to the littoral encompassing Ghana, Togo, and Benin. See Susan R. Stein's *The Worlds of Thomas Jefferson at Monticello*, listed in the bibliography.

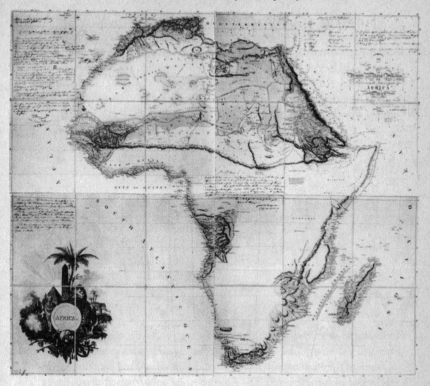

Aaron Arrowsmith map of Africa, 1802. From the collection of the Library
of Congress. Photo courtesy of Monticello/Thomas Jefferson Memorial
Foundation, Inc.)

2

◎   ◎   ◎

Sierra Leone:
From Graham Greene
to Thomas Malthus?

THE MINISTER'S EYES were the familiar two egg yolks, the effect of endemic malaria and other illnesses. There was also an irrefutable sadness to them, as though they *had seen too much.* He spoke in a slow and creaking voice, the voice of hope expired. His flowing white robe clashed dramatically with his blue-black skin, so that his face appeared like a disembodied spirit. We were in downtown Freetown, the capital of Sierra Leone, a long way from the Liberian border from where I had come. But more of that journey later. Flame trees, coconut palms, and a ballpoint-blue Atlantic were in the background.

"In forty-five years I have never seen things so bad. We did not manage ourselves well after the British departed. But what we have now is something worse—the revenge of the poor, of the social failures, of the people least able to bring up children in a modern society. The boys who took power in Sierra Leone come from houses like this," he said, jabbing his finger at a corrugated metal shack a few feet away, teeming with children. "On Wednesday they took over, on Friday they robbed the central bank. In their first three months in office, these boys confiscated all the official Mercedeses, Volvos, and BMWs and willfully wrecked them on the road." The minister mentioned one coup leader, Solomon Anthony Joseph ("SAJ") Musa, who shot the people who had paid for his schooling, "in order to erase the humiliation and mitigate the power his middle-class sponsors held over him."[1]

Crime was what my friend—a top-ranking official in a West African government whose life would be at risk were I to identify him fully—really wanted to talk about.[2]

"You see," he told me, "in the villages of Africa it is perfectly natural to feed at any table and lodge in any hut. But in the cities, this communal existence no longer holds. You must pay for lodging and be invited for food. When young men find out that their relations cannot put them up, they become lost. One step leads to another. They join other migrants and slip gradually into the criminal process. They steal. The women become prostitutes, whom the men beat mercilessly." He continued:

"In the poor quarters of Arab North Africa, there is much less crime because Islam provides a social anchor—of education and indoctrination. The fundamentalists in Cairo are often highly educated people—not like most West African politicians. Here in West Africa we have a lot of superficial Islam and superficial Christianity. For instance, there is no organized Islamic or Arabic education. Western religion is undermined by animist beliefs not suitable to a moral society since they are based on irrational spirit power. Here spirits are used to wreak vengeance by one person against another, or one group against another." (While Western religion may in some aspects be no less irrational—Catholics believe bread and wine turns into the body and blood of Christ—it does not usually sanction immoral behavior.)

In civil fighting in Sierra Leone, for example, the BBC had reported in its magazine *Focus on Africa*, the rebels had "a young woman with them who would walk to the front naked, always walking backwards and looking in a mirror to see where she was going. This made her invisible, so

[1]A coup on April 29, 1992, in Sierra Leone forced President Joseph Momoh to go into exile. A group of young junior officers assumed power.
[2]After the beginning of this chapter appeared in *The Atlantic Monthly* in February 1994, the Sierra Leonean cabinet held a meeting to determine who among them had the most yellow eyes: My need to conceal this man's identity is, therefore, quite real. One thing I will reveal to the reader: This African minister is not a Creole. So his views cannot be dismissed as those of a Creole sneering down on a culture increasingly influenced by indigenous tribes.

that she could cross to the army's positions and there bury charms . . . to improve the rebels' chances of success."[3]

"And of course," said the minister, "the greatest magic is the radio." He tapped an old transistor on the table. "This box, it talks to you, in your own language. Yet it has no wires connecting it to anything. Now, that's magic! Therefore, whatever comes out of this box must be true. This box is how Sekou Toure ruled Guinea for so long.[4] The only thing that functioned in postcolonial Africa was the radio—a way to control a population through magic."

Finally, my friend mentioned polygamy and extended families. Arising from a pastoral culture where men work in distant fields separated from their families for long periods, these loose, albeit complex, family structures thrive in sub-Saharan Africa even as polygamy has all but died out in Arab North Africa. Most youths I would meet on the road in West Africa told me they were from "extended" families, with a mother in one place and a father in another. Translated to an urban environment, extended families may well have contributed significantly to the world's highest birthrates and the explosion of HIV on the continent. Like communalism and animism, non-nuclear family structures provide a poor defense against the corrosive effects of cities, where African culture is being redefined as deforestation tied to overpopulation drives peasants out of the countryside.

But my friend the minister had no sympathy. Like other West Africans I had met and would continue to meet, terrified at what crime was doing to his own society, he railed at the leniency with which the West treats its criminals. "Listen to me," he ordered, leaning over the small, corroded wooden table, his face in my eyes. "I read in one of your American news magazines about a young black man, a solidly built Negro chap—a criminal—and how a woman supports him and bears his children. The article was about how he had learned to paint and write stories in jail, while admitting he was still a hustler. The journalist obviously had some sympathy for him. But that's a worthless fellow! A typical piece of scum!" the minister hissed. "I have no sympathy for him! If I, or another one of my countrymen, had his chance in America, we could be rich. Look at how well West Africans do in America, going to school by day and driving

<hr/>

[3]See Matthew Tostevin's "Sinking to the Depths," listed in the bibliography.
[4]Sekou Toure ruled Guinea from independence in 1958 until his death in 1984. His presidency was characterized by massive brutality and a steep economic decline.

cabs to support themselves by night . . . I've had a lot of meetings with them [African-Americans] in my capacity as minister and I don't always like what I see. They're searching for some mythical West Africa while we West Africans are walking blind into disaster."

I sighed. Having lived in Israel and Greece, I had heard Israelis express exasperation with American Jews, and Greeks with Greek Americans. It was a familiar story.

"What are you reading?" I asked.

"Aeschylus, the *Oresteia* trilogy," he responded. "Modern novels don't hold me. Too many authors nowadays have no experience in the outer world. They focus only on themselves." I wondered if he had read Joseph Conrad's *The Nigger of the "Narcissus,"* which I had been reading, and what he had thought of it. "Is it a racist novel as many claim?" I wanted to know. As in the case of Richard Burton, Conrad's own words incriminate him. The author describes his main character as having "a face pathetic and brutal: the tragic, the mysterious, the repulsive mask of a nigger's soul."

"No, the book is not racist," the minister stated easily, as though I were a fool to think otherwise. "Conrad's protagonist is progressive for his time. The 'nigger' is not passive. He couldn't be played around with. He had the capacity to force the white men around him into actions, which betrayed their inner weaknesses."

Notwithstanding the mean-spirited depiction of the "nigger," James Wait, Conrad's story is a tale of today written a hundred years ago. It is a sea tale, and the ship, the *Narcissus,*

> went on lonely and swift like a small planet. . . . A great circular solitude moved with her . . . The sun looked upon her all day, and every morning rose with a burning, round stare of undying curiosity. She had her own future; she was alive with the lives of those beings who trod her decks; like that earth which had given her up to the sea, she had an intolerable load of regrets and hopes. On her lived timid truth and audacious lies; and, like the earth, she was unconscious, fair to see—and condemned by men to an ignoble fate.

The progress of this ship is bedeviled by the illness of one deck hand, James Wait, an African dying of tuberculosis. Like the crew's confused and divided response to Wait's illness, our own failure to respond intelligently to the issues raised by Africa's decline betrays our own inner weaknesses.

Conrad indicated to his critics that he was willing to stand or fall on his depiction of the *Narcissus*'s voyage. While all ideas are subject to attack, one's personal experience—what one has actually seen and heard and felt in the course of a journey—is impregnable. *The Nigger* was the fruit of Conrad's own experience. In the book's preface the author said that his aim was "before all, to make you *see* . . . [especially] that glimpse of truth for which you have forgotten to ask."[5]

I could do worse than try to emulate such brutal honesty. If I incriminate myself in the process, then the reader may more accurately judge my other observations.

The minister and I sat on a terrace in Freetown. The favorable prospect—the peace and solitude of the view—gave no hint of the chaos all around and below us. Admiring the heartbreaking beauty of the palms and the blue water, I had a sense of perfect well-being, a drowsy stirring that left me with only one urge: the need for a short nap.

It had been a long journey from the Liberian border to the minister's terrace.

◎   ◎   ◎

FROM THE LIBERIAN border I had gone back to Danane—my taxi driver wouldn't cross the border with me, and I had no luck getting a lift with a relief-agency vehicle into Liberia. So from Danane I returned to Abidjan. Getting from Abidjan to Freetown, Sierra Leone, meant flying, since inland travel across Guinea to Sierra Leone is slow and uncertain in the rainy season—washed out roads and unpaid soldiers demanding bribes. Also, the border regions between Guinea and Sierra Leone (and between Sierra Leone and Liberia) are made unsafe by unruly soldiers and war. Within West Africa, though, flying is often no less an adventure than traveling by land, which is why people in a hurry have a tendency to fly from one place in Africa to another via Europe.

Sierra Leone Airways went bankrupt in the 1980s. Ghana Airways, which had flights from Abidjan to Freetown, was notoriously unreliable: Flights arrived not just hours but sometimes days late, and were often overbooked. In 1993, WISWAS, a small, unaccredited company run by a Spaniard out of Monrovia, the war-racked Liberian capital, with help

---

[5]See Cedric Watts's introduction to the Penguin edition of *The Nigger of the "Narcissus,"* listed in the bibliography.

from South Africans, and employing Russian pilots and old Antonov planes, offered the safest connections to Sierra Leone from elsewhere in West Africa. But I decided instead to buy a one-way ticket from Abidjan to Conakry, the capital of Guinea, on Air Ivoire (fairly reliable) and to hope for the best from there. Alone, with only a light rucksack, I could make further plans on the spot.

I landed in Conakry in the late afternoon under a leaden, end-of-rainy-season sky. From the air, the capital of Guinea looked like a canvas of tin-foil wrappers discarded on a bed of wet mud and surrounded by glistening forest, a floating, liquidy green film bordered by the sea. Never had the earth appeared so fragile. Outside the terminal, the taxi drivers fought over me. The winner led me to an old stripped-down Renault, its yellow paint peeling, with gaping, skull-like cavities where the headlights used to be. The forty-five-minute journey in heavy traffic from the airport to the city center was through a single, never-ending shantytown: a nightmarish, Dickensian vision that Dickens himself could probably never have imagined. The corrugated-metal shacks and scabrous walls were coated with black slime. I could think only of Burton's remarks about "the mildewed cankered gangrened aspect" of West African settlements. Stores were built out of rusted shipping containers, junked cars, and shaky contraptions of wire mesh. The streets were a long puddle of floating garbage. Flies and other insects were everywhere. There were multitudes of children, many of them with swollen bellies. Pregnant women sat silently on wooden crates, watching their children play amid the mud and broken glass and other refuse. At the end of the taxi journey there was no downtown, just a few forlorn streets and a few dilapidated office buildings. Conakry was a city and a national capital only in the technical sense. What I saw, rather, was a steamy, sprawling growth on the edge of the Atlantic.

The tide had gone out and I noticed dead rats and an automobile chassis exposed on the mucky beach. By 2020 Guinea's population would double at current rates. On average, women in Guinea give birth to over six children. The infant mortality rate is nearly 15 percent.[6] Meanwhile, aid workers told me that hardwood logging in the interior was continuing at great speed and that people were fleeing the Guinean countryside for Conakry. It seemed to me that here, as elsewhere in sub-Saharan Africa, man was challenging nature beyond its limits and that nature might in the

[6]See the Population Reference Bureau, listed in the bibliography.

future demand its revenge. As African birthrates continue at high levels and slums like Chicago, Washington, and Conakry proliferate, diseases spread rapidly and experts worry that viral mutations and hybridizations might conceivably result in a form of the AIDS virus easier to contact than the present strain.[7] Conakry might symbolize the new strategic danger—the Fulda Gap of the future: a disease breakthrough far more serious and likely than the Russian army breaking into Europe.

A cute, miraculously healthy looking teenager smiled at me from a zinc shack. To thrive in this miasma, merely to survive, indicated a vitality that I would never be able to muster. I smiled back at what I knew to be my genetic superior.

It was dark now. I pushed through a crowd of destitute people to the door of an unfinished cement hulk—a hotel run by tough and friendly expatriates from the Sahara Desert country of Mauritania. I soon found myself in another small room with a loud air conditioner, a broken window, and mosquitoes everywhere. Through the window I saw a jagged collage of zinc roofs and plastic sheeting held down, as usual, by tires. Below, inside the locked courtyard, were a late-model Mercedes-Benz and a BMW.

Later I would meet a Lebanese businessman, also staying at the hotel. He was dressed in a designer shirt and tapered pants, and wore a gold watch. An ostentatious leather money bag hung around his waist. He smelled of expensive cologne. He said that he had been chased by stick-wielding thieves only a block from the hotel. "This country is rich," he told me. "There are diamonds, forests, you name it. But the people are lazy, feckless. They'll never come to anything." This fellow came regularly to Conakry from Beirut "on business," which he did not care to explain further.

There was an Arab mercantile community throughout much of West Africa. When a character in Graham Greene's *The Heart of the Matter*, set in 1940s Sierra Leone, asks, "What do the Syrians do?" the reply is: "Make money. They run all the stores up country and most of the stores here. Run diamonds too." Like the Indians and Pakistanis in East Africa, and the Jews of pre–World War II Eastern Europe, the Arabs in West

[7]Dr. Alan Greenberg, who ran the Centers for Disease Control's bureau in Abidjan, is one of a number of specialists tracking the spread of the AIDS virus. He worries about its ability to mutate in such conditions as obtain in places like Conakry.

Africa were a classic "middleman minority."[8] Though they might at times seem sleazy and arrogant (as my encounter shows), they were highly organized as well as exceedingly ambitious, especially for their children's sakes: Africans, I thought, could do worse than emulate their example. I would get a better feel for the Arabs' predicament in West Africa when I got to Freetown, Sierra Leone.

Freetown was only one hundred miles south along the coast, but the Atlantic Ocean catamaran service had not operated for four months, and nobody knew exactly when it would resume. I could find no one who had made the trip overland. Everyone said it was too risky, due to government soldiers along the road in both Guinea and Sierra Leone.

"Gambia Airways has three flights a week. But they have canceled all their flights for ten days," said a strikingly beautiful and articulate young woman at a local travel agency.

"What about other airlines?" I asked.

"There is a Ghana Airways flight today at 1 P.M. It's completely booked but it doesn't matter. They're so disorganized you might get on anyway—if the plane arrives, that is. Try it. If it doesn't work, I'll refund your money."

Trusting her smile, I bought the ticket and grabbed another battered taxi back to the airport.

Arriving at the airport in Conakry from Abidjan the day before had been easy: too easy. A run-down terminal building with large crowds at the edge of a shantytown, the airport was a grimy and perspiration-soaked bedlam. Immigration and customs officials just waved me through. The wall of people now in the departure area in the midday tropical heat told me that leaving would be more difficult.

The Ghana Airways booth was obscured by a large crowd of Africans laden with old suitcases and burlap sacks pleading and waving their tickets in the air. One rotund woman with several large sacks and shopping bags was nearly in tears, explaining to anyone who would listen that she simply *had* to get on this plane. With my small rucksack I squeezed through to the front. Behind the counter was a lone, morose-looking ticket agent, staring straight ahead at no one in particular. Despite the shouts of abuse, the horror stories being loudly related, and the tickets being waved in his

[8]I encountered the term in Thomas Sowell's article "Middleman Minorities," in the May/June 1993 issue of *The American Enterprise*.

face, he remained absolutely calm, wordless, his mind elsewhere—completing a fond memory perhaps. I marveled at his mystifying reserve and the stores of arrogance it must have required. I tried, using a calm and distinctive voice, to ask him if the flight was canceled. Delayed? Overbooked? It was no use. He wouldn't answer. His face was a mask. He must go through this two or three times a week, I thought.

People kept shouting. The woman with the sacks and shopping bags started crying and repeating her story to me, as if I could help her. The notion that Africans have some sort of inner wisdom and are, therefore, not obsessed with time and schedules the way Westerners are now struck me as utter nonsense. I was bathed in sweat but dared not give up my place in front of the ticket agent.

I waited thus, wet arms and elbows in my chest and backside, for about half an hour. Then another ticket agent quietly walked up and whispered something to the fellow behind the counter. The screams intensified and another round of ticket-waving began. With reptilian slowness, the second agent began accepting tickets and writing out boarding passes. No line had formed, and consequently there was no pattern to who got his attention. I noticed he was not checking the tickets to see which were confirmed, with an "OK" written on them, and which were wait-listed. There was no computer, or even a passenger list, in front of him.

I held out my ticket, whispering in his ear, over and over, "I'm alone. I have no luggage." It wasn't working. So I lied. "I'm alone. I have no luggage. *Diplomat.*" After I repeated this mantra a few times, he turned to me and wrote out a boarding pass. I proceeded to immigration and customs.

"Let me see all your money," said the customs official.

I opened one pocket, revealing my traveler's checks.

"No, I want to see all your pockets. Open them."

I showed him my dollars and some Guinean francs. "Where is your customs declaration for those dollars?" he asked.

"Nobody gave me a form to fill out."

He shot back: "Then give me your dollars. They're illegal. And your Guinea francs, too. Don't you know you cannot export them?"

I lost my composure and began shouting about how I had brought the dollars from America and that he was not going to get them. He relented, but still confiscated the Guinean francs. Thus, I could not buy even mineral water at the duty-free bar. (The smallest bill I had was twenty dollars and the bartender had no change except in the worthless local currency.)

I was lucky. Every seat in the Ghana Airways plane was occupied and people with confirmed tickets had been left on the ground. Twenty-two minutes after takeoff we landed in Freetown. A friend who had lived years in Africa would later describe Freetown airport and its immigration officials accurately, if cruelly, as "a junkyard guarded by growling junkyard dogs."

"What are you doing in this country?" a woman immigration official demanded.

"I've always wanted to see Sierra Leone, hearing how beautiful it was. Also, I have a friend here."

"I'll give you fourteen days," she said.

"But the visa I got at your embassy in Washington is good for a month," I complained.

"I didn't ask you what the visa says. I can read," she shot back, writing *14 days* in my passport.

The taxi from Freetown's Lungi Airport was no better than the Renault in Conakry. The airport gate was guarded by rifle-bearing soldiers. One soldier came up to the battered taxi and stuck his head inside. His eyes were bloodshot and he smelled of alcohol. "What are you doing here?" he asked. I told him I was visiting a friend, "a diplomat." He stared at me for a moment and said, "Welcome," turning his head to spit on the ground.

Africa offered several realities, I noticed. One was what I term the "VIP bubble," within which the highest-ranking diplomats and visiting emissaries experience Africa. In this version of reality, you are met at the airport by an embassy expediter, who escorts you to a waiting area while he gets your passport stamped and afterward hustles you and your luggage through customs. Then a late-model air-conditioned car, protected from soldiers by diplomatic license plates, takes you to a five-star hotel or the ambassador's residence. This experience puts you in one frame of mind about Africa. To negotiate airports on your own puts you in another. At home once, I attended a Washington-area conference and listened to an extremely high-ranking former State Department official talk about positive developments in Africa, neglecting to mention such details as birthrates, resource depletion, and thuggery. I found myself thinking, *How did he arrive at the airport?* (Lower-level diplomats, of course, often have travel experiences similar to mine.)

Hardy diplomats and adventurers, journalists among them, laugh off these airport hellholes, saying, "It's part of the fun and romance of African travel." A favorite dictum of foreign correspondents is, *Journalism in Africa is 90 percent logistics and getting to the story and 10 percent actual reporting*. Very true, but also somewhat intellectually dishonest. Such airport experiences as mine are, in fact, part of the story.

There was no shantytown here as there was in Conakry. Instead, I saw a botanical paradise unroll outside the cracked window, a smoky greenery so lush it appeared almost blue, with trees and plants that had an unreal quality, like a diorama. Again unlike Conakry, or any of the other places along the West African coast, in Freetown there were mountains. After a quarter-hour of fast driving came the people.

The taxi suddenly halted and joined a long line of vehicles waiting for the next car ferry that would take us across a two-and-a-half-mile-wide lagoon, where on the far side lay Freetown. On the stretch of road where the cars waited was a corrugated-metal market, teeming with people who approached me with yams, mangoes, papayas, and boiled eggs for sale. Rather than picturesque traditional cloth, people wore synthetic leftovers from some long-past rummage sale, but the earth looked bountiful. Here, you could have serious social collapse, but unlike the people who lived in more ecologically fragile regions like the Horn of Africa, fewer here would starve. The ropy muscles of the men and the ample breasts of the woman were proof. But as the discolored eyes showed, there were also disease and dietary deficiencies. Obviously, not everything needed in a wholesome diet grew wild or was easy to cultivate.

I heard the screech of tires. Rounding a curve and breaking into the open lane reserved for cars coming off the ferry in the opposite direction was a new, gleaming Mercedes of a subtle gray hue, racing at high speed. The crowd quickly fled from its path. A little girl was nearly run over. Another screech. The car stopped suddenly at the front of the queue. Then, like the others, it just waited for the ferry. Because of the tinted windows it was impossible to see who was inside. The engine continued running, for the sake, no doubt, of the air conditioner. "Who's in the Mercedes?" I asked the man who had sold me a Coke. "Someone from the military government," he replied under his breath. I thought of Haiti.

Yes, Sierra Leone did seem, at first glance, to resemble Haiti. It was beautiful, romantic, leavened with both sadness and evil and, most crucially, self-contained: There were mountains and fields, an ocean, a lagoon, and a port town in the distance—an entire world in miniature. This heightened the feeling of isolation, for Sierra Leone was so hard to get to, so hard to enter, and (I suspected) so hard to get out of. Elsewhere in West Africa you felt you were on a continent. Here you felt at once as though you were on an island. Two of Graham Greene's most memorable novels, *The Comedians* and *The Heart of the Matter*, were set in Haiti and Sierra Leone, respectively. I sensed this was no coincidence.

The ferry arrived: a rusted, blackened hulk riding dangerously low in the water. The cars filed aboard bumper-to-bumper, with just enough inches on either side for passengers to squeeze out of their cars. The Mercedes's doors remained shut, its engine running. I scampered to the mid-deck, where I found a bar filled with rowdy soldiers guzzling Guinness stout. "What are you doing here, man?" one asked me. They reminded me of Serbian soldiers that I had seen a few years earlier in Bosnia drowning themselves in plum brandy. I bought a Guinness and headed for the open air of the upper deck. Rain clouds converged on the sunlight refracted on the water; what had seemed from the shore a shimmering pan of turquoise became a dull and sullen vat. I thought of a few lines from *The Heart of the Matter*: "The sky wept endlessly around him; he had the sense of wounds that never healed."

The breeze picked up. Freetown swept into focus as the ferry approached. The sheer joy of travel momentarily surged through me, an emotion harder to summon as one grows older, as more chapters of one's life accumulate, and experience crowds out raw feeling. Here at last was a dramatic cityscape, built on hills fronting the sea, the very verticality and concentration of its settlement pattern suggesting a richer past and tradition than the flat godowns by the Atlantic at Abidjan and Conakry, which reeked of temporariness, however much larger than Freetown they may have been. Those cities were mere accidents. Freetown seemed, by contrast, a place that was meant to be.

Even its squalor was picturesque. Here too were the usual corrugated metal, charred wood, black plastic sheeting, and old tires. Yet the materials were ingeniously shaped into gabled gingerbread houses leaning drunkenly—yet they stood, each the product of innumerable repairs.

In the space between these houses, as my taxi left the ferry and crawled in traffic, I saw the milky-blue Atlantic melding with the sky. Palm leaves filtered the view. Freetown was an easy place to fall in love with, a place about which you could easily suspend judgment for a few moments. I wished I had been younger and more naive, and that I was not addicted to political analysis.

I noticed freshly painted murals on many of the walls, of young military officers in battle fatigues and dark sunglasses. This was the "beautification campaign" about which a Western relief worker in Abidjan had spoken to me enthusiastically. To me it seemed more like a budding personality cult.

The taxi pulled up to the foreign mission where my friend Michelle worked as a diplomat, a first secretary who specialized in politics and economics.[9] I gave my passport to the guard, who phoned her extension. She came down and stared at me. "You're the only person I know who just, well, dropped in! It's not the easiest place in the world to get to!"

It was not Michelle but another Western friend, a relief-agency director, who showed me the way to the minister's terrace, where I talked with him about *The Nigger of the "Narcissus."* In the coming days we would talk often.

◎   ◎   ◎

THAT SAME NIGHT Michelle took me to dinner with an ambassador from another Western embassy. We went to a Lebanese restaurant right on the beach, with thatched-wood awnings, stylish men and women (mainly white Europeans and local Arabs), and a crowded bar buzzing with that desperate bonhomie common to happy hours the world over. The men and women in the flowered cottons reminded me of Key West or the South Seas. The Lebanese food was excellent. So was the local Star beer. So, too, was the tropical sunset with the required blood-red hues. Peddlers in straw hats plied the beach, jauntily hawking local fabrics to the diners. We joked with them for a few moments. The changing color of the sea and the beer were tranquilizers. The beach was the usual pristine strip of ocher sand braided by a line of coconut palms, common through much of West Africa. I had to remind myself that this was the same beach where military officers had recently taken twenty-nine suspected coup plotters to be executed, after cutting their ears off at a "slumber party" in SAJ Musa's driveway.[10]

The ambassador wore shorts and a colored T-shirt. Still, his formal handshake and slight reserve throughout dinner made it clear that this was a briefing and off-the-record. Here are the highlights:

[9]Michelle is a pseudonym for this European diplomat, whose local contacts might be endangered if I identified her better. Occasionally, to protect people, I use pseudonyms.
[10]The incident occurred in December 1992, nine months before my visit.

- The government, run by a twenty-seven-year-old army captain, Valentine Strasser, despite its considerable brutality, controlled only "half or part" of the rural interior. In the "half or part" of the country that the regime did not control, units of two separate armies from the war in neighboring Liberia had casually taken up residence, alongside a third army of Sierra Leonean rebels. Worse yet, the government forces charged with suppressing the rebel insurgency were full of renegade commanders who had aligned themselves with disaffected village chiefs. Clearly a premodern formlessness governed the battle-field, recalling the wars in tribal or feudal Europe before the Peace of Westphalia introduced the era of organized nation-states.

  It was in Sierra Leone that I first considered the possibility that just as states and their governments were meaning less and less, the distinctions between states and armies, armies and civilians, and armies and criminal gangs were also weakening; that the volume and intensity of the savagery permeating third-world conflicts during the Cold War, whether in El Salvador, Afghanistan, Cambodia, Burundi, the Iraq-Iran border, the Indian subcontinent and Sri Lanka, and elsewhere, were only in varying degrees connected to the ideological struggle of the superpowers.[11] They were part of something else. These "low-intensity" conflagrations were not merely sideshows of the Cold War; they were harbingers of the post–Cold War world, which would include more of the same in Bosnia, the Caucasus, Somalia, Liberia, Kashmir, Sierra Leone, and so on.

- As a consequence of the mayhem, 400,000 Sierra Leoneans were internally displaced; 280,000 more had fled to neighboring Guinea; and another 100,000 had fled to war-torn Liberia, even as 400,000 Liberians fled to Sierra Leone. The third largest city in Sierra Leone, Gondama, was a displaced persons camp, whose inhabitants were generally healthier than the population at large.[12] With an additional

[11]The December 1981 massacre of over five hundred civilians, many of them women and children, in the Salvadoran town of El Mozote is a case in point. The atrocity is documented in Mark Danner's *New Yorker* article of December 6, 1993. Though the author concentrates on America's culpability in training the rightist death squad, he also demonstrates how the killing—not to mention the whole war—bared wells of primitivism for which the local culture itself must also be held accountable.

[12]Catholic Relief Services reported that the camp's 11 percent gross mortality rate was half that of the rest of Sierra Leone; and while 16 percent of the camp's children under five years old were malnourished, the figure for the whole country was 23 percent.

600,000 Liberians in Guinea and 250,000 more in Côte d'Ivoire, the border regions of these four countries had become largely meaningless. Even in quiet zones, none of these governments save for the Ivory Coast's adequately maintained the schools, bridges, roads, and police forces necessary for a functioning sovereignty.

- The flight of peasants to Freetown and the raising of a large army to fight the various insurgencies were factors in the steeply rising crime rate. Elements of the army were deserting with their weapons and turning to armed robbery. The beaches, except in the immediate vicinity of this and a few other restaurants, were considered unsafe after dark.

- Electricity was a sometimes thing, unlike thirty years ago, when Freetown residents had reliable electric current.

- Sierra Leone was, in some ways, more isolated than Albania had been under its Maoist regime. Eighty percent of the Sierra Leone population was illiterate. Unlike Albanians, many of whom had access to television sets and could watch programs from nearby Greece and Italy, including CNN, the overwhelming majority of people here had no televisions. Many had no electricity. Local radio was government-controlled and, more important, carried only local news. The situation was similar in many parts of Africa, alleviated only by shortwave radio.

- Despite all the wars in Sierra Leone, the population was growing at anywhere from 2.6 percent to 3.9 percent annually—nobody knew exactly. The average woman conceived six children over her adult lifetime.[13] However, while 60 percent of the country was nutrient-rich, tropical rain forest at independence over 30 years ago, only six per cent was rain forest now. Disease was out of control.

- Several members of Sierra Leone's elite, or what was left of it, had asked Western officials if, maybe, the United Nations or some other international coalition could send in "20,000" troops to straighten the country out.

In other words, I was visiting a failed society. Almost anyone with real ambition and talent had left, or was attempting to leave, for the United

---

[13]If the population growth rate is, as suspected, much higher than 2.6 percent, that might hike the fertility rate upward, though the growth rate is affected by other factors, such as life expectancy.

States or Europe. Dynamic Sierra Leoneans could be found in many a nation, but rarely in Sierra Leone. In Israel, India, and other places there had been a "brain drain" to the West, but there were always enough top-quality people left behind so that the loss was never fatal. In the fragile states of West Africa the loss of talent was more serious—a selecting-out process at the end of the dock or runway, stranding those who couldn't make the grade.

The sunset was finished. The beach was completely empty, and the atrocities committed on the beach nine months before now seemed vivid, as if they had just happened. The dinner broke up. I was exhausted, and the diplomats had to be at their embassies early the next morning. Beyond the lights of the bar just starting to vibrate with "beautiful people" was the surly darkness of the parking lot, with its menacing youths guarding the vehicles for small change. I looked back at the bar, at the perfumed women and men with expensive watches, relaxing from another day of accumulated untaxed wealth, and had the vision of a tiny planet in space in the last moments before being extinguished by an on-rushing meteor. I felt vulnerable. *Why didn't they?*

Before falling asleep in Michelle's house, I looked out the window at a line of palm fronds, their black tentacles swaying silently against the iron-gray ocean of night. Sierra Leone, Senegal, Gambia, Guinea-Bissau, Guinea, and Liberia: together, they form the bulge of West Africa at the narrowest point of the Atlantic, only three hours or so by airplane to the coast of South America. Yet here was an isolation such as I had rarely encountered, a limb of humanity cleaved from the larger blood flow of civilizations. This whole region had been known to sailors as the Windward Coast, because of the strong winds that drove sailing vessels—first those of the Portuguese explorers, afterward those of the slavers—so quickly around the West African bulge. "For two centuries," my new friend the minister had told me earlier in the day, "Freetown was the most important point for collecting fresh water and vegetables on the route from Europe to the Cape of Good Hope. We were at the center of the explorers' journeys—not at the margins of the earth. The English, led by a man named Hawkins, collected the first slaves here in the sixteenth century."[14] I wondered whether Sierra Leone was finally moving back toward the center of things, given the problems it represented.

[14]Sir John Hawkins, 1532–1595, an English admiral, was the first Englishman to break the Portuguese monopoly on the slave trade.

WHEN YOU READ the history of Sierra Leone you cannot help but realize how much the past was decreed by geography and climate. Here was a trading post, Freetown, and behind it an ill-defined, disease-ridden interior. As long as the sea route around the southern African Cape was the only way to India, Freetown was a main focus of human events, including the evil slave trade. The end of slaving was soon followed by the construction of the Suez Canal, offering a shorter route to India. No longer a victim of slavers, Sierra Leone now became a victim of its location—a backwater attracting only dregs and mediocrities from Europe. The interior jungles led only to savannahs, which, in turn, led only to the Sahara. The Atlantic that had once brought slavers and a rudimentary measure of contact with the Western world now brought almost nothing. Sierra Leone was a metaphor for geographical destiny. Sierra Leone helped me feel what it is like *to be cut off*.

The territory's first contact with Western civilization came in 1462, upon the arrival of the Portuguese explorer Pedro da Sintra, who gave it the name Serra Leao, Portuguese for "Lion Mountain," because the mountains near Freetown resembled a lion when seen from an approaching ship.[15] Despite a visit by Sir Francis Drake during his voyage around the world from 1577 to 1580, contact with the West was intermittent until the late eighteenth century, though the British had built a trading post on Bunce Island in the seventeenth century that became a notorious holding point for slaves en route to the Americas. (John Newton, the British minister who wrote the hymn "Amazing Grace," was a slave trader at Shenge, south of Freetown, before he found God, renounced his profession, and joined the church.)

The American War of Independence provided a way for slaves to gain their freedom by fighting for the British crown. Following the war, many of these freed slaves made their way to England, where they lived in abject poverty. In 1787, a group of English philanthropists purchased a fifty-two-square-kilometer bit of land from the Timni tribal chief Naimbamma in Serra Leao in order to establish a "Province of Freedom" for the former slaves. Thus, "Freetown" came into existence. Of the first set-

---

[15]By sheer coincidence, I once lived for two years in the village of Sao Pedro da Sintra, north of Lisbon. Another version is that an Italian drew a map of West Africa with the name Sierra Leone: hence the name.

tlers—several hundred former slaves and a hundred whites—Richard Burton reports that "many died of disease, some drank themselves to death, others ran away . . ."[16] Within three years, only forty-eight of the original settlers remained. Sierra Leone soon acquired the nickname "the white man's grave."

But the British philanthropists were dogged. Their reaction to this catastrophe was merely to dispatch to the new African settlement twelve hundred more ex-slaves from Nova Scotia (where these slaves, having fought for the British, sought refuge after the British defeat in the Revolutionary War). Of the twelve hundred settlers, within a few years eight hundred went to the grave. The philanthropists then dispatched several hundred more ex-slaves, this time from the West Indian island of Jamaica. The ex-slaves joined with the criminal class of whites in the slave trade. It was the beginning of a fissure, which would continue to this day, between the former American slaves and their descendants (who adopted English names and manners and stayed close to Freetown) and the indigenous African tribesmen living in the interior.

In 1807 the British outlawed the slave trade, and in 1808 Sierra Leone became a full-fledged British colony, to provide both a base for intercepting slave ships and a home for the newly liberated captives from all over the Atlantic coast of Africa, fifty thousand of whom the British brought to Freetown between 1807 and 1864. While popular myth holds that behind the establishment of every African colony lay the cruelest and crassest of motives, Sierra Leone's official founding by the British was largely governed by the urge to help the captured, as well as to prevent ensuing chaos in Freetown. In this respect, the British endeavor was rather like those of the Americans in Haiti in 1915 and in Somalia in 1992.[17] That liberated slaves from over a hundred ethnic groups lived in relative harmony in Freetown throughout the nineteenth century reflects both the peaceful and cosmopolitan nature of these Africans and the able British administration, which provided Sierra Leone with the requisite security.

---

[16]The last part of Burton's account is oddly vague: cut off by ocean and desert, to where would they run? And how would they get away?

[17]In 1915 President Woodrow Wilson sent U.S. Marines to Haiti to restore order after 102 coups and revolutions over the preceding seventy-two years. (See Robert and Nancy Heinl's *Written in Blood*, listed in the bibliography.) In 1992 President George Bush dispatched troops to Somalia to provide security for famine-relief operations.

Yet this harmony and prosperity were relative. Burton quotes a diarist, Captain Chamier, as saying:

> . . . I never knew and never heard mention of so villainous or iniqui-
> tous a place as Sierra Leone. I know not where the Devil's Poste
> Restante is, but the place surely must be Sierra Leone.

Burton's own description of 1860s Freetown indicates that he agreed. Freetown was a malarial pit. "At a distance it is not unpicturesque, but the style of beauty is that of a Rhenish Castle, ruinous and tumbledown. . . . Men come out from Europe with the fairest prospect, if beyond middle age, of dying soon," he writes.

The descendants of the freed slaves, the "Creoles,"[18] were then beginning to emerge as a distinct, wealthier class of Africans who both competed with and depended upon the British. Outnumbered fifty to one by the indigenous Temne, Mende, and other tribes of the interior, the better-educated Creoles were terrified of a British withdrawal, especially after a violent uprising by the interior tribesmen following the imposition of a "hut tax."

Also competing with the Creoles were Lebanese merchants, who began streaming in toward the end of the nineteenth century. The Cre-oles, and to a much larger extent the Lebanese, formed a rudimentary middle class amid the large body of African tribesmen.

The British began preparing the inhabitants for self-rule in the 1920s with the formation of a legislative council, dominated by Temne and Mende. As in so many other places, independence in 1961 began with high hopes for democracy, to be quickly followed by a political melt-down along tribal lines, with the Temne of the north, the Mende of the south, and the Creoles of the coast breaking into separate factions. In one thirteen-month period in the 1960s there were three coups. Elections were so violent that they often erupted into mini–civil wars. Dissidents were publicly hanged. From 1967 through 1985, Siaka Stevens was the "Big Man" ruling Sierra Leone, despite several assassination attempts that forced him to import specially trained bodyguards from pro-Soviet

---

[18]The Encylopædia Britannica; Graham Greene, in *The Heart of the Matter;* and San-ford Ungar in his book *Africa: The People and Politics of an Emerging Continent* use the term Creole for the colony's original inhabitants. However, some guidebooks and Sierra Leoneans themselves prefer Krio.

Guinea.[19] His resignation due to age brought on only greater chaos, which included the large-scale smuggling of diamonds from the country's mines.

If any group can claim to be keeping the economy afloat it is the Lebanese, who form the core of middlemen and store owners. In 1994, the United Nations rated Sierra Leone the fourth worst country in the world to live in. (Guinea was the worst.)[20]

SOLDIERS, ARMED TEENAGE boys actually, stared at Michelle's car until their eyes worked their way down to the diplomatic license plates. One soldier then lifted the rusted bar that served as a gate over the laterite track, allowing us into a hilltop area where one of the junta leaders had a house. We went only as far as the house of a director-general of a ministry. But she was not in, and we headed back down the hill. This house impressed me. It was a magnificent old British structure, a gingerbread pile straight out of a fairy tale, but if you removed the romantic filter from your eyes, you saw the details: a rusted roof, rotting green latticework, gaps every-where like a house in a shack town, and walls askew as though damaged by an earthquake. It was a wreck. This was the home of a high government official, and in truth, because of its size and hilltop location overlooking the Atlantic, it was a palace by Freetown standards. Just looking at the house made me feel, once again, the unfathomable economic distance between Africa and many other parts of the world.

Michelle and I continued on, to an even more remote and beautiful hilltop, along a series of dips and crests with packed-together tropical slum houses on one side and the welcoming blue nothingness of the Atlantic on the other. We were headed for a tryst with Sierra Leonean history, a finely wrought chapter of the literary past that deserves mention.

Between 1941 and 1943, Graham Greene was stationed in Sierra Leone, working for the British Foreign Office, which feared a Nazi takeover of West Africa from the Vichy French base in nearby Senegal. Greene's sojourn in Sierra Leone resulted in *The Heart of the Matter.* Of his twenty-five-odd novels and mysteries—not to mention his travel writ-

---

[19]The term "Big Man" is taken from Blaine Harden's *Africa: Dispatches from a Fragile Continent.*
[20]The UN's "Human Development Index Ranking by Country."

ing, children's books, plays, collected short stories, biographies, and auto-biographies—*The Heart of the Matter* is often viewed as Greene's most memorable work. It is a novel suffused with troubled conscience, the story of a colonial official in Freetown, a Roman Catholic, who faces a spiritual and religious crisis after committing adultery with an Englishwoman while his wife is away in South Africa. Considering all the places through which Greene had traveled, why did he choose Sierra Leone as the setting for this particular morality tale? My new friend the minister, with whom I had been talking of late, provided the answer to a question that had puzzled me:

"Ah, yes, *The Heart of the Matter.* That's the one about the fellow who yields to sex in a place where sexual mores are not very strict."

But how could I have known this without coming to Sierra Leone? *The Heart of the Matter* is a morality tale set in an "evil" place. Given the heat, the liquor required to sleep at night—this before air-conditioning—and the seminudity dictated partly by the climate, adultery for a man whose wife was away was an unremarkable sin. The intense, sustained guilt it generated in Greene's protagonist, Scobie, may have been necessary for the preservation of Scobie's cultural identity: For him, guilt was an artificial life-support system in a "hostile" environment, without which he would have disintegrated from drink and debauchery, the way so many expatriates have done in such places.

Michelle's car kept ascending what Greene had called "the great loops of the climbing road," until a sprawling stone-and-corrugated-iron structure appeared in the clearing—the Hill Station club, where Scobie had come to drink and talk away the lonely nights. A sign over the bar said "Licensed Dealer in Intoxicating Liquors." For a literary-minded traveler, this was hallowed ground and lived up to my expectations. The lacquered paneling, the dart board, the polished trophies, the Ping-Pong table, and the vast array of greenish liquor bottles on the shelves—as warming to the heart as old book bindings—were testimony to the club's meticulous upkeep more than three decades after the British had departed. Here nothing had really changed. Colonialism lived on. The Hill Station was still for the privileged few. The only difference was that they now happened to be Africans.

"Things are wonderful in this country. I can't believe how good things are," said one of the regime's chief civil servants, one of three Sierra Leoneans who were alone at the bar when we walked in. The three, including a medical doctor and the chairman of the Sierra Leone Electrical Power Authority, stood us a drink of ice-cold Star beer.

"How can things be wonderful given the—you know—the situation?" I stuttered. I didn't want to mention the unmentionables: the arrests, the poverty, the wars, the crime, and so on.

"Yes," said the power-authority chairman. "I suppose we do need some sort of a face-lift in the country." His manner was breezy, jovial. It was obvious they were in too good a mood to discuss politics. I didn't pursue the subject.

Given that one of the men was a doctor, I brought up the subject of malaria.

"Yes, everyone here has malaria. I get a recurrence every few months," said the civil servant.

The doctor said that he prescribes an antimalarial agent to an African only if it is a serious case; otherwise, the medicine would make it harder for the patient's body to build up a natural immunity, necessary for someone who lives here.

The conversation wandered from malaria to cholera. I asked the doctor why some African nations still insist visitors show proof of a cholera vaccination, even though it has long been known that the vaccinations are not very effective. Before I came to Sierra Leone, I had gone to a Washington, D.C.–area clinic specializing in tropical diseases, where a nurse gladly stamped my yellow vaccination booklet for an anticholera injection that she had no intention of giving me, saying: "These people [she meant Africans] are like children—they love stamps. We've been telling them for years that the vaccine is not really effective, yet they keep insisting on proof of it."

What was the opinion of the doctor at the bar?

He expressed genuine surprise, some doubt even, about the news—known widely in the West—that the cholera vaccine is largely ineffective.[21] "If that's true, why doesn't our government tell us these things?" he asked. "I have not read about it in any journal. I never knew there was a problem with the vaccine." He shrugged, unruffled. What was I to do—give him the phone number of the nurse in Washington, or tell him to call

---

[21]As part of a survey on U.S. tropical-disease clinics, Nichole Bernier reported that "experts agree" the cholera vaccine is "less than 50 percent effective" and, therefore, "superfluous." See the bibliography.

the Centers for Disease Control in Atlanta? Phoning overseas from Sierra Leone was exceedingly difficult, and costly. Moreover, all this was beside the point, which was that here was a man, a doctor, a reputable physician in Freetown, isolated from knowledge that any hippie backpacker or other budget traveler had easy access to.

More disturbing was that I hadn't really stirred him. The doctor's easy, noncommittal manner suggested he was not going to investigate the subject further.

It was one of those devastating little moments when you realized the sheer irrelevance of discoveries in medicine and agriculture for a region where the most rudimentary clinics and outdoor water pumps had been vandalized within a year or so after they opened; where massive amounts of foreign aid had disappeared over the years while the government spent fifteen cents per capita annually on health care—not enough to buy a syringe, or even alcohol for slide smears for identifying malaria. In many clinics the alcohol had been stolen. A map I had seen in the Freetown headquarters of Catholic Relief Services told the story: Of the thirty-two places around the world where this charity, which helps the most helpless and destitute of societies, has bureaus, eighteen were in Africa, two were in Haiti, eleven were in Latin America, and one was in India. "If the NGOs [non-governmental organizations—Western aid agencies] pulled out, disease would explode out of all proportion," a Peace Corps doctor had told me.

Some relief workers, usually the most idealistic and sympathetic to Africa of any Westerners, were openly admitting the uncomfortable implications of their record in Sierra Leone. In the 1960s, after President Kennedy had established the Peace Corps, both Sierra Leone and India required basic agricultural know-how. Thirty years later, while India had become a net food exporter and a producer of high technology—with no further need of assistance in simple farming—Sierra Leone was where it had been in the 1960s, with Peace Corps volunteers teaching the same basic skills. The message of Sierra Leone was brutal: The end was nigh in the failed battle, fought valiantly by the liberal West, to equalize cultures around the world. The differences between some cultures and others (regarding the ability to produce exportable material wealth) appeared to be growing rather than diminishing.

Rather than Graham Greene, whose *Heart of the Matter*—set in a somnolent and charmingly seedy Freetown of the 1940s—implies a certain romance, it was now Thomas Malthus, the philosopher of demographic doomsday, who seems to have more to say about what is happening in West Africa. At a dinner party at Michelle's, I watched a Sierra Leonean official, a young and intense man with friends high up in the military regime, react angrily, his eyes flaring, as Michelle told him: "It may be that in future years Western aid will be given on the basis of a government's ability to get its birthrate down and to stop destroying its rain forests" rather than on the basis of a government's friendliness to us and of its hostility to communism. The words *birthrate down* were what made this official almost hiss in hatred. Michelle's mention of the rain forests merely implied that African governments didn't have their houses in order, and may have been involved in dirty deals with logging companies: nothing new there. But the birthrate was—to judge from the fellow's reaction—a bit too personal.

◎   ◎   ◎

MICHELLE'S DINNER PARTY was both a charming and foreboding icon of a soon-to-be-gone golden age of diplomacy in the third world. It was charming because here was a diplomat who, though neither an ambassador nor even a chargé d'affaires, was nevertheless able to attract some of the most important people in the country to her house, where a fine meal was prepared with the assistance of a housekeeper. The style in which Michelle was able to live in Freetown and the rank of officials she was able to attract were indicative of the gap between a wealthy Western land and a poor African one. Were this inequality any less than it was, only officials of her own modest rank would have been at the party. Yet Michelle had more influence in Sierra Leone than any Western ambassador could hope to have in a country like France, Greece, or even, say, Malaysia. There were quite a few Michelles in Western embassies around the world, diplomats who, back in Washington, London, or Paris, had been ordinary, anonymous bureaucrats occupying cubbyhole houses in suburbia, taking the metro to work. But transpose them to tropical capitals and they occupy an enviable position in the social pecking order, with a driver and a housekeeper, and a romantic view from a balcony. As far as a diplomat's life is concerned, Greene's West Africa is still alive in the mid-1990s.

But there is another side to the story.

Michelle's dinner party was not your typical embassy reception calculated to "show the flag," with all the polite, vacuous chatter such efforts so often entail. Her remark about birthrates touched one of several nerves, which lent the evening an unremitting tension. For example, the young official who didn't much like Michelle's insinuation about African men fathering more children than they could afford to raise delivered a monologue about oppression. I had asked him about the human rights record of his and other African governments. "You talk about repression," he shot back in a calm, even, and crisply enunciated tone, the tone of suppressed rage. "Let me tell you about what happened to an African student in the so-called free society of England." He then told a long story about a student, associated with the leftist independence movement of the late Congolese leader Patrice Lummumba, who had gone into political exile in England, where the student had been—as it turned out—unfairly imprisoned. To me the sad tale demonstrated what I well knew—that even in free societies justice is imperfect and tinged by racism. But to him this injustice was sufficient to justify the evils of some African regimes throughout the continent. About his own government, he said, "We have been doing some pretty wonderful things in Sierra Leone that you [the West] don't take notice of." He then mentioned the beautification campaign in Freetown, which included the large mural paintings of the coup leaders, including one of Solomon Anthony Joseph (SAJ) Musa, responsible for the atrocities on the beach. As for the large amounts of money the government was spending on arms—which had precipitated the crime wave in Freetown when deserting soldiers formed robber gangs—the young official answered, "You must remember, we are fighting a war to protect our sovereignty." Another government official at the party then complained that the West was not coming through with more loans for Africa. As with the requests for twenty thousand Western troops to sort out matters here, it was hard explaining to people whose sources of information for years had been limited to the Sierra Leonean media and the BBC Africa Service that in the West, interest in Africa had always been slight, while the international community's experience in Somalia had further diminished enthusiasm for the kind of help some in West Africa demanded.

The Cold War had been Africa's best opportunity to garner attention, and therefore money, from the West—since no matter how small and inconsequential the country, if the Soviets expressed any interest in it, or in any place nearby, the West had to be there too. Take away the Soviet threat and there is nothing with which to interest the West.

Of course, there is *something*—the spread of disease, of crime; the destruction not just of rain forests but of whole societies. But those things are opaque, inanimate almost. They don't fit the parameters of hard-news copy, the way a particular coup or an atrocity or a drought does. So the West can't focus on them until it is too late.

The guests departed. Upon retreating to the living quarters, Michelle slammed shut and carefully locked a steel gate that separated the bedrooms and toilets from the kitchen, living room, and adjoining balcony near the front door. This created a secure area in the back of the flat from which the special embassy communications gear could be used to call the embassy security officer or marines for help in case of a break-in, since the private security guards outside the building could not be expected to stop a band of armed robbers.

"What about the police?" I asked, lamely.

Michelle shrugged. "The police have no gas for their vehicles. The government in Sierra Leone has no writ after dark."

When I emerged for breakfast the next morning, Michelle had "some news." She had just been informed over the walkie-talkie that a member of the small foreign community, an American, had been robbed during the night. Eight men armed with AK-47s had broken into his house, tied him up, and stolen everything of value.

THE NEXT DAY at dusk, Michelle and I sat on her balcony looking through the screen of palm fronds to the soothing Atlantic. To most people, especially to Washington careerists, the idea of being a middle- or low-ranking diplomat in a place like Sierra Leone would represent the ultimate in underachievement, unless it came very early in one's career. A posting in Africa is, according to one writer, like having gone "missing." Yet I envied Michelle. I knew that her job was far more stimulating intellectually than almost any job a capital like Washington or London had to offer. As she herself put it: "Waking up each morning in a place that's on the verge of anarchy provides a unique insight into humanity. There are never any lulls." Moreover, it is an experience that exposes one's liberal beliefs to the most severe challenges.

Yet in Michelle's home capital, her political cables from the Freetown embassy enjoyed a lot less attention than the cables about embassy security and evacuation plans. Among diplomats in Africa I heard much talk about closing embassies. In Freetown, the Russian, Italian, and South Korean embassies had all recently shut down. The Israelis, who in the 1970s were desperate to have an embassy in any African country that would have them, were also closing their missions. "There's little economic activity here, and there are so many new opportunities for us in Moslem Central Asia," an Israeli ambassador told me. One American official on a visit from Washington in late 1993 told me: "We closed the embassy in the Comoro Islands without an outcry. So we've got a precedent. Now we're working on closing up Equatorial Guinea. Then we can start on places like Sierra Leone. In the future, we'll have a smaller number of magnet embassies that will handle the whole continent." Michelle was the last of a breed. The future would probably be far less generous to diplomats: There would be fewer of them, and those few would be overworked and living in big cities.

◎   ◎   ◎

"FRIEND TODAY, ENEMY Tomorrow" read the sticker emblazoned on the inside windshield of the truck I was riding in. We were carrying oral rehydration salts, school notebooks, wheat, and corn-soya from the Catholic Relief Services warehouse in Freetown to the town of Bo, 160 miles away, more than halfway across the interior of Sierra Leone in the direction of Liberia and near the edge of government control. The driver, Simeon, was a Christian. But to judge by the sticker and amulets, he was taking no chances. Theoretically, Simeon worked for Catholic Relief. Theoretically, I was riding in a Catholic Relief truck. But the actual distance between the neat, air-conditioned office of Catholic Relief in downtown Freetown, with its affable director, fiddling with his desktop computer powered by a private generator and fielding long-distance calls from CRS's Baltimore headquarters thanks to a rooftop satellite dish, was immeasurable. In reality, CRS's humanitarian lifeline to the Sierra Leone interior depended, like so much else here, on the Lebanese, who ran a trucking company employing African drivers, which CRS contracted to deliver its relief supplies.[22] Here's how it worked:

---

[22]Today in Sierra Leone, people usually refer to the Arab middle class as "Lebanese." Graham Greene, in *The Heart of the Matter*, refers to them as "Syrians." The confusion is mainly due to the fact that through the end of World War II, Lebanon was often thought of as part of Syria.

A CRS official in Freetown would phone one of two Lebanese managing the trucking firm, who sat all day in designer shirts in another spic-and-span, air-conditioned office with a filtered water cooler—a few square meters of efficiency amid the sweaty bedlam of the Freetown docks—to say he wanted a truckload of relief supplies delivered. The Lebanese would then order an African driver into their cologned and air-conditioned midst, hurl insults at him like a sergeant screaming at a fresh recruit, and say, in effect: "Load up your truck and deliver the food *there*." Getting *there* involved many menacing roadblocks and mechanical breakdowns. The driver then slipped out the door, argued and screamed at the loading crew, jumped into his sagging truck, touched two wires together beneath the wheel two or three times until the truck started, and set off.

CRS, because of its idealism and the money it supplied, took the credit. Though the drivers were, as individuals, forgotten heroes, as a group at least they were occasionally mentioned in media coverage of third world relief operations. Moreover, as Africans they were also victims. The only people whom everybody had license to despise were the Lebanese, without whom—whatever their faults—there might not have been a trucking firm in the first place.

These Lebanese truck owners reminded me of the Greeks I had met in Khartoum during the Sudanese and Ethiopian famines of the mid-1980s. The Greeks had been kinder to the Sudanese than the Lebanese were to the Sierra Leonian drivers. Nevertheless, the Greeks also made the relief effort "work," while gaining almost no credit for it. The Greeks were no less cynical than the Lebanese. I remember a Greek merchant telling me during the 1985 rebellion against Jaafar Nimeiri's military regime: "You journalists think there will be democracy. Wait a few years, democracy in a place like Sudan will lead to anarchy." (It led to a confused and incompetent Islamic dictatorship.)

"How long will it take us to get to Bo?" I asked Simeon.

He shrugged. "I don't know, sir. Depends on the road, and on the soldiers."

This was what the Lebanese and the CRS official had told me. Sierra Leone was, on the map, a tiny country, smaller than South Carolina. In reality it was vast. Anyone could calculate how long it would take to drive from New York to California. But nobody here knew how long it would take to get from Freetown to Bo.

Near the outskirts of the city, Simeon brought the truck to a halt outside a checkerboard of corrugated-iron shacks. Out of one shack, in which I had counted twenty people, charged Abdul, naked from the waist up but carrying a shirt in his hand. Abdul introduced himself as Simeon's assistant and substitute driver. CRS paid the Lebanese, who paid Simeon, who in turn paid Abdul. (Moslem Africans often have Arabic names.)

Leaving Freetown we arrived at the first roadblock, a one hundred-yard series of shoulder-high hurdles, built from tree barks like an equestrian course, lined on both sides by soldiers with assault rifles and crowds of civilians lugging canvas sacks. Battered cars, bush taxis, and trucks were pulled over by the side of the road as soldiers sifted through their contents while the civilians used the opportunity to hitch lifts. Women traders sold bananas and boiled eggs. It was like a vast bus stop. Until our truck was made to pull over, that is.

Soldiers jumped all over the sacks of wheat and soya. Simeon leaped out to make sure that none of his cargo was being stolen and to plead with the soldiers that it was only "food for the refugees." He waved his carbon copy of the manifest at them. The soldiers laughed. One came up to me, pointing his assault rifle through the window. That didn't frighten me as much as his eyes—swollen, bloodshot, groggy eyes, the eyes of a drug user.

"What yawr name?" the soldier demanded. "I'm Mustafa. You got something for me? I want some money for that soya you got."

Abdul leaned over and calmly explained that we were carrying CRS supplies, guaranteed free passage. Abdul identified me as a *lokotu*, "an important white man," working for CRS. I stayed silent. It wasn't Abdul's words so much as the lullabying quality of his voice that impressed me. Abdul was all efficiency and intelligence. He was engaged in a holding pattern—calm the goon until we could get away.

Simeon leaped back into the driver's seat. With permission to pass, he touched the wires and we pulled away. The soldier harassing us jumped off the truck, swearing. Abdul shook his head. "These soldiers no good, sir. I'm sorry you must go through this trouble."

"What do you want to do in the future?" I asked Abdul.

"Get to New Jersey, where my sister lives," he said.

Gradually, the shantytowns thinned and we left the city behind. We entered a monotonous bush intersected by pitch-black languorous streams, where women naked from the waist up quickly became a familiar sight. Gears grinding, the truck lurched; the dashboard soon became too hot to touch, and dust flew in from the windowless doors. I quickly learned that in Africa a dirt road was far preferable to a paved road that had been potholed by rain.

The second roadblock consisted of a circular holding pen bordered by logs. Here, too, a gang of soldiers swarmed over our truck. Simeon and Abdul both jumped out this time, pleading, waving manifests, "CRS relief, food for the refugees!" The soldiers laughed. They were a bit drunk and pushed Simeon and Abdul. One soldier grabbed my wrist through the window.

"Hey, that's a nice watch you got. You gonna give me a lift, chap?" He poked his gun through the open window. Following Abdul's example, I just talked calmly, inventing all sorts of things about being a diplomat, on a special mission, not allowed, unfortunately, to take passengers, etc.

Other soldiers came to the truck door, demanding that I order Simeon and Abdul to let them ride in the back with the wheat and soya. This was an "army" without vehicles—rather, an armed rabble without vehicles. The whole concept of military aid to states like this now struck me as criminal. It was like arming a gang whose khaki uniforms were the equivalent of street-warrior insignia. While trying to reason with these young men holding guns, I spotted some four-wheel-drive Toyotas belonging to Western relief officials and diplomats, their windows rolled up, breeze easily through the roadblock. The soldiers, glancing at the license plates, waved them through. Those people will have a different account of their journey in Sierra Leone from mine.

We pulled away. This time, however, a few of the soldiers jumped on the back with the wheat and soya sacks. Simeon and Abdul shrugged. What could we do? CRS had a policy forbidding its vehicles from being used to transport soldiers. But here CRS was only an abstraction. Free-town seemed far, far away. The truck sagged and jerked to a stop. We had a flat tire.

The soldiers jumped off the truck. To my relief, they waved over another vehicle, threatening it with their guns, and jumped aboard. We found ourselves in a village. The tortured metal hulk of the truck, half concealed by all the sacks, had caved to the ground, splitting what was left of the tire. Some youths appeared, wearing baseball caps and cheaply made sneakers without laces. They immediately jumped onto the truck, and helped us unload enough of the supplies so that the tire could be replaced. The jack proved to be inadequate. We needed a bed of rocks to raise the back end of the truck sufficiently to slip the tire off. The whole process took close to two hours, giving me time to look around the village, which consisted of about twenty-five wattle huts and collapsing, fire-trap storefronts, hot and dusty.

It was no different from many of the settlements I had seen—and would see—throughout my journey in West Africa. One could describe this village as "picturesque" or "exotic," and a talented photographer could do wonders with its yoked oxen and bare-breasted pregnant women pounding cassava—provided, of course, that he carefully cropped other sights.

Which were: the piles of garbage, the empty shelves in the single store, the buzzing flies, the vacant and surly stares of the numerous young men hanging out until our flat tire gave them something useful to do, the sheer nothingness of it all. Life went on, babies were being conceived and born, and yet little was created, or even repaired, beyond the bare necessities. This was a timeworn way of life based on high infant mortality and low life expectancy. But with the average woman in Sierra Leone now bearing at least six children over her lifetime, sheer numbers had been mounting over the decades despite all the disease-related and war-related deaths. Sub-Saharan Africa was suffering the ironic side effects of Western aid—rudimentary sanitation in some areas and processed food close to the cities, which were enough to increase life expectancy but insufficient to help the inhabitants adapt to modern times. So the numbers mounted while the daily culture did not change. As awful as a West African shanty-town looked, I could understand why people were flooding to places like Chicago and Washington. In villages like this it was the old story: Close to the city something might happen, a different life perhaps; in the village, nothing happened.

That's partly why the village had a deserted aspect. True, men were working in the fields a few miles away. But many others had fled to the Freetown shanties. I looked over at the garbage: plastic wrap, tin cans, cardboard milk containers, a discarded chicken skin, all mixed with feces—a blend of rural and industrialized waste. Only in the eyes of a hell-bent romantic could this African village still be seen in majestic isolation. The sprawling urban magnets on the coast were changing the reality of villages like this one, whether it was the export of crime (the vandalization of rural health clinics, for instance) or the wearing of baseball caps and laceless sneakers or the milk containers and canned food. As I watched Simeon and Abdul hand out money to these rollicking youths, I had the sense of convergence, blending: city and town, war and crime, soldiers and convicts. Here, too, borders were crumbling, and they weren't all geographical.

When we pulled away, it had begun to rain. The windshield wipers didn't work. Simeon wrapped tin foil around a cigarette to fashion a makeshift fuse. The wipers started working. Simeon didn't boast or bare his teeth in self-congratulation. He was all purposefulness. Force a challenge upon a human being and he will usually rise to the occasion. Though poverty in Sierra Leone was forcing all kinds of daily challenges upon people, in the larger sense, perhaps, the earth here had been too generously abundant to demand the exertions a culture required in order to develop the self-discipline that peoples of less favored climes had been forced over the eons to learn.

Now this abundance was drying up, and few seemed to be aware of it. All day long on the road, I was to see human beings lugging bundles of firewood on their backs, some of it to be used locally and much of it to be taken to Freetown. The bush grew fast, but not fast enough for the increasing numbers of people. Between 1980 and 1990 alone, 20 percent of West Africa's forests had vanished.[23]

The truck again broke down. This time it was an overheated radiator. We waited for the radiator to cool, then topped it up with water from a nearby stream where people of varying ages, males and females, were bathing. The water was stagnant and probably carried schistosomiasis (bilharzia). The hovering flies were likely carriers of onchocerciasis (river blindness). But where else were these people to bathe?

The truck lurched and panted forward up a long, potholed incline for a few more miles, then stopped. The radiator was still overheating. This time Simeon and Abdul drained all of the water out, then filled it all up again with cooler stream water. Another half hour gone. We started up again. Twice more we stopped because of overheating. Including the tire, we had had five breakdowns. Finally, we assumed the worst—the radiator had a leak. We drained it yet once more. Simeon, using a mix of tar, chewing gum, and tin foil from a box of cigarettes, plugged it temporarily, and we proceeded.

---

[23]See World Resources Institute in the bibliography.

We talked and argued our way past two more roadblocks, each as threatening as the previous ones.

By the time we finally entered Bo, darkness had fallen. It had taken twelve hours to come 160 miles. I walked through the unlit streets, bought some boiled eggs and beer for my dinner, then searched for the Pastoral Church, run by Irish priests, hoping to find a place to sleep. A truckload of soldiers backed out of an alley. Just as I made eye contact with them, a young man grabbed my elbow and nudged me along, fast.

"I am Fuad," he said. "Can I help you find someplace?" Fuad wore thick glasses and a purple baseball cap. He was carrying books. I trusted him. He walked me to the office of the Pastoral Church, where I found a priest meeting with a group of locals in a dimly lit hovel of a room. The priest directed me to the church hostel, where I could find a place to sleep.

Fuad stayed with me until I found my room, in a small barracks-style building at the edge of the bush. With running water and an air conditioner, it was surprisingly adequate. I used my iodine-filter cup to drink the tap water.

After the first hour of darkness came the gunfire. Not far beyond Bo was the barely charted territory of the wars. It was unclear what this gunfire was. Was it a robbery, a series of robberies, or just "soldiers" shooting into the air? Fuad shrugged. He didn't know. Too keyed up to sleep, I sat outside the barracks talking with Fuad. He showed me one of his books, *The Christian and Demon Spirits*, by Jimmy Swaggart. "This book," he explained, "teaches me how to keep the devil away from my heart. You must always be vigilant." I didn't laugh. In Sierra Leone, social dissolution was all around. The government, as either a moral force or an organizing factor of public life, simply did not exist. Fuad lived with his mother and seven brothers and sisters. His father had been "away a long time." He had a "diploma" but no job prospects. Without money, he could probably not get into a college. Yet Fuad appeared gentle, calm. Rather than angry, he was determined, repeatedly asking me to write a recommendation letter for him, to help him with a scholarship to a college in Freetown. If Jimmy Swaggart was in some way responsible for this strength of character, who was I to judge?

Fuad was one of thousands of young African men trying to obtain a scholarship to a local college. Yet even those fortunate enough to gain admission had no job prospects awaiting them when they graduated. Sierra Leone was full of Fuads, destined to hope—and try—and be bitterly disappointed in the end.

It rained during the night. The green and black earth was freshly rinsed. As the sun rose, the invigorating scent of rainwater gave way to the smell of mud, and finally to the defeating odor of dust. Jim Ashman was the Catholic Relief representative in Bo. I searched him out for a briefing on what was going on here.

Ashman lived in a bungalow on the outskirts of town. I knocked on his door at eight in the morning. Half-naked and sleepy-eyed, he told me to wait in the living room for ten minutes until he had washed and dressed. The smaller and more out-of-the-way the place, the less formality was required. I had figured I didn't need an appointment to bang on his door so early in the day and his friendly, enthusiastic voice told me I was right. As he quickly informed me, his phone hadn't been working for months.

While waiting I looked around. It was a dusty house, barely furnished. On a shelf were a few African novels and a worn paperback of Graham Greene's *Journey Without Maps*. Balanced against the books was a photograph of some Liberian rebels smeared with blood, dressed as *juju* spirits, standing by a jeep with skulls mounted on it. An African woman emerged, Ashman's wife, who kindly cooked me a breakfast of two scrambled eggs and Coca-Cola. Given my thirst and the destabilizing effect coffee can have on one's stomach in a hot climate, it was a welcome combination. In the postindustrial temperate zone, with its myriad juices and bottled waters, I rarely touch Coca-Cola. In the tropics, I live on it.

Ashman came out and formally introduced me to his wife and their kids, now running around the room. He had been a pharmaceutical engineer working for an American drug company who had found suburban life dull, joined the Peace Corps, and served in Sierra Leone. Unable to re-adjust to America, he worked for a variety of relief agencies until he landed a job with CRS in Bo. Ashman was the relief-worker equivalent of a "stringer": a free-lance journalist working in some minor dateline, who, while less formal and professional-appearing than a staff correspondent— having, to a degree, "gone native" with the local population—also boasted knowledge and a *feel* for the local scene that few intelligence-service bureaucrats in a Western capital could muster. I remember a British stringer in Khartoum in 1985, Jill Lusk, who a few days before the April coup unreservedly announced that Nimeiri, the military ruler, would "very shortly be overthrown, because in my neighborhood, everybody is suddenly talking politics for the first time in years." She was right while many of the local diplomats, with their official cars, pension plans, and secure salaries, turned out to be wrong. In London and Washington, the knowledge chain about the third world often began in far-flung outposts with people like Jim Ashman and Jill Lusk. Information was progressively diluted, less interesting, and off-the-mark as you ascended upward towards "civilization."

Ashman began talking about the nearby Gondama refugee camp and how, with its Western-supplied medical services, newly built toilets, wells, birth huts, steady shipments of bulgar wheat and soya from agencies like CRS, and neat rows of clean, thatched huts, it offered one of the highest living standards in Sierra Leone. "The people at Gondama were expelled from the southeastern part of Sierra Leone. The area is claimed, sort of, by Liberia. The whole issue of nationality and boundaries out here is neb-ulous. The tribal boundaries are not the official ones, and increasingly the only borders that matter are those separating the Mende, Vaj, and Gola tribes. There are villages which the Sierra Leonean army has been afraid to enter, where invading soldiers have cut off people's ears. I know, I vis-ited one village . . ."

I asked Ashman about the flow of people to the cities. He said, "All the students from my Peace Corps days in the countryside are now in Freetown, without jobs." I asked Ashman about malaria: "In August alone at Gondama there were 675 recorded cases of serious malaria. Everybody here has malaria at a low level. I've also noticed a steady increase in the volume of sexual diseases."

"Is Sierra Leone a country?" I ventured.

"Is it a country? Well, that's an interesting question. Let's see . . . I told you about the area of Sierra Leone close to Liberia. I lived in Kabala, in the northeast. The Fula [tribesmen] there are more connected to Guinea than to Sierra Leone. It seems a lot of things are breaking down. Governments here since independence have corrupted the village chief system, by replacing hereditary chiefs with politically friendly ones who have little long-term legitimacy. As the central government weakens, power descends to these chiefs, who can't deal with the responsibility. There is a West African saying—"who would spit a sweet morsel from his mouth?" In other words, Who would part with a bribe? And there are just so many guns around. That's a new phenomenon. Is Sierra Leone a coun-try? It's interesting . . ."

I thought of what a German diplomat had remarked: "In the twenty-first century German ambassadors heading for Africa may again be authorized to sign treaties of cooperation with whatever coastal kings or leaders are able to assert some sort of control over the interior."

Ashman had a final thought about the culture into which he had married. "It is hard to gather wealth here, because as soon as you acquire some rice, for example, your neighbors want it. It is dangerous to save anything, because everything must immediately be shared. The [African] social system works to level everybody down to the same standard: It is a system that works against ambition."

◎　　　◎　　　◎

AS TIME PASSED, I began to distrust my memory. Had the journey from Freetown to Bo really been so bad? Then, in January 1995, came reports of widespread violence and hostage-taking outside Freetown on the very road I had taken. A BBC film crew had taken the same route. Their video footage showed mutilated bodies and a man pulling a finger out of his wallet, claiming it made him "disappear." The model refugee camp at Gondoma had been overrun by murderous rebel troops. The BBC crew interviewed the U.S. ambassador in Freetown, Lauralee Peters, about the state of Sierra Leonean society. She said, "What happens here gives me a shiver down my spine . . . I don't like seeing heads on sticks."[24]

On the other hand, in October 1995 came reports that the fighting in Sierra Leone and Liberia was truly winding down, thanks to the intervention of Africa's own peace-keeping units and private security consultants. As a result, elections were scheduled for early 1996 in Sierra Leone. The chaos, rather than expanding, may, in fact, be bottoming out. That should not make us complacent, however. High birthrates for the past few decades in Sierra Leone mean increasingly large numbers of young people here will be seeking jobs well into the next century. Just keeping people here afloat will require the kind of help and investment that the world is not likely to provide in a market-driven, globally linked economy in which West African countries no longer compete only with each other, but also with developing states in the Indian subcontinent, Southeast Asia, and Latin America.

[24]The on-camera interview and reportage were done by BBC correspondents Stephen Bradshaw and Mark Dowd for the show *Panorama*. The interview with Ambassador Peters did not make it into the final version, which aired March 20, 1995.

It may be easy to say that a place like Sierra Leone does not matter, but if we don't care at all about such places, why should, for instance, suburbanites in Tucson care about the inner city in Philadelphia? To be completely heartless about Africa, I mean to suggest, is to start down a path which imperils our own nationness.

◎ ◎ ◎

BACK IN FREETOWN a few days later, I enjoyed a pizza and a Coca-Cola at the spotlessly clean Crown Bakery, run by Lebanese. There were shiny glasses, designer sandwiches behind the counter, piped-in soft music, lacquered walls and furniture, a freshly painted ceiling, and silent air-conditioning. The dust and rot—the very air of West Africa—was excluded: a feat requiring nonstop cleaning, which the government-run hotels by the beach, charging over one hundred dollars a night for a room, could not manage. Here were international standards of cuisine, cleanliness, and management without the need of foreign advisers. Here was a pretty storefront amid the wreck of downtown Freetown, a place to which aid workers and diplomats could retreat, where Sierra Leoneans could at least see what the outside world looked like and how it worked. Though nobody said it, aid workers and diplomats knew that if all the ten thousand Lebanese ever left Sierra Leone, so might they. The Lebanese were a life-support system for foreigners, whether it was by arranging truck transport for refugee relief or offering lunch in a Western-style place.

But in Sierra Leone, many Africans often saw little good in the Lebanese.

"Fuck the Lebanese" read the graffiti on a wall near Michelle's apartment house. Freetown newspapers were purveyors of blatant ethnocentrism regarding the Lebanese. Lebanese houses were frequently broken into, their occupants occasionally killed. The home of one Lebanese man was burgled three times. The police were not interested in investigating, but demanded a bribe from him nevertheless. Robbing Lebanese was not rebuked as sternly as other crimes in Sierra Leone. "They are dirty Lebanese, involved in dirty corrupt business," was a usual complaint. The Lebanese comprised the middle class in a place where an indigenous middle class was very weak. So while desperately needed, they were also hated.

Through the window of the Crown Bakery, three soldiers were peering at the customers, their faces pressed agains the glass, their expressions covetous. Army shakedowns were part of the price of staying in business for the Lebanese. Meanwhile, a trend was emerging: These Lebanese shop owners were increasingly sending their children abroad for education, and to acquire foreign citizenship. The three soldiers pressing against the window embodied the onrushing meteor that I had felt on the night of my arrival in Sierra Leone at the beach bar. The Lebanese at the bar that night could afford to be jovial because their community was quietly preparing to depart. The future here could be sadder than the present.

3

Along the Gulf of Guinea

STEAMY BREEZES LIFTED off a black nighttime ocean. I sat at poolside in a faded beach chair, observing a group of French tourists frolicking in the water and calling out to an African waiter garbed in colorful *kente* to bring them more beer, which the tourists swam over to get. Finishing my own beer, I felt pleased with myself. This was West Africa as a novelist like Ian Fleming would have it: first-class 1950s-style accommodations rather than the sanitized luxury of the 1990s; service at the snap of a finger; lovely women in the pool; the tinkly sound of Afro-Brazilian music; the gentle swell of a tropical ocean; and the ground beneath you ready to collapse from political chaos.

I had come by airplane from Freetown to Lome, the capital of Togo, a country that may be less fact than fiction. Only thirty-five miles wide along the Atlantic coast, it is 340 miles "tall," stretching from the Atlantic Ocean northward to the Saharan frontier with Burkina Faso. Togo, more than other West African countries, illustrated the region's geographical quandary: Population belts in West Africa are horizontal, and human habitation densities increase as one travels south away from the Sahara and toward the tropical abundance of the Atlantic littoral. But the borders erected by European colonialists were vertical, and therefore at cross-purposes with demography and topography. For example, the Ewe people, who live near the Togo coast, are divided between Togo and Ghana. In addition, Togo has been bedeviled by tensions between its southern peoples and the Voltaic peoples of the north, whose culture is influenced by the Sahara. In 1963, Togo became the first independent African country to undergo a coup, the result of tensions between President Sylvanus Olympio, a member of the Mina people who live on the coast, and soldiers from the Cabrais group, from the north, who assassinated him.

Togo, rather than an organic outgrowth of geography and ethnicity, was a result of late-nineteenth-century German greed. As the slave trade crumbled, European colonializers began to exploit West Africa's commodity resources, such as cocoa and various palm products. In 1884, the Germans landed a ship here and staked out a claim. That was the basis for the national identity of Togo.

The tourists frolicking in the pool beside me had not been here a few months before, in early 1993, when the army rioted, some of the diplomats cleared out, and the French, who replaced the Germans as the colonial power after World War I, once more supported the military dictator, Étienne Eyadema. (Something similar had happened in 1991, after rioting by what the London-based magazine *West Africa* called "Soweto-like stone-throwing adolescents.") A few months after I left Togo, sixty-seven people were killed in a failed coup, and three opposition leaders were murdered during an election process, whose results led to more political conflict.

Lome, which is, according to the maps, the capital of a recognized country, is in fact no more than a charming and overgrown market town of wooden stalls shaded by beach umbrellas, amid crowds of unemployed youths. Spread out lengthwise along the beach without much of a city center, Lome seemed to lack a foundation. But here was a setting so serenely beautiful that as soon as the looters tired, the package-tour groups from Europe returned, ignorant of the mayhem that had devastated the city a few weeks earlier. I noticed that many tourists rarely wander far beyond the hotel.

The next morning I had finished my breakfast by nine. I paid the bill and left the climate-controlled airlock. The damp heat hit me like a fist. Thanks to the Coca-Cola for sale every few hundred yards along the beach, I soon got used to it. I was heading for the international border with

Ghana, just a mile or so away at the edge of town. My plan was to travel by foot, taxi, or bus and to hitchhike along the Gulf of Guinea back to Abidjan, the Ivory Coast capital, four hundred miles away to the west.[1]

In Abidjan, a few weeks before, I had seen satellite photos of the entire Gulf of Guinea, from Lagos to Abidjan, showing one burgeoning population zone that by any rational economic and geographical standard should have constituted a single sovereignty rather than the five (Nigeria, Benin, Togo, Ghana, and the Ivory Coast) into which it was divided. I wanted to see on the ground what the satellite had captured from space, to experience what Africans who regularly travel along this corridor have to go through in order to get from one part of this coastal community to the other. Historian Basil Davidson says that Africans must suffer "the curse of the nation-state." I wanted to experience that curse.

Of all the artificial frontier crossings, the Aflao border station must be near the top of the list. The beach road—the city of Lome, in fact—simply ended, as if lopped off by a giant saw. What came next looked like the entrance to a warehouse or a junkyard. It was a chaotic scene: a rusted and clanging gate, charred and corroded barrack houses, dirt, sand, flies amid piles of mangoes hawked by a small crowd of women, and lots of teenage boys armed with wads of cedis, the Ghanaian currency, which they were selling in exchange for CFA francs.[2] A variety of grazing animals, including goats and sheep, and women with baskets on their heads were passing back and forth through the gate, without stopping. There was no line to wait in. It was a bit like being pulled underwater: You just waded close enough to the crowd until one of the boys grabbed your arm and pulled you over to a window opening in the barracks, where an immigration official sat. I thought of what Ryszard Kapuscinski wrote about this border in 1965:

"At the border between Ghana and Togo there was a large padlocked gate, and when I drove up, a policeman wandered around it for a considerable time, looking for the key. Against this fence two years ago, Silvanus Olympio, the president of Togo, was executed by a firing squad of several officers."

[1] As mentioned in an earlier footnote, the Gulf of Guinea, or what the 1802 map of Africa owned by Thomas Jefferson labels the "Coast of Guinea," is not to be confused with the country of Guinea, located on the Windward Coast.

[2] All the former French colonies of West Africa except Guinea and Mauritania are members of the *Communauté Financière Africaine*, or CFA.

The immigration officer said I needed an exit permit from the Ministry of the Interior to leave Togo. But this was Sunday and the ministry was closed, so he agreed to let me pass if I paid an *amende* (fine) of five thousand CFA francs, about eighteen dollars. I gave him a five-thousand-franc note. He quickly put it in his pocket. "Now you change some money with this boy," the immigration officer told me, pointing to a lad of twelve or thirteen standing beside him. The boy and the officer smiled at each other. I exchanged some francs for some cedis, which I needed to do anyway. It was a scam. No such exit permit was required. I looked around and saw Africans with bags and suitcases also handing over money to immigration officers. The women with the baskets paid nothing, the more prosperous Africans paid something, and I paid more than something. The border existed to tax the wealthy, and to provide jobs and supplemental income for government bureaucrats. It was a wealth-transfer mechanism. There appeared to be no real control; few people were having their bags inspected. Inspections here were less severe than at army checkpoints within the individual West African countries.

The boy with the money then escorted me to the Ghanaian side of the frontier station, where I had my passport stamped and, unlike in Guinea, was given a currency declaration to fill out, so that I wouldn't have difficulty reexporting my dollars. Then the boy walked me to the taxi and minibus stand. I tipped him. He left and walked back to Togo. Nobody stopped him or the countless other youths walking in and out of the gate.

Between the border and the Ghanaian capital of Accra there were four checkpoints, where my fellow passengers and I in the "shared" taxi were stopped and searched and where markets, small villages almost, had formed to offer drinks and snacks to people while their cars were halted. At one checkpoint, I wandered away from the road to urinate. Looking around, I saw the same sight that I had seen in Togo, Sierra Leone, Guinea, and the Ivory Coast: corrugated shacks, laterite teeming with lizards, armies of small children, and pregnant women amid the flies. Ghana at first glance did not appear to be better off than its neighbors. This surprised me. After the Ivory Coast and Kenya had fallen upon hard times, Ghana was acclaimed by some Africanists as the new African "success story," with a relatively stable government, led by a charismatic and somewhat-benevolent military dictator, Jerry Rawlings.

Ghana ranked near Pakistan and India on the UN scale of human development. Yet in February 1994, not long after I visited Ghana, thirteen thousand people fled tribal fighting over land rights, which claimed the lives of between one and three thousand people in the north of the country. Officials said sixty-seven villages were destroyed in riots between Konkombas and Nanumbas.

Accra, however, was full of construction, a sign of economic growth. There were several excellent middle-priced hotels—a measure of civilization considering that there were many cities in the third world where the choice was between a flophouse at a few dollars a night and a luxury life-support system cut off from everything around it for two hundred dollars a night. More impressive, it was safe to walk around Accra after dark, which was not true of other sub-Saharan cities, or of many American cities for that matter. Yet there were other things that didn't so much disprove the "success story" claim as weaken its relevance outside sub-Saharan Africa. There was not much of a downtown, or even an "edge city"—as in American cities where the downtowns had become dangerous and the middle class had moved to the outskirts. I saw only a meandering grid of broken streets, open sewers, laterite, mustard-colored walls in various stages of decomposition, and corrugated-iron roofs. Urbanity was missing. The national museum in Accra was "one of the best museums in West Africa," according to the Lonely Planet Travel Survival Kit. What did that mean, exactly? It meant a rather small, deserted, unlit building of dusty exhibits in cracked-glass cases where for an hour, in the middle of an afternoon, I was the only visitor eyeing the *kente* cloths, wooden masks, drums, stone tools, and other artifacts on display. The duty guard had unlocked the door of the museum when I knocked to enter. After I paid my entrance fee, he returned to a stool by a television set, where he continued to watch a rock video that echoed throughout the museum.

◎   ◎   ◎

I TOOK A room at the medium-priced Sunrise Hotel, which featured a British-style pub restaurant catering to a variety of hustlers and small-time businessmen from Europe taking advantage of Ghana's miniboom. "The Green, Green Grass of Home" was playing loud on the speaker system when I checked in. Individual white men were sitting at separate tables, drinking, eating, and reading foreign newspapers. Nobody was talking to anybody else. In one corner sat a neo-Nazi look-alike with a blond crew cut, a scar on his pit-bull face, and a tatoo on his arm. He got up and started throwing metal tokens into the slot machine. He dumped token after token into the machine for a few minutes, with no effect. Then he called for more tokens. The splendid Ghanaian bartender with corn-rows working behind the bar was occupied with another customer, and didn't answer him immediately. "You people asleep or *vat?*" he thundered. She hurried over with more tokens.

At the bar I met Kenny, a short fellow with a Joe Palooka build and an Andy Capp face, wearing a loud tropical-print shirt.

"I'll stand ya a cold piss," he said.

Two beers came over. Kenny was the caterer for the Sunrise Hotel. He had been a caterer in the British army and the merchant marine for three decades, and specialized in bringing English pub food to third world spots where foreign workers gathered.

"Now, you take this place. It's all right. But if this were my hotel, I'd build a pool. A pool, a whore, a cold piss, and a dartboard is all a gent needs. And I'd make it a real British pub, with all the lagers and you know what. You see," lowering his voice, "you don't want any Ghanaians here, because they got no *fooocking* money.

"I been everywhere: Kyrgyzstan, Archangel. I like the company of men. I was in Qatar when the crown prince came off the plane drunk. The British press said he had the flu—green-bottle flu would be more like it. Now, you take your Arab—he's got no respect for human life. Why, the Yemenis will kill ya for fifty quid, they will.

"You know that in Tasmania it's legal to marry your sister—to *fooock* your own sister." He bobbed his head.

"Concerning this country, you take your Ashanti who lives up north. He's a good bloke. But there's no hope here, mate. Take what you can get, that's my philosophy. Why, up north they're eating lizards, monkeys, rats. I saw only two cats the whole time I was in northern Ghana. The Ghanaians say that cats and monkeys make good chop.

"You see." Kenny lowered his voice again. "I was up north catering for the loggers. Why, they're taking out whole mountains of trees: mahogany, ebony, you name it. There are traffic jams of trucks carrying nothing but tree trunks. Some of the trunks are so big they require a whole truck just for one of 'em. But the money is being stolen, mate. The people here see none of it." His voice became maudlin. "And the gold and diamond camps—why, they're stealing plenty. Nothing goes for your average Ghanaian, I can tell you that. It's all dash [bribing] here. All dash."

Kenny left. I picked up a local newspaper at the bar, *The Ghanaian Chronicle.* The headline read "Rawlings Commandos Killed in Togo." The story was about a failed attempt by the Rawlings government in Ghana to overthrow the regime in Togo. The editorial sharply criticized the Ghanaian leader for engaging in cowboy antics over the border rather than attending to affairs in Ghana. The article was feisty, well written. I looked at the masthead and noticed the editor's name, Kwaku Sakyi Addo, and the paper's phone number. I phoned him immediately, and told him I was a writer from Washington. He promised to come over to the hotel in thirty minutes.

Addo looked to be in his late twenties, clean-cut, with a pressed white shirt, red tie, suspenders, and wire-rim glasses. I apologized profusely for my unshaven face, jeans, and sleeveless fishing vest, explaining that it was impractical to travel by land through West Africa while lugging around formal clothes. His smile told me that he well understood the difficulties of travel through Africa. Nevertheless, his conventional formality and cleanliness made me feel like a fraud in my war correspondent's attire.

"How do you get away with your criticism of Rawlings?" I asked.

"Rawlings needs us," Addo explained. "By tolerating us, he impresses Western donors. Also, by tolerating us he learns how to deal with a free press. Don't get me wrong, I understand that Rawlings is a lot better than any other ruler in West Africa and that Ghana is better off than all of its neighbors. But why should we be satisfied with what we have? When we criticize the government, the government tells us we're being ungrateful. They say, 'Look at Togo and how much worse it is there.' I say: 'We shouldn't compare ourselves to those in the gutter but to those on the balcony.' To South Korea, for instance. In 1957, when we obtained our independence from Britain, Ghana had the same GNP as South Korea. Now the Koreans are giving us aid. That's a failure of political culture in Africa.

"We've got so far to go. Look at the rest of the world! The CFA countries around us are going downhill. The French won't continue to prop up their economies. What prosperity there is in West Africa is mainly artificial. . . . Yes, it's true. There is a lot of deforestation taking place, too much. Rawlings now speaks about the environment. He has created a ministry for the environment. At least, the mentality is changing. But is it too late?"

◎   ◎   ◎

THE EIGHTY MILES westward along the ocean from Accra to Cape Coast took only two hours. The bus was comfortable, it left on time, and there were some empty seats. It was a long-distance bus continuing on to Abidjan. The problem on the Gulf of Guinea was that if you wanted to make stops along the way, as I did, you were often at the mercy of uncomfortable and unreliable bush taxis.

The Gulf of Guinea might also be considered part of the infamous "Coast of Slaves," though that designation more often denotes the area further east along the gulf, where the African state of Benin, formerly Dahomey, is now located. Many of the slaves dispatched to the Americas from West Africa left from a series of rambling European-built forts dotting the shore between Accra and the Ivory Coast border. The castle at Cape Coast, where my bus let me off, is one of them.

The bus stopped along the main coastal highway and I walked the two miles toward the ocean and the town of Cape Coast. Soaked with sweat, I struggled through quiet and forlorn streets, favored with salt breezes eating away at pastel walls. The town was like a series of shipwrecks: collapsed stalls, houses with no roofs, kids in the ocean using pieces of broken wood as surfboards. Man's creations were dying as vegetation prospered. Cape Coast was picturesque with its pounding aquamarine surf, black artillery pieces, and castle walls fronting the sea. By any other standard, it was depressing.

Cape Coast Castle was built by the Swedes in 1653.[3] It changed hands five times before being permanently captured by the British in the 1660s. Alone in the pitch-black dungeon, I thought of the cries of the slaves as I listened to the roar of the sea. In the musty cell that functioned as a gift shop, the handful of visitors, mainly African-Americans on a coach tour, were buying copies of *Beyond the Rivers of Ethiopia: A Biblical Revelation on God's Purpose for the Black Race*, by Mensa Otabil, the pastor of the International Central Gospel Church in Accra. I bought a copy and glanced through it. On page 87, it said:

> Whenever the world has been in a crisis the black man has always appeared on the scene. After the flood, when the world needed a leader, He called Nimrod the son of Cush. When Moses was taken out of Pharaoh's camp, it took a black man Jethro to teach him the ways of God. . . . When Jesus was going to the cross it took a black man to carry the cross.

[3] See Albert van Dantzig's *Forts and Castles of Ghana*, listed in the bibliography.

As I was about to leave Cape Coast Castle, en route to the fort at Elmina, a few miles westward along the Atlantic shore, a Ghanaian women approached me, casually asking if she could give me a lift. "Yes," I said. Her name was Alice. She was a private tour guide for an "American visitor."

The American visitor's name was Yaw Mensah, a Ghanaian who had immigrated to the U.S. a quarter-century before and was back in his homeland for a visit. I had noticed him inside the castle. He had tortoise-shell glasses and a gray-white beard and was constantly taking pictures of the castle with his video camera: just shooting walls, walls, walls for minutes at a time, like a machine-gunner aimlessly spraying bullets into an empty field. At first he was upset by my presence, but Alice said, "Come on, we've got room for him in the car." At last he gave me a business card: "Yaw Mensah, Staff Development Specialist I, Texas Department of Human Services." Yaw Mensah's English, however, was a bit halting. He said he was gathering information for prospective African-American tourists and showed me his diary. He had taken notes about mileage between each town, next to which he had written only "this place OK" or "this place not OK." I showed him my Lonely Planet Travel Survival Kit on West Africa, which already had all the mileage information as part of a fifty-eight-page section on Ghana, in encyclopedic detail, with town maps included. Though this and other guidebooks on Africa were easily available in the U.S., he professed surprise at their existence. Nevertheless, he showed no curiosity about my guidebook. "I'm doing my own book," he said. I got the feeling that Alice was bored with him and that she had asked me along to have someone else to talk to.

The three of us set out for Elmina. As it was lunchtime, she pulled over to a restaurant on the beach. It was a postcard setting: grand empty stretches of ocher sand; thick, towering palm trunks; and kids in loud *kente* shirts playing inside dugout canoes. We sat down at a table and ordered grilled fish and Coca-Cola.

As we waited for the fish, Yaw Mensah delivered a monologue on how white racism was the root of crime and underdevelopment in American inner cities. "Everything would be so perfect in America if this problem of racism could be solved." Alice interrupted, "But he's"—referring to me—"not a racist, I think." I was embarrassed. "Everyone is a little racist," I said. "The trick is to recognize your lapses and fight them." Something was missing here. Yaw Mensah's monologue, like his videotaping of the castle walls, lacked a narrative sense. No thread led from one point to another. *If only whites would change what was in their hearts, then inner city gangs would disband,* was what he seemed to be saying. Yaw Mensah then added, "But America is still the greatest country on earth. I could never be an African again. I'm an American. I take my malaria pills and drink only bottled water. After twenty-five years, my body is no longer accustomed to Africa." Alice sighed with exasperation.

We got back in the car. St. George's Castle loomed in the distance, a massive white pile perched at the end of a rocky headland. Guidebooks describe Elmina as small, vibrant, picturesque, charming, etc. It all depends on what you want to see. There were, of course, the blue fishing boats, a pounding surf, and mounds of fruit. But I saw much else besides that no sensible person could ignore. I saw children, who should have been at school, dozing in the mud and groups of men sleeping on rotting boards or playing checkers and drinking beer. It was Monday, the middle of the day, yet with the exception of women beating clothes against the stones and selling fruit, there were few signs of people doing productive work. The town itself, despite a topographical situation more favorable than Conakry's, looked no less squalid than the Guinean capital: a rusted black meshwork of crumbly walls and scaffolding teeming with small children.[4] For Ghana to be a "success story" required closing your eyes to the town of Elmina, and seeing only the blue sea and the picturesque slave castle.

The castle was badly in need of restoration. "The castles are all going down," Yaw Mensah said. "I don't know. At independence in 1957 the government said it would do something and never did. We need money from someone." He hoped that refurbishing this slave fort would create jobs for the local people.

St. George's Castle was nevertheless a stirring piece of architecture, more impressive than the castle at Cape Coast. My eyes met a thrusting babble of massive white bastions, salt-mottled and with distinctive Portuguese arches and windows braided with inlaid brick. The castle was guarded by a double moat and had its own fresh-water supply from an extensive underground reservoir, completely brick-lined. The Portu-

[4]As recently as 1993, Ghana had a population growth rate of 3.1 percent, with a population-doubling time of twenty-three years. But the picture is unclear. Steve Coll reports in *The Washington Post* that a 1994 survey showed a "sharp decline" in these statistics.

guese had built St. George's in 1482. The Dutch captured it in 1637 and built the reservoir. In 1872 they sold the fort to the British. The underground dungeons that served as the slave quarters admitted no light. Standing in the dank blackness, I tried to summon up the unimaginable terror of an African child being separated from his mother as the slavers divided up their wares; but these were terrors that my imagination could not reach.

"What cruelty, what cruelty!" said an African-American woman whom I had seen at Cape Coast. When the Ghanaian guide matter-of-factly pointed out a sign in the fort's Dutch chapel that read "Zion is [the] resting place of God," the woman said angrily: "No God could ever have existed in this place as long as the slave trade went on!"

Yaw Mensah was busy with his video camera. Alice drew up beside me, hissing in my ear, "Did you hear that woman talk? These American blacks come over here just so they can get angry. For us it's history. For them it's pain. We weren't taken to America as slaves. It's their past more than ours. Anyway, all this emotion makes them feel good. They go back to America, hating whites more—it's no good. They want to be like me, a free African. But they can't. They're Americans."

I stepped outside the chapel onto the white ramparts. The beach extended for miles in both directions like a necklace laid out on the Atlantic's blue skin. I craned my neck to take in the town of Elmina, which was—I could see—without architectural permanence, without sufficient material proof of man's presence. What the Portuguese had built has lasted more than half a millennium, but Elmina would disappear under the tropical vegetation within a few years, were its inhabitants ever to leave. There was life here, but there was no development. The Slave Coast was ready to be recolonized, if only the Portuguese, the Dutch, and the English would agree to come back with their money.[5] (I thought of how Burton would feel were he alive to see the stark images offered by Elmina, Conakry, Chicago, Washington, and similar places in West Africa. In 1863, Burton wrote: "When the slave has once surmounted his dread of being shipped by the white man, nothing under the sun would . . . induce him willingly to return to what he should call

---

[5]While the entire littoral along the Gulf of Guinea can be labeled the Slave Coast, the stretch of coastline in Ghana is also known as the Gold Coast, due to the inland gold deposits, which—along with the slaves—drew the European colonialists.

his home . . . our West Indian colonies were lands of happiness compared with the Oil Rivers; as for the 'Southern States,' the slave's lot is paradise when succeeding what he endures on the west coast of Africa."[6])

THOUGH THE PORTUGUESE arrived in Senegal in 1445 in a bid to outflank the inter-African slave trade across the Sahara, it wasn't until the following century, perhaps, that the scale of the European slave trade in West Africa reached that of Africa's own slave trade, according to University of London professor Roland Oliver in *The African Experience*. Among the places where the Europeans landed, nowhere was slaving a novelty. The taking of slaves was part of the despotism of the Ashanti, Dahomey, and Yoruba states. Many scholars, however, call this rendition of events a distortion. For example, in *Africa in History*, Basil Davidson points out that the slaves held by other Africans were "never mere chattels, without rights or hope of emancipation . . . they were integral members of their community. . . . 'A slave who knows how to serve,' ran the old Asante [Ashanti] proverb, 'succeeds to his master's property.'"

In the seventeenth and eighteenth centuries, as the Dutch, the British, and others became involved in the Atlantic slave trade, it mushroomed. According to scholarly sources, some 10 to 12 million African slaves arrived in the Americas. But these figures capture only part of the crime: "Several tens of millions of Africans over three or four centuries," writes Davidson, may have suffered "deportation or death" because of the slave trade. The Europeans essentially roamed the shores of West Africa, taking advantage in turn of the collapse of the Jolof empire in Senegambia, of the conquests of the Mane[7] and Fulani peoples in the region of Sierra Leone and Guinea, of the expansions of the Benin and Oyo states in the vicinity of Yorubaland, and of the conquests of the Ashanti and various Akan peoples along the Gold Coast of Ghana. All of these expansions and contractions produced slaves, slaves, and more slaves. Even some of

[6]Keith B. Richburg, an African-American and the former Africa correspondent for *The Washington Post*, came to a related conclusion in his essay "Continental Divide." The horror of sub-Saharan Africa, writes Richburg, made him grateful that his ancestors had come to the new world as slaves, so that he could become an American. See the bibliography.

[7]The Mane people are a subgroup of the Mande.

the freed slaves who had returned to Ghana and Togo from captivity in Brazil[8] became slavers, working as middlemen for the Europeans. Political, economic, and moral factors finally brought the transatlantic slave trade to an end in the nineteenth century.

One school of thought argues that European involvement in Africa was less than it appears. Only rarely did the Europeans' presence inflame the fighting between African kingdoms. According to Oliver, "the causes of warfare were essentially local . . . the wars would have occurred even had there been no ocean trade to carry away the captives." The power of the Oyo empire, for example, according to historian Robin Law, rested on two forces: the wageless labor of war captives for agricultural production and the extraction of tribute from subject peoples. European colonialism in sub-Saharan Africa was, on the whole, often of shorter duration than in the Indian subcontinent and Indochina, and it was mainly limited to the coast.

But the truth is probably more ambiguous, since the overseas slave trade, as Davidson persuasively argues, was "an early type of colonial economy" that came into existence hundreds of years before the establishment of colonies and protectorates. The ability to buy European goods by selling human beings inhibited the establishment of cash economies based on local industries. In the nineteenth century, in the northern Nigerian city of Kano, Davidson writes,

> handicraft production of textiles had reached such a high degree of "cottage industry" as to be able to supply the whole of the Western Sudan from Senegal to Lake Chad. Far outside the slaving network of the Atlantic trade, Kano had clearly developed to the point where a new economic development could begin to unfold.

Besides hindering the evolution of early capitalist economies, the slave trade, according to Davidson and others, encouraged warfare between African kingdoms, since only through battle victories could the kings hope to obtain captives in the numbers required by the Europeans. The need for captives led to a need for firearms, which African potentates could buy from the Europeans only by supplying them with more slaves. A vicious circle ensued.

---

[8]These Afro-Brazilians brought back with them the musical influences noted at the beginning of this chapter.

◎   ◎   ◎

BUT THE GREATEST burden inflicted on Africa by the Europeans was probably the political map, with its scores of countries, each identified by the color of its imperial master. This map, with which all of us have grown up, is an invention of modernism, which began with the rise of nation-states. The map offered a way to classify these new national organisms as a neat patchwork devoid of transitional zones. ("Frontier" is itself a modern concept that didn't exist in the feudal mind.) Because European nations were carving out their far-flung domains at a time when print technology was making map reproduction cheaper, cartography created facts by ordering the way we look at Africa and the rest of the world.

In *Imagined Communities: Reflections on the Origin and Spread of Nationalism*, Benedict Anderson, of Cornell University, shows how the map enabled colonialists to think about their holdings in terms of a "totalizing classificatory grid. . . . It was bounded, determinate, and therefore— in principle—countable." To the colonialist, country maps were the equivalent of an accountant's ledger books. Maps, Anderson explains, "shaped the grammar" that would make possible such questionable concepts as the Ivory Coast, Guinea, Sierra Leone, Togo, and Nigeria—and, for that matter, non-African places such as Iraq and Indonesia. The "state" is a purely Western notion, one that until the twentieth century described countries covering only a small part of the earth's land area. Nor is the evidence compelling that the state, as a governing ideal, can be successfully transported to areas outside the industrialized world.

With the help of the map, the census (allowing colonialists to invent millions of "Togolese" and "Nigerians" at the expense of Ewes, Yorubas, Ibos, and so on), and the museum, which invented a "national" past, Africa was artificially reconceived. The "national" museum I had visited in Accra was a lonely, dust-ridden Chatsworth, perhaps because, as it arose from a European mind-set, it meant little to the local inhabitants.

Three decades after independence, the interplay between exploding populations, the willful destruction of natural resources, and the profusion of automatic weapons was leading to a return to Mr. Jefferson's map. But instead of reconstituted tribal kingdoms modeled on the past, what was emerging were neoprimitive shanty-domains, which put additional pressure on societies that already faced an erosion of values. In 1992, for example, the equivalent of $856 million left West Africa for Europe in the form of "hot cash," presumed to be laundered drug money.[9] The past was being cut off as people deserted traditional villages for anarchic cities. The future loomed as a possible abyss.[10]

Loafing along the beach on the Gulf of Guinea before returning to Alice's car, I admired the spectacular beauty of the white Portuguese-built castle against the panel of blue ocean. I had once lived in Portugal, and the architectural details evoked fond memories of bougainvillea, rich wines, faience tiles, and noble Iberian headlands and seascapes. However, for Americans of African descent, that castle could evoke only bitterness and tears. While for many white Americans, Elmina's squalor and destitution might appear as a statement by itself, African-Americans, as well as other whites, would see the town's distress as a *result* of what that castle had wrought. On the mental map of America's racial anguish, the Gulf of Guinea was much closer than the five thousand miles shown on the Mercator projection. Ben Okri had once told me that "you cannot conquer without you yourself being overrun." In other words, by taking human booty from the Slave Coast, America had unwittingly begun the process by which the problems of West Africa could one day become its own.

Alice dropped me off at the bush-taxi station in Elmina, where I squirmed my way into the backseat of a battered and overcrowded mini-van. Yaw Mensah was flabbergasted that I, an American, would travel so humbly, rather than hire a guide and a driver as he had. Alice understood. "That's the only way to get to know Africa," she said as we waved our goodbyes.

[9]See *The London Observer* in the bibliography.
[10]Once population growth and land degradation reach critical levels, even seemingly rational development schemes, rather than redress imbalances, run the risk of igniting more group strife. The case of the Senegal River basin offers an example. Drought and overpopulation in the region led to overtilling of the soil, overgrazing, salinization due to overirrigation, and other environmental stresses, raising the possibility of chronic food shortages. Senegal and Mauritania, consequently, sought international financing for a dam network to expand agriculture along the river. But as anthropologist Michael Horowitz, of the State University of New York at Binghamton, has demonstrated, plans for the new dams caused a surge in land values in soon-to-be-irrigated areas. So the Mauritanian government, composed of white Moors (Arabs), rewrote the laws affecting land ownership, thus invalidating the rights of the black African farmers living on the Mauritanian side of the river. In 1989, ethnic violence erupted in Mauritania that spilled over into Senegal, where black Africans retaliated by closing thousands of shops owned by the Moors. The two nations nearly came to war and seventy thousand black Mauritanians were expelled by their Arab government, taking refuge in Senegal.

It was a ninety-minute journey westward from Elmina to Takoradi, a big seaport in western Ghana. Convoys of logging trucks stretched for miles along the road, en route to huge depots, where the hardwood trunks, like stricken dinosaur limbs, were being collected for shipment to Europe, where they would end up as modern furniture. I remembered what Kenny had said back in Accra: "Why, they're taking out whole mountains of trees . . . But the money is being stolen, mate. The people here see none of it."

I squirmed out of the minivan, lathered in dust and sweat, and walked up and downhill for a mile and a half into the sunset. Another panorama of corrugated-iron shacks and red dust, with women balancing heavy loads on their heads while men sat around and joshed. People smiled at me. Children followed and said hello. The Westline Hotel came into view. Kenny had recommended it. "In Takoradi, it's the Westline where you want to stay, mate. Air-con, cold piss, and good chop."

Kenny was right. But how lonely his life must be, I thought! After I had knocked on the restaurant door in the musty heat, one of the waiters beckoned me into a small, freezing dining room with loud air-conditioning. I was the hotel's only customer. I had my cold beer and Indian curry dish in the empty restaurant as three waiters stared at me.

I rose at six the next morning, as I planned to get back to Abidjan that day. I arrived at the bush-taxi station in Takoradi at 6:45 A.M. The van for Abidjan already had four passengers. I was the fifth. I counted seven other seats waiting to be filled. I bought some yams, boiled eggs, and Coca-Cola to fill my stomach and waited, and soon the driver filled his seven empty seats. But we continued to wait. By 10 A.M., the driver had stuffed nineteen people into his twelve-seat dented crate. The roof was punched down with bundles, and the windshield was partially obscured by smaller bits of luggage. A youth of about twenty came up to me. "You, me, we're not the same. You're white, I'm black. The customs people won't check you, so hold this for me." He handed me two bottles of whiskey, which I stuffed in my rucksack.

The bush taxi crawled out of the station at 10:20 A.M. My elbows were pinned to my ribs by people on either side. Loud music blared from the van's cassette player. The driver's eyes were bloodshot. Driving slowly with one hand, he argued and gesticulated with the other, trying to console two passengers he had been forced to leave behind.

Between Takoradi and the Ivorian border, a distance of seventy-five miles, there were three checkpoints, where some of the luggage was searched and everyone, except me, had to show identification papers. The Ghanaian-Ivorian border was a sprawling market stretching for over a mile, with crowds as dense as those in Lagos, Cairo, or Delhi. Money changers assaulted us as we all fell out of the bush taxi like bedraggled clowns falling out of a circus car. "Lunchtime," the driver yelled, walking away toward a line of food stalls, where unknown meats bubbled in greasy baths. "Be back here in an hour." I noticed that the line of vehicles stretched for over a hundred yards at the immigration and customs station. *We might be here for hours.* I bought CFAs with my leftover cedis. Then I grabbed my rucksack and took out the two whiskey bottles, leaving them where my rucksack had been. I quietly walked away from the bush taxi, melting into the crowd, heading on foot for the immigration station.

The border between the Ivory Coast and Ghana was more organized than the border between Ghana and Togo. There was a narrow dirt walkway with rusted rails serving as a sort of obstacle course, where you presented your visa stamp, your passport, your luggage, your vaccination papers, etc. In Guinea, no currency form had been provided upon entering the country, but one was required upon leaving; in Ghana, a currency form had been given to me upon entering, but nobody asked to see it as I left.

I left Ghana and walked over a small stream into the Ivory Coast. After the immigration and customs procedures on the Ivorian side, I spotted a crowded bush taxi, its engine groaning, about to depart. It had an empty space and I squeezed myself into it. In an hour, after one more checkpoint, I arrived at the eastern Ivorian town of Aboisso. There I bought a reserved seat on a bus due to arrive in Abidjan before sunset. I had made it, I thought.

After forty-five minutes of driving we reached a roadblock. Ivorian policemen unzipped and emptied every suitcase and bundle except mine. This liquor bottle, that fabric, that pathetic pair of trousers, etc. were all illegal, apparently. The policemen's palms were literally out. *What do you have for me?* they suggested to each passenger, who, in turn, slipped small bills into the outstretched palms. Defeat registered in every pair of eyes. Africans are supposed to be—and usually are—extremely talkative. Now there was silence. After the luggage was repacked, the policemen stretched and leaned back on their heels. One yawned. After a minute of staring and talking, they waved us away.

We passed through Grand-Bassam, where the French had built their first capital before its population was wiped out by a yellow-fever epidemic in 1899. It was a collection of rotted buildings, spacious and balconied, punctuating ocean and sand. Palm jungles abounded. On the outskirts of Abidjan there was another roadblock and still more arrogant policemen, who gave the same order to unzip and unpack everything as they held their palms out. At the other end of this checkpoint I noticed two empty taxis with Abidjan license plates. I grabbed my rucksack and, in full view of the policemen, slowly walked away.

It was a twenty-minute taxi ride to the house of a friend where I planned to stay. The four-hundred-mile journey westward, within one coastal community, had involved two international borders and an additional eleven customs stations. It was no better elsewhere in West Africa, or in Central Africa. Between Abidjan and the Ivory Coast's northern border with Mali were eighteen customs stations. One traveler I knew counted "fifty-two customs stations" manned by men "with guns and portions of uniforms" from `N'Djamena to Sarh in southern Chad, a distance of three hundred miles within the same country.

◎   ◎   ◎

A FEW DAYS later in Abidjan, I dined with a foreign ambassador who told me about a visit he had made to the extreme northwest of the Ivory Coast, near Guinea and Mali, to observe an international-aid project supported by the United Nations, designed to eradicate onchocerciasis (river blindness). Black flies hovering over the rivers of interior Africa cause the disease, biting Africans as they bathe and wash their clothes. The program's aim was to eradicate the larvae of the flies by spraying repellent along the waterways.

It was easier said than done. The helicopters doing the spraying had to fly upwind at high speeds, near the water, over rivulets not much wider than their rotor blades, with trees on either side. Landsat satellites beamed down computerized pictures showing the state of each river and rivulet. Highly sensitive computers monitored the chemical content of the river water, requiring constant readjustments in the ratio of the six chemicals comprising the spray repellent. The pilots came from the U.S., Canada, Peru, Portugal, and the former Yugoslavia. The ambassador told me he was "moved" by their "esprit de corps" and militarylike discipline. Though the pilots succeed in eradicating river blindness from the immediate region, the disease could easily return through Liberia and Nigeria if the project ever ended.

"This is what it takes," said the ambassador, full of awe. "The highest levels of technology, attention to the finest details, and the most extraordinary talent and work ethic" are required to halt one disease, in one part of Africa, temporarily. The ambassador then described how the pilots had been rising every day before dawn for several years to be briefed and to study the computer printouts that would determine their flight plans. Western food was flown from Abidjan and trucked to their compound. The pilots had their own generators for electricity. The whole setup was like a base on the moon.

PART II

◎   ◎   ◎

The Nile Valley
The Hollow Pyramid

. . . I am traveling at a time when man's soul, enslaved to the machine and to hunger, struggles for bread and freedom. Today, the cry of the laborer—hoarse from drink, smoke and hatred—is the cry of the Earth. And this heartrending cry accompanied me throughout my journey, from one end of Egypt to the other, and guided me.

—NIKOS KAZANTZAKIS
Journeying

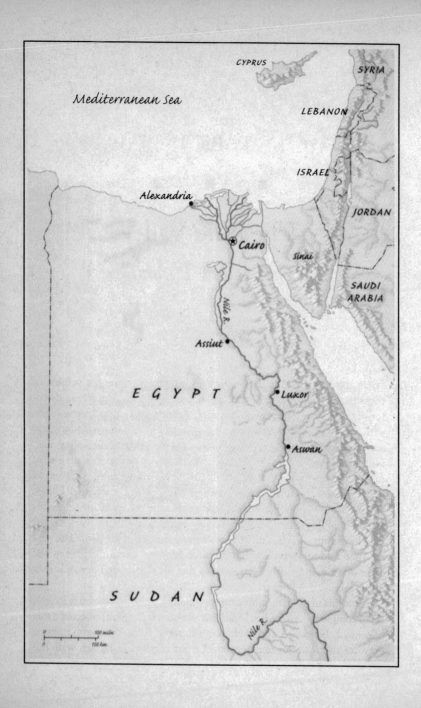

4

"Oriental Despotism"

"IT IS LIKE a pyramid! Before your eyes is eighteen times the volume of rocks used in the Great Pyramid of Cheops!" Ali Abdel Razag, the director of the Aswan High Dam Authority, a short, dark-complexioned man with a gray mustache, rose up on his toes as he pointed out the great sweep of rock and compressed sand that has turned the Nile Valley from southern Egypt to the Mediterranean—a distance of almost six hundred miles—into one big irrigation ditch. "The compressed dune sand beneath the rock-filled outer core is like a spring," explained Razag, "which would allow the entire dam to shift in the event of an earthquake." Razag pointed to the gardens, with neatly clipped trees shaped like doughnuts, that beautify the road along the top of the dam. The gardens, he told me, have another purpose: Moisture from the garden soil seeps down into the dam's clay core, so that the clay doesn't dry and crack in the intense desert heat.

But this man-made mountain, 111 meters high and two miles long, is small compared to what lies beneath it. Russian technicians injected a mix of cement, bentonite, and aluminum silicate at thirty times atmospheric pressure to create an underground "grout curtain": a hidden wall 140 meters deep that prevents subterranean filtration of Nile water from one side of the High Dam to the other.

I rode an elevator to the top of a seventy-meter-high poured-concrete lotus flower built to honor "Soviet-Egyptian friendship." Each of the five lotus prongs looked more like a sword than a flower stem. The relief carvings were a Pharaonic version of socialist realism, the ultimate totalitarian aesthetic, I thought.

I gazed out over the Nile, the world's longest river, 4,266 miles long, a thin blue vein parting a knife-carved moonscape of yellow-ocher sand and black volcanic rocks. The waters I saw coursing into the dam's twelve turbines had originated as far south as the great lakes of tropical East Africa. The still, dust-ridden offices of the High Dam Authority, inhabited by robed and toweled Nubians reclining on torn upholstery were a reminder that Egypt has always been among the most African of Arab lands. The engineering marvel outside had been built by Russians. Egyptian Arabs from Cairo now managed its upkeep, with technical assistance from Americans. But this office building in Aswan was closer in both distance and tempo to the Sudan than to northern Egypt. Within these leprous walls there was not one computer. Instead of laser-printed type, I saw only worn ledger books filled with laborious cursive writing. The only modern machine in the building was the photocopier in the director's office. It was covered with dust.

The Nile is a cultural organism, mingling African, Arab, and Mediterranean civilizations. Its route approximates early humankind's emergence from Africa into the Near East almost 2 million years ago.[1] In the course of subsequent journeys north along the Nile, humankind may have first formed political communities. Like the pyramids, and like the monumental dam that now tames these waters, individual rulers have for millennia dominated the inhabitants along the Nile, numbing them into submission.

⊚   ⊚   ⊚

KARL MARX HAD a name for such tyranny as persists here: "Oriental despotism."[2] In an article appearing in the June 25, 1853, edition of *The New*

---

[1] Regarding dates, I cannot emphasize how confusing the picture of humanity's ancestry and early wanderings are, due to recent discoveries. For instance, current humans may descend from a group only 270,000 years old. By early humanity, I therefore mean a close genetic predecessor of our species.

[2] See *The Marx-Engels Reader*, edited by Robert C. Tucker, listed in the bibliography.

York Tribune, Marx observed a connection between the need to organize vast waterworks and the emergence of authoritarian government.

> This prime necessity of an economical and common use of water, which, in the Occident, drove private enterprise to voluntary association, as in Flanders and Italy, necessitated, in the Orient where civilisation was too low and the territorial extent too vast to call into life voluntary association, the interference of the centralising power of Government. Hence an economical function devolved upon all Asiatic Governments the function of providing public works.

Marx explained how so-called "idyllic village communities" in the Near East and Asia, each isolated from the other, each of which "restrained the human mind within the smallest possible compass," provided no resistance to this overarching despotism, based on the need to coordinate water use over large tracts of territory.

In sub-Saharan Africa, tribal units may have been too often weak—amorphous puddles, seeping and contracting over the terrain—but at the lower reaches of the Nile, these political organisms gradually hardened, like fired clay, into states that were composed of both African and Egyptian peoples. Was this geographically determined? Would it always be like this?

My journey through the Nile Valley came at a time of reckoning for Marx's vision. Violent brushfires, stoked by false, fundamentalist prophets, were lighting up the night skies with tracer bullets over valley towns. In Cairo, there was a profusion of boutiques, Mercedes-Benzes, cordless phones, and slums—and, thus, a recipe for discontent. The Egyptian "state" seemed no longer sacred. Yet with population growth, urbanization, soil deterioration, air pollution, and the contamination and overuse of water all afflicting Egypt, what else but the state (and a strong, austere one at that) could hope to manage the delicate relationship between man and nature? Marx is about to be proven either very wrong or very right about the destiny of great riverine civilizations in the Near East and Asia.

Reading Marx, I inferred an even more pessimistic subtext: that a place like Egypt is just too old, too set in its ways, to change. Communism proved a failure in the twentieth century. But would Marx be proven right in the twenty-first, for having foreseen the intractability of Oriental despotism? Inside the High Dam offices, I stared at the gold plaster cast of Gamal Abdel Nasser, the pharaoh who built the High Dam, and wondered.

Marx never fully elaborated upon his theory.[3] He was a prolific writer, and "Oriental despotism" was just one of many provocative ideas he tossed out. Had he not become famous for having written *Das Kapital*, nobody would remember his article in *The New York Tribune*. Karl Wittfogel, a one-time German communist who immigrated to the United States to escape the Nazis, took Marx's kernel of an idea and developed it in *Oriental Despotism: A Comparative Study of Total Power*. Wittfogel claims that there are certain institutional features in the Near East, India, and China that did not exist in medieval and modern Europe—namely, an absolutism "more comprehensive and more oppressive than its Western counterpart." Wittfogel argues that this absolutism forms the basis for "hydraulic society."

Wittfogel suggests that the oppressive bureaucratic nature of hydraulic society makes it distinct from the feudal states of medieval Europe. "In 19th century Egypt," he notes as an example, " 'the whole corviable population [unpaid and underpaid laborers] worked in four huge shifts on Mehmed Ali's hydraulic installations." This bureaucratic tyranny led, in turn, to the raising of large armies and to the building of massive defense works and other architectural immensities. The "masters" of hydraulic societies were "great builders," Wittfogel writes. Their architectural style was "monumental." The aesthetic effect was achieved through "a minimum of ideas and a maximum of material." And this, of course, is exactly what the Pyramids evoke.

Islam, after it appeared in Egypt in 642 A.D., abetted these cultural and architectural tendencies. Much like Eastern Orthodox Christianity in Ethiopia, Romania, and the Slavic zones of Eastern Europe, Islam has usually been a state religion. "The position of the Islamic sovereign . . . underwent many transformations, but it never lost its religious quality. . . . The centers of Muslim worship, the mosques, were essentially administered by persons directly dependent upon the sovereign . . . and the religious endowments, the *waqfs*, which provided the main support for the mosques, were often . . . administered by the government," writes Wittfogel. Later in my journey, when I reached Cairo, I would notice the soldierly monumentality of Cairo's medieval mosques and Koranic institutions—minarets of

---

[3]Marx's collaborator, Friedrich Engels, discusses "Oriental despotism" in his own writings. The idea was obviously a joint one.

skyscraper proportions emphasizing sheer volume and space arrangement rather than the superficiality of mere color. These were clearly "state" shrines, "political" in nature, honoring Fatimid, Tulunid, and Mamluk rulers and, as such, logical architectural extensions of the Pyramids.

Wittfogel concludes that Marx's Oriental despotism is *despotic power—total and not benevolent*, employing *total terror* and *total submission—* though in some places, Wittfogel admits, Oriental despotism may take the form of a "beggars' democracy," where people talk at will, in groups even, but can never expect to change anything.

Oriental despotism is a fascinating concept that, like many fascinating concepts, is seriously flawed. John Waterbury, a Princeton University scholar, writes in his own book about the relationship between resource management and political systems, *Hydropolitics of the Nile Valley*, that it is not clear that irrigation works in Pharaonic Egypt were even controlled by a central authority. The theory of Oriental despotism also lacks precision. Stalinism, for example, seems a perfect candidate for Marx's and Wittfogel's Asiatic tyranny. Yet Stalin's regime did not arise from a hydraulic past.

Or did it?

It might have, if you accept "hydraulic society" as less a provable theory than a way of suggesting that for civilizations so sedentary for so long, and so perpetually tyrannized, their personalities are difficult to alter, even by the most extreme methods, and that these cultures are shaped, often in ways that are hard to discuss, by material factors. Both Stalin and Mao uprooted ancient cultures, but for all the blood spilled, the outcome was two more despotisms on the hydraulic model, updated for the purposes of large-scale industrialization. Stalinism and Maoism were, Wittfogel later inferred, Pharaonic in their application of terror, Pharaonic in the architectural grandeur of their personality cults, and Pharaonic in their emphasis on massive public works projects—including dams and irrigation systems—through the use of slave, or prison, labor. Thus, the political future of Egypt—the source of Pharaonic despotism—was, for me, a critical issue at the turn of the twenty-first century. The Nile was still pivotal to the story of humanity.

TO PREPARE FOR my journey up the Nile I read a lot. The more I read about a place and about issues that affect it, the more I feel I am traveling alone.

In an age of mass tourism, adventure becomes increasingly an inner matter, where reading can transport you to places that others only a few feet away will never see.

But there were very few tourists to be seen. On a clear February afternoon, toward the end of my sojourn in Egypt, with the temperature hovering around a perfect seventy, as snow and ice layered the northeast coast of the United States—in the middle of what should have been Egypt's high tourist season—I visited the Pyramids at Giza. When there should have been dozens of buses filling the cluster of parking lots, I saw two half-filled buses and one minivan. A large herd of camels, there to convey tourists around the ancient monuments, had no riders.

Because of attacks against foreign visitors by Islamic terrorists, the Egyptian economy was losing more than a billion dollars yearly in tourist revenues. Was such terrorism ephemeral, an aberration like the Red Brigade terrorists in Italy in the 1970s, who once they were snuffed out simply disappeared? Or did the attacks suggest something deeper?

◎　　　◎　　　◎

I BEGAN WITH the High Dam, "Nasser's pyramid." But to grasp the full meaning of this most ambitious of waterworks in seven thousand years of Egyptian history, I turned to the work of a noted specialist, John Waterbury, whose *Hydropolitics of the Nile Valley* became my guide.

Waterbury explains that whereas settled life began here between five and seven thousand years ago, it consisted of little more than independent communities, built on sand escarpments and deltaic outcroppings above the floodplain. A political authority higher than the village level may not have come into place until 3400 B.C. This is when basin irrigation originated in Egypt. Basin irrigation, Waterbury explains, "established a remarkable ecological balance *at moderate levels of population density*" (emphasis mine). When this system began going out of fashion in the first quarter of the nineteenth century, Egypt's population was 4.23 million— one fifteenth of what it would be in the year 2000.

As sure as the turning earth, the Nile flooded in late summer. More than 80 percent of the river's discharge occurred between August and October. The other nine months accounted for only 20 percent. Under the system of basin irrigation, as the Nile rose, teams of villagers dug canals, directing the water into large basins, connected to sub-basins downstream. For two months or so, the water sat in these basins, seeping into formerly dry and cracked soil on what were to become cultivated fields of barley, lentils, *bersim* (clover), and the other crops that would be grown in succeeding centuries, like cotton and sugarcane. As the annual flood receded, the excess water was released. Only in the past 160 years, under the rule of Ottoman khedives, was this system replaced by a year-round irrigation regime, called "perennial irrigation."

Perennial irrigation required a state authority to build more sophisticated earthworks and manage water allocation throughout the Nile Valley so that water could flow in the canals throughout the year. More significantly, explains Waterbury, "once one moves beyond basin irrigation, a new set of motivating factors comes into play: the production of agricultural surplus, state-building and the generation of revenues. . . . The Aswan High Dam is but the most recent (and surely not the last) manifestation of Egypt's struggle to dominate rather than coexist with the Nile Valley."

By the end of the nineteenth century, Egypt's population had risen to 10 million, and the British constructed a dam above the First Cataract of the Nile, at Aswan, in order to control the river's flow and to put more land under cultivation. Thus ended the yearly flood. By 1960, with the population at 26 million, the Russians—the new foreign protectors of Egypt—began erecting the High Dam, which increased cultivable land by 30 percent, doubled the country's electric power supply, and created a reservoir (called Lake Nasser in Egypt and Lake Nubia south of the Sudan border) that guaranteed a strategic water reserve for Egypt in times of drought. Over three hundred miles long, an average of 6.25 miles wide, and up to ninety meters deep, this reservoir took five years to fill up after completion of the dam in late 1970. The reservoir raised the water table under the Sahara as far away as Algeria.

With each increase in population has come a new engineering feat more costly, more complex, and more fraught with risk if something were to go wrong. Humanity's attempt to alter nature in the Nile Valley so as to sustain more human life has led to a quiet, growing revolt by mother earth. (Of course, whether attempts to control the Nile also abetted higher population growth is not known for certain.)

To wit, salinization—the process by which salts accumulate in the soil through saturation from slow-moving or stagnant water—first became a problem in Egypt when perennial irrigation replaced basin irrigation. By 1980, a decade after the High Dam's completion, salinization and waterlogging afflicted between 28 and 50 percent of Egypt's productive land. Almost all of Egypt's irrigated land is now on the verge of being "salt-affected." As much as 10 percent of Egypt's agricultural production may be lost each year to deteriorating soil fertility.[4]

More dramatic is the threat posed to the very existence of the Nile delta, the most densely populated and richest agricultural area of Egypt. Since Roman times, the level of the Mediterranean has risen two meters. But with the annual floodwaters now dammed at Aswan, the Nile is no longer able to carry off excess sediment, and the delta is beginning to sink under its own weight.[5] Because of the absence of sediment flowing into the Mediterranean, the delta coastline is eroding by between one and one hundred meters per year,[6] a problem that will be aggravated in the event of global warming. The National Academy of Sciences reports that

> . . . as many as one billion people, or 20 percent of the world's pop-
> ulation, live on lands likely to be inundated or dramatically changed
> by rising waters. . . . Low-lying countries in the developing world
> such as Egypt . . . where rivers are large and the deltas extensive and
> densely populated, will be hardest hit. . . . Where the rivers are
> dammed, as in the case of the Nile, the effects . . . will be especially
> severe.[7]

In addition, Egypt's population has grown at such a rate that despite the dams and other water projects, the amount of cultivated land per person fell by 80 percent between 1821 (when Egypt was switching from basin to perennial irrigation) and 1975, when the Lake Nasser reservoir was filled up.[8] Though the population growth rate has dropped to around 2 percent, even that lower rate means Egypt's population will have grown from 65 million at century's end to 100 million in the second decade of the twenty-first century. In Egypt, resource scarcity and population increase—to say nothing of the possibility of climatic shifts—could even-

---

[4]See Janet Welsh Brown's *In the U.S. Interest: Resources, Growth, and Security in the Developing World* listed in the bibliography.
[5]The situation is aggravated by the stripping away of soil to make bricks and the overuse of wells, which is depleting the ground water on which the delta rests.
[6]See Cheryl Simon Silver's *One Earth One Future: Our Changing Global Environment*, listed in the bibliography.
[7]*Ibid.*
[8]See the table on page 36 in Waterbury's book, *Hydropolitics of the Nile Valley.*

tually produce political chaos on a truly biblical scale. The October 1992 Cairo earthquake, in which the government failed to deliver sufficient relief aid and slum residents were in many instances helped by their local mosques, showed how Islamic factions can fill a vacuum created by the government's failure to respond to natural catastrophes.

I had come to Egypt because this is where the relationship between the environment and local politics may be about to move beyond previous boundaries. The High Dam, despite its failures—salinity, waterlogging, the dislocation of indigenous Nubian settlements, and the difficulties in reclaiming desert land[9]—seemed an inevitable outcome of humanity's upping the ante against nature at the point where Africa threads into the Near East. As Razag told me, along with other experts I was to meet in Cairo, without the dam Egypt would surely have suffered the horrific results of the drought and famine that devastated the Horn of Africa in the mid-1980s, not to mention an earlier drought in 1972 and severe flooding in 1964 and 1975.

In fact, as monumental a project as the High Dam was, it still wasn't enough. With the population increasing, though at a slower rate, we have come to the point where the water needs of Egypt and the Sudan are greater than what the Nile can now provide. Bolder engineering schemes must be developed, such as storing off-year water in the great lakes of East Africa and building a canal through the Sudd swamp in southern Sudan, where considerable Nile water is lost through evaporation.[10]

Then there is the issue of sharing water with Ethiopia. Eighty-six percent of Nile water comes from the fast-flowing, clear waters of the Blue Nile, whose source is the highlands of Ethiopia, while only 14 percent comes from the sluggish, muddier White Nile flowing through the Sudan and originating in the equatorial lakes. Boutros Boutros-Ghali, the UN secretary-general and Egypt's former minister for foreign affairs, has said that "the next war in our region will be over the waters of the Nile."

So, assuming these gargantuan needs and related undertakings, how can central authority not remain essential to survival? At the turn of the twenty-first century, the purely "hydraulic" nature of Egyptian society appeared to be intensifying, especially since Egypt might eventually

[9]Desert land reclaimed through irrigation in Egypt has proven more costly and less productive than anticipated, since much of the new soil is of poor quality and requires special treatment.
[10]See Waterbury.

acquire even more territorial responsibility—for example, over Libya (a land rich in natural resources, yet with a small population and weak historical legitimacy as a state) or over a dissolved Sudan, where the Arab north has made war on the African south much as one country makes war on another, and where a tyrannical Islamic government may prove unequal to the task of national survival.

But is it possible for the Egyptian state to control its environment without becoming even more despotic?

THESE WERE THE thoughts I brought with me to Egypt. They were the only baggage I had, literally, since my lone rucksack had been misplaced by the airline.

5

◎   ◎   ◎

Islamic Coketown

WITHOUT POSSESSIONS TO distract me in my hotel room—I had neither a book nor a shortwave radio now that my bags were missing—I wandered in the streets until dark. Things, like people, slow you down. To travel well, you should carry nothing except the clothes on your back and the pages of a few books photocopied and stuffed in your pocket.

◎   ◎   ◎

THE ASWAN SOUK (market), with its displays of leather-sheathed swords, ivory knives, beaten-metal shields, carved-wood serpents, arrows, walking sticks, woven baskets, and spices, resembled a cross between a supply depot for a medieval army and a tourist trap. One merchant was playing a cassette recording of a speech by a fundamentalist Saudi cleric, calling the faithful to battle against "America!"

Another merchant, Peter Hosnani, had iron-gray hair clipped very short, cocoa-butter skin, and a look of panic in his eyes, as though he had been caught in the act of counting up his change just as a mob appeared at his stall. He was a Coptic Christian, and his expression reminded me of the Lebanese I had met in West Africa.

"The people here are stupid. In school, they learn only to memorize, not how to think or how to analyze."

"You mean they learn by rote," I interjected.

"Yes, that's right. They learn by rote. There are strict quotas for Copts in all the schools. It doesn't matter how much smarter we are. I know, I used to be a school principal. I quit to open up this private shop. But now there is no business, on account of the Moslem extremists.

"You see, if the government privatizes, everybody knows it will help the Copts more than the Moslems because the Copts are good business-men. This is what the people are really thinking. So the government will only privatize a bit, just enough to satisfy the Americans. . . .

"The government says that 6 percent of the people in Aswan are Copts. It's really 20 percent. . . . I own a seven-hectare sugarcane field north of here, near Kom Ombo. The Moslems came in the night and burnt it."

"How do you know it was the Moslems?" I asked.

"Because I know. . . . Can I tell you a story?"

"Yes," I said.

"I fought in the 1967 war against Israel. During the war, a general came up to me and asked, 'What's your name, soldier?' 'Peter Hosnani,' I answer. 'Oh, you're one of those from the West, a Crusader like the Jews.' In other words, he thought that because I was a Christian, I was not really on the same side as him. This was a general in my own army during a war. What kind of a country is this?"

◎   ◎   ◎

I TRAVELED NORTH, along the Nile.

At first, my train window was like a time machine. I stared for hours at the network of furrows, the creaking water wheels, the cereal fields, and the entire green panel of cultivation; I stared at the wispy palm husks and the branches of the palm that curve out from the bases like the stone leaves atop Pharaonic pillars, at the peasant women with their dazzling lavender scarves washing clothes in stagnant irrigation ditches, at the water buffaloes the color of mud and occasional dromedaries walking along elevated embankments, like bas-reliefs on the walls of a lighted tomb, at the whole monotonous yet engrossing pageant hazed and, in effect, memorialized by dust.

And, of course, I stared at the river itself, crystalline, glistening with the mucus of life. Some have associated such pastoral scenes with the Coptic Christians, who were here first, direct descendants of the pharaohs. (The Moslem Arabs arrived later, in the seventh century, and predominated in the cities of the Lower Nile.) But I saw the tableau simply as a "tourist's Egypt." Nevertheless, as I approached the geographical center of the country, halfway between Aswan and Cairo, this "tourist's Egypt" came to an end.[1]

Soon I began to see a sprawl of crowded redbrick blockhouses. Redbrick, more expensive than the traditional mudbrick, is indicative of the wealth of absentee landlords: Egyptians who labored in oil-rich Arabian Gulf states in the 1970s and 1980s had been putting their money into real estate. However, because the redbrick is sturdier, these buildings are taller than buildings have ever been here before, boosting population densities and, as it happens, social tensions. "The Gamaa Islamiya [Islamic Group] wishes the people a happy Ramadan" read a sign in Arabic as we approached the railway station in Assiut. There were still water buffalo to be seen, but now they were making their way through city streets.

Assiut had become a symbol, a cliché almost, for the fundamentalist violence frightening tourists away from Egypt.[2] Even in the 1970s and early 1980s under President Anwar Sadat, Assiut, racked with poverty and resentment, was a problem, erupting now and then into street riots against a Western-oriented Egyptian regime composed of wealthy Arabs from Cairo. Islamic fundamentalists assassinated Sadat in 1981. The vice-president who succeeded him, Hosni Mubarak, would have even more trouble with Assiut, and with what Assiut represented.

By the mid-1990s, antiregime violence in Assiut and other towns of Upper Egypt was endemic. The loss of three or four security officers per week to extremists' bullets and knives was now assumed to be normal. So were the potshots the fundamentalists from Gamaa Islamiya fired at tourist ships cruising the Nile, and the bombs they occasionally planted

[1]Geography here is confusing. Northern Egypt is also Lower Egypt, since it is down-river near the mouth of the Nile; while southern Egypt is also Upper Egypt, since it is "upriver," closer to the river's source. Central Egypt, equidistant between northern and southern Egypt, is variously referred to as Middle Egypt and also Upper Egypt, since it is still upriver from Cairo. Given the increasing proclivity of journalists to refer to towns in the center of the country as Upper Egypt, I will adopt this phrase.

[2]I am uncomfortable with the term *fundamentalist*, which, as the Princeton Near East scholar Bernard Lewis informs me, is really a word meant to describe a particularly fervent type of American Protestant at the turn of the twentieth century. Lewis prefers the Turkish word *Islamci*, meaning "he who peddles Islam," in order, in this case, to gain political power. Still, given the reader's familiarity with *fundamentalist*, I feel I am stuck with it, as well as with the more neutral term *Islamist*.

on night trains carrying tourists from Cairo to the Pharaonic sites at Luxor. The few tourists who still came to Upper Egypt traveled by air. As for the tourist ships that normally ply the Nile in great numbers, I had counted dozens of them in Aswan, all empty, forlorn, and docked.

I got off the train and entered a dreary gridwork of sand-colored apartment blocks whose cramped passageways, lined with refuse and consisting of mud forever crumbling into choking dust, were stuffed with people and battered cars belching the residue of heavily leaded fuels. The gray and liver-brown building fronts were peeling like diseased skin. The clothes on people's backs were the same shades as the buildings. It was as if the whole city and its inhabitants had been dipped in a vat of liquid mud and set out to dry in the smoke-filled air. The only primary colors I observed were provided by the oranges and other fruit on sale. The faces I saw were tense. The women wore dark head scarves. I soon learned that any woman wearing makeup and exposed hair was—or, more crucially, was assumed to be—a Copt. The only fresh paint anywhere was on the Arabic signs on many an alley corner, advising people to fast during the holy month of Ramadan (which had begun a few days before) and ordering women to wear the *hejab*, the traditional scarf.

I shared my dented Fiat taxi with two other men: Mohammed El Dakhakhny, a news photographer and translator I required for interviews in Assiut, and the driver, a Copt.

"Why is the Gamaa Islamiya shooting tourists? I asked the driver. Mohammed translated my question. The driver answered:

"Because the Egyptian government has made peace with Israel, in the minds of the extremists the tourists must obviously all be Jews—an extension of the Mubarak regime. If you can beat up a *kafir* [infidel]"—he displayed the Coptic cross tattooed on the inside of his wrist and told how he was nearly attacked by a Moslem gang—"you can kill tourists.

"This situation with the extremists is like the evil eye," the driver went on. "We don't know why God has brought it. But we have all known about it . . . we felt it . . . since 1982, after Sadat died. Why did it take the world another ten years to realize?"

He drove us to the Assiut Hotel near the Nile, an oasis of fresh plants, lacquered wood, and bottled water you could drink even during the daytime during Ramadan—Copts ran the hotel, so inside its doors the rules of Moslem Ramadan, whereby you can't eat or drink until sunset, did not apply. The receptionist eyed my U.S. passport and Egyptian visa suspiciously, flipping slowly through the stamped pages. I was worried. The government did not want Westerners in Assiut for fear of violence. Journalists were supposed to get permission before coming here.

"You are not a resident of Egypt?" the receptionist queried.

"No, I'm a visitor," I said.

"Then you must pay ninety-two Egyptian pounds per night instead of forty-six," a matter of twenty-seven dollars.

In my room, I had nothing to unpack except for some Egyptian pajamas that I had bought, which I carried in a plastic bag. But the room offered a fine prospect of the Nile. I stuck my head out the window and smelled the river. Instead of the rot and grit that I had smelled in the street, I now felt the caressing touch of moist, rinsed air, as though a recessed memory were suddenly coming to light.

"The Nile is like a virgin [who has been violated]," Mohammed had told me earlier. "They should never have built the dam. I wish there were still the yearly flood. There would be less people, less problems." Mohammed was from Alexandria and had gone to the best schools. His features ran with all the bloodlines of the Mediterranean, past and present: Saharan, Andalusian, Greek, Arab. He was a cultural buffer between the street and me. I would have no choice but to experience much of the coming hours through his eyes and ears.

The Ramadan fast lasts from sunrise to sunset. It was winter, and darkness came early. So at five-thirty in the evening, everyone would gather for *iftar*, the meal that breaks the fast, beginning with fruit juice and a cup of lentil soup, followed by platefuls of skewered meats. During Ramadan, mosques feed the poor for free, so large crowds gather at prayer time. Then, as evening wears on, people nibble on sweets washed down with tea. With midnight comes another meal. People then sleep a few hours before getting up around four-thirty for breakfast before dawn, and then everyone goes back to sleep. No one shows up for work until 10 A.M. or later. And by 2:00 P.M. many offices and stores are closed. Ramadan days are dreary. People drift in slow motion. But late nights are full of gaiety and strung with colored lights. People gossip under bright dreamy canvases, specially set up for this time of year. There is a fairy-tale quality about the holy month. Little gets done or, more important, produced—especially when Ramadan falls in summer, when the days are long and the heat is at its most intense.

Yet, in these times the holiday is associated with tension. In medieval times, a town like Assiut, much like an isolated Moslem khanate in Central Asia, could have locked its gates to visitors for a month and live off the food it produced during the rest of the lunar year. No longer. Assiut and many other urban concentrations in the Islamic world are now *developed*— badly industrialized blockhouse towns of poured concrete and black fumes. Production must continue and products must be shipped. Now people must work, even during Ramadan. Privatization and the need for production weigh more heavily on religious Moslems than on secular ones, or on Copts. And because people now have to work while fasting, they are cranky, particularly in the late afternoon. In the street, when I asked a man for directions, he clucked his tongue in disdain and pushed on. A second man: same thing. The third finally helped me.

Sunset came. Mohammed and I stuffed ourselves at *iftar*. When it was completely dark we went outside and began to walk. I wanted to walk for a few miles and to get lost, to see what Assiut was really like.

Thus, I stepped into a film noir, right down to the black-and-white television sets in cafés with sawdust-covered floors, zinc kitchen tables, and dim, scabby walls illuminated by single weak bulbs, which gave the squeezed alleyways a somber institutional ambience, as if Assiut were a sprawling penitentiary and each storefront a separate cell. *Kadis* delivering prayer sermons filled the television screens. People seemed bored, but nobody changed the channel. Merchants stood in doorways, dressed in sooty galabias (homespun robes) and fingering prayer beads. They seemed utterly relaxed, even as groups of soldiers rolled by in the open backs of slow-moving white Toyota trucks clutching their AK-47 assault rifles. The dull green uniforms didn't fit. The soldiers looked like raw recruits. The troops were so closely crowded together in the trucks that their elbows almost touched each other's eyes and their rifle butts knocked each other's foreheads on bumps in the road.

"It's a joke," said one merchant. "Someone can lob a grenade from a rooftop and a dozen soldiers would be killed at once. Assiut is dangerous for the government and its soldiers, but not for us." I imagined a fire-fight, and soldiers struggling over each other in a rush to escape from the truck.

Kids kicked soccer balls in the alleys. An earth-mover came rumbling down the street, a few inches of space on either side between it and the front of buildings. In its cavernous mouth were two rusted bicycles and a wide-eyed little girl. Mohammed scrambled to take a photograph. We negotiated an obstacle course of stripped Daihatsus and Isuzu trucks, and battered Russian Ladas. Cassette tapes competed with the televisions, blaring out scratchy rhythms and hypnotic sermons, particularly those of Sheikh Kishk, the Cairo cleric who has declared it wrong for a Moslem to touch the hand of a Christian. Then there were the sandbagged emplacements, with more troops, and the occasional plainclothesman—young men with tight-fitting jeans and pistols in their hands, or, in one instance, a middle-aged gentleman in a galabia, carrying an AK-47. But it was those with guns whose faces showed fear. They seemed the occupied, not the occupiers.

The mosques were the tip-off. I saw very few well-constructed *houk-oumi* (government) mosques, but many streetcorner *ahli* (people's) mosques, which served as local bases for radical clerics and extremist groups. This is what the map fails to show us. Were Egypt shown, let's say, in green, then an ever-lengthening strip of Upper Egypt, including Assiut, should be colored in an even darker shade of green and labeled "Islamic Egypt."

Assiut wasn't pretty, but as a dark-haired, unshaven man in the company of an Egyptian friend, I felt safe, for there is no random crime in Assiut. In that sense, Egypt's is a far more civil society than America's. However, to keep it that way in the face of both increasing urbanization (the number of shantytowns has tripled in twenty years to 370) and for-eign cultural influences—evinced by the profusion of television antennas that beam in not just Moslem sermons but Western-style soap operas—requires an increasingly conservative social glue, which, in turn, can provide an ignitable surface for the spread of Islamic radicalism.

Whereas rural poverty is age-old and consistent with an ever-turning planet, urban poverty like Assiut's can be socially destabilizing. As Iran has shown, Islamic extremism is the psychological defense mechanism of urbanized peasants threatened with the loss of traditions in pseudo-modern cities, where their values are under attack, even as basic services like water and electricity have broken down. The American ethnologist Carleton Stevens Coon wrote in 1951 that Islam "has made possible the optimum survival and happiness of millions of human beings in an increasingly impoverished environment over a fourteen-hundred-year period." Beyond its stark, clearly articulated message, Islam's very mili-tancy makes it attractive to the downtrodden. It is the one religion that is *prepared to fight!* A political era marked by scarcer resources, increased cul-tural sensitivity, unregulated urbanization, and refugee migrations is an era divinely created for the spread and intensification of Islam, already the world's fastest growing religion.[3]

The grim, aesthetically unsatisfying environment of Assiut was, in itself, radicalizing.

◎   ◎   ◎

MOHAMMED AND I were in the midst of a discussion with a gun dealer on a narrow street of the souk when we realized we were late for our appointment. The gun dealer sold only Lee-Enfields, a turn-of-the-century single-action, British rifle of no use to militants but in popular demand by local farmers, who, lacking telephones, fired rifles in the air as a form of communication. But he also sold bullets, and these were of use to militants. Our discussion, convoluted as it was, resulted in a single discovery: that despite government regulations, if you wanted bullets you could get them. I gulped my obligatory tea and made a fast exit.

During Ramadan, a reporter conducts his interviews at night, between *iftar* and the midnight meal. Professor Dr. Mohammed Habib" (this is how he asked to be identified) greeted us at the door of the doctors' union building. He was punctual, arriving at exactly 10 P.M. A geologist at the University of Assiut, Prof. Dr. Habib is one of the leaders of the Ikhwan el Muslimin (Moslem Brotherhood) in Assiut. The Moslem Brotherhood, like the Gamaa Islamiya, was fueling Egypt's Islamization. But, unlike the Gamaa's, its extremism was subject to doubt. Like the Egyptian landscape, whose pigments are dulled by the dust from the surrounding desert and the mud of the Nile, the Brotherhood is concealed in layer upon layer of ambiguity and historical complexity. The Brotherhood might thus be a useful barometer for gauging Egypt's political direction.

The Ikhwan was founded in 1929 by Hassan el-Banna, and quickly adopted terrorism as a tactic. In the late 1940s the Brotherhood was responsible for the murder of an Egyptian prime minister, and in 1954 for the attempted assassination of Nasser. The late president Anwar Sadat opened a dialogue with the Brotherhood, as a wedge against leftist Nasserists who wanted to overthrow him. The Brotherhood then ended its violence and has not been implicated in an attack since 1970. For many

[3]Though Islam is spreading in West Africa, it is being hobbled by syncretization with animism: This makes new converts less apt to become anti-Western extremists, but it also makes for a weakened version of the faith, which is less effective in combating crime.

Egyptians, the Ikhwan is a benevolent neighborhood force, operating clinics, welfare organizations, schools, and hospitals that arose to fill a void created in particular by Nasser and in general by modernism.

Nasser's land reforms ended the latifundium system of landed estates and partial servitude of labor, which integrated, however unequally, the rich and the poor in a traditional social structure. The wealthier classes, especially the new rich, now have less personal contact with the poor than their parents' generation had. In other words, Egyptian life and anxieties have become increasingly similar to our own. Groups are increasingly isolated, but within groups, people have learned to cope with less and less government. And while class fissures widen and other problems mount up, the Nasserist state, composed of over three hundred state-owned firms and 1 million bureaucrats, is a calcifying, Ozymandian monolith. In the earthquake of October 1992, when tenements crumbled into powdery dust, this monolith was nowhere for the first few days. Mubarak was out of the country. A bureaucracy that numbers 1 million persons and does twenty-seven minutes of work per individual per day, according to a United Nations report, was accustomed to taking orders from a pharaoh. So it did not respond to the emergency. But those like Prof. Dr. Habib organized food for the poor, distributed blankets, and shepherded people into the protective enclosures of neighborhood mosques. Such is how the Ikhwan fills the void.

The Moslem Brotherhood's numbers are uncounted, its popularity unpolled since it is officially proscribed as a political party. An overwhelming number of Egyptians and Western diplomats I asked said that if truly free elections were ever held in Egypt, the Moslem Brotherhood would probably obtain the most votes. That's as specific as the information gets. Are there formal links between the Ikhwan and the extremist Islamic organizations, such as the Gamaa? It is hard to say, though in the past, the Brotherhood maintained links with radical groups like Takfir Wa Hegira (Purging and Spiritual Passage) and Jihad (Holy War), the latter of which carried out the assassination of Sadat. Though the Brotherhood has been around for decades and is well rooted in the Egyptian political-social fabric, information about it remains murky.

Prof. Dr. Habib, I was told, is a typical Ikhwani. By that I mean he appeared highly disciplined, and also somewhat proud. With stylish glasses, a cream-colored corduroy jacket, and a perfectly trimmed white beard, he was fastidious as well as didactic, speaking in a nasal, crisply enunciated Arabic that Egyptians call "Islamic" speech. "The Islamists have their own language, their own way of speaking Arabic," explained Mohammed, in an opinion seconded by other Egyptians I would meet later in Cairo. They commonly remarked upon the *Koranic speech* of Ikhwanis like Habib, and particularly of the followers of radical sheikhs, such as Omar Abdurrahman, who was implicated in the bombing of the World Trade Center. This type of Arabic has several distinctive features. While the overwhelming majority of Arabs speak a regionally based, colloquial Arabic—reserving standardized, "classical" (or literary) Arabic for written communications and other formal occasions—Islamists use classical Arabic more regularly. In addition, they flavor it with allegories and symbols peculiar to the Koran. More crucial is the way they pronounce Arabic: Whereas spoken Arabic is usually a flowing language, in which one word easily connects with the next, Islamists appear to meditate on each individual word, separating the word out from the one before it and from the one after it, to savor its meaning. This is a speech mannerism akin to praying, or to memorizing. Because in Arabic substance is conveyed by the actual sound—and not just by the meaning—of the words, it is therefore not uncommon for Islamists to mimic the accent and intonations of a favored cleric as a show of respect. This is not strange in a culture where rote learning is common. An English speaker cannot be judgmental about these things. He can note, however, that they exist.

Habib ordered freshly squeezed orange juice for us, followed by tea. Habib's hospitable manner appeared to be a rebuke to the very surroundings into which he had led Mohammed and me: distinctively grim Assiut surroundings—a massive room of plate-glass walls caked with dust and covered with brown, machine-made carpets and boxlike upholstery. He shook our hands warmly. He never raised his voice. He never interrupted me or Mohammed. He confronted each of my questions straight-on, with a polite and detailed answer. Much of what he said I agreed with. For a moment, I fell into a trance of shared idealism. *If only more people in Egypt were as rational as this man.*

"The government police, unfortunately, behave like barbarians. They arrest and mistreat large numbers of people who aren't even connected to the extremists. We can only solve problems through a political dialogue. The torture must stop. Elections must be free for all the people. Now, as you know," leaning toward me as one friend to another, "the elections are rigged.

Mubarak does not feel secure. So he closes the door completely in the face of peaceful change, and he runs toward America, where his allies are."

"What about the terrorist attacks against tourists?" I asked.

"The government applies tremendous pressure against the militants through torture. So the militants are forced to probe where the government is weak and vulnerable. The militants have nothing against the tourists personally. Their actions are merely intended to minimize the pressure of a regime backed by America and Israel. But these killings of foreigners are against Islam and Egypt. We condemn them. But look, the Somalis kidnap people in order to pressure America. This is exactly what the militants are doing when they attack tourists."

"You have spoken about America. But how does the Ikhwan see Israel?" I queried.

"For [Yasser] Arafat and other Arab governments to make peace with Israel changes nothing. That is just another reason why many regimes in the Arab world are discredited and will collapse. We know the Jews have always been troublemakers. They destroy societies from the inside."[4]

"Are you saying that the government in Qatar, which is considering a natural-gas-pipeline deal with Israel, is discredited? Are you saying that Syria's president, Hafez al-Assad, whose government is negotiating with Israel, is not loyal to the Arabs?"

"Yes, that's what I'm saying. These dictators represent nothing anymore. Revolutions to come will destroy their agreements with the Jews."

He shook my hand with kindness, thanking me for soliciting his opinion.

Habib appeared to me as a "type" increasingly familiar in this awkward, volatile century. His confident, learned manner is eerily reminiscent of educated Hindu and Sikh militants I had once seen in India; of the cultured university professors who spearheaded the Romanian fascist movement; of the self-educated and highly disciplined members of Louis Farrakhan's Nation of Islam—of Farrakhan himself, even; of Dr. Radovan Karadzic, the Bosnian Serb with a degree in psychiatry who suggests that the elimination of Moslems holds the key to his Orthodox Christian people's happiness; and of Dr. Baruch Goldstein, who also had a medical

---

[4] I interviewed Habib nine days before the Hebron mosque massacre, which occurred on February 25, 1994. His remarks cannot be attributed to the emotional climate resulting from that incident.

degree, who relied on biblical references to justify his murder of innocent worshipers in a Hebron mosque: all men with grandiose visions acquired through an exceedingly limited range of books and experience. Because these men are educated (indeed, the use of fine literary Arabic is something Nasser himself never quite mastered), they feel their people's distress all the more deeply. Yet, as one Egyptian businessman in Cairo, hearing my observations, noted: "They have been narrowly educated. And narrowly educated people cause the worst sorts of upheavals." A retired Egyptian diplomat added: "The Jews these people think they know about are the Jews of the Koran, who spurned Mohammed. The Brotherhood's knowledge of Judaism since the medieval era is nonexistent."

There was another unpleasant aspect of this conversation, and of others I was to have with Islamists who complained about the human rights abuses of the Mubarak regime. In Egypt I saw how the defense of human rights could be manipulated for cynical purposes, by people who might be expected to inflict far worse abuses if they ever got control of a government. This was a difficult realization for an American: While Americans have examples in their own society of how religion is exploited for the basest motives, they still perceive the advocacy of human rights as an undefiled cause.

◎   ◎   ◎

CONCERNING THE COPTS, Prof. Dr. Habib told me that "we live peacefully with them, unlike with the Jews. The Copts and we are like fibers in the same tissue." Yet many a fundamentalist preacher—Sheikh Kishk, for example—railed against the Copts. Another member of the Moslem Brotherhood with whom I spoke, Dr. Essam el-Erian, a leader of the physicians' union in Cairo, told me "air strikes against Bosnian Serbs are the only thing that can save this Coptic Christian man, Boutros Boutros-Ghali, who is condemned throughout Egypt for the pain he has caused Bosnian Moslems."[5]

The Copts are direct descendants of the Pharaonic Egyptians. The Coptic Church is among the oldest in Christendom. The Evangelist Saint

---

[5]The word *Copt* stems from the Arabic *Qibti*, a shortened form of the Greek *Aigyptios* (Egyptian). Jill Kamil, in her book *Coptic Egypt*, explains that the seventh-century Arab invaders called Egypt *dar al Qibt* (home of the Egyptians): "since Christianity was then the official religion of Egypt, the word *Qibt* came to refer to the practitioners of Christianity as well as to the inhabitants of the Nile Valley."

Mark is said to have preached here in the first century A.D., and established churches in Alexandria. Saint Anthony, an Egyptian hermit, became the father of Christian monasticism, when, in 313 A.D., he fled into the "Interior Desert" not far from Assiut in order to become *perfect*.[6]

This religious fervor was born amidst the steady deterioration of Roman rule in the third and early fourth centuries A.D. As Rome's grip on the Nile Valley died, its oppression of its Christian subjects worsened. Egyptians had to provide documentary proof that they were not practicing Christianity. Waves of brutality sent Christians farther upriver into southern Egypt, away from the Roman authorities. Ultimately, Roman rule here collapsed and Christianity in Upper Egypt triumphed—until the next wave of fervor, brought upon by invading Arabs three hundred years later. From this example—and others, such as the collapse of the New Kingdom three thousand years ago, when local priests gradually overwhelmed the pharaoh and semianarchy prevailed—it is apparent that there have been parallels in Egyptian history, however crude, in which an increasingly discredited state apparatus has been swept away by a movement claiming legitimacy directly from God.

The Copts fled not only from Roman proconsuls, but later from Arab horsemen, too. Because the direction of the seventh-century Moslem armies was east to west, across the top of Egypt toward Libya and the Maghreb, the Copts fled southward, into Upper Egypt, which is why the Coptic presence in places like Assiut is proportionally higher than in Cairo, Alexandria, and the intervening delta—20 percent of the population in Upper Egypt as opposed to 10 percent in Lower Egypt is Coptic. The prosperity of Coptic businessmen makes the Coptic position in this poor Moslem society akin to that of Korean grocers in south Los Angeles. They are despised as a "middleman minority," somewhat like the Lebanese in West Africa. The quick-step enlargement of the pilgrim center at the Convent of the Virgin Mary, outside Assiut, built with donations from Copts throughout Egypt and the world, is a not-too-subtle reminder to Moslems of Christian wealth—with a giant cross and curved arches of yellow and lime-washed cement dominating the nearby villages. An Assiut merchant told me, "The Christians have inspired jealousy. They are doing well, building forts all around us."

[6]For an exquisitely written, scholarly work on the birth of Christian monasticism, see Derwas Chitty's *The Desert a City*, listed in the bibliography.

Like most of the Coptic monasteries in the Nile Valley, the Convent of the Virgin Mary is built over a cave where Mary, Joseph, and the boy Jesus are said to have sojourned during the Holy Family's flight into Egypt to escape King Herod, a journey mentioned in the Gospel of Saint Matthew. The Holy Family came to Assiut in August, the time of the flood, when the valley was inundated. Thus, the cave is located inside a mountain above the flood plain, overlooking the western bank of the Nile. It is, like the other Coptic redoubts, a desert monastery. The monastery, carved into the dun mountains, is across the road from the last of the green, irrigated land. Nikos Kazantzakis, the Greek author, has said of this place, "Nowhere on Earth" is there "such violent and sensual contact of life with death . . . the green and the sandy gray."

Mohammed and I drove up the steep entranceway, alongside tall apartment blocks housing the thousands of Coptic pilgrims who come here for the August feast that commemorates the Holy Family's legendary stay. I met Father Bishay inside the cave: a yawning black cavity glistening with gold-leafed icons and lined with terra-cotta pots filled with water for baptisms. Here thousands took refuge during the floods of antiquity, making the cave sacred in pre-Christian times. Father Bishay, like all Coptic priests, wore a black robe and a black pointed hood covering his hair and ears. He had dark mahogany skin and a wispy black beard.

Life here is good, he told me. The problems with the Moslems are being exaggerated by foreign writers like myself. The convent was growing, with more donations and more buildings. The massive retaining walls surrounding the complex were but a quaint architectural tradition, I was informed. This was nothing especially difficult about this moment in history. There were no bad trends. Politics did not concern him, he said.

I was told the same thing at the Coptic monastery of Deir el-Muharraq, a rambling desert fortress northwest of Assiut where the Holy Family is also said to have sojourned, in another cave. The word *muharraq* is Arabic for "a hurt caused by fire," a reference to the burning of sections of the monastery by Moslem intruders in the Middle Ages. The architecture pointed to a historical need for security. Sweeping crenellated walls offered the barest of prospects of what lay inside. Inside the walls, I entered an almost Grecian world of white domes and belfries. Here were lemon and olive groves graced by songbirds; frescoes of the Virgin Mary, St. George, and Jesus; gold-leaf icons, brilliantly bound volumes filled with illuminated manuscripts, and religious tracts in Coptic, Greek, Arabic, and Amharic. The monks showed me the artifacts. I was insufferable, plying them with political questions. "No," one of them smiled, forbearingly. "There could never be any trouble between Copts and Moslems. We are protected by God himself. Moslem women even come to the monastery to sacrifice animals if they have trouble getting pregnant." There was no hint of nervousness in his voice. Nor did his eyes avoid mine. I had no reason to doubt him.

Two weeks after my visit, on the night of March 11, 1994, Moslem militants shot and killed five Copts outside the gate of the Muharraq monastery just as the group was waiting to enter the compound. Two of those killed were monks.[7]

◎   ◎   ◎

HOSNI FARAG HAD a glass eye and a crudely manufactured artificial arm. He wore a soiled green galabia and a brown cloth wrapped around his head. The walls of his family room in the village of Manchiet Nasser, north of Assiut, were unadorned gray cement. In the room, where we sat on a mustard-toned sofa, were an old and rusted refrigerator, a fake-gold clock, six naive pictures of Jesus Christ, a glass table smeared with cigarette stains, and a machine-woven brown carpet (handmade carpets are only for the wealthy, and for Western tourists). A fluorescent light hummed loudly from the ceiling. Chickens and turkeys ambled in the gray cement hallways amid a mound of *bersim*. Flies were everywhere. I was inside what statisticians called a "lower-middle-class" Egyptian home, whose squalor conveyed much more than statistical categories could tell me.

At 9 A.M. on the morning of May 4, 1992, Farag was in the field with some other Coptic farmers when "a group of men with beards and rifles" sprayed them with bullets. Moslem militants claimed credit for the attack, in which seven Copts were killed. Farag crawled away, losing an eye and a forearm. "Whenever I go into the field, I'm still afraid of them," he said.

It was a Christian home, and tea was brought out even though it was Ramadan. There was also a woman present, her hair uncovered, seated next to the men. Her eyes, highlighted by black kohl, were sad but fierce, reminding me of the dusky figures I had seen in the icons at Deir el-Muharraq. "Will it get worse?" I asked no one in particular. There was

[7]The Reuters report of the killing was dated March 12, 1994, and was published in *The Washington Post* on March 13, on page A27.

another one of those interminable silences. Finally, the woman answered in the indirect and frustrating manner to which a traveler becomes accustomed in this part of the world.

"The Moslems recently shot a policeman dead for no reason. This policeman had five children. Nasser was good because Nasser arrested these fundamentalists. But Mubarak is only a politician. He cannot protect Christians on every street corner. The government is good only when it is tough."

Farag just stared at me. His one functioning eye was like the stony bottom of a crater: a view without mystery, or hope.

◎ ◎ ◎

MOHAMMAD AND I left Farag's house and walked toward our taxi. Manchiet Nasser was called a village, but it was really part of the same bustling sprawl of automobiles and cement paving that has become the new traditional landscape of Upper Egypt. There was no quietude, only the hot, fetid breath of others on your neck and fingers poking you in the back, nudging you along in the crowd. Officially, there was water in the pipes, but a man with a donkey was selling cans of water because there wasn't enough pressure to carry the water to the upper stories. Was Moslem militancy more than what it seemed? I wondered. Were the bullets that had lodged in Farag's eye and arm, in fact, a harsh background noise partially triggered by deeper, more complex environmental forces?

Yes, one could provide a purely political explanation for the Copts' plight. In *The Arab Predicament*, Fouad Ajami explains how Arab nationalism has always been "at its core 'covert Islam,' and covert Sunni Islam to be precise." As the "secularist impulse" weakened in the 1980s, due to the failure of Arab nationalist regimes to provide either democratic freedoms, economic rationalization, battlefield victories, or any combination of the three, Arab populations were "culturally Islamized."

"There was no use denying it, or retreating, as some Christian Arabs did, into hyper-authenticity. Christian Arabs were on the run," writes Ajami. Boutros Boutros-Ghali, the Coptic Christian married to a Jew who had been Egypt's state minister for foreign affairs, was a poignant example of this. Boutros-Ghali's tough bargaining with the Israelis in the late 1970s earned him frequent rebukes, insults even, from the Israeli government. But he was a man in the middle, distrusted by Egyptians, too. When, as the United Nations secretary-general, Boutros-Ghali resisted military intervention on behalf of the Bosnian Moslems, Egyptians did not judge his beliefs about the Balkans on their merits. Within the Ikhwan, he was seen merely as a Coptic Christian supporting his fellow Orthodox Christian Serbs. Boutros-Ghali's hard line on Israel's treatment of the Palestinians now counted for nothing.

But could politics—ethnic or otherwise—ever exist in a vacuum, outside the larger environment? This was the question I returned to throughout my travels. After all, floods and droughts had a terrific political impact in Pharaonic Egypt. In *Revolution and Rebellion in the Early Modern World*, University of California sociologist Jack Goldstone makes an excellent case for how the English revolution of 1640, the French Revolution of 1789, the various revolutions in Central Europe in 1848, the *jelali* revolts in the Ottoman empire,[8] and rebellions in imperial China all emerged from the inability of regimes to deal with the problems arising from sustained population growth and natural resource depletion. Goldstone uses an earthquake as an analogy: Though the havoc is unanticipated, stresses that build up gradually over the years cause the layers of crust to shift suddenly.

Demographic pressures never reveal themselves as such: People don't demonstrate in the streets or attack others because they believe their region is overcrowded. The crush of humanity invites scarcity, whether in food, water, housing, or jobs. Scarcity fuels discontent, wearing the mask in this case of politicized Islam. Was it only accidental that attacks on Christians, as well as on passing tourist trains and boats, occurred mainly in the most polluted and badly urbanized part of the Nile Valley? In recent decades, the Assiut area had become home to petroleum refineries, cement factories, and food processing plants. Farmland is disappearing as once-distinct villages meld into each other. Assiut's population of 300,000 is three times what it was in the Nasser years. The state, whatever its problems in 1957, when a census revealed the city's population to be 104,000, is even less able to govern now. No wonder Arab nationalist regimes have failed to satisfy their populations! The specific problems of Arab nationalism notwithstanding, there are larger forces at work.

Ajami, too, in an earlier part of his book, notes that of three hundred Moslem conspirators arrested by the Egyptian authorities in the wake of

---

[8]The *jelalis* were armed irregulars in central and eastern Anatolia who revolted against the central authority of Constantinople in the late sixteenth and seventeenth centuries. Many of their supporters came from the ranks of the unemployed. See Lord Kinross's *The Ottoman Centuries*, listed in the bibliography.

Sadat's assassination, over 90 percent came from urban centers, and particularly from the urbanized peasantry living in shantytowns.[9]

◎   ◎   ◎

A FRESH BREEZE: a few minutes' walk in Manchiet Nasser had brought us to the Nile. Egypt is still a riverine civilization, geographically viscous: the railway lines, telephone lines, and most of the roads connecting one end of the country with the other all run along the river. To get to Cairo from Manchiet Nasser, I first had to get back to the Nile. The Nile makes Egypt, like a wooden staff, easy to grasp, to control. Ninety-five percent of Egypt's people live on less than 5 percent of its land, along a river corridor over six hundred miles long but never more than ten miles wide, apparently substantiating the Egyptians' claim that only they among Arabs possess genuine national identity. But what if this wooden staff is rotting, slowly being eaten away by what Kazantzakis calls "this multicolored anthill of humanity beside the Nile"? What would happen? Would the staff simply crumble in the ruler's hand?

[9]This would seen to substantiate the notion, mentioned in Chapter 1, that the urban environment may come to represent the locus of future conflict.

6

Ⓞ   Ⓞ   Ⓞ

Voices of the "Tormented City"

AMID THE HILLS where the stones for the Pyramids were quarried four thousand five hundred years ago is a terrifying sight. Mountains of garbage, leading into valleys and furrows of garbage, form a patchwork of streets on the southeastern edge of Cairo, inhabited by snorting black pigs and wild dogs who pick at the flesh of dead donkeys and snarl at your feet with their bleeding gums. Human beings also live here—thousands of them, many of them children. They are called *zabaleen*, "the people of the garbage."

Work for these children begins at dawn, when they pile into rickety donkey carts and fan out through a city of 13 million, collecting garbage. At day's end, they sift through it, selecting bits of plastic, cloth, and other items suitable for recycling. The items are then sold to "garbage barons," middlemen who in some cases have made small fortunes off garbage, enough at least to replace their zinc shanties with mudbrick or cement. In this way, much of the garbage of Cairo is collected daily. The *zabaleen* are a private-sector success story, filling the gap in a municipal service where the government is ineffective.

The *zabaleen* are mainly Copts, an irony for a group whose relatives in the fundamentalist strongholds of Upper Egypt reminded me of

Korean grocers in the Los Angeles ghetto. The *zabaleen* are a constant in the life of Cairo, much like the half-million Egyptians who inhabit tombs in Cairo's Northern and Southern cemeteries (collectively known as the City of the Dead).

In the late 1980s, it was estimated that as many as 50 percent of the *zabaleen* children died before adulthood of malnutrition, disease, and pollution. The *zabaleen* are now a cliché: Journalists in Cairo yawn when you mention them. They are a regular part of the suffering that Egyptians have been familiar with for thousands of years. *Zabaleen* collecting garbage amid parked BMWs are just another facet of "eternal Cairo," a juxtaposition with which the West cannot grapple, like the marble boutiques rising from the ground like exotic plants, elevating the gray cement and sheet-metal shanties to the second story. In Cairo, as in Istanbul and other developing cities at the end of the twentieth century, many forces are colliding. The future steps over the bones of the past before they have been properly buried. A medieval world coexists with a postmodern one.

After a visit with the *zabaleen*, Embaba appears almost prosperous. Embaba is a new slum area of northwestern Cairo, built by squatters on agricultural land. Like Assiut, it has television sets but no running water. This is where those connected with the assassination of Sadat had been reared. Embaba has become another kind of cliché for Cairo journalists, symbolizing the upheaval of rising expectations rather than the constancy of poverty and suffering. In Embaba, and also amid the *zabaleen*, one may hear "the cry the inhabited tormented city had nailed in the middle of" Kazantzakis's "heart." But which cry would win out: the cry born of fatalism or the one of revolt?

I would begin to find out in Istanbul, later in my journey, where I would get to know such slum dwellers personally. In Istanbul, their voices were the most consciously resonant regarding the future. In Cairo, meanwhile, there were other voices that I remember, voices that shifted in their well-upholstered chairs: anxious voices.

◎   ◎   ◎

"IT'S THE POOR . . ." I began.

"No, it's not the poor," the diplomat said, a bit exasperated. He had been in Egypt for a few years and had his lecture down pat. Though it was midday in a semitropical city, his shirt and tie were fresh in the air-conditioned embassy. "The poor never start anything. It's the upper-poor, the lower-middle class. They're the ones who are dangerous: young guys with degrees who aren't plugged into any power network, so they're driving cabs or waiting on tables, and are full of resentment.

"Here's the situation," he continued.

"You cannot look at things here in Egypt in a linear fashion. For long periods there is stasis, then events seem to zig and zag for a while, ultimately arriving at point B from point A. The journalists going down to Assiut see revolution coming. We here in the embassy see merely inertia. The question is, Where is the threshold beyond which things explode?

"You see, we're now in the late twentieth century, a time of skill-oriented economies. These people have no skills. Mubarak can only move slowly toward privatization. He's looked at Gorbachev and concluded that Gorbachev fell not because he moved too slow, but because he moved too fast."

I was now deep inside the airlock of "Fortress America," the new United States embassy in downtown Cairo, built in the 1980s—a well-socketed tower surrounded by long, high walls. Soon there would be two towers. And there were plans for moving the ambassador out of the white neocolonial mansion with the garden he occupied across the Nile, and relocating the official residence inside the walls. While the American government was doling out over $2 billion a year to the Egyptians, the architecture suggested how much these benefactors feared the Egyptians. The diplomats worked all day in the embassy, eating American food in the embassy cafeteria. Two decades after reestablishing diplomatic relations with Egypt following the 1973 Middle East war, Americans had taken on the character of the Russians during the Nasser era—a presence too big and too isolated, one that engendered distrust.

When I mentioned this to the diplomat, he was annoyed.

"Look, we're sending a message, not just a soundbite! The fundamentalists say we are propping up Mubarak from inside this building! Well just look at that human rights report next to you on the sofa! Take it home and read it! It's substance." I leafed through the twenty-three-page report, full of details about electric-shock torture inside Egyptian prisons and other abuses. "That report is an example of what we're really doing inside the embassy. How many embassies in this city have an officer who works full-time, doing nothing other than investigating the human rights offenses of the government? I wish those folks criticizing us would realize this."

He added: "And don't believe that stuff about how those opposed to this regime are just anti-Zionist, without being anti-Semitic. Go and hear the parliamentary debates, where they mix up the words *Jews* and *Zionists* all the time. . . . There is no secularism here. Neither the Mubarak government nor any other in the Arab-Islamic cultural sphere has ever been 'secular.' Religion infuses daily life here to an extent that the West hasn't known since the days when it was called Christendom. But Mubarak is seeking to champion an apolitical Islam. Is that so bad? What are his opponents offering?"

The diplomat wanted a level playing field for the battle over Egypt's future, where reason and substantiated facts would prevail over what many Egyptians actually thought.

As I left through the embassy's main security gate, retrieving my passport in return for the laminated security card I had been issued, I had a sense not of power but of fragility, as though this stone-and-poured-concrete fortress were a beach house facing a gathering storm whose direction could barely be calibrated, let alone controlled.

◎   ◎   ◎

"AMERICANS TALK A lot about human rights because they are fools. Human rights is a joke. The human rights organization in Egypt is run by ex-Nasserists and Ikhwanis, the same people who wanted to throw the Jews into the sea in 1967. Now they see an opening to topple the government and human rights is their weapon. So they meet with these stupid apes—the foreign journalists—and pour shit in their ears about poverty and torture." One of Mubarak's advisers was speaking. It was still Ramadan. He was sipping coffee in his neat, functional office with a good reading light. He wore a leisure suit. His bluntness and informality were thoroughly Western.

"You Americans have a cultural problem. The people here have a different nature—they are not worried about the environment or overpopulation. Look at the warm weather. Look at the river Nile, how slowly it moves. This is Egypt. Egyptians don't want progress overnight. We know our people; they can help themselves. They are sedentary, passive. This is not uprooted Arabia, where the real revolutions will be."

"What about the terrorism?" I asked.

"The terrorists are idiots, a bunch of painters and plumbers. They tried to blow up a bank in Cairo. Don't they realize that very little money is actually kept in banks! We have fundamentalism because some genius in the CIA decided to use Moslem zombies in Afghanistan to fight communism, and now some of the zombies are here. The military will finish them." This adviser to the Egyptian president had gone well beyond conventional cynicism and into a realm where nothing seemed to matter any-more. He had an answer for everything. He believed that the government had to do nothing more for its people than it was already doing.

◎   ◎   ◎

"WE HAVE ANOTHER model for life on the globe," said Dr. Essam el-Erian, a Moslem Brother who was one of the leaders of the Cairo physicians' union. He had a dark crescent-shaped mark on his forehead, from bang-ing his forehead to the ground thousands of times throughout a life of prayer. His office was not well lit and not well air-conditioned. "This model is the Islamic way. The question is, Can the West, can the U.S. embassy, accept moderate Islam?

"We are an occupied people. Look at Bosnia, look at Kashmir, look at Palestine. They are killing Moslems everywhere and the West supports the dictatorships." Dr. el-Erian was the one who told me that "air strikes are the only thing that can save this Coptic Christian man, Boutros-Ghali, who is condemned throughout Egypt for the pain he has caused Bosnian Moslems." The implication was that the Moslem Brotherhood identified more with Moslems in the Balkans than with their Christian neighbors who were Egyptians.

"The door of hope must be open, not the door of violence. We are the alternative. And there is nothing to stop us. The pharmacists, the engineers, the scientists, the lawyers—all have elected Ikhwanis to head their unions. We are condemning the violent atrocities of the regime backed by those inside the U.S. embassy. The people of Egypt are not interested at all in peace with Israel. Since the 1979 peace treaty the econ-omy has gotten worse, corruption has gotten worse."

Dr. el-Erian offered me a sour candy from a mother-of-pearl box. "I am fasting. But you see, I am not a fanatic." Unlike the diplomat and the Egyptian government official, Dr. el-Erian was looking forward to the political future.

◎   ◎   ◎

THE GREEK ALEXANDRIAN poet of the early twentieth century Constantine P. Cavafy wrote a poem about the fall of Alexandria to Moslem Arab armies in the seventh century.[1] His poem "Exiles" is set two centuries later, in the ninth century:

[1] See Jane Lagoudis Pinchin's *Alexandria Still*, listed in the bibliography.

It goes on being Alexandria still. Just walk a bit
along the straight road that ends at the Hippodrome
and you'll see palaces and monuments . . .
Whatever war-damage it's suffered,
however much smaller it's become,
it's still a wonderful city. . . .
In the evenings we meet on the sea front,
the five of us (all, naturally, under fictitious names)
and some of the few other Greeks
still left . . . our stay here
isn't unpleasant because, naturally,
it's not going to last forever.[2]

In the nineteenth and early twentieth centuries, the West staged a resurgence in Alexandria under the rule of the British-influenced Ottoman khedives. By 1917, seventy thousand foreigners were living in Alexandria, thirty thousand of them Greek. This was Cavafy's generation. Kazantzakis ends the diary of his trip in 1927 to Egypt with an account of a meeting with Cavafy. Kazantzakis writes:

Cavafy is among the last remaining flowers of a civilization. With double, faded leaves, with a long, sickly steam, without seed.
Cavafy has all the typical characteristics of an exceptional man in an age of decline—wise, ironic, sensual . . . Reclining on a soft couch he gazes out of his window and waits for the *barbarians* . . .

Cavafy, "brimming with memory," who makes the very process of remembering the theme of his poetry, is the perfect poet to help the West come to terms with its loss in Egypt.

When I arrived in Alexandria, it was only a five-minute walk from the railway station to the Mosque of Nebi Daniel, built, it is claimed, over the tomb of Alexander the Great that had been erected in the Ptolemaic period following Alexander's death. Mealy cement, white bathroom tiles, and institutional brick assaulted my eyes. On wooden stalls, Moslem religious books were piled high. Old posters decrying the slaughter of Moslems in Bosnia were in tatters on the peeling walls. I also noticed the

[2]Translated from the Greek by Edmund Keeley and Philip Sherrard. See C. P. Cavafy, listed in the bibliography.

German fashion magazine *Neue Mode* and computer advertisements. Battered, locally built Fiats exhaled dark fumes. Grit blew up from the pavement and into my eyes. It was impossible to determine from this tableau where civilization was headed. Which would win, the religious books and posters of Bosnia, or the fashion magazines and computer advertisements—or would there be a strange synthesis of both? All I knew was that for the moment it appeared physically ugly, like bad interior decorating.

The Alexandria of 1914, the year Cavafy wrote "Exiles," had a population of only four hundred thousand. There were large gardens and stylish villas and none of today's poured-concrete monstrosities, and "above all, room to breathe."[3] Alexandria's visual beauty was enough to ignite Cavafy's nostalgia about the past. Now, with 3 million inhabitants, ranks of tall apartment blocks along all the landward entrances to the city, and continuous traffic jams, Alexandria is best when recollected from afar.

The interior of the Mosque of Nebi Daniel was anticlimactic. Instead of fine Oriental carpets, there was only a machine-made green felt. The prayer hall was populated by youths wearing jeans and polyester shirts, praying. A man unlocked a door for me and pointed down toward the tombs beneath the floor where a medieval Sufi sheikh was now interred. "*Iskander* [Alexander] finished," the man said loudly. "Only Islam."

◎   ◎   ◎

OF COURSE, THE Near East has long since ceased to be an exotic backdrop for literary-minded Westerners. An urbanized peasantry that has crowded into Egyptian cities has withdrawn into religion, unable to fathom the issues of overpopulation and resource scarcity confronted in the 1970s by the Western rationalist John Waterbury. These issues will have to be dealt with, however. Central power can deteriorate only so far before another gravitational force emerges.

Thomas Homer-Dixon, who writes intelligently on the security implications of environmental degradation, believes that in places like Egypt there will be environmentally induced praetorian regimes, or, as he puts it, "hard regimes." A society experiencing chronic internal conflict because of resource scarcities, rapid urbanization, pollution, and other "environmental stresses" will, according to Homer-Dixon, "probably evolve along one of two paths: the state will either fragment or it will

[3]See Jacqueline Carol's *Cocktails and Camels*, listed in the bibliography.

become more authoritarian," with democracy a superficial "epiphe-nomenon" having little to do with such long-term processes as a growing population and a shrinking resource base, just as "emerging democracies" in sub-Saharan Africa may turn out to be.

If, indeed, that turns out to be true, what would the new Egyptian pharaohs be like?

◎   ◎   ◎

THE NEW PHARAOHS might combine the values of the late Pakistani dicta-tor Zia ul-Haq and the father of the Singapore economic miracle, Lee Kuan Yew. Like Zia, they would successfully wear the mantle of the Islamists—thus co-opting them—while privately cooperating with the West. Like Lee, they would install a meritocracy in government to better withstand the ravages of less water to drink and less soil to till. They would make the wealthy pay income taxes, and would, in other ways, rationalize the economy. Like both Zia and Lee, they would be harsh to dissidents, since democracy in Egypt, given its poverty and its despotic past, could lead to chaos. Such pharaohs would likely emerge from the officers' corps of the military. But, unlike Mubarak, they would look to East Asia for a model of corporate authoritarianism to replace a dying socialist kleptocracy. However, given the cultural differences between the Nile Valley and East Asia, this scenario, rather than cynical, is probably far too hopeful.

Another scenario would be an authentic Islamic government, which, once it became clear that it had no answers to humanity's struggle with the environment, would descend into tyranny, as in Sudan. Then, the state itself would die slowly, with neighborhood "Ikhwans" continuing to draw power away from a decaying, Cairo-based bureaucracy. The Nile Valley is geographically friendly to a cohesive state. But a few decades of semianar-chy would not be unprecedented in Egypt's long history; nor would a tyranny far, far worse than that of the late twentieth-century Nasserist pharaohs.

PART III

◎   ◎   ◎

Anatolia
and the Caucasus
The Earth's Stratigic Core?

I should tell you that all the provinces that I have been speaking of, from Kashgar forward, and those I am going to mention, as far as the city of Lop, belong to great Turkey.

—MARCO POLO
The Travels of Marco Polo

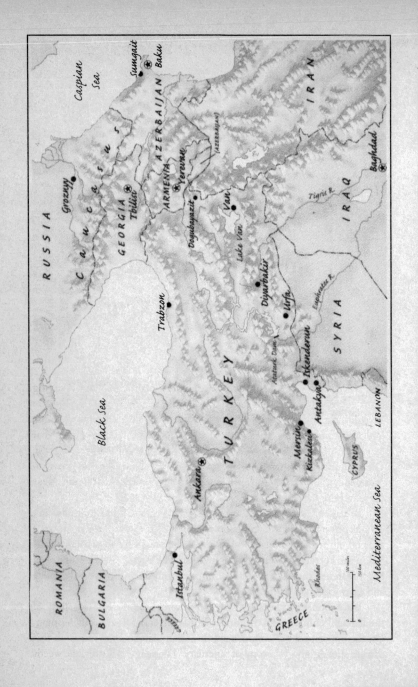

7

◎　　　◎　　　◎

"The Still Point of the
Turning World"

THE WIND, LIKE time itself, raced through the plane trees and towering black cypresses as I walked across a vast walled enclosure of the Topkapi Seraglio, coming at last to the porphyry columns, the conical towers, the gold leaf and cupolas of the Felicity Gate—the *Sublime Porte*, that exquisite French phrase which served as diplomatic shorthand for the Ottoman Turkish sultanate (as the White House stands for the American presidency), an entire universe encompassing North Africa, the Near East, and the Balkans.

Because the Ottoman empire took so long to die, its decrepitude sank deep roots among its subject peoples. This helps to explain why, toward the end of the current historical ice age—the one marked by totalitarianism in the Fertile Crescent and communism in Eastern Europe—upheaval has threatened the sultan's former domain, from Bosnia to the Nile Valley and eastward to Mesopotamia.

I stood on a promontory, "Seraglio Point," the eastern extremity of the Balkan Peninsula and the former headquarters of the Ottoman sultan. On the opposite shore commenced the Asian plateau. The mood on this *charged* spot, as always, is one of sanctuary. The seagulls flutter, the weeds grow between the flagstones, the wind blows in from three converging bodies of water: the Golden Horn, the Bosphorus Straits, and the Sea of Marmara. Here, in T. S. Eliot's words, is "the still point of the turning world."[1]

Geography is destiny. Astride two continents and two climatic zones—the Tartary gloom of the Black Sea and the warming currents of the Mediterranean—Istanbul near the turn of the twenty-first century was a lesson in the ramifications of plate tectonics, from where the plates of the Greek-Slavic Orthodox world (European, yet somewhat Oriental) and the Turkic world (Asiatic, yet Westernizing) collide, recoil, and collide again. Greek Byzantium reigned a thousand years here before it was overwhelmed by Turkish nomads migrating from Central Asia. Now there are new nomads, the last of the peasants from eastern Anatolia, completing their conquest of Turkey's westernmost city, while still other seismic waves emanate from this spot, promising to be even more unsettling, more traumatic.

THE STORY OF man is the story of nomadism: According to much-disputed theories, the migration begins in black Africa, proceeds up the Nile Valley, then into the Fertile Crescent, and eastward along the Indus and Ganges rivers to the Orient and beyond. To glimpse the broad outlines of the early twenty-first century—a time that promises an unprecedented degree of nomadism, or refugee movements if you like—I had chosen to follow, albeit approximately, a likely path of early man. So from sub-Saharan Africa and the Nile Valley I traveled to the northern arrowhead of the Fertile Crescent—Anatolia, where Asia begins, a place the Turks call *Anadolu*, which might sometimes be translated as "mother lode." Anatolia is the primary land bridge across the historical migration route to Europe, Asia, and Africa. At Catal Huyuk, in the heart of this often dry and bony fault zone, archaeologists discovered the world's oldest-known landscape painting, drawn nine thousand years ago. It shows a volcano erupting.

Since Istanbul's importance rests primarily on its location, it was absent from history during the Cold War, when Soviet power artificially

---

[1]This phrase, from Eliot's "Four Quartets," was pointed out to me by Turkey's former prime minister, Bulent Ecevit.

divided Eurasia. But after 1989, Turks were no longer cut off from the Balkans to the west and from their Turkic cousins to the east in the Caucasus and Central Asia. Classical geography had returned. The Turks, history's perennial nomads, could ride back into history.

I am a time traveler, but not necessarily a romantic one. Topkapi belongs on my map. There are other parts of the city that don't. I don't include the Grand Bazaar or the Church of "Divine Wisdom" (Hagia Sophia) or the café up the Golden Horn, where the nineteenth-century French novelist Pierre Loti wrote a steamy romance about falling in love with a veiled Circassian harem girl, Aziyade. Instead, I chart places where a literary tourist would rarely go.

◎　　　◎　　　◎

ARA GULER, A local photojournalist, has chronicled the architectural development of Istanbul in the twentieth century. "I am a visual historian," he told me. "At the end of the twentieth century I find almost nothing left to photograph in my city. There are no aesthetics left here. Look at this scene out of the car window. It's not a village, it's not a city. It's just shit."

This "shit" is where the future is being decided, the part of the map I mean to chart.

I left Topkapi and began driving. I crossed the bridge over the Bosphorus, from the European side of Istanbul to the Asian side—from the Balkans to Anatolia. I drove for almost an hour and was still in Istanbul, but not the Istanbul of romantic memory. My guidebook was atypical: *Tales from the Garbage Hills*, a brutally realistic novel by a Turkish writer, Latife Tekin, about life in the city's shantytowns. The novelist describes complete neighborhoods "fathered by mud and chemical waste, with roofs of plastic basins, doors from old rugs, oilcloth windows and walls of wet breezeblocks."

Sultanbeyli is such a place.

First came the watery dust and the endless unpaved roads with spine-jarring craters no different than those in Africa. I stared at peeling walls, rusted iron entrails, weird urban sculptures of cinder block and corrugated iron, the lightning flashes of welders, tire stores, sheet-metal signs, and sludge: fields and mountain ranges of refuse heaps. Trucks were double-parked everywhere. Factories belched black smoke. A shepherd led his flock of sheep through the mud a few feet from a construction site. There was no focus to any of this development, no downtown. A neither-nor of a landscape, which, as Guler had warned me, was not a village, not a city, just *shit*.

"He listened to the earth and wept unceasingly for water, for work and for the cure of the illnesses spread by the garbage and the factory waste," writes Tekin. But the most revealing passage of *Tales from the Garbage Hills* tells of when the squatters are told "about a certain 'Ottoman Empire' . . . that where they now lived there had once been an empire of this name." This history "confounded" the squatters. It was the first they had heard of it! Though one of the squatters knew "that his grandfather and his dog died fighting the Greeks," nationalism and the encompassing sense of Turkish history is the dream-burden of the Turkish middle and upper classes, and of foreigners like myself, who feel it necessary to have an *idea* of Turkey.

But what did these squatters know about the armies of Turkish migrants that had come before them—the Seljuks and the Ottomans? What did they know about *The Book of Dede Korkut* (the Vulgate Bible of Turkic civilization)? What did they care?

For these newly urbanized peasants—not just in Turkey, but in Africa, in the Arab world, in India, and so many other places—"the world was new," writes V. S. Naipaul in *India: A Wounded Civilization*. "They saw themselves at the beginning of things: unaccommodated men making a claim on their land for the first time, and out of chaos evolving their own philosophy of community and self-help. For them the past was dead; they had left it behind in the villages."

Everywhere in the developing world at the end of the twentieth century these new men and women—flowing into the cities, turning them into grotesque villages—were remaking civilization. To these empowered millions, national borders, nations themselves, even the idea of a nation, were vague. To them the real borders were the most tangible and intractable ones—those of culture. They knew, for example, that the Christian Orthodox Greeks had once been their enemy. And that was enough to establish identity of a sort.

In Iran these new city dwellers had made a revolution. But the revolution would have been impossible without the oil boom that had preceded it, which hastened development and compressed the culture shock. By the late 1990s, however, the old Iran was reemerging: altered, yet recognizable, as I would see for myself later in my journey. What, then, of Turkey, which had had no oil boom and where secularism was part of the national myth? In Turkey everything was more subtle and, therefore, less apparent.

In 1980, 43.9 percent of Turks lived in cities.[2] In 1990 it was 59 percent. By the turn of the century the figure would be 67 percent and climbing. Istanbul, the largest city in Europe, with a population of 10 million in 1993, was growing at the astonishing rate of 4.5 percent a year.[3] Each year, 450,000 new citizens were arriving from *the great out-there*—Anatolia. "Rather than Anatolia being Istanbulized, Istanbul and the other urban centers are being Anatoliaized" is a lament I kept hearing. Even in Turkey's so-called "wild east," former frontier "towns" like Diyarbakir, Van, and Erzurum were doubling in size every half decade, becoming teeming cities, even as villages in these remote regions were being deserted. Turkey in the last decade of the twentieth century was in the midst of a social-economic revolution far more important than any change of government.

Sultanbeyli, on the eastern fringe of Istanbul, was originally founded by ethnic-Turkish immigrants from Bulgaria. In 1985, its population was 3,500. In 1993, 150,000 people lived here. The houses are called *gecekondus* (literally, "built in the night"). Leaky iron roofs are held down by stones. The walls are of mud, unplastered brick, or cardboard tied by string to the roofs. There is no running water in the homes, no sewage lines.

Ayse Kucukhiyali came to Sultanbeyli from Erenkoy, a tiny village in Anatolia's bleak north. Her hands were thick and callused like a man's, and caked with dust. Gripping a hoe, with a blue kerchief over her hair in the traditional Moslem style, she was turning the soil next to her mud-walled house, preparing to plant eggplants and potatoes in view of an automobile junkyard, when I approached her. "Our family are farmers," she lamented. "But there is little future in farming anymore. We came to the city expecting a better existence. My husband works in construction. I am confined to the house—in the city, only the men have a life. For my three children it was necessary to come here. The village school had no teachers. It is for the children that we suffer."

Seyhan Besoluk came from another distant Anatolian village. "The children must be well educated. I want my sons to be doctors or engineers. It is impossible to do that in a village." Like that of the other men and women I met in Sultanbeyli, her *gecekondu* had a television set, though no running water. "We watch the news, but some of the other programs offend us. We are traditional people."

[2]These statistics are based on the 1990 Turkish national census, further elaborated upon by a leading Ankara demographer, Aykut Toros.
[3]Actually, about two thirds of Istanbul lies on the European side of the Bosphorus and about one third on the Asian side.

I walked through a field of mud where some boys were playing soccer with a ball fashioned out of rags. I passed two women veiled from head to toe in black—walking blankets. I tried chatting with them. They giggled; they were teenage girls. They said that they had moved to Istanbul from a village in eastern Anatolia. In Sultanbeyli, for the first time in their lives, they had regular access to television. I, too, had become familiar with Turkish television. It was a copy of the American variety—full of glitz and glamour and sexually provocative, reflecting the values of nouveau riche, Westernized Istanbulis. How were such programs affecting these girls? Did the images reflect their secret dreams? After all, the *gecekondus* were the seed ground of the Turkish lower-middle-class—halfway houses, both physically and socially, between peasant and city life. The bawdy, orgasmic *arabesk* music performed on television and heard on Turkish buses was, in fact, a product of the *gecekondus*. Or did these girls mean to tell me that they were offended—like the other woman with whom I had talked—by what they saw on the screen, turning them against the wealthier class of Turks, and thus, by inference, against the West? Or perhaps it was not that simple; perhaps television was just another disorienting detail of urban life, pulling these girls in different directions at once. I had no time to ask. Embarrassed by their encounter with me, the veiled teenagers fled. The answers to my questions were not going to be given up easily.

In 1989, the same year as the collapse of communism in Eastern Europe, the people of Sultanbeyli elected their first mayor, a member of the extremist Islamic "Welfare" party. This was no coincidence. The *gecekondus* had been a bastion of the Turkish left, whose credibility had been undermined by the revolution in Eastern Europe. In the postcommunist world, discontent was no longer ideological but religious—in other words, cultural. To paraphrase Naipaul, out of the chaos of the end of the twentieth century the ideals of community and self-help were being reinvented by newly settled migrants. At the headquarters of the Islamic Welfare party in Sultanbeyli, in a spotlessly clean room where I was made to take my shoes off upon entering, an official told me—in the same breath almost—how Israel must be destroyed, how Turkey must sever its ties to the West, how the party delivers water in summer and coal in winter to needy families, how gifts of food are made during the Moslem holidays. In this neighborhood, Islam filled the gap vacated by a political establishment that could not keep up with the changes overtaking a society in the midst of upheaval.

FROM ISTANBUL, I traveled eastward to Ankara, the Turkish capital, where shantytowns are built on steep, muddy hills and are visually dramatic in ways that the flat, sprawling shantytowns of Istanbul are not. Altindag (Golden Mountain) is a pyramid of dreams, fashioned from a babble of breeze blocks and corrugated iron, as though each shack were built on top of the other, all reaching awkwardly, and painfully, heavenward—the heaven of wealthier Turks, who live elsewhere in the city. Nowhere else on earth had I seen such a poignant architectural symbol of man's striving, with roofs wedged in by rows of rusted cans, and leeks and onions growing on verandas assembled from planks of rotting wood.

Golden Mountain is invisible to a late-twentieth-century travel industry concerned only with the myths of the nineteenth century. Golden Mountain is an aspect of Turkey, and of the world, that the travel magazines instinctively hide, even as the future is being written inside the heads of Golden Mountain's inhabitants. Think of an Ottoman military encampment on the eve of the destruction of Greek Constantinople. That is Golden Mountain.

"We brought the village here. But in the village we worked harder—in the field, all day. So we couldn't fast during [the holy month of] Ramazan. Here we fast. Here we are more religious." Ayshe Tanrikulu, along with a half-dozen other women, was stuffing rice from a crude plastic bowl into vine leaves. She asked me to join her under the shade of a piece of sheet metal. She gave me a cup of tea, which was soon flecked with dust. Each of these women covered her hair in a kerchief. Ayshe, the oldest, in her thirties, did the talking. Her voice was loud and blunt, like a carnival barker's.

Slum quarters can appear picturesque from a great distance, but otherwise terrifying and repellent. In Turkey it was the opposite. The closer I got to Golden Mountain, the better it looked and the safer I felt. I had fifteen hundred dollars' worth of Turkish lira in one pocket and a thousand dollars in travelers' checks in the other. But I felt no fear. Golden Mountain was not so much a slum as a real neighborhood. The interior of Ayshe's house told the story:

The architectural bedlam of cinder and sheet metal and cardboard walls was deceiving. Inside was a *home*—order, that is, bespeaking dignity. I saw a working refrigerator, a television, a wall cabinet with a few books and lots of family pictures, a few plants by a window, and a stove. The floors were spotless. And there were no bad odors.

The other homes were like this too. Though the streets were rivers of mud when it rained, they overflowed with a protective embrace. Schoolchildren ran along with briefcases strapped to their backs, trucks delivered cooking gas, a few men sat inside a café sipping tea from countless small glasses. One man sipped beer. Alcohol is easy to obtain in a secular state even if 99 percent of the population is Moslem. But there is no problem of alcoholism. Crime is infinitesimal. Poverty and illiteracy are milder versions of what obtains in Algeria and Egypt. Slums—in the sociological sense—are rare in Turkish cities. Here the mortar within and between family groups is strong: It is a civilization with natural muscle tone.

My point in bringing up a rather wholesome, crime-free slum is this: Its existence demonstrates how formidable is the fabric of which Moslem Turkish culture is made.

Ayshe Tanrikulu continued: "My son has a university education. He is a computer engineer. But he doesn't make enough money. I have another child in primary school. We have no money for his books. I don't know if he'll go to a good secondary school. The kids from rich families with connections—they get all the places. The government says school is free, but it isn't really. . . . Life is so impersonal in the city; the air is so filthy. My hopes are dashed. But the children will not live in a *gecekondu*. Education, that is everything!"

In Golden Mountain I saw a more complex and varied reality than the one I had seen in Sultanbeyli. The overwhelming truth about the *gecekondus* was not religious fundamentalism: These shacks were filled with ambitious people, with middle-class desires. A competent secular government in Ankara can co-opt them.

I drifted to another street. Some kids were playing with an old wheel just like the kids I had seen in Africa, wonder in their eyes, as though inventing the thing for the first time.

Suna Karabiyik asked me to remove my shoes as I entered her cardboard-and-mudbrick *gecekondu*. The carpets were cheap, machine-made, but free of dust. Again, I was struck by the antiseptic cleanliness surrounded by an ocean of mud. Suna is twenty-five, from northeastern Anatolia, with black eyes and black hair: a harsh, handsome face, seething with grit and determination, a face Steinbeck would understand. Suna pointed down an eroded hillside to a row of grim modern apartment blocks, all cheaply constructed. "That's where my family is headed. Every day I look at those houses and want to live there. My husband and I have only one child. We don't want any more. We want to give our child a life we never had. We can't depend on the government. We've got to do it ourselves."

"What about your neighbors here? Will you miss them?" I wondered, because those buildings look so cold and impersonal.

"It's good to get acquainted with different people throughout life. We met new people when we moved from the village to Golden Mountain, and we'll do the same thing again."

I marveled at this modern peasantry, for which life was a social adventure, where the government was not even asked, let alone expected, to provide for you. The difference between refugees and nomads is this: Refugees flee a place because they have no choice, but nomads are pioneers *on the make*. Nomads are makers of history. Refugees are its victims.

◎   ◎   ◎

WHO ARE THE Turks? There may be few more important questions for the early twenty-first century.

The word *Turk* first makes its appearance in the sixth century A.D., in the Chinese form *Tu-Kiu*, to denote a nomadic group that founded an empire stretching from Mongolia to the Black Sea. These nomads spoke an agglutinative tongue, which, like Mongolian, Hungarian, and Finnish—languages spoken by peoples vaguely related to the Turks—belongs to the Ural-Altaic group and stems from the region between the Ural Mountains in eastern Russia and the Altai range in Mongolia. It was the Chinese, a mortal enemy of the Turks, who gave definition to this nomadic organism that spread like water over the bleak tabletop of inner Asia. The Great Wall of China, begun in the third century B.C., may have been built to keep these Turkic tribesmen at bay.

The succeeding centuries witnessed a series of Turkic migrations over the Central Asian steppe that involved such obscure horsemen as the Uighurs, the Oghuz, and the Khazars. Empires briefly coalesced, leaving little residue as they compounded with yet another Turkic onslaught. "On the black earth he pitched his white pavilion; his many-coloured tents reared up to the face of the sky. In a thousand places silken rugs were spread." So goes *The Book of Dede Korkut*, a collection of stories set in the heroic age of the Oghuz Turks: a wine-consuming horde—whose women were expert riders, archers, and wrestlers—that succumbed to Islam simply as a religion, not as a complete social system. This latent paganism, common to all Turkic groups, would help the leader Mustafa Kemal Ataturk secularize Turkey in the 1920s and 1930s.

These footloose Turkic tribesmen pressed against the walls of China, as well as northward and westward against Russia. It was the Russians, another historical enemy, who invented the term *Tatar*, as a catchall for Genghis Khan's Mongols and their Ural-Altaic cousins—the Turkic tribes. The Mongol Golden Horde subjugated Russia in the thirteenth and fourteenth centuries, shielding it from the Renaissance. The Tatars were, by and large, responsible for Orientalizing Russia. Ever since the days of Ivan the Terrible in the sixteenth century, the Russians, burdened with feelings of cultural privation and a thirst for revenge, have been on the offensive against the Turkic peoples. Stalin's assault on Turkic unity in Central Asia and his imposition of the Cyrillic alphabet on his Turkic subjects—in order both to Slavicize them and to cut them off from fellow ethnics in Afghanistan, northern Iran, and Turkey—were examples of this hatred. So was the Russian war against the Moslem Chechens in 1995.

In the ninth and tenth centuries, the Finns and the Magyars became the first Ural-Altaic peoples to arrive in Europe. The cultural genius of these horsemen of the steppe was apparent: Within a century or so they had adopted European manners and customs. In the second half of the eleventh century, eastern Anatolia saw its first Turkic nomads, the Seljuks (named after their founding chieftain), who annihilated a Byzantine army in 1071 at the Battle of Manzikert. The Byzantine Greeks held out at Constantinople until 1453, when another Turkic tribe, the Ottomans, having vanquished and absorbed the Seljuks, conquered the city and later called it Istanbul.

The Ottoman Turks were to establish a polyglot empire stretching from the gates of Vienna in the north to Yemen in the south, and from the border of Morocco in the west to Mesopotamia in the east. The Ottoman threat soon made the word *Turk* a European synonym for savagery. Martin Luther, in the sixteenth century, prayed for deliverance from "the world, the flesh, the Turk, and the Devil." Yet the romance of the Ottoman court in Istanbul's Topkapi Seraglio fashioned another, more benevolent, stereotype: that of the "Grand Turk," with evocations of harem girls, tulip festivals, love poetry, brocaded silks and rich carpets, trays of sherbet and other sweets, and pencil-thin minarets reflecting in marble pools—the most sensuous and indulgent of Islamic civilizations.

Topkapi was, originally, a nomadic court, its turrets reminiscent of tents on the Kara Kum Desert in central Asia, its military campaigns each year in Europe reflecting seasonal wanderings on the steppe. By the dawn of the twentieth century, however, Topkapi was a calcified theocracy, much as Greek Byzantium had been prior to the Ottoman conquest four and a half centuries earlier, and like some of the Arabian Gulf sheikhdoms at the dawn of the twenty-first century.

Modern Turkey, which arose from the death throes of the multinational Ottoman empire after World War I, was the dream of one man, Mustafa Kemal Ataturk (Father Turk). Kemal Ataturk was an authentic revolutionary—one of history's handful—because he changed a people's value system. He divined that the European powers had defeated the Ottoman sultanate not on account of their greater armies, but on account of their greater civilization. Turkey would henceforth be Western, he said. Not coincidentally, no Moslem enjoys so high a historical reputation in the West as Ataturk. In the 1920s and 1930s, Ataturk abolished the Moslem religious courts. To wrench Turks away from their traditional Islamic past, he forbade men to wear the fez and discouraged women from wearing the veil. He moved the capital from Istanbul—the symbol of a backward Islamic empire—to Ankara, rooted in pagan Anatolian Turkism, where the bull god reigned over the Crescent. By replacing the Arabic script with the Latin one, he oriented Turkish culture to the West. Even Ataturk's definition of nationality was startlingly modern. "Ataturk declared that whoever says he is a Turk, speaks Turkish, and lives in Turkey is a Turk," I was told by Altemur Kilic, an Istanbul newspaper columnist whose family roots go back to Georgia, Abkhazia, Uzbekistan, and Aegean Rhodes. Ataturk's emphasis on language as the arbiter of nationality made Turkey not only a melting pot of Balkan, Caucasian, and Central Asian Moslems, but also a hospitable place for Turkish-speaking Jews. Ataturk made Turkey not a blood republic but a modern one.

"Kemalism is a desire to be identified with the West, a way of life showing contempt for the Arab world," said Nilufer Gole, an Istanbul sociologist and feminist. "Kemalism celebrates paganism over Islam, it provides Turks with an emotional, nation-building myth that is completely secular and therefore has no equivalent in other Moslem societies, where all the powerful myths are religious." In other words, Kemalism enables secular Turks to fight just as strongly for their beliefs as the newly religious Turks in the *gecekondus* fight for theirs.

Ataturk's mausoleum in Ankara, the Anit Kabir (Great Tomb), is an assertion in marble and stone of this secular *will*—which aims to utilize, and to subsume, the dynamism of the *gecekondus* within the grand vision of Ataturk's "Republican Turkey." A gigantic Hellenistic temple, the Great Tomb is architecturally pagan, with sculptured torches by the walls, wolf tracks carved into the floor, and relief etchings of soldiers embracing mother goddesses. It is a ferocious place. As I walked around this temple precinct, guarded by white-helmeted troops, I felt that had Adolf Hitler died a natural death, this is the kind of tomb he would have had.

But there is another tomb in Turkey: not in Ankara, but in Istanbul—the city of magnificent mosques, of Islam, the Ottoman capital that Ataturk spurned that came back onto the strategic map after the fall of communism. This is not a "great tomb." The view from its humble precincts is of a modern highway; the sound you hear is that of automobile acceleration. But they come, *they come*, the slippered men and kerchiefed women of the *gecekondus*, to pray at this *turbe* (tomb of a Moslem holy man). Here lies Turgut Ozal, the prime minister and later president of Turkey, who died in office in 1993—the second great Turkish revolutionary of the twentieth century.

While Kemal Ataturk was an aloof general, a ladies' man with a well-cultivated taste for Scotch whisky, Turgut Ozal was a short, fat, scruffy peasant whose neck disappeared within his shoulders; who talked while he chewed his food; who never learned properly how to use a knife and fork; and who was not ashamed of his faith:

"Though Turkey is a secular state, I, the president, am not a secular man."

And if Ozal could be a Kemalist while still being a religious Moslem, why couldn't the people in the *gecekondus*? Why should there necessarily be a contradiction? Secularism, as Ozal redefined it, meant just that—not atheism. Not that these people in the shantytowns knew, or cared, what "Kemalism" was. They just knew that, under Ozal, they were part of the system. Ozal, who loved the American notion of social mobility, who traveled with both a Koran and a laptop computer, deeply intuited the dreams of his people: They merely wanted a better life without spurning their religious traditions. The supreme monument to Ozalism is the Kocatepe Mosque in Ankara, one of the largest religious shrines in the world—built with a supermarket complex beneath it.

Ozal softened Ataturk's fierce, Western-oriented secularism. Whereas Ataturk ignored the Turkic east in the Caucasus and Central Asia in order to turn his people westward, Ozal saw the East as a new market for Turkish goods. Whereas Ataturk looked westward for a cultural standard, Ozal lifted Turkey out of its self-imposed isolation by trying to assert a Turkish Moslem power bloc in the Balkans. But Ozal's most important contribution was his rediscovery of the multinational past, rectifying the tragic flaw in Ataturk's vision.

Ataturk's Turkey was a crucible in which Moslems (as well as some Christians and Jews) from throughout the Ottoman empire could be equals, through the adoption of the Turkish language. However, Anatolia had always been a land of three peoples and three languages—Turkish, Kurdish, and Armenian. The Turks, with assistance from Kurdish mercenaries, annihilated almost all the Armenians during World War I, before Ataturk's takeover, leaving only small communities in a few cities.[4] But the Kurds remained: At least one out of six citizens of the Turkish Republic is a Kurd. The failure to adequately acknowledge their existence was the great flaw in Ataturk's vision. In the early and mid-1990s, a war has raged between the Turkish army and Kurdish separatists in southeastern Anatolia; it has left fifteen thousand casualties. It is a war that threatens Turkey's social peace, since large Kurdish communities exist in all the major cities, especially in *gecekondus*. Ozal died just as he was moving toward a compromise with the Kurds. In the wake of his death, though, a hard Kemalism returned that sought to crush the Kurds through military means.

To learn more, I headed east, toward Kurdistan.

[4]Christians, including Armenians, number two tenths of 1 percent of the Turkish population.

8

◎   ◎   ◎

Mother Lode

AT THE END of the twentieth century, one of the last vestiges of the Golden Age of Travel was the Turkish bus. Like the American transcontinental railroad in the late nineteenth century and Europe's Orient Express in the early twentieth, Turkey's network of long-distance buses offers personalized comfort through a primitive and spectacular terrain. The buses are clean and air-conditioned, and offer snack service. The Ankara bus terminal is the most alluring of Oriental bazaars, where departure times and destinations peal in swooshy Turkish syllables. Neon signs proclaiming dozens of private bus companies brighten the passageways—proof of an entrepreneurial economy. As I approached the departure gates, drivers revved up the engines of Swedish- and German-manufactured double-decker vehicles painted in slick graphic designs, like new age versions of flying carpets.

Soon I was rolling south over a calm sea of green spring steppe, whose spareness and desolation were broken only by the rare shepherd with his flock. Once more I felt the joy of travel. An hour later, these grasslands gave way to desiccated saline flats rimmed by the snow-creased Sultan Mountains. I was in the heart of Asia Minor—Anatolia, the "mother lode." Here rise the headwaters of the Tigris and Euphrates, which sustained the earliest civilizations. Hittites, Assyrians, Phrygians, Lydians, and other ancient peoples made Anatolia their base. Abraham is said to have dwelt in southern Anatolia; Noah, in eastern Anatolia. The Trojan War was fought in western Anatolia and along its northern coast roamed Jason and the Argonauts. Herodotus was born in southwestern Anatolia. So was St. Paul. Xenophon, in 401 B.C., led his defeated army of "Ten Thousand" Greek mercenaries back through the bitter snows of Anatolia from Persia. The Persian armies of Cyrus, Darius, and Xerxes marched west through here; the army of Alexander the Great marched east. A branch of Marco Polo's Silk Route passed through Anatolia. So did Mongols and Crusaders. If the earth's dry land has one principal crossing point, Anatolia is it.

In the second half of the eleventh century A.D. the first wave of Turkish nomads from Central Asia arrived in Anatolia. They were called Seljuks, after their founding chieftain. Konya, the capital of this medieval Seljuk state, was my first destination.

◎ ◎ ◎

THE SELJUKS WERE fixated on the color that the French call *turquoise*, which they may have seen first in the cratered lakes that punctuated the desert plateau on their journey to Anatolia from Central Asia. In Konya, the fluted, rocket-shaped dome covered in luscious turquoise tiles above the tomb of Cellaledin Rumi, the preeminent religious mystic of the Seljuk era, represents the ultimate in Seljuk architecture. The fourteenth-century dome seems to levitate above the surrounding cupolas and walls, like a hallucination with height and width but no physical depth. This dome supplies the sense of mystical awe that religions desperately require yet rarely attain.

Along with a throng of pilgrims, I removed my shoes and entered Rumi's blue-domed mausoleum. A sign in English greets visitors with Rumi's words: "Come, come whoever you are, whether you be fire-worshipers, idolaters, or pagans. Ours is not the dwelling place of despair. All who enter will receive a welcome here." Turkish women wrapped in red head shawls and men with beards and woollen hats mingled easily with Western tourists amid the overlapping Oriental carpets and gold-leafed Koranic calligraphy framed by colorful tiles. Not just the tourists, but the pilgrims too, were happily snapping photos. Rarely had I been in a holy place with such a welcoming climate. "Islam in other countries is often based on fear of God. This breeds despotism, since fear of God implies fear of authority. But Turks, due to the influence of Rumi and other mystics, are moved by love of God, which breeds tolerance," a former Turkish prime minister, Bulent Ecevit, had told me in Ankara.

Actually, Rumi wrote in Persian. Persian literature and architecture had a great influence on the Seljuks. It may be telling that Rumi was a cult figure among hippies in the 1960s and 1970s. He was born in 1207 in Balkh, in the northern, Turkic, part of Afghanistan. As a boy, he traveled with his father for several years across Persia and eastern Anatolia to Konya (the hippie route to India, in reverse). Travel, evidently, leavened Rumi's spirit, and his tolerance. A flower child of his time, he believed that men, regardless of race or religion, were united, and linked to all of nature by love. This view, which may have had roots in the pre-Islamic past, was expressed in Rumi's characteristically sensuous poetry:

> And I am a flame dancing in love's fire,
> That flickering light in the depths of desire.
> Wouldst thou know the pain that severance breeds,
> Listen then to the strain of the reed.[1]

Rumi believed that love of God transcends particular religions and nationalities and that Moslems are by no means the only people to whom God has revealed himself. Rumi said that we should simply say "farewell" to the "immature fanatics" who scorn music and poetry. He cautioned that a beard or a mustache is no sign of wisdom—if anything, travel (the nomadic life) will bring wisdom. Rumi was an ascetic, the opposite of a religious activist like Mohammed: He thought that men and women should shun politics and concentrate on discoveries of their inner selves. He favored the individual over the crowd and spoke often against tyranny, whether of the majority or of the minority. When Rumi died in Konya on December 17, 1273, Christians, Jews, Arabs, and Turks poured forth from the surrounding countryside to mourn. They cried en masse and tore their clothes as a sign of grief. His tomb became a site of pilgrimage. In a part of the world associated with fanatics, he is one of history's truly ecumenical figures.

[1]From the verse introduction of Rumi's *Mathnawi*, his magnum opus. See Ozturk in bibliography.

Rumi helped define *Sufism*, a word that comes from the Arabic *suf*, or wool. According to a Koranic *hadith*, a man who wears wool lacks an ego. While submerging the ego through mystical dances[2] and other practices, Sufism nevertheless emphasizes the importance of the individual, making some Turkish Sufi orders the most liberated of Moslem groups. They dance, occasionally drink wine, and admit women to membership, though not really as equals. One Sufi group, the Bektashis, supported Ataturk's secular nationalist movement, though some Sufi orders have worked against Ataturk's secularizing trend. Turgut Ozal, Turkey's late president and prime minister, was a devout Sufi. Ozal's deep religious commitment, combined with his intense dislike of Moslem dictators such as Iran's Ayatollah Khomeini and Iraq's Saddam Hussein, would have warmed Rumi's heart. Turkey's political future will be, in part, determined by how Sufism evolves. That evolution, in turn, will be influenced by urbanization—the pressures brought upon individual Turks as they fight to maintain their traditions in big cities, particularly in the *gecekondus*.

On April 22, 1993, the day that Turgut Ozal was buried in Istanbul, I knelt on the carpets in the mosque next to Rumi's tomb and talked with Ali Erhun, a twenty-eight-year-old religious official. He wore a white skullcap and a polite expression, and held prayer beads in his hand.[3]

Erhun began by apologizing. He could not offer me the traditional cup of tea that Turks sip throughout the day from countless small glasses, because it was forbidden inside a mosque. Hospitality is a trait that Turks ascribe to their nomadic past, when survival depended on offers of kindness from strangers. But this kind of hospitality has another side: It sets very high standards for friendship, meaning it is easy for the West to fall short. That was the theme of Erhun's talk:

"My family is descended from the Oghuz Turks, who migrated into Anatolia from Central Asia and captured Anatolia from the Byzantines.[4] I was born in Cumali Koyu, not far from Istanbul. Here the first Ottomans arrived and needed a place to wash before praying. An old Sufi, someone like Rumi, pointed out a water source with his staff. Underneath that spot they found water. There they built the town . . .

---

[2]This includes Konya's famous Whirling Dervishes.
[3]I traveled in Turkey in 1993, a year before my sequential visits to Egypt, Iran, Central Asia, the Indian subcontinent, and Southeast Asia.
[4]*The Book of Dede Korkut* is based on the stories of the Oghuz Turks.

"Central Asia is the country of our grandfathers. The end of Russia's domination in Central Asia means the eventual reunification of what used to be whole—Turkestan, the Turkic world . . .

"Turgut Ozal, *may peace be upon him*, prepared us for this great transitional moment. Ozal softened the secular edge of Kemalism so that religious Turks now feel included in the system. This new freedom allows Turks to unite the present and future with the old cultures of the past, Seljuk and Ottoman. Islam is a serious component in this process."

But Erhun warned that the Western orientation of the Moslem Turks, nourished by Rumi's openness, was being eroded by the West's "desertion" of besieged Moslems in the Balkans and the Caucasus. As Erhun spoke against the oppression of Moslems, bearded men with skullcaps, who had gathered in the small anteroom of the mosque to hear our conversation, nodded their heads in agreement. The fighting in the Balkans and the Caucasus had suddenly riddled the atmosphere with tension.

"You, the West, are only a fair-weather friend." The prayer beads snapped through Erhun's fingers, but his voice remained calm:

"As hard as we try to be like you, you have always alienated us. Before helping the Catholic Croats and the Orthodox Serbs, you were on the side of the Greeks in Cyprus. You are forcing us to look eastward, toward the Turkic world, but only so much. We will continue to cooperate with America and Europe when it suits us. We will be a big player."

Erhun's eyes did not blink. He was ready for his final point.

"Islam was born in Arabia. The Arabs, for a long time, carried the banner of the Prophet. But Arab civilization was not strong enough for this. So the Turks took over. For a thousand years, since our Seljuk ancestors defeated the Byzantine Greeks, we have carried the flag of Islam with honor. Konya, the Seljuk capital, is where we sit now. The *Mevlana* ["Teacher," a reference to Rumi] is buried a few feet from us. After the collapse of the Ottoman empire, the Arabs again picked up the Prophet's banner. But this was temporary. We, the Turks, are ready again for this role. Don't assume that just because Arabic is the language of the Prophet and of the Koran the Arabs will lead Moslems in this world. We too can lead Moslems. Our Islam, because of the *Mevlana*, is different from that practiced in Egypt and Saudi Arabia."

Was he right? Would the banner of the Prophet move north, from Mecca to Konya, the city of carpets—the essential furniture of the wanderer?

FROM KONYA MY direction was southeast, over the spine of the Taurus Mountains to the Mediterranean. The bus rolled over wave upon wave of yellow limestone peaks and intricate valleys enfolding their own smaller ranges. On these reforested slopes were olive and fir trees, cedars and poplars. This was the soft, manicured skin of Anatolia, close enough to the sea to be part of the Greco-Roman world. Muddy streams cut through scooped-out hillsides, the offspring of geologic upheavals caused by the movement of the Eurasian, African, and Indo-Australian plates colliding here. By ceding territory in the Balkans and elsewhere, Ataturk focused Turkey's nation-building energies on this magnificently varied yet easily definable geographical unit. D. G. Hogarth, the great British orientalist and role model for T. E. Lawrence, declared in 1915, even before Ataturk's revolution, how geography makes the Turks (he refers to them as Osmanlis) a nation:

"Asia Minor [Anatolia] is the nation. . . . Even a military occupation by Russia or by another strong power would not detach Anatolia from the Osmanli unity; for a thing cannot be detached from itself."

But would Turkey's war with the Kurds spoil everything?

I SPENT THE night at Kizkalesi, a Mediterranean town known to Herodotus as Corycus and later renamed for an offshore castle that, according to legend, was built by an Armenian king to protect his daughter from being bitten by a snake. But a snake arrived in a basket of fruit from the shore, and the girl died. A modern version of the tale was now being reenacted. The snake this time came in the form of tourism development. The girl who died was the town itself.

From here, the Mediterranean shore seemed on the brink of becoming one vast Brighton—a toxic holiday camp for the working class on seven-day package tours.

"We are just a bunch of peasants trying on our own to figure out what tourism is," lamented a leathery old man who bought me a cup of Turkish coffee in the town's last coffeehouse. "Until 1987, this was a sleepy village where we grew green beans and lemons. The government is nowhere. It does nothing except light up the castle at night." He was shouting into my ear, having to compete with welding guns, jackhammers, electronic music, and wailing motorcycles with sawed-off exhaust pipes. Trashy three-star hotels were in various stages of completion, separated by mucky, garbage-strewn paths—a few feet from a blue and caressing sea.

The hotel where I checked in, built in 1985, was the oldest in town and filled with pink-faced German factory workers and their wives (or girlfriends). They shouted, banged the Formica tables, and put their arms condescendingly around the Turkish receptionist, as though he were an old friend. The walls between the rooms were paper-thin. Rather than the lapping sea rocking me to sleep, I heard the loud German voices and even-worse music. The shower dripped a little cold water only. The correlation between the rash of hotel building and the availability of fresh water was nil. Nor was there any sewage-treatment facility. Nor was this hotel, and this clientele, substandard. Kizkalesi had become a dormitory for the European package-tour industry—the Brits, whom I also saw, behaved no better. In winter the population of the town was three thousand. But from May through October it was tens of thousands. The visitors appeared to have no idea—nor did they care—where they were. For them, it was a week to let off steam under the sun before another fifty-odd weeks on the assembly line.

The beach was littered with beer cans, wrappers, and breeze blocks from the nearby construction. Redbrick high-rises rose in the distance behind an onshore archaeological site, whose Roman remains dated from the first centuries of the Christian era. Refuse floated in the water. The following morning, I took a taxi to the bus station in Mersin, further east along the Mediterranean coast. The driver was a local Turk, around thirty, who wore cowboy boots, an unbuttoned black shirt, and several medallions around his neck. He didn't talk—he shouted—above the rock music playing on his cassette radio, complaining that after a year he was still waiting for a visa to Canada to visit his girlfriend. Cheap high-rises, stacked one alongside the other, flashed by the window. He was born to tailgate.

The taxi driver was one of a growing classification of human beings: the half-formed man between cultures, and therefore of no culture. He stands on the street corner with tight pants, whistling and clucking his tongue at the rear ends of vacationing women as they pass by. He apes the West, is frustrated by it, and often winds up hating it. Men not much different from my taxi driver had become foot soldiers for the fundamentalist risings in Iran and Algeria. They are a product of the new Mediterranean and Near Eastern landscape: package-tour hotels, late-night discos, and the weed-fields of neon signs.[5]

◎   ◎   ◎

AT MERSIN, I took a bus south toward the Syrian border. Both the sea and mountains receded as I felt the hazy heat-film of the Middle East. Though Anatolia is easily definable, Turkish geography is not without contradictions—notably, the Hatay. The Hatay is a lush, sprawling field of cultivation, a panhandle sandwiched between the northeast corner of the Mediterranean and Syria. Here, Arabs and Armenians always outnumbered Turks. But in July of 1938 the Turkish army moved in, forcing many of the Arabs and Armenians to flee, and preparing the way for Ataturk's government to annex the region. The French, who held the mandate for Syria after World War I, did not protest, and the occupied Syrian population could not. Syria never relinquished its claim on the region. Syrian maps always included the Hatay, as well as the Golan Heights, as part of Syria. Antakya (old Antioch), the Hatay's principal city, was where my bus next pulled in.

Taxi drivers shouted at me in Arabic, offering their services, including rides over the international border to the nearby Syrian city of Aleppo. There was an atmosphere of dusty chaos at the terminal that recalled my visits in the 1970s and 1980s to Syria and Iraq. Arabs still formed a significant part of the Hatay's population, and complexions were darker. As in Arab cities, but unlike in major Turkish ones, the taxis had no meters and I had to haggle over the price: another minor, telltale sign of the victory of culture over official borders. "I'm not from Turkey, I'm from Antakya," the driver informed me. Did he mean to say, I wondered, that he thought himself a Syrian?

In the local park I got a different perspective. It was a Saturday afternoon. Young couples and families strolled through an avenue of dark pines and cypresses. Some teenage boys were calling at girls. All were wearing

[5]On another journey, in order to see a different aspect of Turkish tourist development, I went to Antalya. West of Kizkalesi, Antalya caters to a slightly wealthier class of tourist. The old part of the city has been sensitively restored. Water is plentiful. The streets are immaculate, and there are clean public toilets. Yet even here, the sheer numbers of tourists threaten to turn the region into an environmental wasteland in coming decades. By mid-May, the hotels and pensions are packed, while the Turks are still building, building . . . As soon as someone in this part of the country—someone raised in a *gecekondu*—acquires capital, he builds a hotel.

frumpy, out-of-date clothes. I saw little wealth but little poverty. Balloons and ice cream were on sale. Just as Turkish and Arabic mingled together, so did Arab appetizers and Turkish main courses at a nearby restaurant. There were few police and fewer soldiers about. Old Antioch exuded a lively multinational tolerance that made me think of the "Levant" before the First World War, which I had read about in books.

In the bazaar I met Naci Garva, a man selling crockery from a battered pushcart. He offered me a cup of apple tea and began talking. "I am an Arab, an Alawite, the same religion as Hafez al-Assad.[6] But I have no loyalty toward Syria. Sure, we've got our problems here. Ozal's reforms did make the rich richer and some of the poor poorer. But in Syria for decades the economy has been much worse. The Syrians cross the border to Antakya to shop. In Syria people need ration cards, but here we have so much more freedom. In Syria you can't even breathe!"

My eyes were next drawn to colorful sacks of purple sumac, red paprika, black olives, and other delights. The vendor, Yasar Afacan, was also an Arab. This was a weekend job for him. During the week he was a school principal, which didn't pay enough. He also offered me apple tea. Afacan was explaining that Syria (as a national-ethnic issue) had been dead for decades. The real problem in Antakya, as elsewhere in Turkey, he said, was not political but social—the migration of peasants into the cities. "These crude people have no culture. They're ruining the atmosphere here in Antakya." I had other conversations with other men who agreed.

Legally, as well as morally, Ataturk's annexation of the Hatay was wrong. But he got away with it. The Hatay was one place at the end of the Cold War where history had not yet come back to haunt the present through an ethnic grievance.

Because Turks had for many years enjoyed more personal freedom and a better standard of living than Syrians, I sensed little nostalgia for Syrian rule. The problems and passions of the two merchants I had met in the Antakya market, Naci Garva and Yasar Afacan, were wholly directed toward life in Turkey. But what if the Turkish economy dramatically soured, with rising inflation and unemployment? What if the problem

---

[6]The Alawites, along with the Druze and the Ismailis, are remnants of a wave of Shi'ism that swept through Syria a thousand years ago. The term *Alawite* means follower of Ali, the martyred son-in-law of Mohammed, who is venerated by millions of Shi'ites in Iran and elsewhere. Syria's Sunni Arabs consider the Shi'ites heretics. The fact that Syria's president, Hafez al-Assad, is an Alawite is highly unusual.

with the Kurds disrupted Turkey's social peace? And what if Syria signed a peace accord with Israel, leading to more Western investment and an expanding economy in Syria? Would the Hatay's political climate still remain somnolent?

◎　　　◎　　　◎

I LEFT THE Hatay by bus, heading northeast into the center of Anatolia, passing farmers waist-deep in wheat fields and streams braided with red poppies and other dazzling wildflowers. The men moved with an insect-like slowness in the unceasing steppe wind. On the horizon, beyond the streams and the wheat fields, was a long granite line of snow-decked peaks, bespeaking the brooding immensity of this fought-over land mass. I gazed at what Freya Stark, in *Alexander's Path*, had labeled the "clean austerity" of Anatolia, but what came to mind were armies, and more armies.

Across the Euphrates, the trees became fewer and the glare of the sun intensified, registering the dust like a great bleaching spotlight. I shuddered at the hills, so sere and bony, like exposed vertebrae. *Gecekondus* and red apartment blocks heralded the outskirts of Sanliurfa (Glorious Urfa), the northern tip of the Fertile Crescent, where Mesopotamia converges with Greater Syria. Here, in nearby Harran, Abraham had sojourned on his way from Ur in southern Iraq to the Land of Canaan. I was in the borderland between the desert of the Middle East and the high, colder plateaus of Asia Minor, an area rich with water. In Sanliurfa I descended from the bus and found a taxi that took me northwest, away from town. An expanse of electric power grids and phone switching stations appeared soon on my left—an intimation of immensities to come.

The Southeastern Anatolia Project—Guneydogu Anadolu Projesi, or GAP—was to be a network of twenty-two major dams and irrigation systems by the first decade of the twenty-first century. GAP impounded the waters of the Tigris and Euphrates, and created new farmland equal to the total cultivable area of the Netherlands. Could this development dilute the fires of Kurdish separatism in Turkey?

In the late 1980s, a Turkish state minister, Kamran Inan, outlined Turkey's escalating ambitions regarding GAP:

"The postwar generation in the United States is increasingly turning away from Europe and toward the Pacific . . . Europe is getting old in population . . . as well as lacking dynamism. Turkey . . . is the largest industrial base between Europe and Asia endowed with abundant natural resources and manpower. . . . The upper valley of the Euphrates and Tigris rivers has been the cradle of civilization since 4500 B.C. Completion of the GAP in the 2000s will mean the rebirth of the prosperity which Mesopotamia enjoyed thousands of years ago . . ." Turkey's "excellent position on the axis stretching from the Far East to the Mediterranean basin . . . will be further strengthened by the Southeastern Anatolia Project . . ."

In other words, Turkey had visions of being a great power and GAP was the centerpiece of this strategy. The centerpiece of GAP itself is the Ataturk Dam, twenty-five miles north of Sanliurfa. Before the dam came into view, I asked my driver to turn off the road. I had an appointment to visit the site manager.

Neatly arranged orange and willow trees surrounded the marble office building, as impressive as any company headquarters in North America or Europe. Behind the building I could see a prim, manicured suburbia complete with schools for the children of the dam employees. The contrast between this and the seedy offices of the Aswan High Dam Authority in Egypt could not have been greater.

I first spotted the dam through the picture window in the site manager's office. I heard no sound through the sealed glass—no sense of the dust and breezes or the atmospheric hum that reveal a landscape. Thus my first image of the Ataturk Dam and the majestic man-made reservoir behind it looked to me like an acrylic painting: fantastic; unreal—the dam itself was a pebbly toy curtain plugging a dark, spreading stain of turquoise water as rich and fathomless as the sky where the atmosphere darkens into the blackness of space.

I turned away and looked at the man behind the desk.

Erduhan Bayindir, the site manager for the Ataturk Dam, the world's fourth largest rock-filled edifice, is known as "Hammerhead." His manner was tough, grumpy. His hair was gray, his blazer gray, and his face utterly forgettable. I remember the features of the hilly limestone outside his window but not the lines of his face. His words were a torrent. Like Ali Erhun in the Konya mosque, Bayindir began from a narrow, anecdotal base, then widened it.

"What will be the ultimate effect of GAP on this area of the country?" Bayindir asked out loud. "The truth is, we don't know. Development will bring cultural deterioration. When I was a teenager, we sat on the ground and all ate from one plate. Then newspapers, electricity, and television arrived, and we were sitting at a table eating from different plates. Women were once able to walk alone in the streets, but now they are hassled by men. Crime also came. You can't stop change, you can only try to steer it."

Steer it he does. "One third of Euphrates River water is being redirected toward Turkey's Harran plateau. Before the dam, Syria and Iraq received nine hundred cubic feet of water per second from the river. Now they receive six hundred. Of course, the Arabs protested when we started planning GAP in the late 1970s. Syria and Iraq worked against Turkey in the World Bank. But then we had real luck: Iraq got into a war for worthless land on the Iraq-Iran border. Water became a secondary issue for Saddam Hussein. More luck came. The Turkish economy boomed in the 1980s, allowing us to finance the dam with GNP increases. Then Iraq got into another war with Kuwait. As for Syria, Assad's Soviet godfather died with the Cold War.

"Water is a weapon. We can stop the flow of water into Syria and Iraq for up to eight months without overflowing our dams, in order to regulate the Arabs' political behavior."

This was the Ottoman past talking, a time when the Arabs were a subject people ruled by Turkish sultans.

"It could well be a Turkic century in this part of the world. While oil can be shipped abroad to enrich elites at home, water has to be spread more evenly within the society. No matter how corrupt and selfish a society may be, it's harder to confine the wealth brought by water than to confine the wealth brought by oil.

"And water crosses boundaries. We're creating a new region in southeast Turkey based on agro-export. [The centralized state structures of] Syria and Iraq will, in the final analysis, be undermined by regionalism."

I got back into the car and drove to the dam itself. The tiny pebbles I had seen were now boulders, each the size of a station wagon. The soaring pile of black volcanic rocks created a sixteen-story-high arcing curtain, whose roadway on top, from one end of the dam to the other, was a mile and a half long. I looked down at the masses of poured concrete forming seven gargantuan emergency spillways, each the size of a jet runway and accounting for only a fraction of the dam curtain's length. Against my face I felt a wall of wind rising off the man-made turquoise lake, which meant that this wind was also man-made. Then there were the basalt tunnels (the largest irrigation tunnels in the world) for the "highways" of water to come. The underground construction complex where the last of the eight massive turbines was being assembled was a scene from science fiction— at a steeper angle in a deeper gorge, the Ataturk Dam was visually even more impressive than the Aswan High Dam.

Finally, I stood at the very base of the dam alongside a row of giant transformers. Uniformed engineers and construction workers moved about, quietly and purposefully. That was the difference, I realized, between this project and the Aswan Dam in Egypt, finished in the 1960s, and the Revolution Dam down the Euphrates River in Syria, finished in the 1970s. Both of those dam projects were directed by Soviet experts. But here were a people who evidently did not need foreigners to build things for them.

I looked at eight pale-orange valves that carried the water from the reservoir down into the turbine complex. From the site manager's office the valves had seemed like toothpicks. Here they were each seventeen feet in diameter, and encompassed the entire vertical horizon. Atop the valves, emblazoned on the dam curtain in massive letters, was written Ataturk's dictum *Ne Mutlu Turkum Diyene* ("Lucky is the one who says he is a Turk").

How lucky? I asked, considering that most of the inhabitants of this region of southeastern Anatolia were not Turkish at all but Kurdish. Every indication was that while Ataturk's inclusive nationalism allowed them to be Turks—even demanded that they think of themselves as Turks—they definitely did not want to be Turks: They wanted to be Kurds.

◎   ◎   ◎

IT WAS A hole-in-the-wall barbershop below street level in Diyarbakir, a town about one hundred miles northeast of the dam, and my Turkish-American friend Gunay Evinch was being shaved. The barber, who was about fifteen years old, boiled water, slapped and massaged Gunay's face, applied the razor, and then doused him with cologne. As a final touch, when Gunay was off guard, the young barber grasped my friend's head suddenly with both hands and turned it. A loud crack rang out. A shave, massage, and chiropractic readjustment all for two dollars in Turkish lira.

Diyarbakir, like Sanliurfa, is a Kurdish city in southeastern Turkey. The barbers and the customers were Kurds, and throughout Gunay's pleasant ordeal they discussed politics. One especially loud customer spoke for everyone when he said: "Of course, it's even worse for Kurds in

Syria and Iraq. Compared to them, we are lucky to be in Turkey. Still, we are Kurds and feel good when Kurds in northern Iraq get their freedom."

I had reached Diyarbakir from Sanliurfa (near the dam) by yet another eastward bus journey. The bus music was no longer the breathy and orgasmic *arabesk*—that rude, endearing music of the *gecekondus*; instead it was the lonely mountain tunes of the Kurds. The landscape gave way to unimaginable vastnesses scarred with breeze-block villages drowning in mud and slag heaps, the spillage of repeated earthquakes. Kurdish women with red bandannas were dots on a grimly rising plain that soon merged with the leaden clouds. I passed convoys of Turkish soldiers with mounted machine guns, assault rifles, and bayonets. I saw a military helicopter land in a Kurdish village. The soldiers looked exactly the way Turkish troops must have looked since the days of the Seljuks: a forward-pressing, disciplined herd, as though each man were still connected to his Central Asian horse, with eyes that were chilling precisely because they were so impersonal, without individuality.

It was a malignant cycle. Each strike by Kurdish guerrillas led to a Turkish counterstrike followed by innumerable searches, further alienating Kurdish villagers. The nation-state system here, erected by the Great Powers after World War I, appeared to be cracking like the dry, mudbaked plateau. The Kurds, ignored by the post–World War I peacemakers, were the drivers of this change.

Kurdistan was more real than several score of the nation-states officially recognized by the world community. Unlike most countries in the African and Arab worlds, Kurdistan cohered in its geography and demography. Kurdish is an Indo-European tongue rather than a Turkic one. The complexions of Kurds are often darker than those of Turks; Kurdish features are Aryan, while Turkish features tend to be Asian. Kurds wear Arab kaffiyehs, but in a style different from the Arabs. Sanliurfa and Diyarbakir, both Kurdish, look radically different from other cities in Turkey. Turkish towns have wide streets and solitary prospects and evoke the lunar austerity and echoing loneliness of Central Asia: No wonder Turks settled here, for Anatolia offered these Central Asian warriors a familiar landscape that, as opposed to those of their original homelands, had natural borders. Kurdish towns had narrower streets and were more crowded, reminding me of the Arab world to the south.

The Kurds, who number around twenty million—more people than in either Syria or Iraq; more than in the overwhelming majority of nations at the end of the twentieth century—inhabit an ellipse of territory spreading over much of eastern Turkey, Iran, the former Soviet Union, Syria, and Iraq. Though Kurds inhabit the desert north of Baghdad, the lower plateaus of Iran, and the higher ones of Turkey, they are essentially a mountain people, deriving their collective personality from life on the ten-thousand-foot massifs of Kurdistan. The Kurds have inhabited the Zagros and Taurus ranges since the second millennium B.C.; two thousand years before the Arabs entered northern Mesopotamia and three thousand years before the Turks entered Anatolia.

In the winter of 401 B.C., Xenophon's army of Greek mercenaries retreated through Anatolia when it was set upon by bands of "Carduchi" (probably Kurds), whose hit-and-run raids damaged the Greeks more than did the Persians during the Greeks' Mesopotamian campaign. Xenophon wrote that the Carduchi lived in the mountains and were not subject to outside authority. Like mountain people elsewhere, the Kurds have always been a law unto themselves, a continuing problem for existing states.

Sanliurfa, for example, a half-hour by taxi from the dam, was architecturally a Kurdish city, and thus an affront to the false, unicultural facade of Ataturk's Turkey. The narrow streets fed into the last great bazaar in Turkey that had not evolved into a modern shopping mall—complete with cobblers, gunsmiths, tailors, spice dealers, and tobacco merchants. Huge heaps of cured tobacco stood near stalls where warlike knives were being sharpened. Tumbledown courtyards were filled with men in traditional clothing at old tables sipping tea, as though Ataturk's revolution against Moslem dress had never happened. The dust and the exhaust from motorized bikes thickened the air. Instead of hand-woven carpets and kilims for tourists with money to spare, this bazaar sold only machine-made items for village people. In physical appearance, Sanliurfa was like an Arab bazaar but with a spontaneity missing from the Arab souks of Syria and Iraq.

It was Ataturk's military successes in carving out a Turkish state that helped convince the World War I victors to ignore the ethnic and geographic Kurdish reality. Ozal and three of the seven Turkish presidents before him had Kurdish blood but were reluctant to admit it. Nor were Kurds confined to southeastern Anatolia. The *gecekondus* of Istanbul, Ankara, and Izmir are full of them. Kurds are everywhere in Turkey.

Kurds in the southeast had been migrating to the wealthier and more developed west of Turkey, where they moved into upwardly mobile *gecekondu* districts. In Syria and Iraq, this Kurdish migration was not so great, for Turkey's half-century-long democratic experiment had allowed for freedom of movement. The diffusion of the Kurds made Turkey more a nation than an unstable compound of regionally based ethnic groups. Democracy, accompanied by a free market, had, in Turkey's case, created a basis for solving the problem. It remained for the political elite in Ankara to recognize it.

Islam might also form the basis of a solution. In a mosque in Diyarbakir, I had met Nabi Karabacak, a dentist, who invited me back to his office. The poverty of the building was obvious: the broken toilets, the bad lighting, the filth. Karabacak used antiquated dental equipment. He ordered cold drinks and sent out a boy to buy fresh strawberries. "I am a Turk from the Black Sea region," he said mildly. "I came to practice in the southeast to give something back to my Kurdish co-religionists. I charge patients only according to what they can afford. Kurds and Turks are all Moslems. Why should Islam be a thing of division? It can be unifying factor in the nation's life." Islamic and Ottoman revivals in Turkey were, ideally at least, inclusive rather than exclusive.

IT WAS AN eight-hour bus trip eastward from Diyarbakir to the shores of Lake Van, a shimmering ash-blue rimmed by long walls of snowy granite. A wildness set in. The bus passed other vehicles by inches at high speeds. The carcasses of big trucks lay half submerged in mud by the side of the road. Some were overturned. The windshields were smashed. Here borders felt less stable and only relief maps seemed to make sense: The inhabitants were Kurdish, and the landscape, with its bad roads, wrecked cars, and armed soldiers, reminded me somewhat of Afghanistan, which I had visited frequently in the 1970s and 1980s, before and during the Soviet invasion. I now felt closer to Kabul than to Istanbul. Fewer buses serviced this remote area. I was now riding in a twelve-seat minivan crammed with seventeen passengers. The luggage was tied down to the roof. The local transport companies were as wild as the landscape.

It occurred to me what a crazy gamble a nation-state was. On such a moonscape as this, where people had migrated and settled in patterns that defied borders, I wondered if the post–Cold War era would see a cruel process of natural selection among existing states. No longer could Near Eastern states rely on the West or the Soviet Union for support. Because the Kurds overlapped with these existing states, they might become, in effect, the ultimate reality check. States that could accommodate the Kurds might survive more easily than those that couldn't.

From Van to the Iranian border, I felt as though I were riding along the bottom of a huge crater: a lunar sea of loose topsoil, mud, and panels of rainwater glittering in the sun, quickly evaporating, about to be mud and then dust once more. I thought of Africa. But in this part of the world, at least, there was an age-old land link with great civilizations—European, Persian, and Indian—that met here on the Silk Route between Europe and China. These volcanic flats, for all their emptiness, constituted a central path of humanity, while West Africa lay on a geographical extremity, a ganglion of peoples cut off to a large extent from other great cultures by the Atlantic Ocean and the Sahara Desert. While traveling in the Near East I could think more clearly about Africa. The problem with many area specialists is that they have no such means of comparison.

The minivan was filled with unfiltered cigarette smoke. One of my knees was jammed up against the door as I crouched in an empty space between it and the seat, writing in my journal. Gunay, my Turkish companion, was nervous. Of seventeen passengers, he was the only Turk— everyone else except me was a Kurd. The day had not begun well. In Van, Gunay and I had dragged ourselves over to the station at dawn—after two days on our backs from food poisoning—in order to get seats by the window. A tough and unfriendly-looking Kurd forced his way into our space. When Gunay protested, this fellow said to his friends, "Turks always think they can get what they want."

"*Leh, leh, leh-leh-leh*" blared from the scratchy cassette. This was the music of Kurdish guerrillas, the Pesh Mergas—"those that walk before death"—and it hurt my ears. The actual border between Turkey and Iran had little meaning, since everyone on both sides was a Kurd, and the cathedral-like ranges that marked the frontier were too treacherous to be adequately policed by either the Turkish or Iranian governments. This dun void, where every ten minutes or so a shepherd crossed the road with his flock, was a land vector linking two ethnic cauldrons, the Balkans and the Caucasus. Here, in this Kurdish area, had lain the fault zone between Armenians and Turks at the turn of the twentieth century, and here, perhaps, lay the fault zone between Turkic and Iranian civilizations near the turn of the twenty-first. How would this ground redivide in the future?

DOGUBAYAZIT, A FEW miles from the Iranian border, was an instance of Turkey's awkward dynamism: a mix between the most primitive and the most modern. On a windswept plateau the hue and constituency of pie crust, I found a mudbrick jigsaw of low dwellings and the heart-rending, lice-shaven heads of third world children, with lip sores and discolored complexions, running through filthy lanes. Everyone's shoes and trousers were caked with mud. The only Turks in town were either the government officials or the soldiers at the nearby base. Ataturk's statue seemed wrong here, the face of the occupier rather than of the nation builder. Yet I also encountered a "Galeria" built of whitewashed cement, where stacks of Sony camcorders, three-way car phones, Siemens carving knives, Canon fax machines, compact discs, battery-operated toys, and other sophisticated consumer goods were on sale. Grocery stores were stacked with local and imported items, from mineral water to kiwis. Across the bottom of the television screen in my local hotel—which had no heating or hot water—was a 900 number to dial, to record your opinion on who should be Turkey's next president and prime minister.

Before the 1980s there was nothing here but the usual mud and dust. Then the Iranian economy contracted because of the war with Iraq, and Dogubayazit grew to eleven thousand inhabitants. It flourished by smuggling whiskey, cigarettes, tissues, and much else that Iranians needed but couldn't get. The Iranians, for their part, brought in drugs.

Kurds ran the cross-border trade. Dogubayazit, which had gone from the Stone Age to a shopping mall without any intermediate stops along the way, was the third world town of the future—a free zone of creative chaos where regionalism had replaced nation-statism.

"Iranians come here to buy things and never leave. The situation is so much worse in Iran," said my taxi driver, Idris Salman. There was an air of knowing superiority about Idris, as though his wreck of a Turkish-built Fiat were a new Mercedes. He was cool: the typical "operator" that the Turkish market mass-produces like carpets and evil eyes. While other drivers shouted at me when I stepped down from the minivan, he just lifted his eyebrows and whispered, "Taxi." Idris talked little. A Kurd, he evinced little passion when I asked him about Turks, Iranians, and Armenians. There was money to be made and that had replaced hate as his new interest.

Idris drove me to the Ishak Pasa Saray (seraglio), a late-seventeenth-century architectural confection built by a Kurdish chieftain, with nipple-like Seljuk arches, exquisitely thin Armenian lattice and filigree work, striped Mamluk masonry, and a Persian dome that—like the Seljuk one in Konya—appears to float. The total effect is what I can only describe as Hindu-psychedelic: a child's sandcastle dyed yellow and pink, which more than anything in Tartary evokes the fantasy aura of the Silk Route. For hundreds of years the entrance to the *saray*—the most beautiful Turkish word I know—had gold-plated doors. They were taken by the Russian army when it swept through this plain in 1917, as part of the Allies' attack on the Central Powers in World War I, and are now on display at the Hermitage Museum in St. Petersburg. I skirted the rooftops that had no guardrails or any other sign of tourist conveniences. There were only a few other visitors. The Ishak Pasa Saray was for me a constructive vision for the future based on a medieval past that lacked artificial frontiers, in which a fusion of cultures—rather than a clash among them—makes for genius. I thought of Rumi, the Persian poet adopted by the Seljuk Turks, whose brilliance emerged from the blending of Persian and Turkish traditions. Inside these walls several national styles overlap. The effect is greater than any of them could muster on its own. Idris stood casually at the entrance, as if indicating that the palace was all his and he was doing us a favor by showing it off.

A Kurdish chieftain had built this palace. Only Kurds lived in this area. Kurds hate borders. They are themselves divided by tribe, and a Kurdish state could be a recipe for anarchy. Yet anarchy is what the early part of the twenty-first century might be about, as the nation-state system weakens peacefully in Western Europe, because of the encroaching political power of the European Union and the economic clout of multinational corporations, and less peacefully in Africa, the Near East, and elsewhere. The post–World War I system was about dividing up dry land into categories, even if there have been few neat fits. As political ambiguity asserts itself in the form of weakened states and central governments, the Kurds may foreshadow the future.

DAWN CAME. A heavy mist was lifting, revealing a dark, seaweed-green carpet strewn with black basalt boulders. I was in another bus. The earth north of Dogubayazit seemed to have emerged from underwater, dripping wet, as if the story of Noah's Ark, which is said to have come to rest on the snowy slopes of Mount Ararat just to my east, were true. I could see

Ararat, its blinding-white cone shooting straight up out of the plain like a new world being created.

As my bus headed northward, I moved away from the Turkish border with Iran and toward the border with Armenia, strewn with black boulders. At Ani, the medieval Armenian capital, where a few examples of archaeological greatness still stand, black clouds attacked the plain from the east. Lightning struck. It began raining hard. I took shelter in the cathedral, built by an Armenian king more than a thousand years before, with stones the color of dried blood. The great dome was missing, revealing a sky more frightful than any an old master could paint. I concentrated on the stone relief work, the thin and powerful lines like lightning in the sky.

"The Kurds and the Armenians are the most ancient inhabitants of Anatolia. Why don't we just admit it!" exclaimed Yashar Kemal, the great Turkish novelist, to me upon my return to Istanbul. Just as the Kurds represented the undigested part of the Turkish melting pot, the Armenians have represented the undigested part of Turkish history. Kemal's point was that until Turks stop lying to themselves about both the Armenians and the Kurds, Turkey will be unable to evolve as a more flexible state, and its stability will, therefore, be threatened.

Eastern Turkey's population, including Van, was overwhelmingly Armenian until 1915, when the "Young Turk" regime—hellbent to create a monoethnic state out of the multiethnic mosaic of the Ottoman sultanate—effected the slaughter of hundreds of thousands, or perhaps even a million or more, Armenians. The Armenians who survived "the Genocide" all inhabited the territory to Turkey's east, in the Caucasus, which came under the control of the Soviets after World War I. When history resumed in the late 1980s, Armenians awoke.

In the 1990s, the war between the two former Soviet republics of Armenia and Turkish-Azerbaijan remained largely invisible to the West. So, for that matter, was the violence throughout the whole Caucasus: north Ossetia; south Ossetia; north Abkhazia; south Abkhazia; the Checheno-Ingush splitting to form the two republics of Chechnya and Ingush. Incomprehensible as this melange may have appeared, it mattered, because Anatolia, the Caucasus, Central Asia, and the Indian subcontinent were all part of one interlocking world from the Balkans to the deserts of inner China. Here, in the earth's continental heartland, the vision of the early-nineteenth-century German geographer Karl Ritter was starting to come true. In his *Comparative Geography*, Ritter argued that the ultimate destiny of human beings was to live in an organically connected flow of topographical regions—like many thin and overlapping broken lines on a relief map rather than the dark, bold lines of nation-states. But the way to this most natural and foreseeable of destinies might prove to be awful.

9

By Caspian Shores

"*Kefouz Nejadi?*" (How are you?)

"*Tchokh pis.*" (Bad.)

Reza, a Paris-based photographer of Azeri Turk descent, with whom I was now traveling, had put that question to ten taxi drivers in the former Soviet oil city of Baku. Ten times he got the same reply. It was the spring of 1993. From Istanbul I had flown to Baku, the capital of the newly independent former Soviet republic of Azerbaijan, where the old communist system was falling through the floor but no new system had as yet taken hold. There were two official currencies, the Russian ruble and the Azeri manat, both worthless. Only dollars got you a room and a good meal. Credit cards were unknown, and God help you if any of your dollar bills had a tear or too many creases in it.

The Hotel Azerbaijani was making a full-scale retreat into the Stalinist past. The lobby was guarded by security heavies in tight-fitting shirts, hands on their hips, showing their biceps. Not long before I arrived, a Turkish journalist had come too close to the Azerbaijani president, and one of these guards floored him with one hard, open palm to the chest. But when some thugs tried to break into the room occupied by an attractive blonde from the U.S. embassy, her calls for help to the hotel security men went unanswered. She had to use her walkie-talkie to call embassy officials, who then badgered the hotel staff to intervene.

Ancient female automatons cleaned the lobby floors with diesel oil. My room was a filmy bath of dust, cigarette smoke, and diesel. The single light bulb didn't work. The water was brown. The lock was broken. A lizard-eyed clerk had opened the drawer of the reception desk with a nail, then fished out the key for me. The only employees who showed any initiative were the prostitutes. One, in particular, Camilla, would call Reza and me every night just as we were falling asleep, begging for business. She had "bought" our room numbers from the desk clerk.

Cokes cost $3.50 each in the "dollar bar" on the eleventh floor. Since there was never any change, the real price was $4. Vodka was cheaper than mineral water, which was usually unavailable. (The tap water was contaminated by oil because of the careless and primitive extraction process, another legacy of communism.) Since the collapse of the Soviet Union, the Hotel Azerbaijani has had a criminal aura in keeping with the social dissolution all around.

Everywhere in Baku there was decay. In the Ministry of Defense, next to a cordless phone I noticed a television antenna made from rusty copper wire taped to a piece of corroded wood. In the Bahr (Sea) Restaurant, one of the few open in this city of 2 million, soldiers danced with heavily made up young girls under dim red lights. You could almost hear the soldiers' thighs moving against the girls legs. There was a sad and nostalgic Götterdämmerung quality, a confused weariness to this place, that was by Baku standards an expensive and respectable eating house. Outside, there was the inevitable blackout. The curfew began at midnight. Armed soldiers forced my taxi to a halt near the hotel and then begged for cigarettes.

The new Azerbaijani state did not function. Reza and I had an appointment to interview the democratically elected president, Ebulfez Elcibey. But the sergeant guarding the building entrance to the presidential offices would not let us pass. He knew nothing about the interview, and the phone line to the president's office upstairs was dead. We had to argue our way into the elevator. A few weeks later Elcibey fled Baku when a self-declared militia leader from western Azerbaijan marched on the capital, forcing the return to power of the former Soviet party chief, Geidar Aliyev.

The Azeri Turks of Azerbaijan are richly aware of their own past, but it wasn't congealing into a focused sense of nationhood. It couldn't. There was no middle class here to nourish the kind of national feeling with which we in the West have become accustomed. Nor was there, as in the Balkans prior to World War II, a nascent bourgeoisie. The Azeri Turks, like all the citizens of the former Soviet Union, save for those of the Baltic states, had no memory, or knowledge even, of such a bourgeois existence. Communism had existed here for seventy years, and before that there were only extremely wealthy people and illiterate peasants, as in medieval society. Now there were only those who were acquiring considerable wealth through mafia connections, and urbanized peasants living in poured-concrete tenements, waking up, shell-shocked, for the first time since that awful day in 1920 when the city was overrun by the Bolshevik soldiery. Nor were there any obvious geographical borders to create an identity for the new post-Soviet state.

Azerbaijan's borders were senseless, including both a flat, windswept littoral jutting out into the Caspian, centered around Baku, and a rugged, subtropical chain of mountains surrounding the Armenian enclave of Nagorno (Mountainous) Karabakh—itself surrounded by vengeful Turkish clans. Karabakh symbolized the blood-feuding Caucasus, with horizons as narrow as the prospects its imprisoning valleys offered. In Karabakh the earth seemed small and petty, a place where every issue outside the intercommunal dispute did not seem quite real. Rather than too small, in Baku the earth seemed too vast. Standing by the Caspian shore, you weren't sure if you were in Russia, Central Asia, Turkey, or Iran. A bigger problem was that less than half of the Azeri Turks lived in Azerbaijan; the rest lived south of the international border, in Iran. In 1828, Russia made a deal with Persia that split Azerbaijan between them. This illogical frontier obviously had no historical or geographical meaning. In fact, the first flash point of the Cold War was here: In early 1946, Stalin tried to grab all of Azerbaijan up to Tabriz when President Truman forced him to withdraw to the international border. Azerbaijan's borders were merely a colonial fiction that had little to do with demographic and ethnic realities.

Moreover, whereas African tribal culture contained enough flexibility to adapt somewhat to the colonialists' map, Armenian and Turkish identities were made of stone. While the British and French in West Africa could make these artificial lines take on a reality of their own through a profusion of maps and census reports, it was such things as maps and censuses that were often difficult to obtain in the Soviet Union. So the emergence of a "state" identity was problematic.

The war with Armenia over the Armenian-inhabited enclave of Karabakh in western Azerbaijan was little help in nation-building. I detected no passion for the war. Even after Armenian forces had taken another 10 percent of Azeri Turk territory in western Azerbaijan—in order to open another bridgehead to their ethnic compatriots in Karabakh—then-President Elcibey refused to blame Armenia for his economic and political troubles. "It is the fault of Soviet totalitarianism and what it did to both Armenians and Azeris," he told Reza and me. However wise and open-minded such thinking was, it revealed a lack of direction, which Elcibey paid for when he was overthrown a few weeks later. Rather than weld the population into a solid mass, the war with Armenia weakened the new state by strengthening local clan-based militias.

Armenians, on the other hand, knew exactly whom they hated. In the craggy mountains of Karabakh they raised their children "to kill Turks." As in the Balkans, the problem in the Caucasus was an Ottoman imperial one: a conflict between indigenous Christians and conquering Turks. The Armenians harbor several memories useful for nationhood. According to legend, they trace their descent to Noah on Mount Ararat. By the sixth century B.C. Armenians had forged a kingdom in eastern Anatolia, which remained independent until conquered by Alexander the Great. Armenia rose again in 189 B.C. under the Artashesid dynasty. In the third century A.D., Armenia became the first Christian state in history, before Rome even. The prey of Persians, Byzantines, Khazars, and Arabs over the succeeding centuries, the Armenians rose once more under the Bagratid dynasty from the ninth through eleventh centuries: It was a Bagratid cathedral in which I had taken shelter during that rainstorm at Ani. If this wasn't enough, hundreds of years of Ottoman Turkish subjugation helped build a distinct national identity, just as it did for the Serbs, the Bulgarians, and the Greeks. In addition, the Armenians had the memory of "the Genocide" in 1915. All this worked to shape an Armenian nationalism that is as passionate and well defined as the nationalism of the Israelis.

The Azeri Turks, as members of a large, conquering Turkic race that spilled over from Turkey to China, were never so specifically repressed. Moreover, while the Turks in Turkey proper were at least becoming a modern people through Ataturk's cultural revolution and Ozal's economic one, Turks in Azerbaijan underwent seven decades of collectivization, regime terror, and enforced poverty under Kremlin rule. Throughout the 1980s, Ozal privatized state companies, liberalized banking, allowed for free and floating exchange rates, and used the bully pulpit to champion the small-time entrepreneur. Foreign investment poured in, and as a consequence, culture in Turkey became exposed more to Western forces. Nothing even remotely similar to what Ataturk or Ozal had done occurred in Azerbaijan. And because many of the communist overlords in Baku were not only Russians but Azeris too, Azerbaijan suffered a disorienting tyranny that divided the inhabitants rather than uniting them (as Ottoman tyranny had united the Armenians). The Turks of Azerbaijan had never become a nation, regardless of what the maps in the 1990s said.

◎ ◎ ◎

BAKU, "CITY OF the winds," is traumatic, unsettling. You are clearly on some fault line, but it is a hard one to identify. The *hazri*, cold and salty, blows from the north; the *gilavar*, from the south. These whining gusts from the Caspian bring no relief from the spring and summer heat, carrying with them dust and petrol fumes. The unceasing, dirty wind conjures up the sensation of a physical vacuum complementing a historical one. You tread upon a diseased earth. The soil, the water, the atmosphere are lethal. Oil spills had raised the petroleum level on the beaches here up to a hundred-times the sanitary limit, leading to an outbreak of skin infections. An aluminum plant north of here had been emitting seventy thousand tons of toxic discharges into the air every year. Petrochemical plants were dumping another sixty-seven thousand tons of waste into the sea. Rather than *Eastern Approaches*, a romantic work of travel set in the 1930s and 1940s by British diplomat Fitzroy Maclean, in which a procession of camels on the outskirts of Baku "reminded" the author that he "was already on the fringes of Asia," I found the most evocative guide to the region to be a book called *Ecocide in the USSR: Health and Nature Under Siege*, by Murray Feshbach, a professor at Georgetown University, and Alfred Friendly, Jr., a former Moscow bureau chief for *Newsweek*.

From the airport to the town, the lunar landscape was covered with tar and oil. In the 1870s came the beginning of an "oil boom." Before there was a Dhahran or a Kuwait City, there was a Baku. The Rothschilds and Alfred B. Nobel made fortunes here. A cosmopolitan metropolis emerged—the hôtel de ville, an opera house, company buildings, and hundreds of fine apartments and villas, now sadly peeling. The old city looked pathetically small, just a flash seen from the battered taxi, compared to the miles upon miles of massive communist-era dwellings.

It was as though a volcanic eruption of communist cement had been poured over the city, burying it as it dried. In Baku I could rarely find my way. The curving bay, behind which the city rose like an amphitheater, was nearly deserted, defaced by fumes and rusted derricks. Few persons braved the winds and the odors to walk along the shore. But there was a past, a personal life.

Reza showed it to me.

Reza is an Azeri Turk, born over the border in the Iranian city of Tabriz. But Reza is many other things, too. He is a multilingual architect, a fine photojournalist, and a master of disguises.

Reza exudes charisma. His eyes gleam and devour, revealing the cunning of a bazaar merchant and the compassion of a relief worker. Reza's photographs see the truth behind the facades. In 1978, at the time of the Iranian revolution, Reza was working as an architect in Tabriz. Photography was his hobby. But the religious upheaval destroyed his business as the fundamentalists attacked the secular Azeri Turkish middle class. The capture of the U.S. embassy in Teheran and the taking of American hostages gave Reza an opportunity, however. He took his camera to the capital and began shooting. *Newsweek* noticed his pictures; so did other publications. Though Americans never knew it, they were seeing the Iranian revolution largely through Reza's eyes. But the mullahs could not be told who, exactly, Reza was—or retribution would surely follow. So Reza remained simply Reza, without a family name, in his photo credits. It was a common enough name in Iran, like John.

Reza's father died of a heart attack when the Ayatollah's secret police came to arrest him. His mother died soon after. He spent the money he made from his photographs on buying his other relatives out of Iran and resettling them in France. In 1982, Reza's photography dominated the coverage of Israel's invasion of Beirut. In 1985, when South Africa turned violent but while journalists were still being barred from entering the apartheid state, Reza got a visa by convincing South African authorities that he was an elephant hunter. When Afrikaner police kept photographers from covering a riot, Reza donned the outfit of a billboard painter to stay on the scene. Later that year, disguised as an Afghan communist soldier, Reza infiltrated forbidden Soviet-occupied Kabul, shooting pictures with a pocket-sized autofocus camera. Reza later took a year off from photography to do relief work in Afghanistan. But Baku was always where his soul was.

Of all Reza's experiences around the world, it was his experience in Baku in 1989, four years before we met, that remains the most vivid in his memory.

The story begins in February 1988, when, after decades of calm, widespread rioting erupted in the then-Soviet republic of Armenia. Armenian crowds were demanding the return of Nagorno Karabakh, the Armenian enclave under Azeri control. Though 80 percent of Karabakh's population was ethnic Armenian, the Kremlin had awarded it to the Azeri Turks of Azerbaijan in 1921, following the consolidation of the Caucasus by the Red Army. This was part of the Kremlin's plan to seed republics that were otherwise ethnically uniform with groups likely to prove hostile, in order to confound attempts at future separation from the Soviet Union. Sixty-seven years later this strategy, predictably, made the divorce process more bloody. The 1988 demonstrations in Armenia against Azeri Turk rule of Karabakh sparked an anti-Armenian pogrom in Sumgait, a predominantly Azeri city on the Caspian, just north of Baku. An Azeri mob rushed through a hospital ward, cutting open the stomachs of pregnant Armenian women. Hundreds were killed. The remaining Armenians fled Azerbaijani cities. A multinational mosaic was becoming a black-and-white jigsaw. As in the Balkans, mixed populations were separating themselves out into monoethnic enclaves.

The hatred quickly spent itself, even in industrial Sumgait, poorer, meaner, and more polluted than Baku. "The violence never happened," I was repeatedly told by horrified Baku residents. "And if it did, we condemn it." On January 20, 1989, passions over Karabakh had been replaced by something unique in the history of the Soviet Union: Thousands of residents of Baku were now openly demonstrating for the overthrow of the republic's communist regime. As a result, hundreds were gunned down by Soviet tanks and troops in the boulevards and alleys near the Hotel Azerbaijani.

But the outside world knew nothing of this. Mikhail Gorbachev's Kremlin had closed off Azerbaijan to Western journalists, sending them to Armenia instead, where the story was merely ethnic unrest, rather than demands for freedom from—and, therefore, the breakup of—the Soviet Union. Reza got the truth out. From Paris, Reza called his best friend in Baku, Ramiz, a former ambassador in the Soviet diplomatic service, to seek advice on secretly entering Azerbaijan. Ramiz made a plan and encouraged Reza to come. Reza flew to Moscow with only his autofocus camera. In Moscow, Reza boarded a crowded third-class train—whose crammed and smelly coaches Soviet police ignored—for the thirty-hour rail journey south to Baku. When the train pulled in, Ramiz and a crowd of his friends simply engulfed Reza to avoid police scrutiny.

Reza next found himself in a room of dark-paneled wood, covered with rich, pomegranate-red camel bags, each over a hundred years old. These were the antique carpets of Turkic horsemen: the ultimate Oriental rugs. There was a large wooden table in the middle of the room, with a dim gas lamp and dozens of old, leather-bound books. It was the home of an eccentric, well-connected friend of Ramiz, an Azeri member of the Soviet elite who now wanted to overthrow the system he had benefited from. Reza looked out through the window into the freezing and spectral January night. The alley was empty, except for a line of Russian troops with assault rifles and fur hats. The blood they had spilled earlier that day was still in the gutters. In the following days, Reza would use this room as a base from which to wander around Baku, stealthily snapping pictures with his camera, small enough to fit inside his shirt pocket.

It was this street he was now pointing to as we both looked out the same window, four years later, in the same room with the same camel bags. A party was in progress and we were on our third vodka. Vodka toasts, I was repeatedly told, were the only Russian custom that the Azeris had permanently absorbed into their culture. Still, there was little drunkenness in Baku. It was hard to say why. Islam offered little in the way of an explanation. Azeri Turks were secular in the extreme compared to the Orthodox Christian Russians and the Moslem Iranians. Perhaps it had something to do with a rich cultural base, that same muscle tone that I had noticed in the *gecekondus* of Istanbul. This culture was deepening even if nationhood was indistinct. Outwardly, it was becoming as if the Russians had never been here. The Cyrillic script was receding as Turkish signs, books, and newspapers—written in the Latin script that Ataturk brought to Turkey—returned. The music was increasingly *arabesk*: *gecekondu* music. Turkish kebab stands were appearing. Ramiz, Reza's friend, declared a fourth vodka toast to Azerbaijan, the hearthplace of Turkish literature. After all, *The Book of Dede Korkut* was written in a dialect closer to Azeri than to any other Turkish dialect. The first democratic Turkish republic of modern times was not established in Turkey but in Azerbaijan in 1918, Ramiz informed me, even if the Bolsheviks crushed it two years later. "Forgotten Turkish words, musical themes that we long ago lost, are now returning to our consciousness," intoned Ramiz.

But Azeri culture wasn't simply Turkish.

Ramiz's very manner, the tender, cloistered expression in his searching eyes, and the fetid dining room full of vodka, rotting cheeses, old photos, and perspiring, very lightly drunken men and women—as if they were in one evening-long communal hug—proclaimed an atmosphere similar to what I had experienced in Eastern Europe during communist rule—places where political life had been so sterile that the vacuum, perforce, had been filled by a personal life, making the latter far richer than people in Western Europe and North America could imagine. Ramiz was bald, with a fringe of gray hair. That didn't matter. It was his eyes that counted, eyes that to me were similar to Eastern European eyes: nostalgic, as if remembering a cultural past before communism. It may only be from such remembrances, even if more imagined than real, that nationhood can take root.

Even more important than an Eastern European–like experience, there was also much Persian influence. As with the Kurds, though in a different way—these things are ever so subtle—the Azeris were more olive-complexioned and more Aryan-featured than the Turks of Turkey. To the degree that the inhabitants of Baku were religious, they were Shi'ites, like the Moslems of Iran and unlike the Sunni Moslems of Turkey. Historically, Baku was more Persian than Russian or Turkish. The Kasranid shahs ruled here in the early medieval period, replaced by another Persianized dynasty, the Shi'ite Safavids. Though the Ottoman Turks captured Baku in 1580, the Safavids recaptured it in 1600. In 1728, Russian czar Peter the Great took Baku. Seven years later, though, another conqueror arrived from Iran, the Qajars. But the Russians retook Baku in 1806 and held it until the upheavals of the Russian Revolution in the early twentieth century, when an independent Turkish republic flickered for two years until the Russians, in the disguise of Soviets, came back. Azerbaijan was not merely an eastern extension of Turkey, but a gray, shaded area where the Turkish, Russian, and Iranian worlds overlapped. Because of seven decades of totalitarianism, which buried this rich legacy, this cultural eclecticism had become a confusing void.

I asked Reza about Iran, where I was headed next. Were the Azeris sufficiently repressed in Iran to create a sense of future state identity? I wondered. Even the Kurds had some sense of national identity, chaotic though it was, because they had been overtly oppressed. Reza shook his head. "You see," he began, "the Azeris were cofounders of the Iranian state. The first Shi'ite shah of Iran [Ismail in 1501] was an Azeri Turk. His capital was in Tabriz, an Azeri city, my city. Later, of course, the Persians dominated. There was constant war between Turks and Persians with the border often shifting. Yet the Azeris were always powerful in Iran. They live not just in the northwest, near the border with former-Soviet Azerbaijan, but also in Teheran. There are big Azeri businessmen, important Azeri ayatollahs. So the oppression of Azeris is hard to pin down. Still, there is this tension," Reza's eyebrows lift in punctuation, "between Azeri Turks and Persians. They are two separate cultures. So let's drink a toast, Bob, to the *real* borders, the borders of culture that will replace the borders of states in the future." We drank another vodka in the stuffy dining room, next to the room with the camel bags.

◎   ◎   ◎

REZA IS AN idealist. When he says "the borders of culture," he means peaceful, porous borders that are not so much borders as indistinct transition zones, the kind that existed in an earlier age, when there were no states and no state bureaucracies producing political maps, only large dynastic realms, such as the Habsburg lands and the Ottoman sultanate:[1] the natural borders of geography and ethnography, in other words—not cultural Berlin Walls. Only in such a world could Azerbaijan find a place.

In *Imagined Communities*, Benedict Anderson calls "nation-ness" an artifact of a fast-receding modern world in which every part of the earth's dry land is blocked off into some neat category. Yet "in the stillness of a summer evening, the world sheds its categories," writes Barry Lopez in his work of visionary travel, *Arctic Dreams*. It is that state of geographic innocence that Reza and other Azeris wanted to return to. I was doubtful that this could ever occur.

[1] See the section entitled "The Dynastic Realm," in the chapter on "Cultural Roots" in Benedict Anderson's *Imagined Communities*.

PART IV

◎ ◎ ◎

The Iranian Plateau
The Earth's "Soft Centre"

". . . the Iranian plateau is a 'soft centre' that panders to megalo-
maniac ambitions in its rulers without providing the genius to sustain them."

> —BRUCE CHATWIN
> from the Introduction to Robert Byron's
> *The Road to Oxiana*

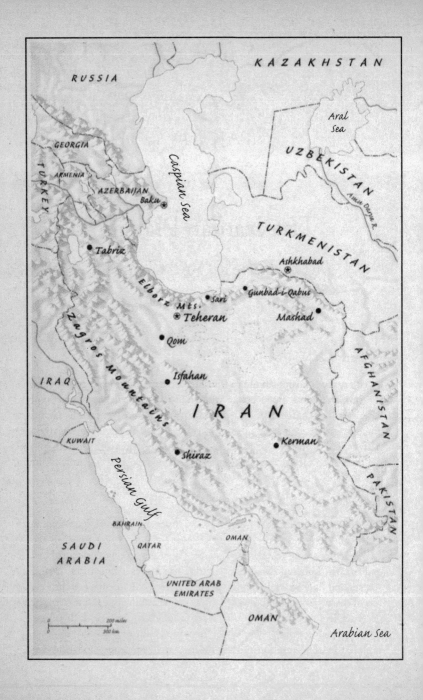

I 0

A Country of Flowers
and Nightingales

IN THE SPRING of 1994, to get to Iran I had to fly from Europe to Teheran, the Iranian capital. But I prefer to recollect my journey from the point where Azerbaijan meets Iran. If I couldn't travel uninterrupted by land, I could at least imagine my journey as continous: that way I would have a better idea of where I was, because of the lands I had to pass through to get there. You lack such bearings when you are deposited suddenly in the middle of a country by plane.

THE RICH AND dark scotch-green of the Elborz mountain range rimming the southern shores of the Caspian Sea near the border of Azerbaijan and Iran, encompassing tea plantations, the glassy reflections of rice paddies, and brown-timbered dwellings, gave way in stages. Vegetation became sparser and uneven, and I could see khaki spaces as I ascended to the very top of the Elborz range heading south, away from the sea and toward the desert. Olive trees replaced tea bushes. The green became drab yellow. The rice paddies disappeared. The luxurious bath of humidity thinned, replaced by the sensation of dust on my forehead. The wooden houses with their tin roofs designed for a wet climate were replaced by structures of stone, mudbrick, and cinder. As I made my way down the other side of the Elborz range in the direction of Teheran, the mountains bore sharp wrinkles rather than soft folds. The fog curled away, revealing the rude, impaling stare of plateau sunlight. Then came the emptiness of rock, sand, and compacted silt.

The change was gradual, yet it was complete. The shift in landscape took place inside of an hour. It was a travel experience similar to the one I had experienced by entering Iran by air from Europe, when, as we approached Teheran one Persian woman, and then another, and another, wiped away her rouge and lipstick and hid her long hair and her leotards or miniskirt beneath the black shapelessness of the *chador*. What had so recently been a lovely garden became a featureless desert.

Were more of Iran—rather than just its north and northwest borders provinces—graced by the moist and moderating influences of the Caspian, then perhaps the history and character of the Iranian people would have been very different, and the transformation of an airplane cabin into a veritable mosque would never have occurred.

◎   ◎   ◎

IRAN'S ISLAMIC REVOLUTION of 1978–1979 was only one chapter in the long history of "Persia,"[1] one of the ancient world's first superpowers, whose empire spanned from Macedonia to India under the rule of Cyrus the Great in the sixth century B.C. For this reason, the Islamic Revolution was not my principal interest. The revolution and its aftermath are the present. I tried to concentrate on the deeper past—and the future. My rucksack contained books like the *Shah Nameh*, the quasi-mythical history of ancient Persia, and *The Adventures of Hajji Baba of Ispahan*, a Don Juan-like epic of late-medieval Persia. I also carried statistical projections of urbanization and population growth.

At the time of the Islamic Revolution, 45 percent of all Iranians lived in cities; by 1994, 57 percent of the population was urban. When the shah was toppled, 5 million people lived in Teheran. A decade and a half later there were 10 million. Since the revolution, Iran's population increased from 35 million to 60 million. Almost half of the population is under fif-

---

[1] *Persia* was the word used by the ancient Greeks for Iran, which is in turn derived from the southwestern province of Fars: hence Farsi, the language of the country.

teen—in other words, not yet born when the mullahs came to power. Many more Iranians are too young to recall those events.

Teheran has, in the meantime, become the fourth most polluted city on earth.[2] The World Bank cautions that air pollution levels in Teheran and other Iranian cities could double over the next decade as villagers flood into the cities at the rate of 5 percent of the population yearly. Clearly, demographic shifts and their attendant problems now overshadow the heady winter of 1978–1979, while the secondary causes of the revolution (modernization, overcrowded cities, etc.) are more intense than ever. For example, though the population has nearly doubled, the number of hospital beds has increased by less than 60 percent. Disease and rumors of plague are rife.[3]

◎ ◎ ◎

YET IT WAS the afterimages of the Islamic Revolution, like the tones of black in a photo negative, that struck me upon my arrival in Teheran.

My first acquaintance was a "Mr. [Asghar] Kashan." Iranians, I quickly learned, are formal, and first names are rarely used. Mr. Kashan was the friend of someone I know in the Iranian government, who agreed to guide me in Teheran. He was bald, with short gray hair and black-framed glasses. Middle-aged, he had gray eyes full of fatigue and half measures—a far cry from the dark and penetrating eyes of Near Eastern revolutionaries.

Mr. Kashan wore the "three-day growth" that Iranians have made famous in the years since the revolution. Like so many other Iranian men, Mr. Kashan looked as if he hadn't shaved. "It is because we are permanently in mourning," another Iranian would later explain to me, "in mourning for Hossein," the grandson of the prophet Mohammed, martyred by the Sunnis at the battle of Karbala in Mesopotamia over thirteen hundred years ago. To a Westerner, such unforgiving Persians may appear obsessive. "It's what makes even other Moslem Shi'ites afraid of the Iranians," a Pakistani friend counseled.

This obsessive behavior reveals itself in other ways, too. For instance, the Iranian "students" who held United States diplomats hostage in

[2]Source: Population Action International. Only Delhi, Beijing, and Calcutta have worse air-quality indexes.
[3]See Shaban and Johnston in the bibliography.

Teheran in 1980 pieced together hundreds of documents that the diplomats had fed to shredding machines just before the siege: tens of thousands of strips of paper, each less than an eighth of an inch wide. Crossing into Iran from a neighboring country is like going from a shop selling crude folk art to a Madison Avenue boutique, for here was an attention to detail—and a degree of artisanship, therefore—which did not quite obtain in Turkey, or in Egypt. Neurotic this culture might be, even psychotic at times, but it was a culture that had to be taken seriously: a capable culture, which, if it turned its mind to, say, car bombs, would display the same meticulousness as in its craft items. I recalled how quickly the Iranians went from little presence at all in Lebanon in 1982, to virtually controlling pockets of the country by 1985 and organizing deadly accurate terrorist attacks through their surrogate, Hezbollah—and they did not have to invade, as the Israelis did. As in the days when Cyrus, Darius, and Xerxes threatened ancient Greece from their stronghold at Persepolis, Persia is still a formidable challenge to the West.

"You must be tired," Mr. Kashan said. "Today is Friday. Everything is closed. I'll take you to the *Hosseinieh*, and to the cemetery, then you can sleep the rest of the afternoon. Tonight we'll have dinner by the river and talk."

Mr. Kashan said very little the rest of the day. He had been part of the religious underground against the shah, someone who had been with the ayatollahs from the beginning. Now Mr. Kashan was an adviser to the governor of the Iranian Central Bank. His manner was low-key—the result in part of a bad heart. His expression told me: *Look around. See for yourself. If you have questions, I'll try to answer them.* Faceless, forgettable Mr. Kashan with his green prayer beads would, by the end of my sojourn, slowly become the face of Iran, a clue to where it may be headed in the twenty-first century.

By *Hosseinieh*, Mr. Kashan had meant the recently completed tomb complex of the founder of the Islamic Republic, His Holiness Grand Ayatollah Hajji Sayed Ruhollah Musavi, from the town of Khomein in central Iran: hence Ayatollah Khomeini. Such exalted titles—*ayatollah* ("sign of God") and the lesser *hojatollislam* ("divine proof of God")—indicate a clerical hierarchy more complex than elsewhere in the Islamic world, one that the Safavids established in the early sixteenth century in the course of building a powerful Persian state that could compete with the well-developed bureaucracy of the rival Ottoman Empire.

Ayatollah Khomeini's tomb is not a mosque, but a more informal "public place of Hossein," the Shi'ite martyr, thus a *Hosseinieh*. This is a crucial distinction. An Iranian mosque may be decorated with hand-woven silk rugs and fine mirrors, but a *Hosseinieh* is more *everyday*. It is a blunt rebuke to "sophisticated" Persia by the industrialized, blue-collar masses who were Khomeini's constituency. The atmosphere inside the gold-domed tomb twenty miles south of Teheran was less that of a holy place than of a sports stadium. The ceiling, rather than exhibiting delicate filigree or mosaic, was composed of unadorned steel girders. The car-pets—in this land of hand-made silk rugs—were machine-made and of coarse wool. I compared it to the mausoleum of Sayida Zeinab, a grand-daughter of the prophet Mohammed, a Shi'ite holy place outside Damas-cus that I first visited in the 1970s. I remembered its fine faience, its gold ornaments, its huge crystal chandelier, and its hand-woven magenta rugs—such a contrast from the crass decorations of this holy place. Chil-dren were now kicking a soccer ball and playing tag a few feet from the green cage that held Khomeini's earthly remains. The smell of kebab min-gled with that of the pilgrims. I snapped pictures of the crowd and took notes. Nobody seemed to care. One man asked me if I wanted to change money. Outside, an enlarged parking lot, a laundromat, a supermarket, and a hotel-restaurant complex were all under construction. People removed their shoes, came inside to see the tomb, prayed for a while, ate, laughed, met friends, and maybe changed some rials for dollars on the newly legalized "free market." This was my first insight into Khomeini's genius as a politician.

Khomeini himself had stipulated that his tomb be a *Hosseinieh*. In other words, *give the working poor what they want, a place where they can feel comfortable*. I noticed that Mr. Kashan was smiling as I scribbled my notes. Later he would tell me that the great accomplishment of the revolution was that "it made corruption egalitarian. Under the shah, corruption was only for the rich."

Next, Mr. Kashan took me to the nearby "martyrs' cemetery," where many of the casualties of the 1980–88 Iran-Iraq War are buried. Here I found Persia, as opposed to revolutionary Iran. Journalists' descriptions of this cemetery are usually limited to a fountain spurting blood-red water, but the cemetery stretches for miles, perhaps the largest graveyard in the world, and it also holds a supermarket, laundry facilities, a computer cen-ter for locating individual graves, and a planned metro station. In other words, the cemetery was less a place of fiery passion than a vast, hum-drum, tightly packed community of the dead with whom the living could commingle while they shopped.

It was Friday and the cemetery was filled with picnickers, who spread their carpets, and laid out their baskets of flat bread, saffron-colored rice, meat, olives, and goat cheese, and their tea kettles. Visits to dead relatives, even youths killed in the war, were the occasion for a family outing. And everywhere—this would be my most overpowering impression of the cemetery—were junipers, evergreens, magnificently tended arrangements of roses and tulips, and an infinity of canals. The scent of fresh water and the stronger perfume of flowers on the border of a suffocating, alkaline desert: such was Persia.

◎   ◎   ◎

IT WAS NIGHTTIME, humming with the sound of fresh water tinkling over rocks. Mr. Kashan and I were walking uphill along the banks of the Darband River, which flows down from the Elborz at the northern extremity of Teheran. We passed a number of teahouse restaurants until we found one that we especially liked. Here Iran revealed its closeness to Central Asia. Along with the orchids, tulips, and roses, bubbling water pipes, and a flute player were the carpets on raised platforms where people ate, as in the Central Asian, *chai-khanas*, or teahouses. On these carpets, leaning against brocaded pillows under the glow of colored lights strung over-head, men and women smoked, held hands, whispered, and flirted. Intrigued, I stared at a woman in a black *chador*, who returned my stare, a challenge. Mr. Kashan noticed this and smiled, again, as if to say: *You see, we are not, exactly, as we are portrayed in the West. Consider the women, for example.*

Indeed. My first impression in Iran was that the female half of the population was draped in shapeless black. But after a few hours my eyes began to adjust to the distinctions. The material for the *chadors*, as I later found out in the Teheran bazaar, was imported from Japan and South Korea. Some *chadors* were silk, others cotton and crepe. Quality varied greatly. A *chador* could cost as little as ten dollars or as much as fifty dol-lars. Most were black, but not all. Yet this was only the beginning. Some women displayed bits of forbidden hair, along with flashy earrings; others wore kohl beneath their eyes, and, in not a few cases, lipstick. Many had finely manicured hands with long red fingernails. Many women also used perfume; occasionally I noticed an expensive French scent, which, unlike flowers in the cheap odor of incense, gave off a provocative animal aroma. Driving through the traffic toward the Darband River on this, my first evening in Teheran, I noticed that many of the Iranian drivers were women, liberally using their horns and shouting from their car windows, badgering other drivers to speed up. What a difference from Saudi Arabia, America's ally in the Moslem world, where women aren't allowed to drive. I saw one Iranian woman draped in black driving a motorcycle. Another rode on a motorbike behind her boyfriend, holding him tightly around the waist, and at the stoplight I could see that they had begun to hold hands, engaging in an erotic finger-play.

Women in Teheran stare you in the face. Their eyes meet you dead-on. Cairo has little of this, and Istanbul much less than Teheran. And while Iranian women are required to cover their hair and conceal the curves of their bodies, a full *burka* dress, or an opaque veil over the entire face, is far rarer in Iran than in Egypt, Turkey, or, as I was later to discover, in Central Asia and Pakistan.

A male journalist could go, for example, to Saudi Arabia, to Iraq, even to Pakistan, with its female prime minister, Benazir Bhutto, and be lectured at length about "the increasing role of women in public affairs," and be obliged to interview a prominent woman who ran this or that league of Iraqi or Pakistani women. And yet, when I entered a restaurant in these countries, I would encounter only men eating their grilled meat. Women were rarely in sight, and usually confined to the "family" section behind a screened partition.[4] In Iran, as I had just begun to learn, women could always be seen in restaurants, and were always approachable. In Iran, a male traveler communicated with both sexes, not just with his own. In Iran, you could point a camera at a woman—as I often did—and she would smile. If you did that in Pakistan, the woman would run away and a man might throw a rock at you. In Iranian homes, even lower-middle-class homes, where women remained in *chador*, women still talked to you, questioned you, and did not politely retreat.

[4]In Benazir Bhutto's Pakistan, female literacy is only 45 percent that of male literacy, according to the United Nations Development Programme in 1994. In fundamentalist Iran, next door, it is 66 percent. In the past two decades, female literacy in Pakistan, relative to male literacy, has risen only 8 percent, while in Iran it has risen 23 percent. In Pakistan, less than half as many women as men reached secondary school: in Iran, 70 percent did.

The Islamic Revolution was supposed to have been cultural as well as political. The *chador*, coupled with the giant posters reading *Marg bar Amrika* ("Death to America"), were visual evidence of this dual purpose. Yet the mores of what was, by Near Eastern standards, a highly sophisticated, urbane, and even northern culture, appeared minimally affected fifteen years after the revolution, or even twenty years later, at the time of my last visit to Teheran. Women, as I was to see, crowded the fancy clothing boutiques in north Teheran and the less fancy ones elsewhere in the city: Uniformity outside of the home served only to increase fashion consciousness inside. Iranian women would not be turned into peasants. And as public life had been circumscribed, I observed that, as in the Eastern Europe I knew well during the communist era, private life here had become richer in order to compensate.

I believe it was Uri Avneri, the Israeli leftist and social critic, who observed that to be genuine, a revolution must radically alter a culture. Zionism, for example, created a new spoken language, Hebrew. It changed people's diets. It forced small businessmen in Europe to become farmers in the Near East. It even changed the way people looked and dressed. Iran's revolution was anemic by comparison. I took the matter up with Mr. Kashan as we sat down to dinner.

"No, it is not so simple. True, the *chador* is only a symbol. At Teheran University, where my daughter studies, where the students once demonstrated against the shah, the male and female students must sit on separate sides of the classroom. But between classes, what happens? They mingle together. Our culture is moving back into the normalized center, that is true. But this would have been impossible had the revolution not allowed us to be ourselves in the first place. The revolution gave us back our self-respect. Of course, there were human rights excesses. But in the days of the worst excesses, we were still more Persian than at any time during the shah's reign." In other words, if I understood his tortured rationalization properly, the revolution was an aberration to counter the aberration of the shah's rule. But these were long aberrations, lasting decades. You had to wonder if normalcy was possible here.

We listened to the flute player entertaining the crowd at the teahouse. The grilled meat and plates of rice came, yellow with saffron, soaked in butter, punctuated with barbary figs. There were the side dishes flavored with tarragon and mint, spinach and yogurt, garlic marinated in vinegar.

And "Meshedi Coca-Cola," a reference to the American Coke made at the Coca-Cola bottling plant in Meshed, the holy city of pilgrimage in northeastern Iran, where the eighth Shi'ite imam, or leader, Imam Reza is buried. Debate had been raging in the newspapers and in the Iranian *majlis*, or parliament, about closing down this bottling plant, symbolizing as it did American cultural influence. But the debate had recently died down. One story had it that Iran's current spiritual leader—Khomeini's clerical heir— Ayatollah Sayyed Ali Khamenei, himself from Meshed, had friends with a financial interest in the bottling plant. So did President Hashemi Rafsanjani's family. Hypocrisy was easily accepted here. Normal relations with the United States are inevitable, more than one revolutionary would later tell me with a casual shrug.

The conversation drifted to other matters, losing focus. As to the Persian makeup of the Pahlevi and Islamic regimes—versus the Turkic makeup of the previous Qajar dynasty[5]—Mr. Kashan told me to be very careful. "Our relations with the Azeri Turks [of Azerbaijan] are subtle." Rather than an either-or, it was more a question of a fine shift in balance. Nine of the twenty-seven ministers in the present Iranian cabinet are Azeri Turks, and sixteen of the twenty-seven ministers speak Azeri Turkish as well as Persian. This is not a hair-splitting issue of interest only to scholars: The Azeri question, more than any other, as I was to learn, was a key to unlocking the future of Iran and the Caucasus. Here was the subtlety that Reza, my photographer friend in Baku, had spoken about.

We were finishing our meal and Mr. Kashan was about to ask the waiter for tea, when I asked him about his thoughts on Salman Rushdie, who was issued a death sentence for allegedly blaspheming God in his book *The Satanic Verses*. Mr. Kashan admitted that the *fatwa*, or edict, issued by Ayatollah Khomeini was a political act as well as a religious one. Mr. Kashan admitted, too, that perhaps—yes, perhaps—the late ayatollah had been somewhat unwise in issuing the edict. "But what of it! In the West, your courts daily issue imperfect verdicts. Some of your judges' decisions are even quite bad. Yet they are carried out. They must be. If they weren't, the legal system, and the society, would descend into chaos. The Rushdie verdict is but another judicial ruling, like the one to extradite

[5]The Qajars were a dynasty of Turkoman shahs who ruled Iran from 1794 to 1925. Though they began Iran's modernization, their rule was also characterized by a deteriorating central control that allowed foreign powers undue influence in Iranian affairs.

the Libyans accused of blowing up the plane over Lockerbie. If you don't like the legal system, work to change it, but in the meantime its rulings must be obeyed. And Rushdie didn't just libel another person, he committed a libelous action against God Himself." The fact that Rushdie himself had often written harsh tracts against the West was an irony of which Mr. Kashan displayed no knowledge—or interest. That was a local issue in the West, of no concern to him.

Mr. Kashan suggested that the dissemination of *The Satanic Verses* was being helped along in some vague manner by the Church of England, and by the archbishop of Canterbury in particular. Mr. Kashan spoke softly in an even whisper about this. He enjoyed my protestations, which provided him with his entertainment. The waiter brought gummy ice cream, flavored with attar of roses.

◎　　　◎　　　◎

BACK IN THE hotel lobby after my dinner with Mr. Kashan, I met an Iranian-American by the reception desk, a woman in her late twenties who had come to Teheran with her brother. Brought up in an American suburb, she came every spring to Teheran. "I love it," she said. After all, the parties were so much better here than in America. The banning of alcohol, the requirement of the *chador*, made what went on *posht-e pardeh*, "behind the curtain," that much more arousing. Liquor wasn't just available in wealthy north Teheran. It flowed. A bottle of Johnny Walker Black was only thirty dollars on the black market. Women didn't simply dress up at private Teheran parties: They dressed and danced and flirted to the nines—in slinky black-satin numbers and under layers of makeup. Parties were not just parties, they were feasts of forbidden fruit. How dull, how unfulfilling, an American suburb must be in comparison! Woe to the society that insists on ironing out its incongruities!

One Western resident here, a woman, would tell me: "You must watch a Persian woman dance in her home before her guests, displaying her gold and jewels to show that her husband is doing well and that he loves her enough to buy her such things. You can see traces of this behavior in five-year-old girls—how these girls move with their bodies! It is implanted in their genes. Politics has no effect over these things."

I went to bed in an eddy of half-formed impressions. Iran was overwhelming. I would need to slow down and concentrate on one aspect of the culture at a time.

MY IMPRESSIONS OF downtown Teheran the next morning were of easy familiarity. Teheran looked so much like Athens, another Near Eastern city, in which I had lived for seven years. Both Athens and Teheran had been decrepit, provincial towns in the nineteenth century and had mushroomed into sprawling, unplanned conglomerations of hard-angled, chalky stone buildings, with few distinctive landmarks, under a glaring sun filtered through lead pollution. In Teheran, Western consumerism assaults you everywhere with signs for Kenwood stereos, Toshiba computers, Swiss watches, and American soft drinks and computer software programs. Teheran is less grubby than the Greek capital. Men and women in orange uniforms clean the streets. Sycamores and sparkling canals line most of the avenues, and the outskirts abound in sleek highway overpasses.

I walked along Firdausi Street, named after Iran's Homeric poet. Here in the early morning the money changers were unpacking their wares. Whole suitcases of U.S. dollars, Iranian rials, Pakistani rupees, and Afghan afghanis were being opened on the street. One man was placing rocks on stacks of cash to keep them from flying away in the breeze. No policemen were in sight. The possibility of robbery was remote. Iran has a very low crime rate, and it is perfectly safe for a visitor to carry large amounts of cash in his pocket.[6] This could not be explained away by totalitarianism—the reason, for example, that the Soviet Union, during its existence, had a low street crime rate. The Iranian regime was certainly repressive toward its political enemies and religious groups like the Baha'is, for which it has earned an abysmal human rights record. But the all-encompassing security control and terror required to discourage common theft was missing. Iran was never a prison-state like Iraq. In Saddam Hussein's Baghdad, survey maps and controversial books were banned, but in Teheran—except, of course, for Rushdie's books—they were sold everywhere.

The sight of stacks of U.S. dollars piled up on the street, in no danger of being stolen, supported my initial views of Iran. Here was a society, like Turkey's, with a strong social mortar, a society that you didn't need to feel sorry for. Foreign diplomats and aid workers did not sit around in Teheran—as they did in Lagos and Nairobi—exchanging stories about this

[6]David St Vincent, in the Lonely Planet guide to Iran, reports that regarding crime, Iran is "one of the safest countries in Asia for the foreign visitor."

colleague who was robbed and that colleague who had just installed iron bars over her windows. Nor did foreign embassies in Teheran advise their nationals that rising crime made it unsafe to use public transport, as embassies in nearby Uzbekistan and other former Soviet republics had begun to do. The U.S. had diplomatic relations with Nigeria and Kenya. And Uzbekistan had even joined NATO's "Partnership for Peace" program. But none of those countries had civil societies in the sense that Iran did.

The U.S. State Department had advised me not to go to Iran, a state with which America had no diplomatic relations. But I felt safer in Teheran than in many American cities. These things mattered, because while governments undermine and commit violence against each other, struggles between governments are only the news of the moment. Ethnic and national characteristics change far more slowly and are, therefore, better guides to future political trends. Just as the U.S. waged war, and then peace, with Germany and Japan, it would ultimately do so with Iran, a country with which our enmity has been far less intense than with the former Axis powers, and with which our military, economic, and educational links run deeper.[7]

In 1829, urged on by their mullahs, Iranians had stormed and destroyed the Russian embassy and decapitated the Russian ambassador, Alexander Griboyedov. But Russian-Iranian relations were eventually restored. Who, now, even remembers the incident? To believe that U.S.-Iranian relations will never be restored because of the hostage crisis would be to ignore history. Iran's revolutionary iniquities were partly the result of fast-forward urbanization and modernization. Its worst perversities may actually be behind it, while the reckoning for the U.S. favorites of the moment, Egypt and Saudi Arabia, might still be due.

◎　　　◎　　　◎

IN 1892, to describe Iranians, Lord Curzon wrote:

> The finest domestic virtues coexist with barbarity and supreme indifference to suffering. Elegance of deportment is compatible with a coarseness amounting to bestiality. . . . A creditable acquaintance with the standards of civilisation does not prevent gross fanati-

---

[7]See the analysis on the long-range trajectory of American-Iranian relations, written by Edward G. Shirley, a Persian-speaking former intelligence officer at the Central Intelligence Agency, listed in the bibliography.

cism. . . . Accomplished manners and a more than Parisian polish cover a truly superb faculty for lying and almost a scientific imposture. The most scandalous corruption is combined with a scrupulous regard for specified precepts of the moral law. Religion is alternately stringent and lax, inspiring at one moment the bigot's rage, at the next, the agnostic's indifference. Government is both patriarchal and . . . Machiavellian . . . the people at once despicable and noble; the panorama at the same time an enchantment and fraud.

Seventy years later, Terence O'Donnell, an American who lived on a farm in Iran, wrote:

Iranians are voluptuaries and delight in the flesh. Their conversation, their poetry—which means everything to them after their God, and sometimes before . . . all reflect a love of earthly pleasures. . . . There is, too, the readiness to engage in revenge and to relish it.

Thinking and reading about Iran, I found it hard to avoid these stark dualities: the poetry of Hafiz—whose sensuous verses about pagan fire, red wine, and alcoholic intoxication presage the great chivalric ballads of medieval Europe—and the torture chambers of Evin prison; the banners proclaiming "Death to America," and the hand-stitched carpets in the hotel gift shops of a U.S. five-dollar bill. Or, as Robert Byron evoked this duality in *The Road to Oxiana*, the fabulous turquoise-blue jar set against the brown desert waste. Iran was nothing less than all the contradictions of the Near East in their most intense form. James Justinian Morier, author of *Hajji Baba of Ispahan*, writes at the beginning of his book that in Persia, an "uncontaminated source of Eastern manners lay before me, and I was delighted with the opportunities which would be afforded . . ."

I felt that Iran now offered something even more tantalizing than in the nineteenth century, when Morier wrote *Hajji Baba*: the incongruities of an Oriental society exacerbated by the beasts of Western consumerism, exploding demographics, and the information age.

I gave Mr. Kashan a list of the people I wanted to see. He said he would try to arrange it.

11

◎   ◎   ◎

The Revolution of "the Hand"

TRY AS I might to focus on "eternal" Persia, I kept encountering the word *enghelab*, Persian for "revolution": a reference to the Enghelab-e Eslami, "The Islamic Revolution." At Meidun-e Enghelab, or Revolution Square, in downtown Teheran, where crowds had toppled a large statue of the shah in 1979, there was now a relief carving of an Iranian religious figure. I cannot be sure if the relief carving was of Khomeini, since the face was indistinct. What I remember clearly is the figure's outstretched and over-sized hand—an opened palm and fingers—dominating the foreground. "It is the Khamseh-ye Al-e Aba [Five Fingers of the Holy Mantle], taking the people up to heaven," Mr. Kashan said, moving his green prayer beads slowly and patiently. The Five Fingers symbolized Mohammed the Prophet, his daughter Fatima, her husband Ali, and their descendants, Hassan and, especially, Hossein, killed by the Sunnis along with his troops at the battle of Karbala, for leading an insurrection to wrest the throne away from the Umayyad caliphs.

Many of the photos of Khomeini that I saw in Iran showed him with an outstretched open hand in the foreground, and a smoldering expression—the face of Hossein, or of Jehovah in the desert, I imagined. The similarity of these images, of God and Ayatollah, in the minds of Iranians would certainly clear up what, to a Westerner, appears to be a basic contradiction: Khomeini is always being spoken about by Iranians as "merciful" and "compassionate" and "understanding." ("I can say definitely that Imam Khomeini was full of love in his heart," said Mr. Kashan.) But there is no photograph of Khomeini smiling, or even with a trace of warmth in his eyes.

Khomeini's "love" and "compassion" were thus godlike: not of this world. "Normal human emotions did not affect the Imam," explained Mohsen Rafighdoost, Khomeini's personal driver and bodyguard, and a friend of Mr. Kashan. When a reporter asked Khomeini how he felt upon returning to Iran, after years in exile, to crowds of hundreds of thousands of people who had come to greet him at the airport, Khomeini replied, "I feel nothing."

Such implacability characterizes Shi'ite clerics in *Hajji Baba of Ispahan*. The main character, Hajji, trying to pass himself off as a holy man, wears "the affected taciturnity of the sour, proud, and bigoted man of the law." Hajji tells the reader, "I found that the profound taciturnity which I had adopted was the best help towards the establishment of a high reputation for wisdom . . ."

Khomeini is always referred to by Iranians as Imam Khomeini. *Imam* means "leader," or, more accurately, "He who guides the *umma* [community] in prayer." Imam is also the title given to the twelve descendants of Mohammed, who, according to Shi'ites, succeeded the Prophet as the spiritual and earthly leaders of the faith. These imams lived in medieval times, except for the twelfth, who is not dead but believed by Shi'ites "to be in occultation," or somehow hidden from view. Since Khomeini is the only ayatollah whom Iranians have ever called Imam, is he the twelfth imam, in occultation since the Middle Ages? "No," Mr. Kashan told me, but not without some equivocation.

The Islamic Revolution, to judge by its ability to unite disparate images of God and man, might represent the culmination of national and religious longings simmering for centuries. For the idea that the clergy had more right to rule than the wine-drinking shahs had, according to historians, been growing gradually, albeit erratically, since the seventeenth century, the time of the Safavids, the first dynasty in Iran to successfully establish Twelver Shi'ism.[1]

---

[1] Twelver Shi'ism is based on the legitimacy of the twelve imams, and constitutes the main branch of the Shi'ite faith.

Or was the revolution simply a cinematic event, not a revolution at all but a coup d'état by antiregime clerics? Listen to this foreign businessman, a fluent Persian speaker, who has lived in Iran for several years and who invited me to his house in north Teheran for dinner one night:

"Wait another five years and they'll be hanging mullahs from lampposts in the streets. It's happened before in Persian history, these incredible political shifts. The revolution is disintegrating. More and more videos, more satellite dishes—the most popular television program in Teheran is *Baywatch*. People are watching MTV. Mullahs in the parliament want to ban the satellite dishes. Like everything here, they'll settle the problem with money: Everyone who owns a satellite dish will pay a bribe, or they'll dismantle some of the dishes and call the media in to film it . . . half of the Iranian cabinet is now American-educated. They know California better than they know Shi'ism. Iranians from L.A. are coming back here and going to court to get their property returned. The boring truth about the Islamic Revolution is that the rich are still rich, the poor are still poor. The only real change is that the middle class was largely destroyed. True or not, the poor feel that Iran lost the war with Iraq and that the clergy are to blame. What you have left is an alliance between radical mullahs and the security services. Together, these two groups can do things like help terrorists abroad and try to acquire a nuclear bomb— actions which allow them to proclaim that the revolution is still alive. But their support is increasingly thin, and the society at home is headed in a completely opposite direction."

In other words, the battle between East and West was not being fought between the United States and Iran but inside Iran itself, between Iranians.

Between the idea of a grand Shi'ite revolution and the businessman's just-another-bloody-disaster-finally-being-undone lay Mr. Kashan's vision of a less dramatic readjustment—"something that allowed us to be ourselves," after which came a long, ongoing period of normalization in a fresh context.

◎   ◎   ◎

I GRADUALLY CAME to share Mr. Kashan's view. The revolution is an important part of Iran's past, but its causes are elusive. There has been too much discussion about the religious roots of the Islamic Revolution, too little about its cultural and historical roots, and even less about the demographic and environmental roots of the event, which contain the important clues to the likely shifts in cartography that will occur in the Near East and Central Asia at the close of the twentieth century, or soon after.

◙   ◙   ◙

"THE PEOPLE OF Iran are like the earth; they require *rishweh* [a bribe] . . . before they will bring forth fruit," observes the author of *Hajji Baba of Ispahan*. The linkage between the soil—its fecundity in some areas and its flintiness in others—and national characteristics in Iran is striking. In *Roots of the Revolution: An Interpretive History of Modern Iran*, Nikki R. Keddie explains:

> Although Iran had been the seat of strong and prosperous states and empires in ancient times, agricultural decline and aridity . . . grew over centuries. Hence when Turkish nomadic tribes invaded Iran beginning in the eleventh century they did not, as had earlier nomadic invaders, settle or fit into interstices between settled areas, but rather, finding arid lands suitable for nomadism, spread that way of life.

Several persistent themes began to emerge a thousand years ago on the Iranian plateau. First, there has been the competition between the indigenous Persian-speakers and the Turkic-speaking tribesmen, who filtered into Iran from the Caucasus—roughly, Azerbaijan in the northwest and Central Asia in the northeast (near the borders of the former Soviet Union and Afghanistan).

These Turkic tribesmen have, in fact, ruled Iran for long stretches of its history. Isma'il, the first shah of the Safavid dynasty, established in 1501 A.D., was a Turkish speaker. Because he relied on Persian-speaking bureaucrats, the Safavids evolved into a Persian Shi'ite dynasty, the greatest of medieval times, with its capital at Isfahan.[2] In 1722, the Sunni Afghans sacked Isfahan; then Nadir Shah, a Persian, ejected the Afghans in 1736. Late in the eighteenth century, there was a brief period of Persian glory under the Zand dynasty, based in Shiraz. By the mid-1790s, however, Turkic speakers were back in power, under the Qajars, who were not

---

[2] The spelling of Isfahan with an *f* is generally more prevalent than the soft *p* employed by James Morier in *Hajji Baba of Ispahan*.

overthrown until Reza Khan, the father of the last shah, established the Pahlevi dynasty, dominated by Persian speakers, in 1925.

Today, Persian speakers form only about half of Iran's population. Turkic-speaking Azeris account for as much as a quarter of the citizenry, and this does not include other Turkic sectors of the population, such as the Turkomens in the northeast, near the former Soviet border, and the Qhashqha'is in the southwest, near Shiraz and the Persian Gulf. This is mainly why the fate of neighboring Turkic-speaking Azerbaijan, in its current struggle with Armenia, as well as the emergence of independent Turkic states in former Soviet Central Asia adjoining Iran, may directly influence Iran's political future more than anything that happens between Iran and the West, or between Iran and the Arab world.

The second persistent theme in Iran's history is tied to the spread of nomadism along vast stretches of desert tableland and higher plateaus, alleviated by many lonely and isolated oases, which led to a tradition of weak central government. This is why the image of a totalitarian state, whether under the shah or the ayatollahs, has never been quite accurate. The Turkic tribesmen and the Kurds—not to mention the Baluchi drug smugglers in the remote southeast, near Iran's border with Pakistan— continue to be a law unto themselves. The inability of the Shi'ite clergy to control outlying reaches of the country since the early, chaotic days of the revolution has meant that, in this respect at least, their regime has turned out to be less oppressive than the shah's. Moreover, the financial and administrative tools of control afforded by oil wealth and modern telecommunications have not improved significantly since the revolution (the price of oil has gone down, in relative terms), yet the clergy must govern a population that has almost doubled in size since 1979. Teheran now has more people than all of Iran had in 1914, and twice as many as Iran had in 1800. Here is where the forces of demography work against tyranny (or against government itself).

Moreover, traditionally weak central government, and the accompanying development of competing power centers in cities separated by vast stretches of arid land, meant that the Shi'ite clergy could evolve independently of the less-religious shahs (whether the monarchs be Safavids, Zands, Qajars, or Pahlevis). As Keddie points out, from the eighteenth century through the 1940s, the Shi'ite clergy had their locus of power in An Najaf and Karbala, that is in Mesopotamia (just west of the Iranian plateau), where the tombs of the first imams are located.

Finally, as the land grew more arid over the centuries, due, among other factors, to the disruption in farming that resulted from the Mongol invasions, the earth of Iran became ever stingier; so that a relatively large number of peasant farmers, living in scattered, remote, and therefore undeveloped regions, was required to produce food for the cities. However, in the twentieth century, as factories sprung up, and as international trade expanded, allowing for the importation of food—spurred further by the modernization programs of Reza Khan and his son, the last shah—this large population of peasant farmers fled the villages for the cities.

With oil wealth, more food could be imported and the price of basic commodities for city dwellers could be subsidized. Farmers became less important, while the attraction of cities increased. Oil wealth also allowed Iranian cities to modernize. Ryszard Kapuscinski writes in *Shah of Shahs*, "Iranian cities became places where "the unpredictable cruel Stone Age coexists with the calculating, cool age of electronics . . ."

From 1956 through the eve of the Islamic Revolution, urban areas in Iran grew 5 percent annually at the expense of rural areas, and the rural labor force grew at a rate of less than half that of the country's total labor force.[3]

"The Shah," writes Kapuscinski, "thought that urbanization and industrialization are the keys to modernity, but this is a mistaken idea. The key to modernity is the village." Kapuscinski adds:

> The Shah got drunk on visions of atomic power plants, computerized production lines, and large-scale petrochemical complexes. But in an underdeveloped country, these are mere mirages of modernity. In that kind of country, most of the people live in poor villages from which they flee to the city. They form a young, energetic workforce that knows little (they are often illiterate) but possesses great ambition and is ready to fight. . . . In the struggle [against the city's entrenched establishment] they make use of whatever ideology they have brought from the village—usually this is religion.

Kapuscinski believes there will be no end to this vicious circle, in which a new generation of migrants will always follow in the footsteps of the previous one, until the villages themselves become modernized and offer as many opportunities as the towns. I saw no evidence of such rural modern-

[3]See M. J. Majd's article on land reform and urbanization, listed in the bibliography.

ization in my journey so far—not in West Africa, the Nile Valley, or Anatolia. Whether in Abidjan, Cairo, or Istanbul, what I saw instead was that cities were being overrun by peasants and turned into huge villages.

But in Iran, the shah had encouraged his people so recklessly, so fast, so lopsidedly, piling contradiction upon contradiction, that they became heady with ambition, and with frustration. When the economy took a temporary nosedive in the late 1970s, the shah was, for one, long critical moment, suddenly without the means to bribe his subjects.

Whereas the Qajar government in the nineteenth century—plagued by the decentralizing forces of a vast desert, nomadism, and an independent clergy united with bazaar merchants—accomplished little of the centralizing "reform from above" seen in such places as Egypt and Turkey, the Pahlevi shahs did succeed at centralization, but in a manner that eventually undid them. Reza Khan, a self-made cavalry officer who seized power in the confused aftermath of World War I, created a greatly enlarged army and civilian bureaucracy, both centered in Teheran. This new governmental class, and the businessmen who fed off it, were at the heart of Reza Khan's modernization program. After the fashion of Mustafa Kemal Ataturk, Reza Shah—as he was known after his coronation—forbade the *chador* and other traditional dress. He ordered Iranian men to wear European suits and hats. He also forbade all photographs of the camel, which he considered a backward beast. But Reza Shah was a third-rate Ataturk, who harbored in his very person the backwardness and contradictions he so hated, sleeping on carpets on the palace floor until the day he died, using his power to amass vast wealth, and ordering a firing squad to execute a donkey that once strayed onto his newly acquired property. Reza Shah's centralized modernization merely created "two cultures" in Iran, writes Keddie, the Westernizing culture of the cities and the increasingly embittered peasant culture of the villages. Then, as oil wealth accumulated and urbanization accelerated, the village came to the city and, in 1979, vanquished it.

◎   ◎   ◎

IRAN WASN'T TURKEY, in other words. The Anatolian plateau, because it was less arid than its Iranian counterpart, held enough interconnected areas of settlement so that the difference between village and town, as great as it was, was still less pronounced than in Iran. Far more important, Anatolia has a thousand miles of frontage on the Mediterranean, besides a long Black Sea coast that linked it throughout history to the Balkans and

European Russia. More compact internally and closer to Europe externally, the Anatolian plateau, despite its many drawbacks, formed a more fluent venue for an experiment in Western state-building than did the Iranian plateau—especially when this Western model of a highly secular and centralized state was imposed upon Iranians at gunpoint and breakneck speed by the Pahlevi shahs.

The toppling of the shah, like the downfall of communism in the Soviet Union, is an example of how when states become too rigid over too great a land mass, they crack open at the seams. Iran under the ayatollahs, with its competing centers of power—the *majlis* (parliament); the elected president and his cabinet; the mullahs and their buddies in the security services; and the governors in the various cities—is far more flexible and chaotic than the Iran of the Pahlevis. The Iranian Revolution and the counterrevolution a decade later in the Soviet Union may therefore foreshadow an era in which other rigid states will collapse, bring varying degrees of chaos, or perhaps newer, more ingenious forms of authoritarianism. Larger populations and intense competition for jobs and other opportunities may make the possibility of stable democracies problematic in lands where they have never existed.

The chaotic interregnum imposed by the Islamic Revolution has weakened the Iranian state even as Greater Persia, in a cultural and economic sense, is emerging after the collapse of the Soviet Union and Afghanistan. The borders, for example, between Iran and the newly independent former-Soviet Republic of Turkmenistan in the northeast, and between Iran and Afghanistan in the east, are porous and bristling with trade and the movement of peoples. Persia thus expands as its central government weakens and Turkic races renew their historic infiltration of the Iranian plateau. These were the issues I would return to in my journey across northern Iran and Central Asia.

◎   ◎   ◎

WHILE THE GEOGRAPHIC and demographic sources of the Islamic Revolution were fundamental, as well as long in gestation, specific ingredients ignited the uprising and determined its precise character.

The distortions of Iranian urbanization were inflamed by the oil boom. From 1963 through the late 1970s, annual per capita income in Iran rose from two hundred to one thousand dollars in real terms, one of history's most dramatic increases, according to Keddie. But the disparity in incomes between rich and poor widened. The poor got richer, but the rich got much, much richer. Then, in 1973, thanks partly to the prodding of the shah, the Organization of Petroleum Exporting Countries (OPEC) quadrupled oil prices. The shah increased government spending accordingly, as 88 percent of development and building funds came from the new oil revenues. The economy overheated and inflation followed. So did further migration to the cities, along with traffic jams and power blackouts, as a pseudomodern infrastructure failed to accommodate breakneck development. In mid-1977 the shah launched an anti-inflation program. Suddenly, large-scale unemployment shook the country after years of dramatically rising expectations. Then *boom*. The rest is history.

The revolution's anti-Americanism had another cause, one peculiar to Persia. Iranians, unlike Arabs, never experienced formal colonization by the West, which led, in the cases of Syria, Lebanon, Jordan, and Algeria, for example, to the invention of states with artificial borders. Persia has been an ethnically defined nation since antiquity, though one with shifting frontiers. But this Persian state was often very weak, partly because of its strategic location between the Russian and British empires in Asia. Thus, in the nineteenth and twentieth centuries, Persia was frequently carved into spheres of economic influence. For example, in 1872, the Briton Julius de Reuter (founder of the news agency) obtained exclusive rights to Iran's mineral wealth, to its railroads and streetcars, to its irrigation works and other agricultural construction, to the running of its national bank, and to major industrial projects. Lord Curzon called it one of the most extraordinary surrenders of a kingdom's wealth to foreign hands in recorded history. Persia evolved as proud and uncolonized; yet Persians themselves had reason to feel especially exploited, precisely because they lacked the protection often afforded by colonial status.

Furthermore, the centers of this nefarious exploitation—the foreign embassy compounds—were situated in the heart of Teheran, hidden behind high walls, which enhanced their mystery. In no other city in the world have walled foreign embassies so dominated the downtown area for so long as in Teheran.

Each morning in Teheran, I drove past the Russian and British compounds; each stretched for one long city block or more. What went on behind those walls? What was it like inside? Since I never once visited any of these foreign embassies, I gradually became as curious as the Iranians. It was easy to imagine the insult they felt. And for a people so long exploited by foreigners, it was natural that the sense of mystery engendered by the fortresslike architecture of these compounds would, over time, give rise to paranoia and ideas of conspiracy.

For instance, the November 4, 1979, seizure of the U.S. embassy by radical Iranian students was, in part, inspired by a belief that the U.S. diplomats inside the compound were planning a coup against Khomeini. Like many Iranian conspiracy theories, this one contained a grain of truth that had been stretched out of all proportion. American diplomats were trying to make the best of a bad situation by developing military and business ties with the new revolutionary regime, hoping to steer it in a more moderate direction. It would be unreasonable, however, to think that these diplomats could hatch a grand "plot" to topple Khomeini. But in 1953, as Iranians never stopped reminding me, the U.S. embassy in Teheran under Ambassador Loy Henderson had spearheaded a CIA coup that overthrew the Iranian premier, Mohammed Mosadeq, because of his attempts to nationalize Western oil companies in Iran. "The anti-Americanism of our revolution would not have been possible without the Mosadeq episode," Mr. Kashan explained. "It told Iranians that the U.S. had replaced Great Britain as the new interfering power."

The long walls of the U.S. embassy compound are now scarred by graffiti, reading "The veto of a superpower is worse than the law of the jungle." Here a people who had never been colonized were saying, *We want our independence.* When American-Iranian relations are reestablished, it might be wise either to tear down the walls of the U.S. embassy or move the embassy to an out-of-the-way suburb.

An Iranian official whom I met through Mr. Kashan got up from behind his big desk at one of the ministries and sat in the chair beside me, so that nothing came between us. He looked down at his red prayer beads and said in the tired voice of a depleted revolutionary: "The shah was the culmination of centuries of foreign interference, and the fear caused by the constant violation of our land by Turkic nomads and others—all further aggravated by what happened to Mosadeq. But this is something we have now gotten out of our system thanks to the revolution, like a boil building up over decades that has been lanced. This is why anti-Americanism is completely gone from Iran. The hard-liners only posture now. The slogan 'Death to America' and the obligation to wear *chadors* will be the last things to go, since they have become the principal symbols of the revolution. But you will see: In the years to come, America will no longer be an issue in Iran. I say this as a revolutionary, as someone who has the deepest affection for Imam Khomeini."

◎   ◎   ◎

AN UPROOTED SUBPROLETARIAT, spawned by the modernization programs of Reza Shah and his son, brought down a monarchy and founded a new state, whose altar was a *Hosseinieh* of stadium lights and machine-made carpets in place of the late shah's "White Palace," with its gilded furniture and hand-made silk. The hand with the Five Fingers of the Holy Mantle replaced the Peacock Throne. Like Turkey, the Persia of the future will be a blue-collar variant of the Persia whose poetry I carried in my rucksack. The twenty-first century not only came early to the Iranian plateau—ahead of its arrival else-where in the Moslem Near East—but it also arrived with a violent jolt.

In the 1990s, the Iranian landscape finally stopped shaking and a new equilibrium could be discerned. The banners of white cloth, with the blood red, slanted Arabic letters peculiar to Persia, that hung from the buildings and street lights in Teheran were not proclaiming the "Great Satan" America, but the need for each Iranian family to have only two children, in order to reduce the 3.49 percent annual population growth rate that threatened to double the Iranian population yet again in twenty years. Abortions are now possible, and Iranian factories are now produc-ing contraceptives. In the same edition of *The Teheran Times* that carried a lead article entitled "Shatter Myth of Everlasting Power of West: Espe-cially that of the United States," there was an advertisement for "Ameri-can conversation taught by an American—please call . . ." in addition to advertisements for airplane and courier connections to Western Europe and the U.S. A popular book in stores near Teheran University is *Contem-porary American Slang*. In the basement of the Central Bank, the crown jewels and the Peacock throne itself have been put back on display for the public, though only for two days a week. The shah's former palace is open too, without a trace of revolutionary propaganda to mar the exhibits. Ira-nians stroll through the adjacent royal gardens to enjoy the roses and the nightingales. Iran has always been a land of harsh contrasts. The rich and variegated hues of traditional Persia are now melding with the stark monochrome of political Islam. Will the hand with the Five Fingers of the Holy Mantle continue to hold sway? Or will that be toppled too? What new forces are emerging? Are new upheavals ahead?

12

Bazaar States

"I REALLY GET A fever when I think of that day. I was prepared to be murdered, if it was necessary to protect the Imam. Three times the crowds shook the car and almost lifted it in the air—once at Teheran University, once in south Teheran, and once at the cemetery. But I was only concerned with the Imam. My own life was nothing. The Imam never showed fear, or any other emotion whatsoever."

February 1, 1979, was the most important day in the life of Mohsen Rafighdoost. On that day, Ayatollah Khomeini returned to Iran by plane from Paris after fifteen years in exile imposed by the shah, who had abdicated two weeks earlier, on January 16. The route from the airport to downtown Teheran was lined with adoring millions. Rafighdoost pulled his car up to near plane-side. He would be Khomeini's driver, as well as the chief of Khomeini's personal security detail.

"What kind of car was it?" I asked.

Rafighdoost's eyes flashed. His face exploded in a self-satisfied grin. "A Chevy Blazer," he said. He continued his recollections of that momentous day:

"One of the oppressed of south Teheran broke open the door of the car as I was driving, and shouted abuse about the shah into the Imam's ear.

I was about to deal harshly with the man when the Imam told me, 'Just drive slowly, leave this fellow as he is, let him express his feelings.' You see how gentle the Imam was with the people!

"Crowds were all over the car, touching and hanging on to it as we moved. I felt the car bump slightly. I thought I had run over someone's leg. The Imam told me to stop, and get the injured person's name to arrange compensation. But the old man whom I had injured said, 'How much should I pay for the honor of being run over by the Imam's car?'

"The first night back in Teheran the Imam slept in a school. Then he moved to a *Hosseinieh*. I remember the crowds watching the Imam pray that first night. Thousands of eyes were upon him. But he prayed as if no one was there. Nothing affected him," Rafighdoost said in deepest admiration, while nodding his head and staring hard at me.

Rafighdoost seemed every bit the bodyguard. Energy and aggression rippled from his compact, slightly stocky physique, marred only by a protruding gut, as he sat at the edge of his chair, tapping his foot and banging his thigh with his fist and nodding his head whenever he had a point to make. He had a short salt-and-pepper beard and thin straight hair of the same color, which was only now, in his mid-fifties, showing signs of receding. His profile was vaguely simian, in a way that made him look more menacing but without making him ugly. His small, beetle-shell eyes radiated a playful dangerousness.

Rafighdoost straddled the border between suave and sleazy. Had he been wearing a tie, he could have passed for a nightclub bouncer rather than the Ayatollah's bodyguard. He wore a designer shirt, a well-tailored black sports jacket, and gray slacks. His beard was neatly clipped. Yet he had no socks and wore a pair of rubber beach thongs: an attractive variety of good quality, like the kind sold through the L.L. Bean catalogue. He apologized for the thongs. "I forgot that a visitor was expected. They are more comfortable to work in."

When I entered his office, Rafighdoost, reclining in his chair, his feet on the desk, was working on his desktop computer. Stacks of notes and documents cluttered his desk, on which a pair of reading glasses—with fashionable frames—lay. Iran, somewhat like Turkey, but less like Africa and the Nile Valley, represented a relatively energetic domain with a cooler climate, where offices were used for real work rather than the display of petty bureaucratic power. In Iran it was not a disgrace to be found actually writing at your desk. Even by Iranian standards, however, this was an impressive desk, and an impressive office, with good olive-gray chairs and a Sony television set.

Rafighdoost was definitely a man of parts, and a very dynamic one at that, as formidable with his computer as he must have been with his fists. As Rafighdoost's rubber thongs indicated, his fashion consciousness ended where his work began. He had not only been Khomeini's chief bodyguard, but he also helped create from scratch the Revolutionary Guards that brutally crushed secular moderates and the leftist Mujahidin Khalq (People's Holy Warriors), among other "enemies" of the Islamic Revolution. Rafighdoost now controlled the Bonyad Mostazafin (Foundation of the Oppressed), Iran's largest holding company, comprising eight hundred different firms, which was established with money confiscated from the shah's family. One Iranian, no fan of Rafighdoost, calls this foundation—ostensibly meant to help the poor—"the greatest cartel in history." Rafighdoost is worth tens or perhaps even hundreds of millions of dollars.

When I had entered his office, he offered me his hand as if extending it to a crowd. He had little modesty. He knew his importance.

◎   ◎   ◎

HOW RAFIGHDOOST GOT to be behind the wheel of that Chevy Blazer the day Khomeini returned to Iran, how he got control of a substantial part of the shah's fortune, and how he converted that fortune into an even bigger financial empire is a matter of socioeconomic class. Rafighdoost is a *bazaari*, the class of people who made the Iranian Revolution.

Bazaaris are the people who work in a *bazaar*, a Persian word that means "market." Westerners use it interchangeably with the Arabic word *souk* for markets throughout Moslem North Africa and the Near East. The bazaar, or souk, is often the first place a tourist goes, to buy souvenirs and to lose him- or herself in serpentine alleys lined with shops that sometimes are under picturesque archways as, for example, in Tunis and Jerusalem. For tourists, such traditional markets evoke the cliché-mystery of the "fabulous" East. Though the worker in a hole-in-the-wall bazaar factory is certainly in a different position from a big moneylender in the market, both the factory worker and the moneylender are *bazaaris*, because they are both involved in petty trade of a traditional, or a nearly traditional, type, centered around the bazaar and its Islamic culture. Although Western goods are sold in the bazaar and *bazaaris* sell souvenirs

to Western tourists and smile before their cameras, Westernization—
supermarkets, department stores, machine-made goods, and large
banks—threatens the *bazaaris*' livelihood, and the smile before the camera, therefore, may often be deceptive.

Bazaaris, as a threatened class, tend to exist in places where the society is in the midst of an awkward modernization, where the bazaar is in
some stage of transition between the world of *A Thousand and One Nights*
and that of the suburban shopping mall, where the lightning sparks of the
welder singe the timeless image of turbaned men inhaling tobacco from
hubble-bubbles.

The Moslem Brotherhood—the Ikhwan—in Egypt is heavily
backed by *bazaaris*, for while it is the university-educated men of peasant
background who constitute that half-formed, "narrowly educated" class
of people so dangerous to pro-Western regimes in the Near East, it is
likewise the educated sons of *bazaaris*, a slight step up on the social lad-
der, who often lead these narrowly educated men in their efforts to topple an established order: again, like the Ikhwanis I had encountered in
Egypt.

The Near East at the end of the twentieth century is a region in great
social turmoil and economic transition. It is a region where *bazaaris*, a
kind of Islamic petty bourgeoisie, are important. "*Bazaaris* have the most
radical prejudices. They deal with foreigners, but only for the sake of
making money. They are the traditional ally of the clergy against the
Baha'is[1] and the Pepsi generation," observed an Iranian friend. "Rafighdoost," explained another Iranian, "is an absolute *bazaari* through and
through": a boy of the streets who learned math with a scratch pad at his
father's fruit stand. In Khomeini's Iran, the close links between mullahs
and bazaar merchants made it possible for a clever bodyguard like Rafighdoost to become a financier.

What distinguishes Iranian *bazaaris* from those in other fast-
changing societies in the Islamic world has been their close links with the
high-ranking clergy, or *ulama*, a relationship that developed gradually

---

[1]Baha'is have been horribly persecuted by the clerical regime, which sees them as apos-
tates, unworthy of the official status that Christians and Jews have enjoyed in fundamentalist Iran. Baha'ism is an offshoot of Shi'ism. Interestingly, it emerged in the
nineteenth century under the early impact of the industrialized West in Iran, and is
therefore especially hated by those Iranians who see themselves as threatened by the
West.

during the nineteenth century under the rule of the Qajar shahs. Nikki Keddie writes in *Roots of Revolution*:

> Ulama and bazaaris often belonged to the same families; much ulama income came from levies paid mainly by bazaaris; the guilds often celebrated religious or partly religious ceremonies for which the services of ulama were needed; and piety and religious observance were among the signs of bazaar standing or leadership. (Even today respectable bazaar shopkeepers are often addressed as "Hajji," whether or not the speaker knows if the addressee has made a pilgrimage justifying this form of address.) Entry into the ulama through study was an avenue of upward social mobility and entailed more respect than entry into Qajar service. Mosques and shrines [located close to the bazaar] were a major area of *bast* (refuge) for individuals and groups that feared government arrest or harassment.

But because the *bazaari*, as one Iranian observed, is a businessman, "his idea of religion is different from that of the cleric. The *bazaari* is willing to bend the rules of religion for the sake of finance." The so-called hypocrisy and corruption of the Iranian clergy often stems from the *bazaari* backgrounds of many of the mullahs.

"Describe a stereotypical *bazaari*," I asked a long-time foreign resident of Teheran who speaks Persian. He answered:

"A *bazaari* is a fat guy with meaty hands and fingers like kebabs, with gold rings on them. He sits in his shop and sips tea. He trades. He makes a lot of money and he prays several times a day. He comes home at night to a big, expensive house with nothing of taste in it, where he has a wife who slaves for him."

"Yes, I am a *bazaari*," a vendor in the Teheran bazaar told me. "I buy and sell things."

"In other words, you are a thief," interjected the vendor next to him, laughing.

"A *bazaari* will say to himself, 'I am a man of God who prays very often, so if I say that such and such a carpet that I wish to sell to you is worth so-many tomans², that is the true worth of the carpet, since a religious man like me would never lie. Because the *bazaari* is religious, he

---

²A toman is a unit of ten rials.

believes that he is always right," explained Vahid, the son of a mullah in Teheran, who then gave me another example of *bazaari* behavior:

"The word for beard in Persian can be *pashm*, which also means 'wool.' The *bazaari*, while stroking his beard, will say to a customer regarding a carpet for sale, 'Yes, this is made of very good wool.' "

The bazaar where Rafighdoost grew up is representative of the awkward modernization common to much of the Near East. It is a labyrinthine world of corrugated-iron roofs, brick archways, and plate glass in the midst of the poor working-class region of south Teheran that lacks any trace of beauty—except for the eighteenth-century Imam Khomeini Mosque (formerly the Shah Mosque) at its center—and filled with every manner of goods, from *chadors* and carpets, to pots and pans, to radios and television sets, to American candy bars.

Rafighdoost is not just a *bazaari* but a *meydani* (a person of the square, or market)—someone who has worked in the fruit and vegetable market and who therefore has few or no business connections of any kind with Westerners or their companies as, for example, a seller of expensive carpets, or of electronic goods in the bazaar, would have. Yet Rafighdoost's clan, while not Westernized, is not unsophisticated: Members of his extended family also number doctors and engineers. Rafighdoost's brother runs another of the large revolutionary foundations established with confiscated money from the shah. Rafighdoost's son is studying to be a cleric.

"I was born in south Teheran, near the bazaar, to a very religious family close to the Imam. I was always pro-Imam. I am a self-made man. I was not allowed to enter university because I was expelled from high school in 1953, when I was thirteen, for pro-Mosadeq activities. Anti-shah sentiment was something I learned in my home growing up. . . . In 1976 I was jailed for political reasons. Four months before the revolution, in 1978, I was released when the people stormed the prisons (as part of the series of demonstrations that culminated in the shah's downfall). Immediately after leaving prison, I became a contact point for antiregime people, and for distributing the Imam's decrees from Paris.[3] I was also hiding people from the shah's police.

"When the Imam first decided to return to Iran [before the shah's abdication], a revolutionary council was organized. I was given the task of

---

[3] In 1978, Khomeini moved his place of exile from An Najaf, in Iraq, to Paris after the shah put pressure on the Iraqi government.

logistics and personal security for the Imam. That's when I decided that I myself would be the Imam's driver. . . .

"It was soon after the Imam returned. I was the minister of the Revolutionary Guards. Myself, along with the head of the civil police and the head of the gendarmes, were to meet with the Imam. As the meeting began there was a commotion at the door. I went to see. There was an old man holding a bag of almonds who said he had a message for the Imam. 'What message?' I asked him. He said he wanted to give the almonds as a gift to the Imam. I related this to the Imam, who then told the three of us to leave: The Imam was now too tired to discuss security issues. Instead, the Imam just wanted to meet the old man. Judge for yourself the goodness of the Imam!" he said, banging his thigh and nodding at me.

"Know that the people in Iran are now completely free, so far as the laws of Islam permit. They have economic freedom and social justice. I have myself destroyed slums and shantytowns with money from this foundation. But there are still foreign elements who want to hurt our democracy." His expression suddenly turned sour. I thought of Morier's description of a holier-than-thou Iranian in *Hajji Baba*—"the downcast eye, the hypocritical ejaculation . . ." But I also thought of what a Washington-based analyst of Iran had told me:

"Rafighdoost is a new-age *bazaari*, with few of the redeeming virtues of his forefathers. He is a mobster-trader—a dark, rootless master-monopolist."

I asked Rafighdoost about the financial particulars of the Foundation of the Oppressed.

"The Bonyad [Foundation] is made up of seven independent organizations divided into eight hundred different companies. Their activities include industrial mining, housing construction, transportation, hotels, and tourism. In 1993, we made a profit of two hundred fifty billion rials," roughly $100 million at the free market rate of exchange. "The first part of our profits go for the victims of the shah and the wounded in the eight-year war with Iraq. The second part is for high schools in poor areas, for public health clinics, for clothes for five hundred thousand needy students. . . . The third part is for re-investing. We have fifteen new plants under construction in poor and remote areas of the country."

The foundation's commitment to the needy and the war-wounded I did not doubt. The amputee who operated the elevator that took me up to

Rafighdoost's office was only one of a number of handicapped young men I saw working there. When I mentioned this observation, Rafighdoost was delighted. "You see how determined I am to help those injured in the war!"

But the Foundation of the Oppressed, as the largest holding company in an oil-producing country of 65 million people, had huge real estate, cash, and other assets. It was a state within a state, in which it was impossible to determine just what was going on. The foundation's headquarters, where I met with Rafighdoost, consisted of three new buildings of polished white stone: One was sixteen stories high and each of the other two buildings had ten stories. I had to pass through two checkpoints, one of which comprised guardhouses and vehicle barriers, in order to enter the complex. It was more impressive than any government ministry I saw in Teheran.

Were the amputees employed inside—along with the charity work and the whole aura of do-goodism as exemplified by the very name, Foundation of the Oppressed—merely facades, like the chemical-weapons facility in Iraq that reportedly operated under the cover of a factory producing milk? Was the foundation's emphasis on helping the "oppressed" the tactical equivalent of putting a terrorist training facility near a school or hospital, as in Lebanon?

I asked such questions because the Foundation of the Oppressed, like the other revolutionary foundations established with the shah's money, was answerable only to the "Supreme Leader" of Iran, Ayatollah Ali Khamenei, at whose home Rafighdoost says he goes to pray. Iran's elected president, Hashemi Rafsanjani, and his cabinet had no oversight or control over the foundation's activities. The Central Bank of Iran's ability to tax, or to affect the foreign currency flows of the foundation, was close to nil. Who knew to whom and to what groups in the Middle East and elsewhere Rafighdoost may have been sending checks? Only Ayatollah Khamenei knew. His photograph hung in a large and ornate gold frame in Rafighdoost's office, next to a similarly framed photograph of Imam Khomeini. Conspicuously absent was a picture of President Rafsanjani, who heads a cabinet that includes American-educated technocrats, some of whom are trying to move Iran closer to the West.

BUT THE POSSIBILITY that Rafighdoost may have been operating a financial and logistics clearinghouse for international terrorists was less intriguing to me than the possibility that the Foundation of the Oppressed represented a new kind of economic organization, in a new kind of emerging state—a state better suited to the porous borders and political chaos of a region where the empire to the north (the Soviet Union) had collapsed into weakly governed mafia fiefdoms in Central Asia; where the state to the east (Afghanistan) had disintegrated into landlocked emirates based on drug trafficking; where the state to the west (Iraq), an artifice of European colonialism, was a veritable penitentiary that soon faced explosion; and where the state to the northwest (Turkey) was engaged in a violent struggle between Turks and Kurds over the future of its Anatolian land mass.

I thought about all of this because while the radical Islamic character of Iran was temporary—the result of a revolution whose effects were eroding—and while the future of Rafighdoost's foundation was dependent upon the survival of the revolutionary regime, the way in which business was now being conducted in Iran was likely to survive, in one fashion or another, whatever happened with the country's politics.

Might the legacy of the Islamic Revolution be an economy that mirrors the informality and directionlessness of the bazaar? *Bazaaris* had created a political and economic system that was a larger version of the labyrinthine world of the south Teheran market. The revolutionary foundations were like huge wholesalers and retailers with which the smaller shopkeepers were not in a position to compete, because they couldn't afford the bribes required and they didn't have the connections. The alliance between the *bazaaris* and the Shi'ite clergy now existed on a macrostate level, between the likes of Rafighdoost and Ali Khamenei, rather than on the street level between the shopkeepers and the neighborhood mullahs. As in the bazaar, the rules were far more flexible than any state system familiar to a Westerner could ever tolerate. Some enterprises could import or export dollars, some couldn't. Some could do it at this rate of exchange, others at that rate of exchange: It all depended upon whom you knew. As in the bazaar, short-term advantage was the rule, long-term investment the exception.

Furthermore, the informal sidewalk-banking system in Iran was often more reliable than the official banks, where you might deposit money one day and find that you couldn't withdraw it the next, unless you bribed the teller a certain percentage of your holdings.[4] Huge profits were

---

[4] See *Wall Street Journal* reporter Peter Waldman's account of the Iranian economy, listed in the bibliography.

being hidden and spent on who knows what. A truly effective income tax system didn't exist for the well-off and even for the not-so-well-off. But that didn't mean the poor were being forgotten. As in the bazaar, all the merchants gave alms. On the streets of all Iranian cities the revolutionary authorities had installed charity boxes in which, I noticed, people frequently dropped money. I didn't see more than a few beggars while I was in Iran.

Rafighdoost, I mean to suggest, was still the fruit seller, one who kept his books with a computer rather than with a scratch pad. As a truly devout Moslem, he handed over a generous portion of his proceeds to the needy. He dealt with the authorities in an informal and after-hours basis: Here was a murky world of deals and mutual favors where written laws had yet to be invented.

     ◎   ◎   ◎

THE BAZAAR WASN'T so much filling the void in a postrevolutionary society as characterizing the society. By the mid-1990s the system of competing power centers bequeathed by the revolution—as a reaction to the iniquities of one-man rule by the shah—was weakening. "We are seeing a disintegration of power in Iran," a cabinet member told me. "There is total confusion. For each small measure you must spend days or weeks bargaining to assemble a coalition." (For example, because there are 1.5 million automobiles in a metropolitan area of 10 million, with 150,000 new vehicles per year, Teheran was registering atmospheric lead concentrations ten times higher than World Health Organization standards. Reducing traffic meant raising the price of gasoline in this oil-rich country, where car fuel, at the equivalent of three American cents per liter, was literally cheaper than water. But a proposal for a marginal rise of fuel prices nearly collapsed during months of parliamentary bickering.)

At the same time, nothing, or no one, appeared likely to provide political stability if the regime collapsed. The monarchy, an institution with which Iranians had a troubled history before the shah, was discredited. The military was said to be somewhat divided. As for democracy, perhaps it already existed: Witness the bickering over the fuel price. The freely elected parliament was a scene of attacks against the regime. So were some Persian-language newspapers. True, the coalition of radical mullahs and the security services could fail, leaving the parliament and the presidential cabinet in control. Such a development would improve the human rights situation, but given the intense factionalism of the 270-member parliament, it probably wouldn't lead to stability. And if, as was much more likely in the short run, the opposite happened? If the power of the mullahs under Ali Khamenei increased, then so would the influence of the *bazaaris*, and of their way of doing things. Nor was there a charismatic figure, like Khomeini in the 1970s, hovering about. The situation recalled the period following World War I, when Reza Khan emerged from the shadows of the military to provide order in the country. Except that instead of 10 million people to control, there were now more than 60 million.

Might this be normalcy? I wondered while I was with Rafighdoost. Might this be *it*? Might Iran be a culture, like so many others, that was too sophisticated for the one-man thugocracies like those next door in Iraq and Syria yet not sophisticated enough for a reasonably functioning and stable democracy? Was Iran, like so many political cultures, evolving into something neither authoritarian nor democratic nor even organized as a state is normally thought to be? Was the twenty-first century to see the implosion of political Islam and the rise of the Islamic bazaar state?

Indeed, nowhere in the Moslem world at the end of the twentieth century had Islam been able to make the conceptual leap from a unique way of life to a unique and successful way of governing and of organizing a national economy. In Iran, political Islam had meant, in practice, a nationalization of state enterprises and the expansion of the welfare state to help the poor. Because that proved too expensive, Iran was now beginning a painful privatization program—a familiar story certainly not unique to Islamic states. Dr. Ebrahim Sheibany, a vice-governor of the Iranian Central Bank who was educated in the U.S., showed me an interesting graph in his office. Whereas in 1977, on the eve of the revolution, the Iranian upper class accounted for 52 percent of total wealth in the country, in 1992 it still accounted for 45 percent. But with inflation now running at 22 percent and the welfare state under pressure, the distribution of wealth was reverting to what it had been in 1977. Contrary to the perception encouraged by the many reports of Revolutionary Guards breaking into wealthy villas in north Teheran, the Islamic Revolution did not destroy the rich "as a class" in the way that the Bolshevik Revolution did, though many wealthy families had been persecuted. In other words, the foreign businessman who had told me that the rich were still rich and the poor still poor was not exaggerating. The revolution was a muddle. The *bazaari*-run foundations, with no real equivalents outside of Iran, constituted the only unique economic institution to emerge from revolutionary Iran.

◎   ◎   ◎

AS A *BAZAARI*, Rafighdoost is nothing if not flexible and expedient. "Was the break in relations between the United States and Iran something that was destined to end?" I asked him. In the Near East, such a question is never answered directly. Still, his circuitous reply was intriguing.

"The United States can't forgive us for the occupation of its embassy here. It's true, the students invaded your embassy against all international rules. Yet they did it because your diplomats were involved in planning a military coup against Imam Khomeini. The documents found by the students prove it. If the Imam wanted to support our young people, he could easily have killed the diplomats. After all, the shah killed thousands of people. But the Imam dealt with the students wisely and dexterously. In the end, not one drop of blood was shed. And the length of time it took the Imam to arrange the release allowed for a crisis atmosphere, which the U.S. manipulated to increase its influence in the region. Your government should thank us.

"We can also prove, quite simply, that the U.S. and Israel intrigued with Iraq to assist its invasion of our territory in 1980, starting an eight-year war.

"U.S. foreign policy is based on superiority. [President Bill] Clinton now says we help the IRA [Irish Republican Army], while he is inviting IRA officials to America. How hypocritical! And because the U.S. still blames us for everything, America is keeping us from solving our economic problems. We have only two demands of you, then everything can be fine between our two nations—one: release our assets and blocked money; two: don't get involved in our internal affairs, and declare this publicly."

"That's all?" I asked him.

He nodded affirmatively.

The two demands were actually interrelated, since the second demand, besides highlighting Iranian sensitivity toward foreign interference in the past, was—I gathered from the context of the conversation—a veiled request for the U.S. to *stop pressuring the Europeans to deny Iran long-term loans.* Iran, in short, needed money.

What about the situation in the Middle East regarding the peace process with Israel? I asked.

No, Rafighdoost had no demands in that area. This was confirmed by an interview I had the following day with Iran's deputy foreign minister, Mahmoud Vaezi. Iranian newspapers were at the moment screaming blood about the "traitor," Yasser Arafat, who had made peace with the despised Zionists. But Vaezi and other officials assured me that Iran would take no hostile action to impede the Palestinian-Israeli peace treaty, especially if it would help normalize relations with the U.S. "For sure, there is no enmity between the Iranian people and the American people," stated Vaezi. As for a larger peace settlement with Israel, the deputy foreign minister said:

"There would be no change in our friendly policy toward Syria even if [Syrian President Hafez] Assad meets with [Israeli Prime Minister Yitzhak] Rabin. We will not interfere with the internal affairs of Syria if Assad decides to have such relations [with Israel] based on his country's interests and the will of his people."

Iran's support of the terrorist Hezbollah in Lebanon and of Hamas in Israel's occupied territories told me that Vaezi and Rafighdoost were lying. I also assumed that the Iranians were behind the spate of bombings in Argentina and elsewhere of Jewish targets, that followed the Washington meeting between Rabin and Jordan's King Hussein in July 1994. Or was this typical *bazaari* behavior—what our culture considers lying and theirs merely haggling? You hold out for a tough price by planting a few explosives, but you also make it known that you are willing to settle on other terms, if you have to. Or was the deputy foreign minister being especially conciliatory because of his own particular politics and background?

Deputy Foreign Minister Vaezi, like the bank vice-governor Dr. Sheibany, like Mr. Kashan and others in the middle and upper levels of the Iranian government with whom I met, were all American-educated, mainly in California. They came from a different world from *bazaaris* like Rafighdoost and the various mullahs, who had a more limited formal education and little or no exposure to the West. (Mr. Kashan, who studied in San Francisco and also worked with the clergy, straddled the two worlds.) Both types of Iranians had worked for the shah's downfall. However, whereas the revolution had turned out more or less the way many *bazaaris* had intended it to, the Iranian students whose American educations were paid for by the shah—and who then turned against him—had been seriously mugged by reality. Rather than the liberal democracy toward which they aspired, they had gotten the skulduggery of the bazaar. The nostalgia these former students, now in early middle age, sometimes displayed for the U.S. was often poignant. One Iranian doctor, who worked with the wife of a cabinet minister at a factory producing medical syringes, confided that he still rooted for the Texas A&M football team.

But the *bazaaris*, Rafighdoost implied, could also make peace with America. After all, when had they ever let religion interfere with their financial interests?

One Iran specialist in the U.S. government believes that men like Rafighdoost will "first use violence in an attempt to sabotage Arab-Israeli talks. Who knows, maybe the bombs will derail the peace process. If they don't, if Syria actually makes peace with Israel, then Iran will be able to walk away from the whole problem. The mullahs can tell the faithful, 'We tried our best,' then reestablish relations with Uncle Sam. In this way, the wider opening of the Syrian track of Arab-Israel negotiations may well lead to the opening of an American-Iranian dialogue."

◎　　　◎　　　◎

ANOTHER *BAZAARI* WHOM I met in Teheran was the president of Iran's chamber of commerce, A.N.S. Khamooshi. In parliament, Khamooshi had represented a clerical faction with ties to "money circles" in the country's major bazaars. While the Iranian government officials who studied in America were always curious about me, plying me with friendly questions, Khamooshi, much more so than Rafighdoost, had only ice in his eyes, and a lecture to deliver.

"If we hear the sound of the oppressed, we in Iran, as a great power for thousands of years, cannot be silent. We will help oppressed people anywhere with money and propaganda. . . . We are the motherland of the Near East, with over 60 million people. We believe we can bring peace to all the surrounding countries if only those troublemakers [in the United States, in Israel, in Saudi Arabia . . .] would allow us. This is the most strategic part of the world, America should not forget that. . . . Remember, too, that Azerbaijan, Turkmenistan, all of these places were once part of Iran. They are all Moslem. Their best way to the warm waters of the Persian Gulf and the Indian Ocean is through Iran. That is why prosperity from new oil discoveries in the Caucasus and in Central Asia will be good for us, especially as we are on the edge of adjusting our economy from a centralized to a market system."

Morteza Alviri, adviser to President Rafsanjani on free trade zones, filled in the details of Khamooshi's lecture. Alviri, like Deputy Foreign Minister Vaezi and others allied with Rafsanjani—but unlike Khamooshi, Rafighdoost, and other hard-line *bazaaris*—did not deliver a harsh speech. Instead, he calmly sketched out Greater Persia's long-range ambitions—ambitions that had much less to do with Islam than with Persia's historic position as a regional superpower. "We are in competition with Turkey over oil and transport routes," he told me. While Turkey was seeking to take advantage of Central Asia's future oil boom with roads and pipelines oriented in an east-to-west direction—that is, from Central Asia across the Caucasus to Anatolia and the Mediterranean— Iran envisaged two north-south trade corridors. One rail and road link would go from Ashqabad, the capital of Turkmenistan, southward to the Iranian city of Meshed, then across the desert to the Qeshm Island free zone in the Persian Gulf. The other Iranian route going south to the Persian Gulf would begin on the Caspian Sea coast, at the border between Iran and Azerbaijan.

"Even without new oil pipelines," Alviri explained, "once Central Asian oil begins to flow, we'll be able to cover all our consumption needs in the northern half of Iran by importing oil from just over our northern border, leaving all of our locally produced Persian Gulf oil to be exported from right where it is being pumped." Deputy Foreign Minister Vaezi chimes in: "Iran is the only bridge for Central Asia to Europe and North America. In history, most parts of this big region belonged to us. Turkey's geographical link with Central Asia is severed by Armenia. We have the advantage. We are ready."

In fact, while the government in Teheran makes impassioned statements in support of Palestinians and Bosnian Moslems, it is the unstable, often violent Caucasus—Armenia and Azerbaijan, Russia and Chechnya, and Georgia—that quietly elicits greater Iranian interest. Whether Turkey is able to establish an oil pipeline through the land of its historic enemy, Armenia, and whether northern, former-Soviet Azerbaijan with its untapped oil reserves can become an economic magnet for the millions of

Azeris inside Iran will affect the future of Iran and regional trade more than anything likely to occur between Israel and the Arabs, or in the Balkans. The modern Western state envisaged by Reza Khan at the beginning of the twentieth century had, by the end of the century, given way to the rule of the medieval bazaar and, perhaps, to the restoration of its age-old caravan routes.

1 3

◎   ◎   ◎

Qom's Last Tremors

TEHERAN SEEMED A city without end. Near its southern extremity stretched mile upon mile of poured-concrete apartment blocks and cheap office buildings, like rows of gravestones in the polluted heat. The air, heavy with sediment, was like a rock quarry immediately after a detonation. The outskirts of Egyptian and Turkish cities had looked no better. For an increasingly larger portion of humanity, such places are now not just home but the end of the rainbow: the ultimate step-up from a zinc-roofed shack in a shantytown. The *Hosseinieh* where Khomeini lay buried not far from these housing projects, was itself an example of this new kind of settlement. I was headed for the crucible of that new aesthetic, Qom, the holy Shi'ite city from which Khomeini had first emerged.

The last of the tombstone apartment blocks finally fell behind me. Then after a short, barren stretch came the gold cupola of Khomeini's tomb. Afterward, for the next two hours, nothing: the awesome nothingness of the Iranian plateau.

It starts with a bumpy, crusty plain the color of sulphur, layered with cracked sandstone mounds and turret-shaped rocks. The sandstone changes to a loose, brownish dirt littered with slag, then a gaunt, asbestos-gray volcanic tableland strewn with white salt deposits. This soon gives way to green outcroppings and lonely red pottery-colored mountain ranges. But all of this is a prologue for the sepulchral stillness of the salt beds: featureless, horizonless blazes of dryness where all perspective is lost. It is a landscape of abstractions, almost two-dimensional, without focal points, a landscape for advancing delusions of sterile glory.

"Another low ridge is climbed, another valley opens out, towards the southern end of which extends the belt of mingled brown and green that in the East signifies a large city," wrote Lord Curzon about the approach to Qom a hundred years ago. But now the approaches to Qom are marked by urban sprawl and the drab modernization that has come with the building of factories. The city now begins slightly beyond its original river location, on a pan of scoured earth and salt beds. First there is an industrial zone dominated by stone cutters; then a messy checkerwork of square houses made of stone and brown brick. The streets, lined with vehicle-repair shops, are crowded with old cars, noisy motorbikes, and Toyota pickups blowing fumes into an atmosphere already thick with dust and other debris. Rising above the haze of pollution looms a dome so spectacularly gold it appears black at the edges. It is framed by volcanic mountains of "peculiar sterility," according to Curzon.

The dome seems more unreal and holy on account of the industrial ugliness surrounding it. The carbon monoxide fumes suck additional air out of the wasteland at the city's edge, making the landscape—what Curzon referred to as the "consecrated dust of Kum"—appear that much more austere, and intolerant. Driving into Qom in 1994, I saw how the very starkness of the mullahs' rage reflected what had been happening in their society as revealed in the landscape. Rather than diminish the appeal of religion, in Iran modernization had escalated it. How much more beautiful, how much more otherworldly, was the dome precisely because of the fumes, a product of the scientific West that engulfed it.

Qom is the burial place of Fatima, the sister of Imam Reza, the eighth Shi'ite imam, who died in the early part of the ninth century. In succeeding centuries, Fatima's grave became a popular pilgrimage site, even after Tamerlane, the Turkic-speaking Mongol, riding south from his base in Samarkand, sacked the city in the late fourteenth century. The present shrine around Fatima's tomb was built by the great Safavid shah Abbas I (the Great) in the early seventeenth century and enlarged by his successors, anxious to provide a counterweight to Shi'ite pilgrimage centers in

An Najaf and Karbala in Mesopotamia, then under Ottoman occupation. Perhaps because Qom lies in the heart of Iran, near Teheran, and at the confluence of many important roads, it developed into a more important center for the Shi'ite clergy than did Meshed, where Imam Reza himself was buried, but which is situated in the extreme northeast of Iran.

As the political power of the Shi'ite clergy increased over the centuries following Safavid rule, Qom became a sort of second capital of Iran, and a place of refuge for holy men who had incurred the wrath of the country's secular rulers. In *The Adventures of Hajji Baba*, a dervish advises Hajji, who is in flight from the authorities: "You must go to Kom . . . as soon as you arrive there, lose not a moment in getting within the precincts of the sanctuary of the tomb of Fatimeh. You will then . . . be safe, even from the shah's power." Qom's aura was enhanced when, under the Safavids, Shi'ism became the official state religion of Persia, and many a Safavid and Qajar shah wanted to be buried in Qom. Qom, in Curzon's phrase, is "Persia's Westminster Abbey."

◎   ◎   ◎

"EVERYBODY LOOKED TOWARD Qom. . . . Whenever there was unhappiness and a crisis, people always started listening for the first signals from Qom. And Qom was rumbling," writes Kapuscinski in *Shah of Shahs*.

The year was 1963. A high-ranking local cleric already in his sixties, Ayatollah Khomeini, accused Shah Mohammed Reza Pahlevi of selling Iran out to the West. "The shah must go!" Khomeini declared. Demonstrations erupted throughout Iran. The shah's troops killed and wounded hundreds of protestors. Khomeini was exiled the next year, first to Turkey, then to An Najaf in Iraq, and finally to Paris, from where he returned to Iran in 1979 to found an Islamic state. The spirit of Qom has, in effect, been ruling Iran since then.

And the atmosphere of the city, I began to discover—comparing Qom to Teheran and, as I would later do, to Isfahan and Shiraz, where I was headed next—was unlike any other place in Iran. Yet Qom was recognizable to me. I had been in other holy cities, less intense versions of Qom, elsewhere in the Near East: Kairouan in Tunisia, An Najaf and Karbala in Mesopotamia (Iraq), and Jerusalem and Hebron in Israel. The late *New York Times* correspondent C. L. Sulzberger said about Jerusalem: "Beautiful as it is . . . one can see hate rising from its rosy-stoned hilltop as tangibly as one can see mystical passion rising above El Greco paintings of Toledo."

Though such intolerance is a feature of holy places everywhere—whether in the Orthodox Christian monasteries of south Serbia or in the Hindu temples of India's Ganges River valley—the relationship between mood and physical landscape is more manifest in the desert Near East, where the ubiquity of dust and the absence of water and greenery reciprocate the severity and self-imposed suffering of the people. In Qom, unlike in the other Iranian cities I visited, I noticed little greenery, few water channels, few attempts, in short, to sensualize the urban landscape in the way that Persians usually do so brilliantly. Qom was indubitably *of* the desert, separated from the Caspian Sea by the ten-thousand-foot-high wall of the Elborz range. Qom also has the grainy, Dickensian quality of industrial Assiut in Upper Egypt.

Qom, Curzon writes, "is much addicted to bigotry and superstition. No Jews or Parsis live here; and English ladies . . . have usually found it prudent to veil in public." Indeed, the wearing of the *chador* struck me as far more natural in Qom, worn as it is over the bodies of shy and frumpy women who eschew the lipsticks, perfume, and designer glasses of the women of Teheran and other cities, where the *chador* seemed artificial, a mandatory costume at a masquerade ball. Qom women tended to walk in packs, unlike women in other Iranian cities.

In Qom, writes Morier in *Hajji Baba*, if people "suppose you to be a *sufi* (free thinker) . . . they would tear you into little pieces, and then feel contented that they had got on another post on the high road to paradise." And here is Curzon: Qom "is one of the places where an accidental spark might still be fanned into a disagreeable flame."

But this had already happened in 1979, and since then Qom's effect on the rest of Iran had been diminishing. Qom seemed smaller and quieter, more provincial than its population of over half a million inhabitants two hours' drive from Teheran had led me to expect.

Then, suddenly, I heard a loud drumbeat. A religious procession was gathering on the eucalyptus-lined avenue, led by turbaned men with long cloaks and scruffy beards. Dozens of somber men crowded together, their hands on their hearts. Two of them were crying. A teenage boy carried a loudspeaker so that a mullah could address the crowd.

"A funeral procession," a passerby informed me.

"For whom?" I asked.

"For Mohammed Gawad."

"Who was he?" I asked again.

"The ninth imam," who died over a thousand years ago.

The expressions of despair did not look simulated. The sadness was real. This was power, faith so strong that emotion for someone dead more than a millennium flowed as naturally as if for a brother who had died yesterday.

As the crowd prayed, I realized that this was the first public prayer I had seen in Iran. Even at Khomeini's tomb, while people milled around, some quite reverentially, not that many actually prayed. Neither had I noticed people streaming into mosques in Teheran; nor would I in other Iranian cities, with the singular exception of Qom. Part of the reason for this is the Shi'ites' tendency to favor private prayer. In every hotel room I occupied in Iran, I noticed a plaque indicating the direction of Mecca, as well as a prayer carpet and a stone for touching your head to real earth while praying. Still, something seemed wrong. The Nile Valley had been oppressive with religiosity and throngs of praying men. So, too, to a much lesser extent, were parts of Anatolia. But Iran, despite Qom, did not seem to me a very religious country at all.

A former U.S. intelligence officer who spoke fluent Persian and a State Department official who served in the Peace Corps in Iran in the 1970s used similar language to explain this phenomenon, which I will paraphrase:

Religion is effectively mobilized into political action in Iran to a degree that you may not find in other Islamic countries. Otherwise, however, Iranians are not fanatical. That's why when the revolutionary fervor died down [in the mid-1980s] many Iranians stopped going to public mosques.

A lack of religiosity helps explain why alcohol at home is forbidden in Iran to a lesser degree than in Saudi Arabia. In Saudi Arabia, under the puritanical Wahabis, what is forbidden is supposed to be forbidden. In Iran, what is forbidden is allowed if it is good politics—that is, if it provides a loose enough atmosphere to help entice Westernized expatriates to return with their money.

In Qom I noticed a strong Arab influence in the way people looked. Many people in the streets lacked the sharp features of the Indo-European Persians, having instead the slightly more exaggerated curves and darker complexions of desert Semites. The Persian spoken here, even by the native Iranians, I was told, often has an Arabic inflection, the effect of years of Koranic study in Arabic. Qom's population is, in fact, composed of a significant number of Arabs, particularly Shi'ites from Iraq and else-where in the Gulf. Here Shi'ism and Islam, more than the concept of his-toric Persia, constitute the big tent under which people initially appeared to unite.

I walked into the sanctuary of Fatima, forbidden to non-Moslems. Because of my dark hair and complexion, I was not stopped by the guards at the door, who did not seem especially vigilant. The inner courtyard was a disappointment. Despite the blue faience, it lacked both the spectacular beauty that I would later see in Isfahan and the intense mystical aura of Imam Reza's tomb in Meshed, which I had visited in the 1970s, before the revolution. But Qom, more than a venue for architectural splendor, was a political power base for the Islamic Revolution. This stemmed, in part, from the religious seminaries where Khomeini himself had studied and taught.

◎ ◎ ◎

"MEN, HUMAN BEINGS, exhibit many different kinds of religious worship on this earth," began the student, his eyes like lit coals, constantly glancing heavenward. The student spoke Persian with a distinct, well-enunciated Arabic inflection, full of guttural stops that I recognized from my travels in the Arab world. I was sitting with a group of seminary students in a lovely courtyard surrounded by three levels of blue faience archways, amid carpets and piles of books, where the quietude was enhanced by the sound of birds. There was the passing, momentary aroma of mint and the crackle of prayer beads through fingers. Here at the Faizieh (Abundance of Goodness) School, Khomeini himself had sat for years, in the same spot perhaps, discussing similar issues. The student, a fellow in his mid-twenties, went on:

"Yet, however varied the ways of worshiping God, only one of them can be the correct way. We examine all of the other religions logically, and philosophically. We respect other beliefs and ideas: Christianity, Judaism. But, logically, we have had to conclude that only Islam is right. The Koran shows the only right way. We always use reason and logic in our inquiries. Still, if someone must use another path to God, it is up to each of us to choose his own fate." The student's black eyes rolled upward, as though thanking God for putting such compassionate and open-minded thoughts in his mouth. The other students nodded, but remained silent. This stu-dent doing the talking had an aura about him. His short, very thick black beard evolved perfectly from the hair on his head. His coffee-toned features were noble. He was short but muscular, and had an air of superiority: a little big man. He also had a way of moving his hand with a rapid lift of his eyes, as if he were preaching to a large audience, even though we were squatting on a carpet a few inches from each other. He appeared to see right through me, as if I were nothing. Continuing, he said:

"The goal of our study is to attain *feqh* [understanding]. We do this through *mobahetheh* [discussion]. A student must be able to show to his fellows that 'I know. I understand.' Our field of inquiry is very broad." His open palms moved outward from his body. "We study elocution, astrology, Greek philosophy, even medicine, since we read the works of Avicenna," the eleventh-century Persian physician and philosopher. He showed me a book, loosely translated as *Nations and Religions*, compiled in the Middle Ages, which he said was used by the students to examine the strengths and weaknesses of other faiths.

"What about history?" I asked.

"We read Ibn Khaldun," he said, referring to the medieval Arab scholar who, in 1377, wrote the *Muqaddimah*, the "Introduction" to history. I, too, had read the *Muqaddimah*, or rather an abridged version of only 459 pages. It contained a bit of wisdom that I thought apt for comprehending Persia and other places in my travels: "The past resembles the future more than one drop of water another." Ibn Khaldun's ideas on *asabiya* (clan-party loyalties) are still relevant to Iranian politics. But such nuggets exist in isolation, in a book that seems to a Westerner at the turn of the twenty-first century like a collection of pedestrian aphorisms lost in a maze of philosophical abstractions.

The discussion brought to mind what V. S. Naipaul had said in *Among the Believers*: Because others in "spiritually barren lands" will continue to produce the equipment necessary for civilization and human material progress, the devout Moslem is free to turn away from such defiling activities and dedicate himself to beautiful ideals.

The dun courtyards of the Al-Azhar University in Cairo are another bastion of medievalism in a polluted and overcrowded city, where, as in Qom, students turn away from the industrial fumes of the modern world and journey inward toward the ideal represented by the levitating gold dome. In Iran and some other Islamic countries this renunciation has, of course, been abetted by oil wealth, which provides a steady income but requires no effort. Islamicists in Qom, and elsewhere in the Moslem world, are like scholars on a long sabbatical, wasting a precious historical moment—paid for by oil—pursuing inquiries that lead nowhere.

"We study much as we did a thousand years ago," the student told me. "After class, we divide up into small groups like this one and discuss what we have learned." How beautiful and naive it seemed. Because such an approach to political and economic problems left them unsolved, tyranny often filled the void.

I visited the home of another seminary student, an Iraqi Shi'ite, a refugee from the rule of Saddam Hussein. It was on a side street, a few blocks from the sanctuary of Fatima, up three flights of stairs. There were a small kitchen, a stand-up toilet, and two rooms, lined with religious books from floor to ceiling on drab metal shelves. Except for machine-woven carpets and cushions, there were no furnishings. He lived with another student, an Iranian.

While the tea was brewing I marveled at the books, an Islamicist's paradise. My host put a question to me:

"You are so interested in us, but what about you? What is your religious background? Americans can be many things, we have heard."

"I am Jewish."

He, his roommate, and Vahid, my translator—himself the son of a mullah—all remained silent, but only for a moment. The Iranian roommate asked if all Jews were Zionists and if I supported Israel's oppression of the Palestinians. I gave standard, diplomatic responses to these questions, which I had parried often before in the Moslem world. They did not reply. Instead, the conversation moved on, with no discernible uneasiness. I couldn't tell if this indicated politeness to me on their part or if the Israel-Palestinian issue had become stale in Iran, as it had elsewhere in the Near East. Later, out on the street, Vahid would say to me, "Bob, you didn't tell me you were a Jew. You know, Iranians have always been fascinated with Jews. They are a very old, very ancient people. We think ancient people are too clever and"—he lifted his eyebrows—"shrewd." I wondered if this implied a self-criticism, a projection of how Iranians secretly viewed themselves, since they, too, are an old people.

While Iranian newspapers gave prominence to the iniquities of the "Zionist entity," the wars in the Balkans and in the Caucasus—where Moslem communities were under attack from Orthodox Christians—elicited more passion. I heard talk of other students from Qom who had volunteered to be freedom fighters in Bosnia and Azerbaijan, and in Kashmir, where Moslem guerrillas were fighting the regular army of Hindu-dominated India. One of my companions asked if it was true that "in the entrance hall of the CIA there is a map showing America's goal of a Greater Azerbaijan carved out of Iran." I told him there was no such map. Then I tried to explain how Americans were turning away from foreign affairs, toward their own problems. But this failed to register with my companions. After all, it was known that America had bombed Iraq, killing many thousands of innocent Iraqis, merely to discipline its own ally, the murderous Sunni Saddam Hussein, whom America still needed in its struggle against Iran. And was it not America that supported the repressive monarchy in Saudi Arabia, where women were not permitted to drive or hold jobs or go unescorted in public—customs that Arab and Iranian Shi'ites found barbaric? Qom bridled at America's hatred of "fundamentalist" Iran, even as Washington assisted an even more conservative Moslem regime in Saudi Arabia. Did these Shi'ites in Qom ever consider, I wondered, that if the Saudi monarchy they so hated were overthrown, a more extreme Sunni regime, even more anti-Iranian, might come to power in Riyadh?

Contradictions abounded. The Qom faithful supported their brother Moslems in Azerbaijan struggling against the Christian Orthodox Armenians. On the other hand, Qomis feared an enlarged Azerbaijani state because, as Persians, their loyalties lay with their fellow Indo-Europeans, the Armenians who were Persia's traditional allies against the Turks. An Azerbaijani victory would help Turkey and endanger Iran. Moreover, as a city of radical Shi'ites, Qom's loyalties were with the Palestinians. But Persia's interests lay with the Jews of the Near East—friends of Persia from the time of Cyrus the Great to that of the late Shah.[1] More complicated yet, as Persians their interests rested with fellow Persian-speaking Tajiks battling Turkic peoples in Central Asia. But weren't the Tajiks Sunnis and therefore enemies of Shi'ite Qom?

Qom seethed with passions that flared as far as Kashmir to the east and Bosnia to the west (the approximate frontiers of ancient Persia), even

---

[1]Cyrus the Great freed the Israelites from the "Babylonian Captivity" and resettled them in Palestine in the sixth century B.C. His motive was to create a pro-Persian buffer state between Egypt and Persia. Similar motives affected the late shah, who saw Israel as a pro-Persian buffer against Persia's traditional adversary, the Arabs. This reality was not lost on Khomeini's regime, which quietly accepted arms from Israel in its war against Arab Iraq.

while the foundations of religious Shi'ite identity were being undermined by a resurgence of traditional Persian identity. It was a world of cross-cutting civilizational loyalties.

◎   ◎   ◎

VAHID AND I were on the road for six hours from Qom to Isfahan. On the way south, we halted for a meal of *dugh* (sour milk), cherries, apricots, and tea. Then we passed through another saltscape of cindery buttes and long canyon walls.

As we entered Isfahan, we stopped at a carpet shop. The most beautiful hand-woven silk carpets in the shop were from Qom. They were the first "Qom carpets" I had seen, identifiable because of the intricate grid-work of squares making up the design. In Teheran, I had simply not noticed them. In Qom, they were hardly in evidence because the market for such expensive rugs is in bigger and wealthier cities. The peacock shades of turquoise, ruby, and pomegranate-red were electrifying. These carpets were exclusively the product of Qom. How could I explain the contradiction between this literally silken sensuality and the suffocating sterility of the holy city and its "consecrated dust"? I turned to Morier's description of the Mollah Nadan in *The Adventures of Hajji Baba*:

> He [Mollah Nadan] continued to talk about...his fasts, his penance, and his self-mortification...but when I compared his healthy and rubicund face, his portly and well-fed body, to the regimen which he professed to keep, I consoled myself...that he allowed great latitude in his interpretation of the law; and perhaps that I should find, like the house which he inhabited, which had its public and private apartments, that his own exterior was fitted up for the purposes of the world, whilst his interior was devoted to himself and his enjoyments.

In other words, an austere Islamic exterior concealed a pleasure-loving Persian core—consistent with Islam as an Arab import from the hot deserts of southern Arabia, introduced to Persia thirteen centuries ago. Superficially, Qom might always be Qom: a narrow, holy city. But beneath the surface, other aspects of Iran's multifaceted personality were struggling to be heard. That, to me, was the suggestion of the carpets.

14

The Heart of Persia

ON MY FIRST evening in Isfahan, Vahid and I had dinner with a group of Iranians from Teheran. The woman seated next to me worked in one of the government ministries and had studied English and American literature. She wore a black *chador*, so her lively eyes, highlighted by cosmetics, were the only feature that I could discern. I wondered what lay hidden beneath her dark shroud.

She told me she had devoured the writings of Edgar Allan Poe, and rhapsodized about the beauty of "The Raven." She quoted by heart a stanza from "The Bells." Daniel Defoe was another passion of hers, she said. We discussed *Robinson Crusoe* and *A Journal of the Plague Year*. Whereas *Robinson Crusoe* is about man building a community, *Plague Year* questions whether man is capable of preserving one. This led to a discussion about moral and social upheaval. She mentioned Henry Miller and Tennessee Williams. Then she brought up *Huckleberry Finn*:

"Twain is so wonderful at showing the irony and hypocrisy of the prevailing social framework, and of the political power structure in society. He exposes the problem with accepted social convention."

For a brief, magical moment, I thought that she might be criticizing Iran's ruling clergy by way of Mark Twain, as the Polish journalist Ryszard

Kapuscinski had criticized the communist rulers in his native Poland by writing about the tyranny of the shah.

However, she quickly retreated to *The Great Gatsby*, praising its depiction of "the violence and aggression in the dog-eat-dog world of American society." She went on:

"How can you be so brave as to live where you do? Aren't you afraid? The crime statistics in Washington are so bad. I can't think of a greater tragedy than to struggle to achieve something in life, in your work, only to be murdered randomly. Maybe we're spoiled and sheltered here. It's just that living in Iran is so safe and secure."

Her passionate voice and the mystery of her black *chador* left me confused and frustrated by America's vast misperception of Iran, a society—it was true—that in some ways was far more civil than my own; where in 1994 the statistical chance of being a victim of violence was probably small compared to America. But I was also sorry for her: I guessed that she was not so much trying to convince me of revolutionary Iran's social superiority as she was trying to convince herself. How could somebody intimately acquainted with the novels of Henry Miller and the plays of Tennessee Williams be so naive as to believe revolutionary Iran was a better place for a reflective individual than America?

This woman, in her twenties, was not from Iran's Westernized and politically impotent upper class. Her background was modest. I would later visit her home in central Teheran and meet her parents, who would complain bitterly to me about how the economic chaos after the revolution had wiped out the value of their savings. What little money they had left was being spent to educate their daughter and other children. Dissatisfaction went deep in Iran. Much less sophisticated than their children, this woman's parents were less willing to lie to themselves—and to me—than she was.

I was reminded of Bulgaria in the mid-1980s, which was being attacked in the West for its slavish aping of Soviet foreign policy while just beneath the surface, Bulgarian society was far healthier than Yugoslavia's and Romania's, whose regimes had better relations with the West at the time. When communism collapsed, Bulgaria became, initially, the most pro-American country in the Balkans, while the West's favorite, Yugoslavia, disintegrated into bloodshed. I wondered if Iran was going to follow in Bulgaria's footsteps, while traditional friends like Egypt and Saudi Arabia might crumble under upheavals from which Iranians were struggling to emerge.

The dinner ended around 10 P.M. Vahid and I weren't tired, so we decided to walk down to the Zayande Rud, the river running through Isfahan. It was thirteen days after the end of the celebrations of No Ruz, the Persian New Year, and the banks of this "rapid and rushing" river (as described by Curzon) were populated with families camping out. (No Ruz is a Zoroastrian holiday whose celebration the clergy had little success in discouraging in the first years after the revolution. In fact, Id al Adha, or the Feast of Sacrifice, the biggest holiday on the Moslem calendar, was minimally celebrated in Iran the year of my visit because it came so soon after No Ruz.)[1]

Because thirteen is an unlucky number, Iranians considered it unwise to sleep in their homes on this night. This was the reason for the crowds along the river with their carpets, blankets, and teakettles. Wherever I looked, along both sides of the wide river on this night I could see little fires. Iranians love fire: another legacy of Zoroaster (Zarathustra). The medieval poet Abdul Kasim Firdausi, in the *Shah Nameh*, calls the first fire ignited from stone "the Light of the Divinity." The last Wednesday of the year before No Ruz, called Rose Wednesday, is celebrated by jumping over bonfires while children set off firecrackers and small bombs.

Wherever I turned I could hear the sound of clinking tea glasses. The crowds were so thick that I had to be careful not to step on someone's carpet or blanket. Vendors sold ice cream and balloons for the children. People were talking in hushed whispers, as though expecting a spaceship to land in the dark field, lit only by hundreds of small fires. As I walked across the Bridge of 33 Arches, built by the Safavid shah Abbas the Great in 1602, my ears rang to the sound of water pouring through stone. Fresh, humid breezes lifted off the river (such a relief from the sandy wastes of the plateau) and mixed with the fragrance of tobacco from hubble-bubbles in a teahouse built within the bridge's medieval archways. If the word *mystical* still means anything, it could be applied to Isfahan on this night. The hometown of Morier's fictional character, Hajji Baba of Ispahan, was living up to my expectations.

As in Teheran, I noticed a lot of hand-holding between young men and women, and a lot of makeup and fingernail polish. Persian sensuality was apparently implanted in people's genes. It struck me that the mullahs

[1]Iranian daily newspapers marked the date not only according to the Moslem calendar but according to the Zoroastrian calendar as well.

had gone wrong by insisting on being both purely Persian and purely Islamic—sneering at the Arabs while insisting that the Arabs' religion dominate Iran. The result was the mullahs' hell-bent determination to be ruler of the whole Islamic Near East, an ambition that the West, with help from Turks, Israelis, and not a few Arabs, was in a position to foil.

The crowds along the river, however, did not seem bent on dominating anything, nor was the scene truly Islamic.

We walked for hours, well past midnight. "You see," said Vahid, "by the standards of Qom, Imam Khomeini was a true liberal reformer. The Imam said it was all right to play such games as chess and to enjoy certain kinds of music. He glorified the *Hosseinieh* over the mosque. This is the Ayatollah Khomeini that the working class of Iran sees, not the radical person seen by the West. . . . The Imam achieved a good balance. We need the supervision provided by Islam because we are under attack from the West." Was Vahid, like the woman with whom I had had dinner, trying to convince himself of something?

Vahid looked anything but revolutionary. He had a normal-length dark beard rather than the usual three-day growth, and wore a cowboy shirt and jeans. Jeans were popular in the Islamic Republic, even though neckties were frowned upon as a mark of Western imperialism. (St Vincent, in the Lonely Planet guide, advised, correctly as it turned out, to bring several pairs of jeans but not a necktie, which I did even though I had scheduled official interviews.) The ban on neckties should logically extend to jeans. But like in Iranian Islam, where alcohol was forbidden yet allowed, practicality ruled. Jeans were functional for the poor and the middle class. Neckties were not.

Vahid was a veteran of the Iran-Iraq war, where as a lieutenant he had commanded troops in battle. Even though the war produced a million casualties and featured protracted trench warfare, in which the Iraqis used poison gas against the Iranians, Vahid emerged from two years of combat unscathed. Soon after being released from the army he got into a car accident and broke several bones. I had seen Iranian drivers who tailgate gas trucks at 80 miles per hour, and Vahid's story did not strike me as unusual.

Vahid lived with his wife in a one-room rooftop flat in a formerly poor district of central Teheran that was undergoing gentrification. Vahid's father was a mullah. Yet Vahid, like almost every Iranian I met outside of Qom, did not seem particularly religious. His flat, which I would visit later in Teheran, was sparsely furnished, with carpets, pillows, and books. As soon as I entered, he and his wife engaged me in a discussion of the comparative costs of living in Iran and the U.S. What continually struck me about Iranian society was how mundane and normal it was. Vahid said, "Religion is being overtaken by other realities here. You will see, the *chador* will go. Our anti-USA posture is a temporary reaction against imperialism. We did it against the British and the Russians in the nineteenth century. My father, a religious cleric, said he would rather pour hot lead into his ears than hear popular music. But slowly we introduced music into the house."

◎　　　　◎　　　　◎

"ISFAHAN IS HALF the world," went the Oriental hyperbole. Curzon notes that in the middle of the seventeenth century, at the height of Safavid glory, there were fifteen hundred villages within the vicinity of Isfahan and the city itself was twenty-four miles in circumference. Inside the walls were 162 mosques, 273 baths, and 1,802 caravanserais. The number of inhabitants is estimated to have been between 600,000 and 1.1 million in that era—an incredibly high figure considering that in 1994 the city's population was estimated to be only about a million. Isfahan did not seem overcrowded and unlivable, because it represented a centuries-old urban organism whose growth had been relatively minimal after Teheran had become the focus of national-political development in the nineteenth century: Teheran's population has grown forty-fold since 1887, when 250,000 inhabited the city and outlying villages.

In his *Road to Oxiana*, Robert Byron had written that the Mosque of Sheikh Lutfullah and the Friday Mosque in Isfahan were two of the "four finest buildings in Persia."[2] Vahid and I visited them.

Byron, a distant relative of Lord Byron, visited Persia exactly sixty years before I did, yet the number of tourists in Isfahan in the spring of 1994 could not have been much greater than when he explored the city. The Islamic Revolution and its aftermath had made Iran, once again, almost a terra incognita for Westerners. Except for a group of Iranian teenage girls, covered in black, on a school tour, I had the interior of the Sheikh Lutfullah Mosque to myself.

[2]The other two buildings that so impressed Byron were the Mosque of Gohar Shad in Meshed and the Gumbad-i-Kabus, a tower, also in northeastern Iran, that I was to visit.

Referring to the interior dome of this Safavid era structure, Byron writes:

> I have never encountered splendour of this kind before. Other interiors came into my mind as I stood there . . . Versailles, or the porcelain rooms at Schönbrunn, or the Doge's Palace, or St. Peter's. All are rich; but none so rich. Their richness is three-dimensional; it is attended by all the effort of shadow. In the Mosque of Sheikh Lutfullah, it is a richness of . . . pattern and colour only. The architectural form is unimportant . . . it is simply the instrument of a spectacle, as earth is the instrument of a garden.

In fact, the various shades of blue faience, highlighted by white calligraphy and conch work, dissolved into a beauty so numbing it appeared to have no borders and likewise no depth, and, therefore, like the Iranian plateau, no perspective. This was a frightening beauty. It reflected authority without wisdom or balance. The calligraphy suggested such an overabundance of the *word* that language itself seemed to lose meaning. It was possible to descry a connection, albeit tenuous, between the artistic values that created this dome and the political values responsible for the excesses of the Islamic Revolution. This dome was yet another lesson in the victory of culture over politics.

The Friday Mosque also left me dumbstruck. Vahid and I were the only visitors in its massive hallways and antechambers, through which Curzon and Byron had passed. This mosque was originally raised by the Arab caliph Al Mansur in 755 A.D. Seljuk Turks and Safavid Persians restored and added to it. Curzon found the palimpsest of styles offputting. I found it reassuring. Like the Ishak Pasa Saray that I had marveled at in eastern Turkey, the Friday Mosque in Isfahan teaches how genius in architecture is often the result of cultural fusion. Here is Byron:

> One wonders what circumstance at that moment induced such a flight of genius. Was it the action of a new [Seljuk] mind from Central Asia on the old civilization of the [Iranian] plateau, a procreation of nomadic energy out of Persian aestheticism?

While cultural differences are basic and undeniable, these edifices illustrate how the interbreeding of cultures (and of races, too) can modify them. Regarding the walls, I watched as the sharp angles of Hellenism merged into the curvatures of Arabism through the medium of Kufic writing. The blue and green Persian tiling and the monumental Seljuk brickwork were so dazzling that I almost missed an alcove of stuccoed vines and flowers, fine enough to form the centerpiece of almost any other building. I sat down in a dusty corner, leaned back against the wall in the warm sunlight, and stared. The *keyf*—the sense of well-being—was as if I had drunk a splendid wine, which Byron had the luxury of doing here at a time when Persia produced wine from the renowned Shiraz grape.

Indeed, inside the Chehel Sotun (The Forty Columns), a pavilion used for palace receptions by Shah Abbas around the turn of the seventeenth century, wine today is much in evidence—in a series of large paintings glorifying the Safavid court. The paintings show turbaned men and buxom women in low-cut dresses pouring red wine from long decanters. The local authorities covered these paintings with scaffolding at the time of the Islamic Revolution, to prevent the pictures from being destroyed by radical mullahs. In 1991, when Isfahanis judged the political atmosphere sufficiently relaxed, they removed the scaffolding.

My strongest memory of Isfahan is of a garden with a reflecting pool framed by cypresses and sycamores, which I peered into from a crowded modern street. Deep in the garden, where only the sound of birds could be heard, a mullah was delivering a sermon about "moral purity." Outside on the street were stores selling tight-fitting Western clothes and music, and pictures in store windows showed Mickey Mouse and Sylvester Stallone playing Rambo.

◎　　◎　　◎

VAHID AND I continued south, toward the ancient ruins of Persepolis and the city of Shiraz. At a desert oasis we stopped for tea, rinsing the glasses in an icy cold sea-green water channel lined with poplars and sycamores. The vegetation and fresh smell of the stream were a relief from the suffocating and dusty waste. This oasis settlement was not really a product of natural forces. Like others on the Iranian plateau, it was fed by a system of underground man-made water channels called *ghanats*, in operation since antiquity. Fifty thousand *ghanats* were estimated to be still in operation in the 1990s. Iran's population has nearly doubled since the 1979 revolution, and never before has this ancient water system been under such strain.

The banners in Iranian cities calling on married couples to have no more than two children were proof of how the acute shortage of resources had forced even a fundamentalist government to rethink its opposition to birth control.

While U.S. policymakers were still obsessed with Iranian-sponsored terrorism, I sensed that the outlaw behavior of Iran's current regime was one of those problems that would soon be submerged—under the pressure of greater, tectonic forces gathering at the turn of the twenty-first century, forces driven by the ability, and inability, of various cultures to manage dwindling resources. Were the mullahs and their successors to prove successful in slowing Iran's population boom, the geopolitical future might partially forgive Iran its current iniquities.[3]

◎   ◎   ◎

"THE WONDERFUL MONUMENTS of Persepolis create a considerable feeling of national pride. . . . In the future, our people will be able to recover their traditional [great power] role and hold up the torch of Islam to illuminate the ways of other nations," declares President Rafsanjani on a signboard at the entrance to the archaeological site. Perhaps more revealing of the mullahs' evolving relationship with Iran's proud—but pagan—past is the statement of the hard-line Supreme Leader, Ayatollah Khamenei, which also appears at Persepolis:

"These ruins show the great power of our nation but also the tyranny and cruelty of a king."

In other words, the Achaemenid kingdom of Cyrus, Darius, and Xerxes, which dominated the Near East from this spot, provides a legitimate basis for revolutionary Iran's current geopolitical ambitions while the cruelty of the Achaemenids justifies the overthrow of the shah.

The late shah provided an example of this cruelty here. The Isfahan-Shiraz road once passed directly in front of the archaeological site, but the shah, in preparation for his 1971 celebration of the two thousand five hundredth anniversary of the Persian monarchy, moved the road and evacuated a village next to the site. A forest was planted in its place: thus

---

[3]Iran's initial opposition to birth-control measures at the 1994 Cairo Population Conference did not affect its vigorous birth-control program at home. Its opposition at the beginning of the conference was strictly political—a means by which the mullahs could bedevil the West, and particularly the United States.

the shah and his foreign guests could enjoy an idyllic ambience for their fete. But the villagers were never compensated for having their homes bulldozed.

I walked onto what had once been the shah's reviewing stand, now rusted and cracked, to scan the vast formation of pale yellow pillars and retaining walls. There was not a touch of shade. I beheld the relief carvings of sacred bulls and cats, toothy demons, oval-eyed charioteers, and captured slaves bearing tribute. I studied a carved portrait of a bearded warrior with a spear, standing beside an upright animal with a horse's head, a bird's wings, the tail of a scorpion, and the legs of a giant carnivore. Another relief carving, of a seminaked woman emerging from a bath with perfume and towels in her hands, appeared to writhe alive from the stone. Her eye, like so many of the other eyes carved into the stone here, exhibited both sensuality and cruelty, beauty and emptiness. At Persepolis, Byron observed the "cleanness [of the stone] reacts on the carving like sunlight on a fake old master; it reveals, instead of the genius one expected, a disconcerting void . . ." Byron added that the relief carvings here "have art, but not spontaneous art . . . Instead of mind or feeling, they exhale a soulless refinement . . ." My impression was of a people whose capacity for self-reflection could not keep up with its ambition— consequently, Iranians, from time to time in their history, got in over their heads. The Islamic Revolution was no exception.

It occurred to me that while I concentrated on the great Persian dynasties of the past, I had not been affected by such formerly great West African empires as those of Mali and Songhai. But for a traveler it is hard to write about what cannot be seen. Those Saharan-based empires rarely had a strong presence in the parts of West Africa where I traveled: Chieftain societies predominated along much of West Africa's coast. Moreover, because mudbrick, rather than stone, is the favored building material in sub-Saharan Africa, relatively little is left of those great civilizations, even in the drier interior. In much of West Africa, environmental degradation leaps to the eye; in Isfahan, Persepolis, and Shiraz it is the architectural remnants of the pagan and Islamic pasts.

◎   ◎   ◎

"WE PERSIANS BELIEVE Hafiz can see our future, that he has a solution to all our problems," said Vahid, the mullah's son, about the fourteenth-century poet who wrote

Flush with red wine the goblets pale,
Flush our pale cheeks to drunken hue . . .[4]

It didn't surprise me. In *Garden of the Brave in War*, Terence O'Don-nell writes "In the end, these [poets], rather than the bullhorns, are the voices that the Iranians heed and venerate." The crowds before my eyes sustained his point. It was sunset. Vahid and I had just arrived in Shiraz from Persepolis. We immediately headed for Hafiz's tomb, where large numbers of Iranians file past every evening at dusk, bearing roses in their hands. At Khomeini's tomb in the southern outskirts of Teheran I saw children playing tag or soccer, but not here in this reverent ambience. A hypnotic melody that sounded vaguely Indian played softly over the loud-speakers. Rather than the drumbeat of Qom, here was a slow-dancing motion. People waited their turn to touch the marble tomb, engraved with the poet's verses, that rested beneath a small and graceful octagonal pavilion with stone pillars and a tiled roof: all this in the midst of a garden suffused with orange blossoms and cluttered with potted plants. Beyond these plants was a series of stone alcoves punctuated by lavender water lilies, where men and women smoked from hubble-bubbles. Framing the entire garden and tomb complex were rows of towering cypress trees: nature's minaret. Vahid and I sat down and watched groups of Iranians posing for photographs beside Hafiz's tomb. The cries of songbirds were more peaceful than any silence. "Deep down we are a nation of flowers, nightingales, fire, butterflies, and wine—that is the pure essence of Per-sia," said Vahid. I took out Morier's *Hajji Baba* from my rucksack and turned to the part where Hajji, drinking wine in bed with his lover, recites from Hafiz:

The double charms of love and wine
Alike from one sweet source arise:
Are we to blame, shall we repine,
When unconstrain'd the passions rise?

I also retrieved Gertrude Bell's translation of Hafiz's *Divan*, flipped the pages arbitrarily, and read:

[4]Selections from Hafiz in this book have been translated by Gertrude Bell. They are reproduced by permission from *The Teachings of Hafiz* (Octagon Press Ltd., London).

From the Shah's garden blows the wind of Spring,
The tulip in her lifted chalice bears
A dewy wine of Heaven's minist'ring . . .[5]

Bell writes in a preface to her translations that these "delicate love-songs were chanted to the rude accompaniment of the clash of arms, and his [Hafiz's] dreams must have been interrupted often enough by the nip of famine in a beleaguered town . . ." Hafiz, which means "one who remembers (the Koran by heart)," was the pen name of Shemsuddin Mohammed, whose loose conduct and wine drinking scandalized the clergy of his day. Hafiz was born in the wake of the Mongol conquest of these lands, and lived under Tamerlane's conquest of Shiraz: a time of anarchy relevant to the present era, when Iran, recovering from a bloody revolution, faces threats from newly liberated Turkic peoples to the north. It was Hafiz's self-deprecating wit that saved him from Tamerlane's wrath, after the conqueror had summoned him.

TAMERLANE: "Art thou he who was so bold as to offer my two great cities, Samarkand and Bukhara, for the black moles on thy mistress's cheek?"

HAFIZ: "Yes, sire, and it is by such acts of generosity that I have brought myself to such a state of destitution that I have now to solicit your bounty."

Tamerlane, his anger cooled, dismissed the poet with a gift.[6]

Hafiz, like Cellaledin Rumi, whose grave I had seen in Konya, was a Sufi mystic. The frequent references to exotic love and wine drinking can also be interpreted as metaphors for the mystical state of mind to which Sufis aspire. Sufism has softened Islam on the Iranian plateau as it has on the Anatolian plateau. Yet perhaps because Iran's historical contacts with Western liberal thought have been fewer than Turkey's, opposition to Sufis is, or has been, more focused here. "Curses on Jelaledin Rumi!" exclaims an assembly of Qom clerics in *The Adventures of Hajji Baba*. But in Shiraz, as in Isfahan, it was apparent that Qom did not rule Iran. And the impressive crowds at Hafiz's tomb—crowds that have steadily gotten

---

[5]Reproduced from *The Teachings of Hafiz* (Octagon Press Ltd., London).
[6]This exchange between Tamerlane and Hafiz is taken from the 1910 edition of the Encyclopaedia Britannica's entry on Hafiz, written by the nineteenth-century English Orientalist Edward Henry Palmer, who was murdered in Sinai in 1882 on a camel-buying expedition.

bigger as the revolution recedes in memory—were not the only manifestation of this.

The tomb of Sayyed Mir Ahmad, the brother of Imam Reza who died in 835 A.D., is the Islamic holy of holies in Shiraz, a city that came into prominence under the eighteenth-century Zand shahs. Whereas Qom signified Islam in all its bleak austerity, this tomb and its many pilgrims reeked of Sufi mysticism and the paganized superstitions of Turkic nomads. Here I saw magnificent tribal rugs, colorful gypsum, and blue-tinted glass mirrors reflecting the rays of high-wattage lights, creating an impression of thousands of jewels and stars in the heavens. Tribesmen from the surrounding desert filed in and kissed the two combination locks on the silver cage holding the tomb. I watched as a Mongol-looking man-boy, with an adolescent mustache, a wisp of chin hair, and a very worried expression, slipped some rials to a turbaned holy man sitting on one of the carpets, with a wooden tray of books beside him. The holy man pocketed the rials, closed his eyes, and turned to a page in the Koran: he then began reading in a nasal but melodious drone. The man-boy listened intently. It was a tribal superstition, similar to fortune-telling, Vahid explained. "You pay a mystic some money and he blindly turns to a page in the Koran. The passage he selects is supposed to guide you in solving your problem. This boy obviously has a problem to which he seeks a solution. In Qom, the religious authorities frown on such practices [even if they are practiced there 'behind the curtain']. But in Shiraz they are common."

◎   ◎   ◎

KHOMEINI'S *HOSSEINIEH*, WITH its machine-made carpets and soccer-stadium lights, represented the new blue-collar Persia, as opposed to the romantic Persia of Hafiz's tomb. But the people waiting in line to touch Hafiz's grave were both poor and rich. Hafiz had clearly survived the Islamic Revolution. But would Khomeini survive the reemergence of historic Persia?

15

◎　　◎　　◎

The Tower of Qabus

AFTER WE RETURNED to Teheran, Vahid had no idea why I wanted to travel over the Elborz mountains toward the Caspian Sea, then northeast onto the Turkomen steppe—a day and a half of steady driving—merely to see an empty brick tower that didn't have any pretty tiles on it.

In the Lonely Planet guide, David St Vincent cites the Gumbad-i-Qabus, or tower of Qabus, as his last entry before the glossary. He writes, "The whole tower is so perfectly preserved that it is hard to believe that it was built almost a millennium ago." Robert Byron claimed it was a photograph of the tower that alone drew him to Persia in 1933–1934.

After crossing the Elborz and coming upon the semitropical green of the Caspian littoral—with desert Iran now but a memory—we stopped for the night at Sari, a nondescript town. We hopped into the car early the next morning, ascending the windswept steppe, leaving the lush Caspian behind us. The temperature dropped. Though fifty miles from the official border with the newly independent former-Soviet republic of Turk-menistan, I sensed that here was the real frontier, and someday, ultimately, maps may reflect this. Here—where, in Byron's words, "bearings, land-marks, disappeared, as they would from a skiff in mid-Atlantic"—was a geographical no-man's-land, after which were to come different faces, with softer, wider features that suggested to me the wildness of Turkic Central Asia. I had met the deepest and oldest of all Iranian fears, what Morier, in *Hajji Baba*, explains as the "apprehension which the very name of Turcoman excites throughout the whole of Persia." Hajji himself thinks of the Turks as "the most accursed of heretics, whose beards were not fit to be brooms to our dustholes . . ." In the *Shah Nameh*, Firdausi recalls an episode of ancient mythical history:

> Long shadows on the plain at even tide,
> The Tartar host had won the victory;
> And many a Persian chief fell on that day . . .

Aside from St Vincent's guidebook, in none of the books about Iran I had perused in recent years was there a mention of the tower of Qabus. The tower had acquired a sepia quality in my mind, existing only through the pages of Byron's *Road to Oxiana*. The veil that descended over Iran after the Islamic Revolution deepened its attraction for me.

According to Byron, the tower is visible from a distance of twenty miles, first appearing as "a small cream needle" on an empty horizon. But at this distance from the tower, I encountered a sprinkling of brown telephone poles, sagging power lines, and oil refineries. Though I was visiting the region in the same season as Byron, I could hardly see twenty miles through the polluted air. On the outskirts of the town of Gumbad-i-Qabus, named for the tower, the air was gritty. There was now a forest of telephone poles. The streets were lined with welders and shops selling spare parts for automobiles. It was like a wintry version of Qom. I remember the first Turkoman I saw: riding a noisy motorbike with an astrakhan hat above his moon face. Byron had mentioned "a small market town." I was thus shocked by the sprawling grid of bustling cement streets that went on for miles in every direction.

We could see no tower. Finally, we asked the driver of an orange pickup truck for directions. He told us to follow him.

He led us to a municipal park with neat garbage receptacles, multi-colored benches, and vendors selling Cheez Doodles and Bond Street American Blend cigarettes next to a smudged picture of the late revolutionary firebrand Ayatollah Mohammed Beheshti, killed in a bomb blast in 1981. The banality of the site devastated me.

The tower of Qabus stood on a green mound by a swirling pedestrian pavement, next to a road crowded with pickup trucks and other vehicles. The tower, which seems so tall in the black-and-white photo taken by Byron's traveling companion, Christopher Sykes, looked so—well, average, compared to the two telecommunication towers in my line of vision, with their giant satellite dishes. A woman pushing a baby in a pram walked by me, not even staring up at the edifice.

I told Vahid I wanted to be alone with the tower for a while. He lifted his eyebrows and ambled away, but kept looking at me, wondering I don't know what. I sat on the ground and craned my neck skyward at the conical roof.

The sun had recently slipped out from behind the line of low, moving clouds, revealing what I had originally come to see, though I did not know it until this moment: The tower was the ultimate tent, glorified in stone by a nomadic race, and preserved thus through the deep chasm of the centuries. A Turkoman ancient with a skullcap, two boys beside him (his grandsons, perhaps), circumambulated the tower, glancing up at it now and then. I thought of the shepherd, or the nomad on horseback, moving across the plateau and glancing at the sky in the same manner, reassured that man is not alone in the universe. The conical roof, so dynamic and harmonious against the moving clouds, expressed the simple awe of the shepherd rather than the forced cries of the proletariat as expressed in the smudged portrait of Ayatollah Beheshti at the park's gate. The definitive totem pole, I thought.

The tower was built by Qabus ibn-e Vashmgir, a poet, scholar, patron of the arts, military general, and prince of the Ziyarid dynasty, who died in 1007, a year after its completion. For Byron, the 167-foot-tall structure of unadorned fired brick was a virile Turko-Persian counterpoint to the dreamy and feminine, purely Persian, architecture of Isfahan and Shiraz. Officially, Qabus and the other Ziyarid monarchs were Persians. Actually, they were a hybrid of Turks and Persians: of Turan and Iran. The tower was a starker, more concentrated version of the Turko-Persian architectural fusion I had first seen at the Ishak Pasa Saray in eastern Turkey, and again at the Friday Mosque in Isfahan. This architectural trail contains a lesson for mapmakers and policy analysts: that the Turkish-Persian relationship is among the most complex of civilizational rivalries.

Though there are clear differences between the two civilizations, there is also overlap. Rumi, who lived in Seljuk Turkey and wrote in Persian, is but one example. While Central Asia is today mainly Turkic, islands of Persian cultural influence abound, and even within the Turkic areas, a rich residue of Persian culture remains. Of Bukhara, now in the new Turkic republic of Uzbekistan, Marco Polo wrote at the end of the thirteenth century, "The city is the best in all Persia." While I found the boundary of Persia well within Iran's current borders, according to Marco Polo, the eastern and northeastern limit of Persia was Balkh, in north-central Afghanistan. Perhaps we are both right, and all of the cartographers since the Middle Ages have been wrong: Rather than borders, there have always been, in reality, moving centers of power and influence. Firdausi, for example, the great medieval Persian poet, lived much of his life outside the present boundaries of Iran, in Turkic eastern Afghanistan.

The bustle and rapid expansion of the town of Gumbad-i-Qabus, I was to learn, were a result of the collapse of the Soviet Union and the ensuing explosion of cross-border trade that brought alcohol and soft-porn videos into Iran from Turkmenistan, and Iranian consumer goods—from canned foods to dental floss—into Turkmenistan. Greater Persia was apparent in Gumbad-i-Qabus, but so was the renewed Turkic incursion.

Iran has been governed largely by Persians since the collapse of the Qajar dynasty. Still, the late shah's wife, Farah, is from a Turkic background, as is perhaps the most brilliant cleric of the Islamic Revolution, Mohammed Kazem Shari'atmadari. The Supreme Leader, Khamenei, is said to be part-Azeri. Indeed, Turkic Azerbaijan in the northwest—the most populous and well educated region of Iran—has often been the political and intellectual vanguard here. After World War II, it was a center of leftist activity in Iran. And the cry "Death to the shah" was first heard in Tabriz, the capital of Iranian Azerbaijan, in February 1978. Instead of melding the two civilizations, however, such factors often refine the distinctions. Reza, the photographer friend with whom I had traveled in Baku, had told me that "the Persians are secretly jealous of the Azeris." Though one must allow for his chauvinism, Azerbaijan is more highly developed and has always paid more taxes than the rest of the country, and received less in return from the poorer Persians. Will the disaffected Azeri Turks of Iran, accounting for as much as 25 percent of the country's population, one day join their fellow Azeris in former-Soviet Azerbaijan? This may be the most sensitive issue in Iran in the 1990s, though little discussed by the Western media. The answer may be provided by the outcome of the conflict between Armenia and northern Azerbaijan, which in turn will determine whether northern Azerbaijan will peacefully exploit its massive oil reserves[1] and thus serve as an economic magnet for Azeri Turks south of the border, in Iran. ("The problem is an old one," Iran's deputy foreign minister, Mahmoud Vaezi, had admitted to me in Teheran. "We cannot afford to be seen as taking Armenia's side against Azerbaijan, or vice versa.")

So the lines of history hadn't changed much since Qabus built his tower at the turn of the last millennium. Whether Byzantines versus Sassanids, or Ottomans versus Safavids, the peoples of Central Asia and the Anatolian plateau had often been in conflict with those of the Iranian plateau, and the Caucasus has recurrently been the flash point. As the competition over future oil pipelines and other trade routes intensified, the Turks and the Iranians had reached a level of conflict greater than at any moment since the last Turko-Persian wars in the early nineteenth century. These two ancient peoples, so alike to an outsider but so different to each other, were quarrelsome neighbors. Here in stone was the magnificent result of their mating.

Across the horizon, separated by a thousand years, were the much taller communication towers, dwarfing the Gumbad-i-Qabus. Around this miserable little park a grim and noisy town had sprung up. The urban landscape had changed more in the sixty years between Byron's visit and mine than in the 928 years between the tower's completion and his visit.[2] I wondered what it would look like in another sixty years considering that half the population of Iran was under fifteen, with similar demographics obtaining in Turkic Central Asia.

Though the pattern of competition between the Turkic and Indo-European peoples (whether Persian, Armenian, or Kurdish) was recognizable—as was the pattern of their fusion, as evinced by this tower—demographic and economic factors had now become paramount. To appreciate this tower, and similar monuments across the earth, would require the mental cropping-out of the landscape around them. As towns like these continue to expand exponentially, the combined effect on politics of growing populations, scarce resources, industrial growth, and

[1]With an estimated 3.3 billion barrels of oil reserves in five Caspian Sea fields, former-Soviet Azerbaijan—along with neighbors Kazakhstan and Turkmenistan—is on the verge of an oil bonanza rivaling that of the Persian Gulf.
[2]Byron disappeared at sea in 1941, at the age of thirty-six, when the Germans torpedoed the ship in which he was sailing to Cairo to take up duties as a war correspondent.

cross-border trade will intensify. The Islamic Revolution may have been an early reaction to problems of population and urbanization, but fundamentalism had failed in Iran, if not yet in parts of the Arab world. What next? Would renewed caravan routes, bolstered by an information highway and weaker governmental oversight, lead to a high-tech medievalism in the twenty-first-century Near East that I imagined when I met the bazaar baron Rafighdoost communicating, for example, with mafiosi in Bukhara and Herat through the latest comm gear and IBM Thinkpads.

I wasn't sure, but I continued to think about French writer Alain Minc's statement that the most important economic class to emerge from the ashes of the Cold War is the mafiosi, a subclass of which are the new-age *bazaaris*.[3]

Yet I felt more certain that just as the tower of Qabus had been overtaken by a landscape Byron could barely have imagined, the issue of "fundamentalism" in Iran, and the West's preoccupation with it, was about to be overtaken by larger shifts in the political-historical landscape that few could yet fathom.

Iran has often been less a state than an amorphous empire, reflecting the richness and dynamism of Persian culture. Its true size would always be greater and smaller than any officially designated national area. While the northwest of today's Iran is Kurdish and Azeri Turk, parts of western Afghanistan and Tajikistan are culturally and linguistically compatible with an Iranian state. It is this amorphousness that Iran could return to as the wave of Islamic extremism and the perceived legitimacy of the mullahs' regime erodes.

Twenty-first-century Iran might bear startling resemblance to a 1760 map engraving of Persia I had once seen. There were no bold lines, only indistinct regions that merged into such places as "Kurdistan," "Balouchestan," and "Tartary" on the Persian periphery. It was time to cross into Central Asia, to see these shifts at work.

---

[3]Minc's book, *Le Nouveau Moyen Age* (The New Middle Ages), presents a similar thesis to the one I offered in my *Atlantic Monthly* article "The Coming Anarchy."

PART V

◉　　◉　　◉

Central Asia
Geographical Destinies

Asia is the mother figure. . . . From her have come the great streams of population. We trace back to her through the Aryans that poured from Central Asia.

—WILLIAM O. DOUGLAS
Beyond the High Himalayas

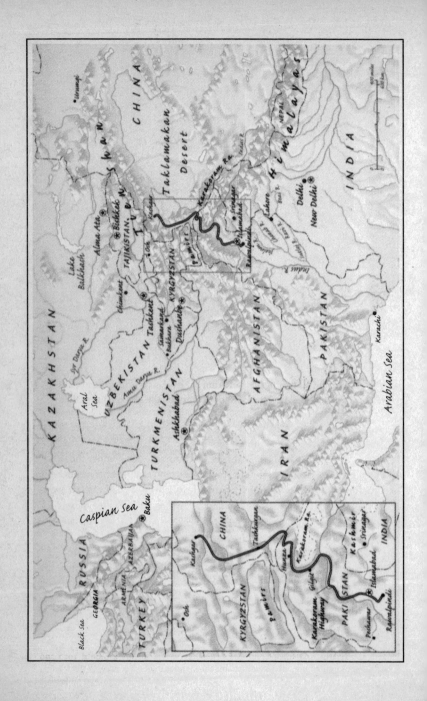

I 6

Russian Outpost

TO IMAGINE THE map of the emerging world you should travel backward from the latest CD-ROM version of the Encyclopaedia Britannica to the eleventh edition, published in 1910. The subject headings in these brittle, yellowing pages still correspond to the world of the late-1990s: "Russia in Asia," "Turkey in Asia," "India (with lesser Frontier States)," "Persia," "Baluchistan." . . . Pakistan, of course, is absent. Its components fall under the rubric "lesser Frontier States." There is, too, an extremely long entry under the word *Turkestan*: "the western limit being the Caspian Sea and eastern Mongolia and the Desert of Gobi." "Turkestan," writes Prince Peter Alexeivitch Kropotkin—the Russian geographer and anarchist—in the Britannica's eleventh edition, is "a name that cannot very well be dispensed with."

Indeed not. It was the Sassanid Persians, in the third century A.D., who may have used the word first to denote the "land of Turks." The four-teenth-century Moorish traveler Ibn Battuta also used it. Russian czarist officialdom in the nineteenth century institutionalized the label. And following the seventy-four-year interregnum of the Soviet Union, the word *Turkestan* has come back into vogue.[1]

[1]This is a relative statement. The word *Turkestan* was in formal use until 1922 and remained in limited use, albeit unofficially, throughout the Soviet period.

But the label, broad as it is, is still too narrow.[2] For within Turkestan are not only Turkic peoples such as Turkomans, Uzbeks, Kyrgyz, Kazakhs, and Uighurs, but large pockets of Persian Tajiks and Caucasian tribes, and much smaller islands of Balti Tibetans and mongoloid races.[3] Prince Kropotkin calls Turkestan "a theater of so many migrations and conquests that its present population could not fail to be mixed." Though the Kyrgyz, he writes, are unrelated to Caucasians, Mongols, and Tatars, they have "intermingled . . . with the Volga Kalmucks . . . and with the Dzungarian nomads . . . all alike of Mongol stock."

Confused about Turkic identity? So are many of the people who inhabit this vast region. A monochrome Turkic power bloc, colored on the map in Seljuk blue, is not likely to arise. Individual and national identities across Turkestan are far too complicated for that.

In the 1990s, the world began to discover in Turkestan a volatile, antiquarian region of medieval city-state identities (Bukharan, Khivan, etc.). In Eastern Europe, history resumed in 1989 after a half-century of dormancy. In Turkestan, it resumed after half a millennium—for the first time since the Portuguese navigator Vasco da Gama discovered the sea route to India in 1498, making it possible for East-West trade to bypass Central Asia. On the eve of da Gama's voyage, Ottoman Turkey and China constituted the world's most important economic and cultural centers, with Central Asia the link between them. A string of Islamic centers, fusing Turkic and Persian cultures, formed a strategic caravan network. It was this caravan network that the Portuguese navigator made obsolete.

As history moved on, Turkestan was left to the mercies of czarist Russia and, later, the Soviet empire. Stalin exterminated the Moslem intelligentsia and deliberately transplanted whole populations, bedeviling each of the newly created Soviet republics with illogical borders and huge, imported minority populations in a region where the lack of natural frontiers had permitted volatile and arbitrary imperial boundaries. While in

[2]Scholars do not consider Kyrgyz and Kazakhs as strictly "Turkestanis" but rather as "Central Asians," because they live to the east of what is normally considered Turkestan.
[3]The conquest of Genghis Khan's Mongol hordes in the thirteenth century had a limited racial effect on the Turkic peoples, since most of the original Mongols went home; the remainder interbred with the local population. It was the Russians who first lumped together the Mongols and their Turkic subjects under the name Tatar.

the Middle East, the Nile and the Tigris-Euphrates river valleys fulfilled their geographical destinies as age-old civilization clusters around which states could be organized, Central Asia was marked by a loose string of cities and towns (Bukhara, Samarkand, Ghazni, and so on) whose food supplies came from adjacent agricultural areas. These primordial city-states embodied "composite" identities—for example, Persian language, Turkic race, and Moslem religion—that didn't easily constitute an explicit ethnic or national identity.[4] Central Asia has been defined as "a vast shatter zone of peoples and cultures," an unorganized world where "national identities are multiple and polycentric."[5]

The crack-up of the Soviet and British empires left Turkestan, or "Tartary" as the Elizabethans called it, a jigsaw of new and artificial states by the 1990s. Besides the newly independent republics within the former Soviet Union, Turkestan now also comprised parts of China, northern Pakistan, and northern India. The U.S. State Department, in a Cold War time-lock of area specialization, divided Turkestan among its former-Soviet bureau, its South Asia bureau, and its East Asia bureau. The guidebook industry, with rare exceptions, apportioned parts of Turkestan among the former Soviet Union, China, and the Indian subcontinent. William O. Douglas, onetime Supreme Court justice and inveterate traveler, had it right in 1952, when he observed, "Central Asia is mostly in Russia and Tibet. But the northern stretch of India and the outposts of Pakistan that nestle in the Karakorams are also Central Asia. They are *one world* . . ." (his emphasis). From the moment I arrived in Uzbekistan, to journey by road through three former Soviet republics, western China, and northern Pakistan, this was a world that I was never conscious of leaving until I had ridden down the other side of the Karakorams into the densely populated frying pan of Punjab, where the Indian subcontinent finally begins.

◎   ◎   ◎

I ARRIVED IN Tashkent armed with Eugene Schuyler's *Turkistan: Notes of a Journey in Russian Turkistan, Khokand, Bukhara, and Khulda*, published in 1885. Schuyler, a member of the Romanian Academy, and of the Ameri-

---

[4] The concept of "composite" identities for Central Asia was originally used by Robert L. Canfield, an anthropologist at Washington University in St. Louis.

[5] These ideas belong to Jon Anderson, an anthropologist at Catholic University in Washington, D.C., who articulated them in an interview with me.

can, Italian, and Imperial Russian geographical societies, settled on Tashkent as his base of operations in Central Asia. So would I, and for the same reasons. Then, as now, Tashkent was a Russian outpost, regional metropole, and a good place to arrange further travel. I was grateful when I first arrived in Tashkent to have brought notes from another, less romantically inclined volume: *Ecocide in the USSR: Health and Nature Under Siege*, by Murray Feshbach and Alfred Friendly, Jr.

The instant I stepped into the arrival building at Tashkent airport I was struck, as in Baku, by the atmospheric and architectural brutishness wrought by the Bolshevik nightmare.[6] The arrival building was a narrow, constricting heap of pebbly poured concrete and cheap slate, with sharp and uneven corners, and glaring fluorescent lights. It was like a network of interrogation rooms. Soviet architects had an unerring ability to create instant squalor with only a few wrong angles and an abundance of cheap construction materials.

Beyond the arrival terminal, the city spread across the flat landscape in a succession of inhumanly wide boulevards and squares. The government buildings were too big and ill-proportioned, with gray concrete skins blown into balloonlike bubbles and trapezoidal shapes. Inside these massive buildings I would later see rows of sleazy little cubbyholes, with crude and oversized light fixtures. The apartment houses were like those I had seen in Baku, and in the cities of Albania and Romania: often unpainted, badly fitted, made of cinder block, with bathroom tiles decorating the facades and drunkenly caving balconies where tomatoes and onions took the place of flowerpots beside the clotheslines. But this was surely the most hideous and alienating example of Soviet design I had seen. It cried out, *We crush the weak.*

I stayed with a friend, a Western diplomat. "Don't drink the tap water," he told me. The guidebooks had forewarned me. In Iran, the water was often safe, but here the water, and much else, wasn't. Feshbach and Friendly write in *Ecocide in the USSR*:

Drinking water . . . is precious but frequently poisonous in many parts of Central Asia. In Kirghizia, with 62 percent of its population

---

[6]I flew to Tashkent from Teheran via Pakistan, since I was unable, as a third country national, to get across the land border from Iran to Turkmenistan, and no air connection existed at the time from Teheran to Tashkent.

rural, one-third has to slake their thirst directly from streams, rivers and primitive wells . . . annually "over 1,500 people die from digestive illnesses . . . more than half are children less than one year of age." . . .

Being an urban Uzbek, it should be noted, is . . . no guarantee against pollution. Of the eleven textile fiber plants in the capital city of Tashkent and its environs, seven have no water purification facilities . . . Their wastes, 60 percent of them untreated, went directly into the Akhangaran River . . . the most dangerous water was to be found in Central Asia . . . The rate of new cases of typhoid, a waterborne disease, ran from over three times the Soviet average in Uzbekistan to thirteen times the average in Tajikistan.

At dusk, the initial shock of communist-era ruination had worn off. I went for a walk, and reflected. Schuyler's *Turkistan* was not, I decided, entirely out-of-date. "As I sat in the porch in the bright moonlight, the first night of my arrival at Tashkent," Schuyler writes, "I could scarcely believe that I was in Central Asia, but seemed rather to be in one of the quiet little towns of Central New York. . . . There are few old buildings and most of the mosques are small . . ." Beyond the massive government edifices and squares, Tashkent was still low-leveled, nondescript, leafy, and provincial-seeming, with a sleepy Indian-summer quality in its outlying neighborhoods. This marchland of the czarist empire reminded me of another marchland: that of eastern Hungary, also overrun by Mongol hordes. In 1966, there had been two major earthquakes in Tashkent, followed by eight hundred tremors in 1966 and 1967. The shattered, ad hoc quality of the architecture intensified the sense of alienation and placelessness. I had to look hard for beauty: I found it in the ornately carved tin rain gutters atop some of the roofs, and in a mustard-colored baroque house, again like those of eastern Hungary. But such examples were not numerous. The mosques, both new and old, were small. If no longer reminiscent of central New York State, as Schuyler found it, Tashkent now evoked a big city in Iowa. Romantic associations aside, Central Asia was "central" Asia, the flat and homespun middle of a continent, reminiscent of the American Midwest.

Schuyler estimated the city's population anywhere from 60,000 to 120,000 in 1885. In the 1990s it was 2 million. But, earthquake-prone and a Russian garrison post, Tashkent was a hollow gridwork that had added miles rather than density. Tashkent, meaning "stone village," had begun as an oasis settlement in the first century A.D. Persians, Mongol hordes, and Turkic khans would exchange control of it over the medieval centuries. In June 1865, the Russians arrived.

◎   ◎   ◎

THE RUSSIANS' DRIVE southeastward, to conquer the Turkic peoples and to acquire warm water ports along the Indian Ocean, gathered momentum with Peter the Great's conquest of the Sea of Azov from the Ottoman Turks in 1696. Over the next century, Russian fur trappers and traders built forts across southern Siberia, arcing down into Turkestan. In the nineteenth century, following its recovery from Napoleon's invasion, Russia began subduing one Turkic khanate after another. As the czar's forces moved closer to India, the British became alarmed. The "Great Game" of espionage between Great Britain and Russia had begun—a nineteenth-century version of the Cold War. The Russian advance into Turkestan was not always unwelcome, for the Turkic rulers were often cruel, not only to Russian merchants and their children whom the khans sold into slavery, but to their own Turkic subjects as well. Stalin's barbarities were still in the future.

With thirteen hundred men and twelve artillery pieces, Russian general Mikhail Cherniaev's troops began scaling the ramparts of old Tashkent before dawn on June 15, 1865. By June 17, Tashkent was part of Czar Alexander II's empire. Tashkent became Russia's base for further conquests in Turkestan, as it would later become a base for travelers like myself.

The Russians built a classical colonial city, a vast checkerwork of right-angled streets that quickly swallowed up the medieval Turkic city.[7] In the early-1990s, only 8 percent of the population of Uzbekistan was Russian, but most of this 8 percent was concentrated in Tashkent, giving Tashkent the flavor of a colonial city.

Thus my first encounters in Turkestan were not with members of a Turkic ethnic group but with Russians and even Armenians, who, like the many Jews who lived here, arrived in the wake of the nineteenth-century czarist conquest and Stalin's subsequent ethnic relocations. The faces on the street—Russian, Turkic, Korean, and the many indistinguishable mixes

---

[7] I say Turkic rather than merely Uzbek because Uzbeks may then have been less numerous than Kazakhs and Kyrgyz in Tashkent.

of Eastern Europe, the Balkans, and inner Asia—testify to this legacy of Stalinism. Here was the opposite of a city like New York or San Francisco, to which immigrants had come by choice, seeking a better life. The forebears of the people of Tashkent had often been conveyed here en masse, by force.

Some writers, including myself, had already described Moslem Central Asia as part of a new and expanded Near East. But Tashkent taught me that my earlier published judgments were rash. The Soviet Union had gone, but Turkestan was still joined to Russia more than to the Near East. For how long, though?

"I GREW UP seeing myself as superior. Now I must find my place in a new society." Sergei was Russian; his wife, Uzbek. Until 1991, when the USSR collapsed, this mattered little politically. Before 1991, he and his wife were both "Soviets" and theirs was, at least officially, a typical "Soviet" marriage, not unlike many marriages between Serbs and Croats in Yugoslavia before it sundered. Now Sergei's intermarriage was potentially dangerous.

Sergei's grandfather had immigrated to Kazakhstan after the Bolshevik Revolution; his father emigrated from Kazakhstan to Tashkent. His mother's family was exiled by Stalin from Russia to Kyrgyzstan, and then to Tashkent. Sergei eventually became a signals intelligence officer in the Soviet military. A blond bodybuilder, Sergei looks every inch a "Hero of the Soviet Union." Except, with the Soviet Union dead, he is merely another Russian: a minority that is steadily leaving Uzbekistan, fearful of its future in a state controlled by those it used to oppress.

Many of these ethnic Russians will stay in Central Asia because they have no place else to go. Sergei is typical. Both sides of his family came to Turkestan two generations ago. He has no relatives in Russia. As he told me, Russian cities are more expensive to live in than Tashkent. Crime, though considerable in Tashkent, is worse in Russia. Living in general, Sergei felt, is harder there than here.

Sergei, like many people I encountered in my travels, expressed himself in ethnic-cultural terms. He explained that since his wife's family was Uzbek and his children half-Uzbek, half-Russian, he hoped at first that the Uzbeks would manage themselves better than the Russians had managed them. "After all, this is a flat country, easier to control than Tajikistan, which is high mountains, and where tribal groups have been separated from each other by deep valleys, leading to civil war. Tajikistan has no future." But Sergei's optimism for Uzbekistan was now faltering. Speaking of the president, he explained, "Karimov is really for his tribe. On the street, in buses, from the statements and actions of the government, Russians don't get a sense that we are welcome, even though we have generally been better educated." (Another Russian would tell me, "Russians are the first to be laid off. We suffer petty harassment. We're shouted at in the buses. The Uzbeks tell us to 'go home to Russia.'") Sergei went on:

"It was comfortable when we were all poor. Now some of us are getting rich and this increases tensions. Equality in poverty can prevent ethnic struggle."

"HOW CAN YOU think of traveling around this country by bus?" Maria asked me in derision. "They'll see you are a foreigner and rob you. . . . This used to be a modern city, but now for the first time there are cows wandering in the streets and squares. These peasants have taken over. The bazaar is full of hooligans. You see that man driving too fast and following too close behind the other car: It is because he is an Uzbek. Yes, I know, you're American, so you think I'm prejudiced. Watch the drivers, watch the cars. The Russians drive bad, the Uzbeks worse. The only civilization you have in this city, to speak of, is on account of one general scaling the city walls in 1865," Maria sneered. She was an Armenian in a society that had just been taken over by a Turkic people. Her dark, penetrating eyes assessed everything and gave away nothing. The first time I met her, she listened to me without responding. The second time, she dissected my ideas piecemeal. "I'm not saying that the Russians were so great. You see a Russian crossing herself in the street in front of you. Is it because she is devout? Maybe. Maybe also it is because she thinks you may give her a little money." Maria's voice was always tired, postcynical. She reminded me of the Egyptian official I had met in Cairo who had told me that human rights was a joke and that Islamic terrorists were just a bunch of "painters and plumbers." These people had given up on the world. But this did not mean that what they had to say, taken in context, did not reveal more about their societies than the bland optimism I heard from others.

"It isn't a question of the government. It is a matter of the society which the government only reflects," Maria said. "Come, I'll show you something real. There were hundreds of them, rough and drunken teenagers. I saw it. The government militia stood by and did nothing." I didn't know what she meant.

Maria took me to the sprawling Dombrabad cemetery, where a sizable minority of the Orthodox Christian and Jewish graves had been smashed and toppled. I looked down at one gravestone, broken into several pieces. It read: "Kostas Nikos Dimakis, March 3, 1914–August 12, 1992." Maria and I walked silently under a high canopy of oak trees for a hundred meters, passing long rows of gravestones on either side, from the Greek and Russian Orthodox section of the cemetery, where the crosses here and there had been bent or broken off, to the Jewish part. The portraits of these dead people had been carved in the headstones, like lingering spirits more real than the living. "The Jews are mostly gone from Tashkent. The last ones are now leaving, selling their carpets and other possessions," Maria explained. "So there is no one to repair their broken graves or to care for their upkeep." In each long row, at least one gravestone had been toppled or broken. Given that I had passed more than fifty rows, this was a lot. The weight of the massive headstones testified to the energy required to damage just one of them; a normal hammer was not going to do much harm. I noticed also that the stone walls of the cemetery had been knocked down in places.

"You see," said Maria, "to the Uzbeks, the Jews and the Christians are seen as the bourgeoisie. Since the cemeteries in Tashkent are nearly all full, Uzbeks must now be buried in cemeteries as far as forty kilometers from Tashkent. But they lack the money for fuel to drive there. So they are resentful at the Jews and Christians buried here in town."

I had come to Turkestan expecting cultured Moslems such as those I had encountered in Iran. I found instead the eerie physical remnants of large Russian, Greek, and Jewish communities being wrecked by drunken roughnecks. Technically speaking, that smashed Greek grave of "Kostas Nikos Dimakis" represented the easternmost flank of a Turkic Moslem-Greek Orthodox civilization clash that stretched from the Aegean and Cyprus in the West, through embattled remnants of Greek communities near the Black and Caspian seas, to Central Asia. In actuality, the desecration was a sordid villainy having more to do with local economic and social conditions, the detritus of communism. It reminded me of the harsh treatment meted out by poor Romanians to the ethnic German bourgeoisie in Romania, and to the awful relations between poor

Africans and the Arab bourgeoisie in Sierra Leone. What these people were driving out were the very role models and financial motors that they needed.[8]

Western diplomats were divided in their sympathies. One said to me, "It's true—Uzbeks do drive more recklessly than Russians. Whatever the past, the Russians are the educated elite. They need to feel welcome." Another said, "Don't you believe all this nonsense about how Russians are oppressed."

But the Russian-Turkic clash was only one of several ethnic conflicts I was to encounter in Central Asia after I left Tashkent.

◎　　　◎　　　◎

BEFORE EXPLORING THE rest of Uzbekistan, I had to make visa applications for further travel. I arrived at the embassy of Kazakhstan only to learn that the staff had just moved to a new building. At the new building I encountered a celebration in progress, and was immediately placed at the head of the table next to the Kazakh ambassador. "We have killed a sheep in celebration of our new building. Eat, eat, eat," the ambassador ordered me.

I couldn't believe my good fortune. In Washington, I had paid eighty-five dollars for a visa to Uzbekistan, which I received, nevertheless, only because a friend knew the Uzbek ambassador. But I had failed to obtain a visa to Kazakhstan. Tashkent had been my last hope. Now that I was breaking bread with the Kazakh ambassador, how could he refuse me?

There was not an inch of space on, or at, the table, around which ten people sat in a closed room without air-conditioning in late May. Mountains of cheese, tongue, strawberries, and other fruit occupied the center, surrounded by bottles of vodka, champagne, and warm red wine. It was ten in the morning. A plate of horsemeat was placed in front of me, along with a sheep's head and a bowl of *kumiz*—slightly alcoholic mares' milk that Marco Polo called "a right good drink." The ambassador poured a glass of vodka into a paper cup for me and said, "Drink. You have brought good luck

---

[8]The Russian exodus from Uzbekistan, numbering in the tens of thousands, decimated the ranks of professionals in the republic, according to Feshbach and Friendly in *Ecocide in the USSR*, "leaving vital installations such as the republic's largest thermal electric power station without skilled maintenance personnel . . . and halving Tashkent's ambulance service staff."

to our new embassy." I drank. He filled the cup. He then ordered me to do likewise with the *kumiz*, and then to help myself to the horsemeat and the sheep's head. The others were looking at me with wide and cratered faces and indeterminate skin colors, blending East and West, North and South— faces reflecting the geographical center of the earth's land mass. When it was my turn to offer a toast, I delivered a short speech on American-Kazakh friendship. Everyone cheered after it was translated. The ambassador poured me another vodka. I asked about a visa. The ambassador told me to return "tomorrow."

The next morning, with severe stomach trouble, I struggled back to the Kazakh embassy. The ambassador was busy, I was told. Instead, I saw a clerk, who said he could not issue me a visa unless someone in Ka- zakhstan sent an invitation. "That way," he explained, "if you are robbed or murdered in Kazakhstan, it will not be my government's responsibil- ity." I arranged for a Western embassy press spokesman in the Kazakh capital to send a fax to Tashkent formally inviting me. I eventually got the visa. The fee: $120. And I had complained about the visa process in West African countries!

Were such hassles the result of an old Soviet system still in place, whereby nobody got visas without prior invitations? Was it mere crimi- nality, with the clerk and ambassador or whomever pocketing the cash? Or was it, as I had suspected it was in West Africa, that the more fictitious the actual sovereignty and meaning of the state, the more determined the immigration authorities are to prove otherwise. Or was it all three?

IT WAS TIME to leave Tashkent.

I 7

◎   ◎   ◎

Pre-Byzantine Turks and
Civilization Clashes

FROM WHERE ULUG BEG and I sat, the Registan appeared across the street like an unreal theme park of painted minarets, ribbed turquoise domes, and glittering faience walls: The walls were like Persian carpets several stories high and several blocks wide that had been frozen upright into pottery glaze. The neat angles and cleanness of these fifteenth- and seventeenth-century structures—their very modernity, in fact, compared with the ramshackle huts of cheap wood, plastic, and concrete that I saw in every other direction—suggested that the Registan in Samarkand had been assembled overnight by people from Disneyland.

The Registan, meaning "place of sand"—sand scattered on the ground to soak up blood from public executions—was the heart of medieval Samarkand. Samarkand, which was captured in the fourth century B.C. by Alexander the Great, made into a junction point of the Silk Route by the Chinese in the second century B.C., sacked in the thirteenth century by Genghis Khan, chosen by Tamerlane in the fourteenth century as his capital, and glorified by Marco Polo and Ibn Battuta, is now a facade. Aside from one or two pretty courtyards, there is nothing behind the high walls that remains from what had at one time been three Koranic schools comprising the most magnificent medieval square in Turkestan. Little is left except these magnificent walls: surrounded by miles upon miles of hovels, battered automobiles, and people in unsightly polyester clothes.

There was no decent place to eat. Ulug Beg, my Uzbek guide, and I were sitting at a *chai-khana*, or Central Asian teahouse, but not the traditional *chai-khana* with rugs on raised platforms, which I seldom found in the big cities of Uzbekistan; this was, rather, the Soviet variety—with dented metal chairs, covered with smudged and peeling white paint with a high lead content. The chairs were chained to painted tables so that they wouldn't be stolen. Piles of cigarette butts were scattered on these tables. On sale, in the thinnest paper cups that I had ever encountered, were hot tea, chemical-tasting soft drinks of neon colors, and vodka, which rowdy groups of men were guzzling at nine in the morning, a sight more troubling than the absence of alcohol in public eating places in Iran.

"What can I do? This is my motherland. I am so ashamed," Ulug Beg told me. Ulug Beg, though an Uzbek, had been as overwhelmed as I was by the squalor we had seen that first day on the road from Tashkent, where I had met him the day before at the university. Nineteen years old, Ulug Beg was an amateur boxer with a Popeye physique, milk-coffee skin, black spiky hair, and wide Asian features reminiscent of the paintings of Mongol warriors. But he was an innocent. His father was connected to the still-surviving former-Soviet power structure, which meant that his family was well-off financially. By the standards of his own society, Ulug Beg had had a sheltered life.

He had studied in Moscow and in some of the Baltic cities. But he had never before traveled to Samarkand or Bukhara, where he had agreed to accompany me. After all, they were Tajik cities, he explained. Why would an Uzbek want to see them, unless he had specific business there? Samarkand—like Bukhara—was, according to the map, part of "Uzbekistan" (land of the Uzbeks), but in a legal sense only.

Samarkand and Bukhara are in the heart of Central Asia. But that's all the map tells us. Because of overlapping Russian, Persian, and Turkic influences, the cultural geography here is confusing. Tajiks are more or less a Persianized people; Uzbeks, a Turkic people. Bukhara and Samarkand are Persianized islands in the heart of a Turkic-run state. They reminded me of a map I had seen once of Central Asia, which showed language and civilization groups: like a child's finger painting that only marginally corresponded with the legal boundaries.[1]

What these differences mean, on the ground, is questionable. Uzbek-Tajik tensions, according to scholars, have been mainly confined to historical arguments fought between Uzbek and Tajik intellectuals. These scholars also note that post-Soviet Central Asia exhibits more tensions between urban and rural Uzbeks, and between urban and rural Tajiks—not to mention local clan rivalries—than between Uzbeks and Tajiks.

The ethnic situation is highly confused. For example, Uzbek president Islam Karimov is rumored to be half-Tajik, though his parentage is closely guarded. But in public Karimov usually speaks Russian, but his regime's hostility to the Russians was borne out in its reluctance to have the poems of Aleksandr Pushkin added to the Uzbek school curriculum. After all, Pushkin was Russian, not Uzbek. Eventually, the government announced that a non-Russian forebear of Pushkin had been identified. Pushkin, therefore, could now be taught.[2]

THE DAY HAD begun at 8 A.M., when Ulug Beg and I headed for Tashkent's long-distance bus station. The original Ulug Beg was Tamerlane's grandson, who ruled in Samarkand from 1407 to 1449. Besides being an enlightened ruler, Ulug Beg was an astronomer, comparable it has been said to Copernicus. Ulug Beg plotted the positions of the moon, the planets, and over a thousand stars, and calculated the length of the year to within fifty-eight seconds.

This Ulug Beg, my guide and translator, was a student at Tashkent's distinguished University of World Economy and Diplomacy. He had never guided anyone before, and seemed more nervous than I was, though his stomach was functioning normally and mine wasn't. But as a future member of the republic's ruling ethnic elite, he must have thought it could be useful to see other parts of his homeland. Ulug Beg, like many of my translators, was young. He was neither a journalist nor a professional guide. His opinions were not fully formed or fully coherent. But he and millions like him were about to write the script for the political future of

[1]The map was produced by Marvin Zonis and Associates, Inc., a Chicago-based international consulting firm.
[2]Pushkin, one of the foremost figures in Russian literature, was also part black. His mother's grandfather, Abram Hannibal, was a black general in Peter the Great's army.

many places around the world. In Uzbekistan, as in Iran, more than half the population were teenagers or younger.

We found a cab that would take us most of the way to the bus station. Ulug Beg and I spoke English en route, which he had learned at school in the Baltic states. The driver charged us twenty thousand soms for the five-minute ride, about eighty cents. "We have been cheated," Ulug Beg informed me. "From now on, no English until we've paid the driver." The second cab got us to the station after five more minutes of rather fast driving. It cost two thousand soms, or eight cents. I was not focusing on economics, yet I assumed that a place where I exchanged a one-hundred-dollar bill and needed a shoe box for the equivalent in local currency was not doing very well. As a rule of thumb, the cheaper it is for a foreigner, the worse it usually is for the locals.

Tashkent's bus station was populated with young toughs in thin fake-leather jackets and polyester shirts drinking vodka. A few weeks earlier in Samarkand, an American backpacker had been beaten nearly unconscious and had his bags stolen. A Western ambassador told me that both his wife and his daughter had had bags lifted from them on separate occasions at Uzbek bus terminals. These victims may have been careless, or their appearance may easily have given them away as prosperous foreigners. Or they may have been simply unlucky. I didn't know. What I did know, simply from looking at the crowd in the terminal hall, and from having a New Yorker's instinct for self-preservation, was that I was back in a place—like some parts of West Africa, but unlike the Nile Valley, Anatolia, and Iran—where the social fabric was thin. Uzbekistan may have been a cultural extension of both Turkey and Iran, but as I would discern, in crucial ways it bore no relation to either of those countries.

"Don't give your bag to the driver to put below. Keep it on your lap or under your seat." Ulug Beg was excited. His eyes didn't stop moving. He trusted his fellow Uzbeks no more than he trusted Tajiks. From Tashkent, the bus journey southwest to Samarkand was four hours and cost the equivalent of sixty-five cents. The seat frames were broken and the upholstery looked as if it had been chewed up by a herd of goats. The passengers were mixed: young toughs with acne and prematurely graying hair and shirts opened to their belly buttons; heavy-set women with flower-print dresses, kerchiefs, hairy legs, and gold teeth; lots of children, some quiet, some sleeping, some screaming. Some of the women seemed to be in pain. There was no air-conditioning. Everyone, even those not sweating, had oily complexions, something I had noticed in much of the Balkans and the former Soviet Union: Was it the dust or the poor quality of the soap?

Though beer and vodka had been readily available at the bus station, mineral water and bottled soft drinks were not. I filled my canteen in the bus station lavatory and poured it through my iodine-filtered cup. I recalled that in West Africa, bottled water and Western soft drinks had been in plentiful supply and the people and landscape were often beautiful to look at.

The road to Samarkand was not "golden" but lined with high weeds and white-painted concrete walls that enclosed fields and factories.[3] For four hours I gazed at the achingly flat, monochrome landscape of loose gray soil, cotton fields, and concrete-lined irrigation canals. What in Schuyler's day had been a "famished steppe," might in the future be called a "poisonous steppe." Feshbach and Friendly write in *Ecocide in the USSR* that

> . . . too much water used for irrigation stayed in the ground. Water tables that used to be twenty-two to twenty-three feet down in many areas rose to within a foot of the surface. Waterlogged soil on nearly 3 million acres of Uzbekistan became so saline that the land could not be farmed. . . . [Central Asians'] health was often further undermined by contaminated water and . . . excessive exposure to agricultural chemicals.

Samarkand, for all its romantic associations, announced itself with rusted pipes, corrugated-iron roofs, unpainted cement and porous cinder block facades, and the whine of diesel trucks. Ulug Beg and I headed for the city's first privately owned hotel to be opened since the collapse of communism. A burly, muscular man, with a beer in one hand and a cigarette in the other, greeted us at the hotel entrance with a "*salaam aleikum* (peace be upon you)."

"Let me do the talking," said Ulug Beg, tensing his boxer's muscles as we walked through the front door. In Moscow and the Baltic cities where he had studied, Ulug Beg had lived in student dormitories. Was this the first time he had ever checked into a hotel?

[3]James Elroy Flecker wrote, "For lust of knowing what should not be known / We make the golden journey to Samarkand."

The receptionist was Russian—in her fifties, I guessed. She was over-weight, and dressed like a twenty-year-old stripper, in a sequined dress with a low neckline that highlighted the cleft between her considerable breasts. Her hair was a bright synthetic orange, her perfume overpowering; her motherly, knowing eyes penetrated, I assumed, through to any man's fantasies, no matter how strange. After a few minutes of haggling, she made Ulug Beg pay eighty cents for his room. I, being a foreigner, paid thirty dollars. She wanted the money up front, in bills dated no earlier than 1990.

By now, several women of various racial hues had drifted over to the reception desk. These women were good-looking and wore heavy makeup. Like the receptionist, they were dressed like trapeze artists, and their eyes, like hers, were cynical cash-register eyes. I was a foreigner, which meant I had money to spend. Was this a whorehouse?

Upstairs, there seemed to be a lot of activity in the corridor. I spotted a man creeping into a room, in which I glimpsed a naked woman with jewelry around her neck and wrists. My room had a red Turkish carpet, red felt chairs, red flowered curtains made of plastic (like a shower curtain), a tea set, a refrigerator, and a double bed with red sheets. I looked out through the window, past a line of uneven, undressed concrete balconies and onto a truck depot, beyond which I could see a row of rose-colored bubble-shaped plastic street lamps. Like the government buildings in Tashkent, these street lamps indicated an ungainly design motif that had arisen from no discernible past or tradition. This hotel was not in an out-lying industrial zone but in the heart of Samarkand.

There was a knock on the door. I opened it. One of the painted ladies stood there with a few napkins in her hand. "Here is toilet paper," she said, staring at me as the receptionist had.

ULUG BEG AND I walked from the Registan, past yawning blocks of nonde-script, depressing architecture to the Gul Emir, or Ruler's Tomb, the burial place of Tamerlane, his grandson Ulug Beg, and other members of the Timurid ensemble.[4] Helped by an army of Turkic horsemen and Turkic-speaking Mongols, remnants of Genghis Khan's original horde, Tamerlane had, by the end of the fourteenth century, established an empire stretching from eastern Anatolia to northwestern India, which included all of Persia.

---

[4] Tamerlane's real Turkic name was Timur Leng ("Timur the Lame").

He died in 1405 while leading an army to China. Perfumed with rose water, musk, and camphor, Tamerlane's body was dispatched back to Samarkand, to this spot, for burial. In 1937, Fitzroy Maclean, the British secret agent and travel writer, slipped into Samarkand and visited the Gul Emir. "In front of the great entrance arch," Maclean writes in *Eastern Approaches*, "an old man had set up his bed under a mulberry tree. Rousing him, I induced him to open the gate for me."

Now, nearly six decades later, the blue-domed building was covered in scaffolding. An armed militia officer in an old Soviet uniform, his shirt hanging outside his pants, told me that if I gave him a dollar, he would turn the lights on inside. For another dollar, he would show us the basement where the real graves were, about which the general public, so he claimed, knew nothing. I gave him two dollars. In fact, the basement graves are described in all the guidebooks.

"I am so ashamed," Ulug Beg repeated as we sat outside on the steps of the tomb. "This may be Central Asia, but it is really the collapsing remains of the Soviet Union. I have to ask myself, what future does my country have if I have to be wary of the policemen, the very ones who are supposed to protect me?"

It was well known in Uzbekistan that police and militia were corrupt. In Tashkent and the other cities in the country, police stopped drivers who had committed infractions and demanded bribes. There was no road offense that wasn't easily fixed on the spot, provided you had the money. But the money almost never went into the public purse. The officers' expressions were always the same: sullen and ravenous, sizing you up. They seemed to be on the lookout not for crime but for opportunity. These policemen rarely walked upright, but shuffled with shoulders hunched forward. Their uniforms were untidy. Everything about them was feckless and askew.

"Even though the Soviets are gone, it hasn't changed the way the people think about their government," Ulug Beg explained as birds chirped overhead in the tomb's courtyard. "The people assume from their history that the government is not there to serve them. And because the government is not a part of them, it can never change. Nor, they assume, should it. For the people, the government is still thought of as *they*. And if *they* persecute us, then *it must be right*.

"You see, it is different in the Baltic states, where I studied. There, the people were ready for independence, because in their minds they had been a real nation long before it was official. Here, we are still not ready.

"Even the professors at my university are affected by this mentality. It is deep in them. It is in everything they teach us. I remember once we had a visiting official from your country, I think it was Brzezinski. He had a Polish name. I learned more from him than from any of my teachers. I can't remember what he said, exactly. But he was an independent thinker. That inspired me."

Ulug Beg asked a cabdriver to take us to one of the world's largest mosques, built between 1399 and 1404 with the assistance of ninety-five elephants, and named after one of Tamerlane's Chinese wives, Bibi Khanym. The young driver didn't know where the mosque was—I was astounded. He was gruff. His breath stank of vodka. Ulug Beg steamed:

"This is bad, it is all bad here in Samarkand. These people are all Tajiks. I don't know or understand these people. How can I like them? We must settle Uzbeks here. We must settle many, many Uzbeks in Samarkand."

Of course, I had noticed other cabdrivers, just as bad, in Tashkent, who were probably Uzbeks. If any characteristic united these incompetent, surly drivers it was age, not ethnicity. They were mainly young. The oldest drivers—those in their seventies—maybe because they had memories, of World War II, the deportations, whatever, seemed more rooted. But this new generation were *proles*, without a history or a culture. While in the 1930s, Maclean could write that "life seemed easy" in Samarkand, "and the inhabitants seem to spend most of their time talking and drinking tea," six decades of communism had taken their toll. Too many young men in the cities of Uzbekistan lived a skid-row version of *A Clockwork Orange*. Ignorance and alcoholism were partly responsible for a fatalistic public response to President Karimov's dictatorship—a less severe, 1990s version of Genghis Khan's and Stalin's absolutism. But given the simmering hatreds here, might Karimov's be a tyranny of necessity? I asked myself.

Here is the historical background to my question:

THE WORD *uzbek* means "independent" or "free"—from *Uz*, meaning "self." The Uzbeks trace their lineage back to Uzbek Khan (1312–1340), a son of Batu Khan, in turn a grandson of Genghis Khan. Uzbek Khan's forebears were part of Genghis's original Turko-Mongolian horde. It was these Uzbeks in the early sixteenth century who deposed Babur, the great Turkic poet and the last of Tamerlane's successors, who consequently fled Samarkand to found the Moghul dynasty in northwestern India. Of all the Turkic literary languages that were born during this confused and momentous period, it was Uzbek that survived longest, replaced only in 1937 upon Stalin's orders.[5]

The Uzbeks are an extremely proud and, according to many, "chauvinistic" people. But their ethnic pride, like that of the other Turkic peoples in Central Asia, as well as of the Persianized Tajiks, never conformed with statehood. "Few peoples in the world have ever been forced [as if against their will] to become independent nations. Yet that is precisely what happened to the five Central Asian republics" in 1991 when the Soviet Union dissolved, writes the American Central Asian expert Martha Brill Olcott. These people wanted civil liberties, but not necessarily freedom as citizens of new states. She adds that "although each republic was named for a local nationality, none was" based on the borders of any state that had ever, in fact, actually existed. Therefore, all these groups now have border claims on one another—and large populations in the other's territory on which to base such claims.

It is not only irrational borders with which Uzbeks and others in Turkestan have to contend: They must also rebuild, even reinvent, a national past out of preconceived myths, compounded by the historical erasures of communism. Another regional specialist, Edward A. Allworth, observes that today in Central Asia, nationalities are being created *retrospectively*. And not always accurately: Statues of Tamerlane are going up in Uzbekistan to honor an "Uzbek national hero," even though Tamerlane was not an Uzbek. In truth, it was the Uzbeks who toppled Tamerlane's dynasty when they defeated Babur.

Furthermore, all of this assumes that regardless of the lies of both history and mapmaking, people still know what they are. Often they don't. Prince Kropotkin's remark in the Britannica's eleventh edition about the "mixed" nature of Central Asia's population finds expression in the fact that as early as 1925, even before Stalin's mish-mash of deportations, farmers in Bukhara could not say whether they were Uzbeks or Kazakhs or Tajiks or whatever. They were *just from Bukhara*.

[5]See Dr. Stefan Wurm's paper on Turkic culture and linguistics listed in the bibliography.

To see how the Uzbeks and Tajiks might appear to each other, I went back to Schuyler:

> The Tadjiks and Uzbeks are readily distinguished from each other, not only in appearance but also in character. The Tadjik is larger and fuller in person, with an ample black beard, and with an air of shrewdness and cunning. He is . . . in every way morally corrupted. The Uzbek is taller and thinner, with a scanty beard . . . He is simple in his manners and dress, while the Tadjik is devoted to his personal appearance, and fond of adorning himself. The Uzbeks look upon the Tadjiks with contempt . . . The Tadjiks treat the Uzbeks as fools and children of nature . . .

As with other groups who have distrusted each other, notably Turks and Iranians, Uzbeks and Tajiks are often more closely related than they—and Schuyler—admit. Intermarriages are not uncommon, and Tajiks speak Dari, a dialect of Persian, which is greatly influenced by Turkic words.

Yet the Uzbek-Tajik divide might be the most significant of the various ethnic divides in Central Asia. This is because Uzbekistan is the fulcrum upon which the destiny of the whole region turns. Uzbekistan, with almost 45 percent of the entire population of former-Soviet Central Asia, is the most populous and centrally located state in the region. A population map of Central Asia would show most of the inhabitants living in—or close to—Uzbekistan. Uzbekistan's population is 23 million, compared with under 4 million inhabitants in Turkmenistan to the west, under 6 million in Tajikistan to the southeast, under 5 million in Kyrgyzstan to the east, and about 16.5 million in Kazakhstan to the northeast. Uzbekistan borders every one of these states, and also shares a small border with Afghanistan in the south. Moreover, there are 6 million ethnic Uzbeks who live outside the borders of Uzbekistan. Uzbeks, for example, form 24 percent of the population in Tajikistan, even as two of the major cities inside Uzbekistan, Samarkand and Bukhara, are populated by ethnic Tajiks. Ethnic Uzbeks also compose 13 percent of the population in Turkmenistan and 12.9 percent of the population in Kyrgyzstan.

In addition to their presence in these other states, Uzbeks account for 70 percent of the population of Uzbekistan itself. They, therefore, enjoy clear demographic dominance in the region. But it is a very fragile dominance. Uzbeks look across their southern border and see war-racked

Tajikistan, where Moslem fundamentalists are fighting ex-communists. Twenty thousand have died and tens of thousands of refugees have fled into Afghanistan. Both Tajiks and Uzbeks wonder if Persian-speaking Tajikistan could be a base for Iranian influence in Central Asia. Some Uzbeks told me that they fear Iran is promoting a Greater Tajikistan, to include the several million Tajiks in southeastern Uzbekistan and the 4 million indigenous Tajiks in northern Afghanistan.

Had the peoples of Turkestan been middle-class for several generations, with two cars in the driveway, a microwave in the kitchen, and mortgages to pay off, these border questions would be irrelevant—when, for example, have you read of separatists in Quebec, or linguistic nationalists in Belgium, arming themselves with AK-47s?

Uzbek president Islam Karimov is, for the time being, the alternative to chaos. I met Karimov twice, not in Uzbekistan where he is nearly impossible to interview, but in Switzerland, where he had gone in search of foreign investment. There, a group of reporters had asked about human rights abuses in his country—Uzbekistan under his rule has the worst human rights record of any former Soviet republic. He barked back that it was none of our business.

Under Karimov, democratic activists are routinely beaten by police. In 1992, Uzbek security officers used an iron bar to crack the skull of Abdulrahim Pulatov, a well-known Tashkent University professor who was demanding democracy. Washington repeatedly nags Karimov about human rights violations. It is questionable, however, how much Karimov cares what America thinks, given that European and Asian businessmen in Uzbekistan show little interest in his human rights record. Considering the volatile mix of alcoholism, unemployment, and potential ethnic conflict in Central Asia, might it make sense, in the short run at least, for Karimov to idolize strongmen like Lee Kuan Yew of Singapore and Alberto Fujimori of Peru rather than idealists like Vaclav Havel of the Czech Republic?

Consider Birlik, the banned political party headed by Pulatov, the fellow who had his skull cracked open. In the West, Birlik is defined as a group advocating human rights and democracy. But Birlik is also an Uzbek nationalist party. Perhaps Karimov watches the throngs of bored and restless young people at Birlik rallies, knows that half the population is under sixteen, and sees civil unrest in the future—not necessarily between Uzbeks and Tajiks, but also between Uzbeks and Uzbeks, like the clan-based tussles between various Azeri Turk groups in Azerbaijan. His strategy is to concentrate on economic development to soak up poverty and attendant social ills like alcoholism. Political liberalization can wait.

But Karimov, who grew up an orphan under hard circumstances, is socially awkward, which adds to the bad impression he makes in places like Switzerland. Insulated his whole adult life within the Communist party hierarchy, he has no grasp of economic modernization. He wants to be like Mr. Lee in Singapore, but he doesn't know how. He fears what has happened in the Caucasus—where economic and social misery parallel Central Asia's—and where two nationalistic democrats, Levon Ter-Petrosian in Armenia and Ebulfez Elcibey in Azerbaijan, both freely elected and lauded by Western human rights activists, promptly entered a war that killed twenty thousand people and created a million refugees. In the Caucasus, as in Rwanda, as in Sudan in the late 1980s, as occasionally in Nigeria and other places, democracy has often institutionalized ethnic and regional divisions. In the Caucasus, it required a Soviet era dictator, Geidar Aliyev—who overthrew the democrat Elcibey in Azerbaijan—to move toward peace with Armenia.

Karimov and others like him are betting that democracy is not the final word in political evolution. The West believes they are wrong. But what if they are right, or even partly right—in their cases? For us it's a matter of principle: for tens of millions threatened by the specter of civil conflict, it is a matter of life and death.

◎   ◎   ◎

THE CABARET AT our hotel did not really get going until eleven, when a male singer, who took long drags on an unfiltered cigarette, crooned, "I'm in hell." The microphone, turned up many decibels too high, rumbled and crackled. In the red velvet darkness, men dangling cigarettes danced with women wearing bedroom slippers and fake satin gowns. Tables were cluttered with salami, cheese, stuffed vegetables, filthy ashtrays, and vodka bottles. A group of professional female dancers took the stage. They were like harem girls, moving hypnotically, their eyes vacant and dilated: They could have been dancing for Genghis Khan. Next came a contortionist.

There was an easy vulgarity about the evening—a Berlin cabaret ambience of the 1930s leavened by sham Central Asian mystery. A militiaman leaned drunkenly against the wall and patted the girls as they left the stage. Shouts and table pounding erupted here and there, but never quite spilled over into fisticuffs. At the table next to Ulug Beg and me sat a group of youths in their early twenties with their girlfriends, dressed like American teenagers from the 1950s. One youth took pulls on a big cigar and kept ordering wine and vodka. He gave a big tip to the waiter. "How can he afford that in this economy?" I asked Ulug Beg. He shrugged. "He must be in some racket, like everyone eating here."

At another table was a group of drunken army officers. "They are bragging about being on good terms with people close to President Karimov," Ulug Beg explained. "It is disgraceful. In Soviet times, officers got drunk in public, sure. But rarely in uniform. Now there is no discipline." At a third table were a group of civilians, all heavyset men, in gaudy three-piece suits and wearing gold rings, talking loud. "What are they talking about?" I asked. Ulug Beg answered:

"They are discussing which is the best country from which to hijack a plane, if one wants a big ransom. Such conversations are common." Ulug Beg's face tightened. He confided to me that he used to be a bodyguard, on account of his boxing skills. "But now it is too dangerous. In Soviet times, only fists were used. Now it's guns."

My guide was less innocent than he had first appeared.

A pretty waitress came over and started talking with Ulug Beg. When she left, he hissed, "She thinks because it is hot in here I want to flirt with her. It is so depressing. These Tajik girls in Samarkand are all so beautiful. Why aren't our own Uzbek women so pretty? I feel strange here, as if I am in Tajikistan."

The waitress reminded me of Schuyler's comment about how, compared to the Uzbeks, the Tajiks fussed over their personal appearance and liked cosmetics. But neither the Persian Tajiks nor the Turkic Uzbeks were like the Persians in Iran or the Turks I had met in Turkey. En route to Turkestan, I had assumed I would soon be encountering people like the Anatolian Turks. But even Ulug Beg, though well groomed and educated, was crude in the way he ate and narrow in his prejudices against Tajiks. And Ulug Beg was among the most Westernized Uzbeks I was to meet in Central Asia. This coarseness might be more than just the effect of three quarters of a century of Soviet communism.

I thought and thought. Could these be *pre-Byzantine* Turks? Could this be what Turks might have been somewhat like before the great Seljuk and Osmanli migrations to Anatolia, where the Turks were softened by the Mediterranean and culturally transformed by the Byzantine Greeks, whom they conquered? (Lord Kinross points out in *The Ottoman Centuries* how the Ottoman Turks had inherited the legacy of Byzantium with all its cosmopolitan fineries, including the eunuch system and the domed churches that the Ottomans converted into mosques—just as the Byzantines had inherited the legacy of Rome.) Abandonment of traditional trade routes after da Gama's voyage, and the centuries of czarist-Soviet tyranny that followed, left the peoples of Turkestan to stagnate. Like other prisoners with the available means, they became bored, and drunk, and occasionally violent.

◎   ◎   ◎

ULUG BEG'S HOSTILITY, however atypical, toward Tajiks reminded me of the cracked Greek tombstone in the Tashkent cemetery, of the Iranians' fear of Turks, of the tensions between Turks and Arabs over the damming of the Euphrates, of the Moslem violence against Copts in Upper Egypt, and other ethno-cultural tensions I had observed in the course of my travels. Was this evidence of what Samuel P. Huntington of Harvard called "The Clash of Civilizations"?

The world, Huntington argues, has been moving in our century from nation-state conflict to ideological conflict and, finally, to culture conflict. I would add that as refugee flows increase and as peasants continue migrating to cities around the world—turning them into vast villages—national borders will mean less, while political power falls increasingly into the hands of less educated, less sophisticated groups. In the eyes of these uneducated but newly empowered millions, the real borders are the most tangible and intractable ones: those of culture and tribe. Huntington writes, "First, differences among civilizations are not only real; they are basic," involving, among other things, history, language, and religion. "Second . . . the interactions between peoples of different civilizations are increasing; these increasing interactions intensify civilization consciousness."

Huntington points to interlocking conflicts among Hindu, Moslem, Slavic Orthodox, Western, Japanese, Confucian, Latin American, and possibly African civilizations.

Because Huntington's brush is broad, his specifics are vulnerable to attack. In a rebuttal to Huntington's argument, Johns Hopkins professor Fouad Ajami, a Lebanese-born Shi'ite who certainly knows the world beyond the ivory-tower America universities, writes in the September-October, 1993 issue of *Foreign Affairs*:

The world of Islam divides and subdivides. The battle lines in the
Caucasus . . . are not coextensive with civilizational fault lines. The
lines follow the interest of states. Where Huntington sees a civilizational duel between Armenia and Azerbaijan, the Iranian state has
cast religious zeal . . . to the wind . . . in that battle the Iranians have
tilted toward Christian Armenia.

True, Huntington's hypothesized war between Islam and Orthodox
Christianity is not borne out by the alliance network in the Caucasus. But
that is only because he has misidentified *which* civilizational war is occurring there. Azeri Turks, perhaps the world's most secular Shi'ite Moslems,
see their cultural identity not in terms of religion but in terms of their
Turkic race. The Armenians, likewise, fight the Azeris not because the latter are Moslems, but because they are Turks, related to the same Turks
who massacred Armenians in 1915. Turkic culture (secular and based on
languages adopting a Latin script) is battling Iranian culture (religiously
militant as defined by the Teheran clergy, and wed to an Arabic script)
across Central Asia and the Caucasus. The Armenians are, therefore, natural allies of their fellow Indo-Europeans, the Iranians.

Huntington may be correct to say that the Caucasus is a flash point of
cultural and racial wars. But, as Ajami observes, Huntington's terms are
too simple. While Turks are growing deeply distrustful and coming to
hate Moslem Iran, they are also, especially in the shantytowns that are
coming to dominate Turkish political life, identifying themselves increasingly as Moslems, betrayed by a West that for several years did little to
help besieged Moslems in Bosnia and which attacks Turkish Moslems in
the streets of Germany.

To go a step further, the Balkans, where nation-state wars flared at
the beginning of the twentieth century, have been on the verge of culture
conflict between Orthodox Christianity (represented by the Serbs and a
classic Byzantine configuration of somewhat-sympathetic Greeks, Russians, and Romanians) and the worldwide House of Islam. Yet in the
Caucasus, Islam is subdividing into a clash between Turks and Iranians.
Ajami rightly asserts that this very subdividing, not to mention the many
divisions within the Arab world, indicate that the West, including the
United States, is not threatened by Huntington's scenario. As the Gulf
War demonstrated, the West can still play one part of the House of Islam
against another.

"The Clash of Civilizations" is a romantic term, conjuring up massive armies divided by race, language, and religion, advancing across battlefields thousands of miles long, wielding banners of the cross and of the crescent. The reality is different. The desecration of Greek and Russian Orthodox tombstones by a Moslem Uzbek mob in Tashkent was an isolated incident ignited by specific, local factors—like other isolated events, such as a war between Moslems and Orthodox Christians in Bosnia; a decades-long war of words, with occasional bloodshed, between a Greek Orthodox government in Athens and a Turkish Moslem government in Ankara; the forced exodus, earlier in the twentieth century, of Greek Orthodox communities from Istanbul, Smyrna, and the Turkish Moslem-controlled Black Sea coast; and the tensions between various Russian Orthodox and Turkic Moslem communities in Azerbaijan, Kyrgyzstan, and Kazakhstan. But these events, taken as a whole, have more to do with historically based religious and ethnic differences than with modern state loyalties. So for such events, Huntington's civilization clash is an appropriate term—as a crude organizing principle.

But the reality is uglier, more complex, and pathetic. Forget about medieval horsemen giving battle; expect instead a fistfight with smashed vodka bottles in a plywood bar. For the moment, a civilizational competition may exist between the Turkic and Iranian peoples for future trade routes in Central Asia—routes, that for the most part haven't yet been built, with the battle so far being fought with charts and anemic statements within bureaucrats' offices. It is a competition that the Russians are joining: The Russians want to upstage both Turkey's plan to transport Central Asian oil across Anatolia to the Mediterranean and Iran's plan to transport the oil to the Persian Gulf with their own plan to ship oil through the Black Sea and the Bosphorus straits. As some states here become increasingly identified with old caravan routes, this might lead to conflict. Meanwhile, what I saw on the ground is a Turkic Uzbek youth, Ulug Beg, pale with anger after being teased by a Persian Tajik woman.

Schuyler's description of the negative stereotypes harbored by Uzbeks and Tajiks for each other may still apply because of the economic and social disorder arising from seventy-four years of communist rule, and the weakening of other constraints. From Schuyler's day through 1991, Uzbeks and Tajiks were all subjects of a single authority: the czar, and then the commissar. There was no territory for them to fight over, just as there was none in the Balkans in the days of the Ottoman empire. But now, with very fragile states with little tradition behind them and little logic to their borders, the tensions a visitor notices in Central Asia are less between states than between groups both within and overlapping such states, or between inhabitants of one traditional city-state region and another. The chance that these states will shatter as a result of intensified Turkic-Iranian competition (leading to strife between Uzbeks and Tajiks), or because of economic competition within the Uzbek or Tajik communities, is probably greater than the threat of a traditional war between, say, Uzbekistan and Tajikistan—neither of whose governments can claim the loyalty of their ethnic minorities in such a circumstance, and neither of whose military frontiers coincide with ethnic ones.

◎　　　◎　　　◎

ALL I HAD learned so far was that states in West Africa, the Near East, and Central Asia were weakening, and that ethnic-religious identities appeared stronger by contrast. Beyond that, I had little proof of anything. Travel was indeed frustrating.

18

◎   ◎   ◎

Clean Toilets and the
Legacy of Empires

I HAD TO use the toilet.

Ulug Beg and I were at the Samarkand station, waiting for the bus to Bukhara. In the upstairs cafeteria, as I was sipping tea, I noticed a hallway with some offices. Maybe there is a toilet there, I thought. In the offices were a few women. I interrupted their typing to ask. They cheerfully pointed further down the corridor to a door. I opened it and went inside.

The floor was flooded. The cracked bowl was indescribably filthy. Flies buzzed. Holding my breath, I relieved myself and left. There was no toilet paper. There was no place to wash my hands.

Weren't these pleasant women offended to use such a facility? Couldn't they have organized themselves to clean the lavatory? It wouldn't have been that much work. This was the filthiest toilet I had seen in Uzbekistan, but some others were about as bad. The question troubled me. Then I read an article about toilets in Romania by Slavenka Drakulic in *The New Republic*.[1]

---

[1]"Lav Story: Romania's Dirty Little Secret" was published April 25, 1994. See the bibliography.

"Romania, like most ex-Communist countries," Drakulic writes, "remains a country of peasants," and "peasants have a different idea of hygiene than city-dwellers: they go here and there, in nature while working in the field or in a wooden cabin in their yard." After World War II and the triumph of communism in Romania, peasants flocked to cities to take part in mass industrialization. But this did not make them *urban*. "The values of a civil society are values created by citizens," writes Drakulic, "and one or two generations of peasants living in the cities under a totalitarian regime had no chance of becoming citizens, politically or culturally."

Regarding peasants, Drakulic may have been uncharitable, since Uzbek peasants often had clean toilets and outhouses in their homes. But her larger point is correct: The condition of a country's public toilets—or the lack of them even—says something about its progress toward civil society. West Africa was still in a pre-toilet phase: you went in an open space, without shame. However, the public toilets I remember from West Africa, even those at bus stations, were cleaner than those I saw in Central Asia. Egyptian and Turkish toilets ranged from pristine to awful. Iranian public toilets were often clean, perhaps because the ayatollahs did less damage to Persian culture than the communists inflicted on Central Asian culture. Could the legacy of communism in Central Asia be as disruptive as the demons of demography, climate, and resource scarcity in Africa? Like the conversations Ulug Beg and I had overheard in the hotel cabaret, the filthy public toilets I saw pointed to a society where few loyalties existed beyond the home. (I couldn't help wondering what a traveler from abroad would say about New York City—based on its lack of public toilets.)

◎　　　◎　　　◎

A BOY CAME onto the bus and recited a Moslem prayer for a safe journey. The five-hour trip westward, from Samarkand to Bukhara, captured Feshbach and Friendly's main concept of Turkestan:

> When historians finally conduct an autopsy on the Soviet Union . . . they may reach the verdict of death by ecocide. . . . For any event except the mysterious collapse of the Mayan empire, it would be a unique but not an implausible conclusion. No other great industrial civilization so systematically . . . poisoned its land, air, water and people.

The bus was a sealed sheet-metal container under a glaring desert sun. The young man in front of me was drinking beer out of a fruit jar. The children behind me were playing with poorly molded plastic tommy guns, pretending to be hijackers. The fields were notched with concrete irrigation ditches, one after another. Alkalinity from overirrigation had made the outermost reaches of the Kizyl-Kum ("Red Sand") Desert look as if the Creator had poured the contents of a giant salt shaker over it and then added some ground chalk for good measure. Rather than red, the encrusted sand and eroded silt of this utterly flat landscape looked ashen and metallic, like mercury. There was no shade. Here and there were the iron-roofed blockhouses of collective farms, with walls of cinder blocks and dried mud. There was no sign that a copse of trees had ever been planted here, or a fence painted; no sign of anything personal—a single fond memory—to distinguish the lives of those forced to grow up, grow old, and die in such miserable barracks.

We passed a soccer stadium: basic poured-concrete with weeds sprouting around it. It might as well have been an archaeological site.

The Soviet Union was officially dead, but its corpse would rot for decades, confounding attempts at civil, political, and environmental renewal. The twenty-first century was nearly upon us, yet policymakers in the Near East and the Balkans were still grappling with the destitution left by the Ottoman empire, dead since 1918. How much more profound and manifold was the impact of Soviet communism on the Caucasus and Central Asia than Ottoman desuetude had been upon the Near East! As cruel as they were, the Turkish sultans never perpetrated anything like Stalin's terror-famines and mass deportations, which, in the words of historian Robert Conquest, made a considerable part of Soviet Central Asia in the 1930s "one vast Belsen." Nor was there anything approaching such environmental disaster in the former Ottoman empire. The destruction here is something completely new in history. Forty percent of the agricultural land in the new Commonwealth of Independent States is considered "endangered." Sixteen percent of former Soviet territory is an "ecological crisis zone." Over 20 percent of ex-Soviet citizens live in regions of "environmental disaster." Twenty to 30 percent of general morbidity in the former Soviet Union is related to environmental factors; in Uzbekistan, writes scholar Nancy Lubin, "between 1970–1986, infant mortality rose by almost fifty percent . . ." Lubin writes: "The Silent Spring that Rachel Carson described in her classic book in the 1960s is now almost a reality for millions of Commonwealth citizens."[2]

To restore the environment to acceptable levels for human habitation will be a long and costly process that will put a drag on future economic development in Central Asia, further hindering the emergence of a civil society.

◎   ◎   ◎

THE SOVIET UNION was alive and well in the Intourist Hotel in Bukhara, where Ulug Beg and I had just arrived after our bus journey from Samarkand. Yes, they had rooms available. No, you couldn't pay later. They wanted to know—for certain—how many nights you planned to stay. And they demanded that the entire bill be paid in advance. There were long forms to fill in and several receipts to collect. No, you couldn't have the key. You would get the key only upon submitting the proper receipt to the charwoman on the eighth floor. It was like checking into a prison. Before 1991, Ulug Beg told me every other word barked at you from behind the reception desk was *nyet*. Now it was *yok*, which means "no" in Uzbek and other Turkic languages, and has an even greater finality about it. "To them, the fact that you are an American only means that you have money to give them. They are too isolated, too ignorant, even to know how to be curious about you as a person," Ulug Beg explained. In the "duty-free" shop beside the hotel elevator, two dusty cans of Coca-Cola lay inside a locked glass display case, like jewels.

◎   ◎   ◎

"BOKHARA HAS REMAINED, and, I think, cannot but remain, so long as it survives at all, wholly Eastern," writes Fitzroy Maclean in *Eastern Approaches*. Rather than a simple glittering facade like Samarkand, Bukhara had volume: Islamic buildings, with baked yellow brick walls and blue faience domes dissolving before my eyes as though I had smoked a pipe of hashish. I encountered these wafer-brick domes at eye level, from elevated stone bridges. Bukhara was full of surprising angles, as though I were crouched on the ground looking upward through a watery lens. Here were *chai-khanas* with raised platforms and carpets, populated by old men

---

[2]The data in this section come from Nancy Lubin's paper "Pollution and Politics in the USSR." See the bibliography.

with embroidered caps and wispy white beards, sipping green tea. From the Kalyan minaret, with its fourteen bands of Kufic calligraphy around its tapering neck, which made it look like a finger stacked with fourteen puzzle rings, Genghis Khan threw his faithless wives to their deaths. "Tower of Death," it is called. Maclean compares it "with the finest architecture of the Italian Renaissance."

Bukhara was hot. In May the temperature was already over a hundred degrees Fahrenheit. My face burned, as if I were standing too close to a fire. "It is because of the Aral Sea and what the Russians did to it. The Russians made the climate worse," declared an elderly Tajik merchant. Other old men agreed. The summers in Bukhara were now hotter, drier, and longer than when they were young, they told me.

The Aral Sea is probably the world's greatest single environmental disaster, and certainly among the most notorious. Once the earth's fourth largest inland lake, in the last thirty years it has shrunk to half its original size and a third of its former volume, in order to provide water for the Soviet Union's cotton monoculture. In 1989, the sea was three times more saline than in 1961: Few fish survive anymore in its waters. By 1981, report Feshbach and Friendly, twenty-nine major storms "of dust and salt" had been caused by the sea's shrinkage. The storms that followed throughout the 1980s carried between 90 and 140 million tons of salt and sand yearly. Human costs have been enormous. According to Nancy Lubin:

> Because of the salination caused by the drying up of the sea and the overuse of pesticides and chemicals in the fields, most inhabitants of that area suffer from a range of respiratory and intestinal diseases. . . . In the Aral Sea region . . . one out of ten children born does not live to its first birthday. Many of those children who do survive are . . . disease ridden . . .

Bukhara, some three hundred miles southeast of the Aral Sea, is, according to some experts, too far away to be directly affected by the sea's shrinkage. However, Feshbach and Friendly note, "the lake that once acted as a huge heat pump and cooling system lost its power to moderate the regional climate. Surrounding deserts gained the meteorological upper hand." Summers are now rainless and hotter in Bukhara; winters are snowless and colder.

A local newspaper reported that hotels in Bukhara would soon start accepting Visa cards, and Western soft drinks and Kodak film were on sale in some places. Ulug Beg, though, was not upbeat. "The only thing we Uzbeks have in common with Tajiks is the sky," he commented, feeling as much a foreigner in his own land as I did.

I found cause for some optimism at the Sufi religious center built around the tomb of Sheikh Bakhautdin, a holy man who died in 1384 after founding the Naqshbandiyah order of mystics. (The sheikh was called *an-naqshband*, "the painter," because of the visual impression of God that the repetition of his prayer should leave upon the faithful.) Twenty minutes by taxi from Bukhara, the complex included a sixteenth-century mosque and a modern museum, which had, among its exhibits, a photograph of the visit here of the late Turkish leader Turgut Ozal, who as a devout Moslem had ties to Naqshbandi Sufis. There were quite a few visitors at the Sufi center, all religious Moslems. The exhibits were in local languages. There was no intention to attract Western tourists. Yet the place was neater and more spotless than any historical site I had visited in Uzbekistan: Because Islamic identity was real and not artificial like the current Uzbek state, it engendered community-mindedness. Though Islamization has proved fertile ground for terrorists, it also offers a path toward civil society that former-Soviet Central Asia desperately requires.

◎　　　◎　　　◎

MY JOURNEY TO Samarkand and Bukhara with Ulug Beg had been a side trip to the southwest from Tashkent. Back in Tashkent, I collected my visas in preparation for a land journey in the opposite direction—southeastward across Central Asia, through Kyrgyzstan, Kazakhstan, western China, and Pakistan. After saying goodbye to Ulug Beg one late May afternoon at 5 P.M., I headed for the Tashkent long-distance bus station. Now I was traveling alone. It would be an all-night ride eastward to Bishkek, the Kyrgyz capital. Because I would now be leaving Uzbekistan, the ticket vendor would not sell me a ticket without a stamp from the police, whose office was upstairs in the terminal building. I gave my passport to the police officer, who motioned me to sit down. He went through all ninety pages of my passport. (I had a forty-eight-page "business" passport with two twenty-one-page "supplements.") He looked at all the stamps.

"You did not register with the police when you came here. You must pay me a big fine. Maybe a hundred dollars." said the officer.

"I'm sorry, I didn't know about registering," I told him. "I was staying with a friend, not at a hotel."

He just stared at me. I looked at him with a pleading expression. Slowly, he licked the stamp that was to go on my exit form. He breathed on the stamp in three long breaths, still staring at me. At last, he handed me back my passport with the exit permission. Had he hesitated a moment longer, I was prepared to give him five dollars and then bargain upward if necessary.

I half-hoped that because of the thirteen-hour journey to Bishkek, and the fact that we would be traveling at night, the bus would be in better condition than the ones I had taken to Bukhara and Samarkand. It wasn't. People stuffed everything, including suitcases, vodka bottles, and fertilizer sacks, under and above the broken seats. Passengers took off their shoes and began smoking. A group of young men who had stripped down to their waists in the dank heat began drinking heavily. They shouted above a scratchy transistor playing pop music. West Africa had revealed social dissolution; but with the exception of the male youths raised in shacktowns, West Africans were often more modest than many Central Asians. By the time the driver pulled out of the station, half an hour behind schedule, the bus smelled of sweat and alcohol. On the panel behind the driver's seat, facing the passengers, was a poster of a nude American pinup whose large and glossy breasts seemed to fill the bus as it bumped along the road. *The promise of the West*, I thought.

The man beside me was Russian. He put a cup of brandy in my hand, then offered me a boiled egg and a tomato. "To Bishkek?" I asked. *"Nyet,"* he responded, a bit angry. "To Frunze!" Frunze—a reference to General Mikhail Frunze, a Russian conqueror of Turkestan—was what the Russians had called Bishkek until the Kyrgyz renamed it in 1991.

Because of the mountainous topography of Central Asia, getting to Pakistan was not simple. Pakistan lay far to the south and slightly to the east. But rather than a straight line southeast, I would have to make a wide clockwise arc around the mountains: first northeast, then far to the east, then back around to the southwest, then, finally, south. The difficult topography was welcome: I would get to see more of Central Asia this way.

In the first stage of my journey I would be traveling northeastward: from Tashkent, the capital of Uzbekistan, to Bishkek, the capital of Kyrgyzstan. Though, according to the map, Uzbekistan and Kyrgyzstan shared a long common border, this frontier was quite mountainous. To get to Kyrgyzstan, therefore, the bus would first go northward into Kazakhstan, then east along the Kazakh steppe before dipping south into Kyrgyzstan. Whatever the map said, the road and railway routes indicated not so much separate countries as a string of city-states stretching from west to east: Bukhara, Samarkand, Tashkent, Bishkek, and Alma Ata. These route patterns were like a geo-political X-ray mapping of the region,[3] revealing what was behind the facade of the current map, a legacy of Stalin.

The bus left Tashkent and headed north, reaching the Kazakh border within an hour. It consisted of a few defaced concrete roadblocks. The bus didn't stop. There were no checks. In an instant I was in Kazakhstan, whatever that meant.

Now the driver turned east. We stopped only once during the night, at a string of shacks where fruit, candy, locally made soft drinks, and alcohol were on sale. A few of us walked behind the wall of shacks to pee. It was dark. A cool breeze moved across the steppe. The maddeningly flat landscape was broken by telephone poles. Back in the bus, the loud snoring made sleep impossible. At dawn, I got my first look at the white flanks of the Tien Shan, the "Mountains of Heaven," which prevent a direct southern approach toward Pakistan. I was now at the edge of the great cluster of mountain ranges that are home to some of the highest peaks on earth. The Tien Shan intersect the Pamirs (Roof of the World), which, in turn, abut the Hindu Kush (Hindu Killers) and the Karakorams (Black Gravel Range), which merge with the Himalayas (Abode of Snow). In the morning, just as I nodded asleep, the bus pulled into Bishkek. I don't remember a border post between Kazakhstan and Kyrgyzstan. But in Kyrgyzstan there were big potholes; in Kazakhstan the roads had been smooth.

◎   ◎   ◎

KYRGYZ NOMADS HAD been part of Genghis Khan's Golden Horde, which subjugated medieval Russia. They must have left a genetic trace. In *The Magic Mountain*, Thomas Mann describes a captivating Russian woman with " 'Kirghiz' eyes"—the eyes of a "prairie-wolf." To split the Kyrgyz nation, Stalin created two republics. He made a region of the Tien Shan

---

[3]This concept belongs to Professor Alan K. Henrikson of Tufts University, who explained it in a 1985 letter to the Central Asian scholar Mahnaz Z. Ispahani. See Ispahani, listed in the bibliography.

mountains "Kyrgyzstan," and the great steppes to the north—the home of the original Kyrgyz who fought with Genghis Khan—he called "Kazakhstan." The differences in language and customs between today's Kyrgyz and Kazakhs are, therefore, minimal.[4]

Nestled high in the Tien Shan glaciers with some three thousand lakes and a population of only 4.4 million, Kyrgyzstan, self-sufficient in both food and water, escaped many of the ravages of communism. Another stroke of luck was the elevation of Askar Akaev in 1990—a mathematician with little belief in communist ideology—to the post of republic leader. Akaev opened Kyrgyzstan to the outside world (my visa cost only twenty-five dollars and didn't require an invitation). He also allowed the International Monetary Fund to practically write the new country's economic program. When I exchanged a fifty-dollar bill at my hotel in Bishkek, instead of a shoe box full of money, I got just a thick wad of bills in return. A more stable currency, I realized, can help create a strong state identity. Any economist could have told me that, but I was learning through experience. Uzbekistan, without a stable currency, had little identity as a state.

Bishkek, like Tashkent, and like Alma Ata, too, is a capital city near the border between two states. Bishkek lies at the very foot of the Tien Shan mountains but it is still part of the Kazakh steppes, a few miles beyond the Kazakh border. Like Tashkent, it is a Russian colonial city with a grid street pattern, but unlike Tashkent, it is clean, quiet, small, and home to many rose gardens against a backdrop of magnificent mountains. The pretty, miniature nature of the capital and of the country itself, and the civility of its government compared to those of its neighbors, have made Kyrgyzstan the "favorite" state in Central Asia for Western diplomats and other specialists—a sort of Central Asian Vermont. But like Ghana in West Africa, the success of Kyrgyzstan is relative to the failure elsewhere in the region.

After checking into my hotel, I went for a walk along streets crowded with Russians selling bad soap, Mars bars, razors, toys, furniture, bathroom scales, cheese, and so on. One elderly Russian told me, "The factories are closed, production has stopped, and people are selling everything just to survive or to raise enough money to return to Russia. The Kyrgyz don't want us. Crime is up—not like Uzbekistan, but for us it's high. No

[4]See Ahmed Rashid's *The Resurgence of Central Asia*, listed in the bibliography, for a fuller discussion of these issues.

one here wants democracy. We want jobs and stability." A European diplomat elaborated: "I don't trust the situation. Technically, there is progress here. Technically, the system is opening. Technically, there is Western business interest. But how many contracts have actually been signed? Why, when an official gives a speech asking for the public's advice, are there no questions from the audience afterward, only silence? And why haven't the Russians stopped leaving?" In *The Resurgence of Central Asia*, Ahmed Rashid reports:

> An estimated 100,000 Russians had left by the end of 1992, but their continued presence is fueling Kyrgyz nationalism. The government is now attempting to implement reverse discrimination by promoting Kyrgyz bureaucrats to senior positions. . . . Despite its intensive pro-capitalist legislation, Kyrgyzstan was still unable to attract major foreign investment. . . . The gross domestic product declined by 15 percent in 1992 after a drop of five percent the previous year. Industrial output declined by as much as 25 percent. . . . Kyrgyzstan's lack of resources and industry means that there is relatively little for the government to privatize.

In that morning's edition of *The Kyrgyzstan Chronicle* (May 31, 1994), the news was mostly depressing. According to one article, the average Kyrgyz family had to spend 69.6 percent of its income on food in 1993, compared to 34.1 percent in 1990. In another piece, written by a Lt. Col. Ahjol Isayev, "tribalism" between warring Kyrgyz clans was rife in the Kyrgyz army. Another article, entitled "Tien Shan Colombia," by Lt. Col. Alexander Zelichenko, deputy chairman of the Republic State Committee for Narcotics Control, reported that there were 229 confirmed cases of "narcotics planting" in 1993, compared to four in 1990. He said opium is grown in farmsteads, gardens, and kitchens. Most of the growers are either below thirty or over sixty, or unemployed—those sectors of the population that are the "least socially protected." Ten kilos of opium are smuggled daily from Afghanistan, where there is no central government, to Tajikistan, where there is a civil war, to Kyrgyzstan. In some sections of Kyrgyzstan, "12 percent of the juveniles systematically use opium," and an additional "42 percent episodically."

And in August 1994, a few months after my visit, Oxford Analytica reported that Kyrgyzstan's triple-digit inflation was a factor behind "social unrest in shantytowns around the capital." Everything was relative. The Kyrgyz currency was stable only compared to Uzbekistan's. To preserve the integrity of the new currency, Oxford Analytica warned, Akaev might have to "shift toward authoritarian rule."[5] Despite its relative physical isolation from the rest of the former Soviet Union and the competence of its economic decision-makers, this country was, nevertheless, slowly becoming trapped in the downward spiral of other ex-communist countries: falling production combined with rising inflation.

These may have been mere problems of transition, similar to those encountered in some European states, like Poland and Hungary. But here too it is Stalin's map that may ultimately determine what happens to Kyrgyzstan:

The most fertile and densely populated part of Central Asia is the ethnic-Uzbek-dominated Ferghana Valley, the real hub of the region. Stalin apportioned the valley to three Soviet republics: Uzbekistan, Tajikistan, and Kyrgyzstan. Uzbekistan got most of it. This is mainly what accounts for Uzbekistan's high population compared to its neighbors, and its critical importance to the rest of Central Asia. The Ferghana Valley is also the center of Central Asia's Moslem religious revival—a threat to the secular Uzbek regime—which may have been why my Uzbek visa didn't permit me to visit there.

As with Macedonia in the southern Balkans, no matter how you divide the Ferghana, each state would be left with unruly minorities, because in every town there are Uzbeks on one street and Kyrgyz on another (and some Tajiks too). In 1990, discontent over rising food prices and a 22.8 percent unemployment rate caused riots between Uzbeks and Kyrgyz in Osh and Uzgen, two valley towns on the Kyrgyzstan side of the border. A video recording in Uzgen showed Uzbek babies hanging on meat hooks in a butcher shop.[6] More than a thousand people were killed. Reconciliation has been slow. In Osh, both the Kyrgyz and Uzbek communities practice ethnic apartheid. So much for Turkic unity.

The Ferghana Valley may be more important than any of the three Central Asia states that divide it, because that is where Central Asia's population is concentrated. Moreover, while these states are fairly artificial, the

[5]Oxford Analytica Daily Brief for the World Economic Forum in Davos, Switzerland. August 3, 1994.
[6]See journalist Vivien Morgan's account, listed in the bibliography.

Ferghana is a historically and geographically rooted region. Will the resurgence of Islam in the valley forge better links among Uzbeks, Kyrgyz, and Tajiks, all of whom are Moslems? Or will Islam, combined with bad economic conditions for years to come, erode the legitimacy of secular state regimes, with unpredictable, but not altogether benign, consequences?

I WANDERED FOR over an hour in Bishkek's outlying suburbs, at a point where the steppe literally ends and the foothills of the Tien Shan begin. Finally I found it: one dilapidated dacha among many similar ones. Inside were four ethnic Russian yuppies with computers, a video, and a fax machine. A cheerful woman with red hair offered me tea and biscuits. It was a mountain-trekking company that had capitalized on the influx of Western embassy staff following the collapse of the Soviet Union and Bishkek's elevation to a capital city. The only activity in Bishkek on weekends was to explore the nearby mountains and lakes—excursions that these young Russians organized.

I told them I wanted to cross the Tien Shan mountains, in order to get to Kashgar in the Chinese-controlled region of East Turkestan. I had an idea: If I cut through the mountains, through the Naryn and Torugart passes, on Kyrgyzstan's southern frontier with China, it would shorten my journey to Pakistan considerably, while also providing new adventures. Schuyler, in his *Turkistan*, mentions this road as a busy trade route. However, in the twentieth century, state borders had hardened, as Soviet Russia and communist China all but closed the passes. Now this route was slowly reemerging, as Kyrgyz people on both sides of the Kyrgyzstan-China border renewed ancestral links. However, like at the reborn crossing point between Iran and Turkmenistan, there were still difficulties for third-country nationals like me.

The woman told me that a jeep to the Chinese frontier could be ready tomorrow, with a driver, food, and other provisions, for a cost of $150. However, the Chinese would not allow me entry unless I was met at the border by a car from an official Chinese tour agency, based in Kashgar. She tried faxing Kashgar, but the line was down. She sent a telex. There was no response. I would thus have to go the long way to Pakistan after all, continuing clockwise around the vast Tien Shan range: by driving northeast to Alma Ata in Kazakhstan, then further east deep into China's Sinkiang province in the vicinity of Mongolia, where the Tien Shan at last lose their great height. Then, I would cross to the southern side of the Tien Shan and retrace the whole journey southwestward to Kashgar, before heading south into Pakistan.

As I left the trekking office, one of the employees asked if I had hot water in my hotel. "It's lukewarm," I said. "That's better than in people's houses. There hasn't been hot or lukewarm water in Bishkek for a month," he said. "Why?" I asked. Nobody was sure. There was one story about broken pipes, another about energy shortages—a small example, perhaps, of the officially dead Soviet Union still dying.

◎   ◎   ◎

THE TREKKING AGENCY gave me a car for the trip from Bishkek to Alma Ata. The driver and I headed north out of Bishkek and in a few minutes reentered Kazakhstan. There were no more yawning potholes: Kazakhstan's oil wealth meant better roads. The border consisted of a stop sign and a few one-story buildings, which my driver ignored. I presented my Kyrgyz and Kazakh visas only when I checked into hotels. Had I stayed at private houses, whatever the law, I could have managed without visas.

As we headed slightly north, away from the Tien Shan mountains and then eastward toward Alma Ata, the sea of shaved green steppe rolled on and on, a drab and brutal ceaselessness of wind, steppe, sky, and an occasional cluster of corrugated-iron rooftops as my driver and I gradually heaved upward toward feathery clouds. Here was the ultimate plain: the essence of "earth" at its Iowa-like center. I could imagine the thunder of hooves. To the south, just over the border in Kyrgyzstan, lay Tokmak, where, in 1206 or 1207, a Mongol chief named Temuchin defeated a rival Mongol army, and afterward assumed the name Genghis Khan (Perfect Warrior). In his *Travels*, Marco Polo writes that Mongol warriors could "go for a month without supplies, living only on the milk of their mares and on such game as their bows may win for them." Genghis's troops would not even dismount in order to sleep, but abided "on horseback the livelong night" while their horses grazed. If the troops got thirsty, they sustained themselves "on the blood of their horses, opening a vein and letting the blood jet into their mouths, drinking till they had enough, and then staunching it."

After four hours of driving we reached Alma Ata.[7] Suddenly, there were advertisements for Fiat cars, Camel cigarettes, and the "Texas-Kazakh"

---

[7]Kazakhs have renamed the city Almaty. But to many it is still Alma Ata, "Father of Apples."

bank. The hotels accepted several kinds of credit cards and travelers' checks. There were casinos. In the midst of a run-down street was a spanking-new Mercedes-Benz dealership displaying the latest models. In the lobby of my hotel I heard businessmen conferring in Hebrew and Japanese. Arriving in Alma Ata was like returning to the outside world after the wilds of Bukhara, Samarkand, Tashkent, and Bishkek.

Big Oil was the cause of all this activity. More than a thousand miles to the northwest, along the Caspian Sea, in a barely inhabited area belonging to Kazakhstan, lay the greatest number of supergiant oil fields outside of the Persian Gulf. Kazakhstan's oil reserves are equal to Kuwait's. In 1992, Chevron signed a deal with the Kazakh government to invest $40 billion in these fields, hoping for "trillions of dollars" in the early-to-mid twenty-first century.[8]

But there are problems. Ground temperatures at the "Tenghiz" oil fields by the Caspian soar to 122 degrees Fahrenheit in summer and drop to around 40 degrees below zero in winter. The hydrosulfide gas seeping from the ground there can kill you instantly. The decaying Soviet pipelines are unusable. Development of the fields will take longer and prove more costly than Chevron thought. Moreover, Kazakhstan itself constitutes a risk. Chevron made a big investment in southern Sudan in the 1970s, assuming it could pump 5 billion barrels of oil, only to see the region implode into civil war, anarchy, and famine.[9] The map of Kazakhstan makes little more sense than Sudan's.

Thirty-seven percent of Kazakhstan's population is composed of ethnic Russians, who live mainly in the north, adjacent to Russia. Logically, Kazakhstan's northern border with Russia should be moved several hundred miles to the south. Of course, Kazakh president Nursultan Nazarbayev has no intention of doing this, and has been removing Russians from key positions throughout the north and elsewhere and replacing them with ethnic Kazakhs. Russians have fought back, with physical attacks on Kazakhs in northern towns. The majority of Russians in northern Kazakhstan have been there for two or three generations and are too poor to return to Russia.[10] Meanwhile, their contiguity with Russia emboldens

[8]See the article on oil by John Greenwald listed in the bibliography.
[9]See Mansour Khalid's *Nimeiri and the Revolution of Dis-May* in the bibliography, for background on Sudan's oil deals and political troubles.
[10]Some Russians have been in the area much longer. There have been Russians in the northwest of Kazakhstan since the 1640s and along the Russian-Kazakh frontier since the 1720s.

them. The Kazakhs, however, will not give in: They have scores to settle. In the 1930s, Soviet Russian authorities murdered, starved, collectivized, and expelled 1.5 million Kazakhs.[11] The Russians also used Kazakhstan as a nuclear test site, causing high cancer rates and hideous birth defects. In the tenth-anniversary supplement of the European edition of *The Wall Street Journal*, in 1993, a projection of future headlines in the twenty-first century included a Russian-Kazakh war escalating into a nuclear strike.

Today, Alma Ata is the quintessential capital city in transition, with high-rolling Western business executives forced to put up at fleabag hotels with shaky telecommunications and little on the menu except artificial orange juice, vodka, cognac, and tough steak. Cabdrivers, whose cars were no better than the wrecks I had seen in Guinea, were charging customers five dollars to convey them a few hundred yards. While Samarkand, with its army of whores, was a would-be Bangkok, Alma Ata with its casinos was a would-be Las Vegas. I had been told that five Western-standard hotels were being built. Sleazy Klondike energy was everywhere. Would sudden oil wealth tranquilize ethnic problems? Or would it lead to massive corruption and economic overheating, as in Nigeria? Would it spark a revolution of ever-rising expectations, and intensify ethnic rage? I know that if I return to Alma Ata in five or ten years, the city will be completely different. There will either be decent hotels, more sophisticated staff, better telecommunications, and an increasingly Westernized and prosperous society or there will be war and ruin. Anything in between seems unlikely.

◎   ◎   ◎

FITZROY MACLEAN WRITES that "over the mountains from Alma Ata lay Chinese Turkestan or Sinkiang . . . an outlying province of China . . . temptingly near and temptingly inaccessible." Kazakhs, Kyrgyz, and millions of other Turkic ethnics live on both sides of the border of the former Soviet Union and China. The hard frontiers of the 1930s had defeated Maclean, the diplomat-cum-intelligence agent, who was turned back by Chinese border guards. Now, with the Soviet Union's demise and the reemergence of old caravan routes, a rail line had begun operating between Alma Ata and Urumqi, the capital city of China's Sinkiang province. Urumqi was more than five hundred miles away, due east along the northern flank of the Tien Shan range—thirty-six hours by train, including an eleven-hour stop at the border. To get eventually to Kashgar,

---

[11]See the separate entries for Conquest, Nahaylo, and Rashid in the bibliography.

I would have to travel eastward to Urumqi, where the Tien Shan lose their height, then double back to the southwest.

I left Alma Ata at nine in the evening. The train's interior was wood-paneled, with red curtains; there were Russian samovars. Its movement rocked me quickly to sleep. In the morning I beheld a flat and yellow steppe. We had been heading north, before turning east for the duration of the journey, thus the Tien Shan peaks had fallen out of view. Here and there horsemen hovered over vast herds of scrawny cattle. Occasionally, a settlement appeared. Rather than the traditional yurts, or circular felt houses of Turkic nomads, I saw broken fences, mounds of torn tires and other junk, and the rusted girders of deserted building sites. Communism had done its work here, too. The Russians had finally paid back the "Tatars" for their preventing Russia from becoming a truly European nation.

Low hills closed in on either side as the train eventually crawled on to high, tabletop grasslands creased with snow. Birds flew at window level. I could see lakes of an unreal cobalt blue to the north. The train pulled into a sprawling rail yard: the Kazakh side of the Kazakhstan-China border.

Workers unhitched the cars, lifted them, one by one, ten feet high with giant jacks, and replaced the wide-gauge Russian undercarriages with narrower ones for the Chinese tracks. Russian gauges, still in use throughout the former Soviet Union, are wider than the world standard. The idea was to prevent invaders from entering Russia by train. The changeover took hours.

A Kazakhstan immigration official, an ethnic Russian woman, entered my compartment. She stamped my passport with barely a glance at the Kazakh visa for which I had paid $120. "How much money do you think I make at this job?" I didn't answer. "Seven dollars," she told me. "Seven dollars a month. I hear it's better in New Jersey. I have relatives there. But I'm married to a Kazakh, so I'm stuck."

Next came a customs inspector, an ethnic Kazakh. His eyes were bloodshot and he seemed drunk. "Fill out these forms," he said. "Open everything. I want to see all the dollar bills you have." I carried most of my cash in a money belt tied below my knee, under my trousers. I figured it was a shakedown and displayed only the handful of dollars in my wallet. "That's all!" he shouted. I explained that I used credit cards. "Let me see!" he again shouted. I showed him. He rubbed the credit cards between his fingers and shook his head, dissatisfied. He went through everything in my rucksack. He stopped every other moment and engaged me in a staring contest. He wanted a bribe. After a tense half-hour he left, not bothering to collect the forms I had filled out. It was worse than Africa.

After eight hours and more attempted shakedowns by various officials, the train pulled out. We entered a wide pass with black rock at the edges. This was the Dzungarian Gap, connecting west and east Turkestan. Through this passage had come armies of Turkic nomads westward to pillage Russia and eastward to pillage China. It was the bleakest earthscape I had ever seen, and seemed to curve at the edges, as if the earth were a smaller planet with no atmosphere of its own.

At midnight the train crossed the international frontier. But the dusk had just expired and the stars were only now coming out. Though Beijing lay nearly two thousand miles—and several time zones—to the east, the communist authorities there had decreed that all of China use Beijing time. In China, for the time being, unlike in the former Soviet Union, the center still ruled.

1 9

◎   ◎   ◎

China: "Super-Chaos" and
"Physical-Social" Theory

THE BACK-ALLEY shabbiness of the Kazakh border crossing, with its drunken, thieving, and slovenly customs guards, was behind me. The train halted in a blaze of floodlights at the Chinese border station. Male soldiers and female customs inspectors stood at attention in neatly tailored green and blue uniforms. The customs inspectors jumped aboard and politely helped the passengers with the forms. The long day, combined with the strange food, the heat, and the altitude, had made me queasy. I ran to the train door, hoping to get to the platform in time. A soldier raised his gun at me, not to shoot, but to prod me back inside: No passenger could step off the train until all customs declarations had been collected. Between my retches, I looked into the soldier's eyes. Like the eyes of the Turkish soldiers I had seen in southeastern Turkey earlier in my journey, they seemed cold and heartless, like the eyes of a machine. Though the guard watched me being sick from two feet away, he registered nothing, as though no one were there. Soldiers like him had obviously observed far worse suffering. I imagined individually the one hundred million tragedies of the Great Cultural Revolution, when deaths, deportations, and family separations were carried out daily by Chinese troops and Red Guard units.[1]

An order was shouted and the passengers were herded into the station building. I was in the heart of Turkestan, but all the faces in uniform were Chinese, or what academic specialists call "Han," after the country's dominant ethnic group, whose dynasty had ruled China from 202 B.C. to 220 A.D. The building was modern and well lit. We had our passports stamped and placed our luggage on a brand-new conveyor belt for X-raying. An English-speaking soldier assured me it was "film-safe." Though similar procedures, plus the changing of car undercarriages, had taken more than eight hours on the other side of the border, here we were back on the train in two hours, preparing to move. I mentioned this to the soldier. "There is chaos over there," he replied. "We fear it."

Much as I have questioned the future dominance of the states in this region, this frontier outpost of imperial China was a lesson in state power. The state could coerce, and it could protect. The instant I crossed that border in the grasslands of the Dzungarian Gap, the crime rate had sharply dropped, and I had to adjust the hour hand of my watch by several revolutions. In 1994, this was still a real border, not at all invisible.

But the state here was also an occupying force. Its sovereignty was more one of military fiat than an organic result of ethnicity and geography. In *Eastern Approaches*, Fitzroy Maclean explains:

> Few inhabited areas of the world are more remote and . . . inaccessible, than Sinkiang, or, as it is called, Chinese Turkestan. On the maps Sinkiang is simply shown as an ordinary province of China, but, though much can be learnt from maps, they do not always tell the whole story.
>
> Geographically Sinkiang is separated from China by the formidable expanse of the Gobi Desert while its inhabitants are for the most part not Chinese but Turkish, akin in race and language and religion to the inhabitants of Russian Turkestan.

Sinkiang, literally, means "New Dominion," and what is dominated by the Chinese is East Turkestan. Though the Chinese state has been in

---

[1] Fox Butterfield, in *China: Alive in the Bitter Sea*, notes that, according to the *People's Daily*, 100 million people suffered "political harassment" from 1966 until Mao Zedong's death in 1976.

existence for over three thousand five hundred years, Sinkiang first became part of China only in the middle of the eighteenth century. Since then, writes Maclean, the history of the province "has been one of sustained turbulence," with Russians and Chinese vying for control of this Central Asian back-of-beyond. There have been revolts and periods of independent Turkic rule right up through the 1940s. The founder of Nationalist China, Sun Yat-sen, had even recognized the right of all Turkic Moslems to self-determination. In 1949, Mao Zedong's communists marched into Sinkiang and have held it ever since. But not even the communists could subdue the region completely. As recently as 1990 there were major riots and bloodshed protesting Chinese rule. The head of the East Turkestan government-in-exile, Isa Yusuf Alpekin, sits in Istanbul and meets regularly with the leaders of Turkey's various political parties. After the breakup of the Soviet Union, the new Kazakh government in Alma Ata allowed an East Turkestan "liberation organization" to be established there.

Though Turkic and other minorities account for roughly 6 percent of China's population, they occupy over half of China's land area.[2] Sinkiang, twice the size of Texas, is China's largest province. It comprises the easternmost part of Central Asia, as the description "East Turkestan" indicates. While the Chinese represent one of the oldest ethnic nations on earth, like the Iranians, another ancient national group, they have watched the size and shape of their map constantly change. Central government in both China and Iran has all but disappeared at times. In the mid-1990s, China's communist gerontocracy may be close to another such historical reckoning. In a recent novel, an Albanian writer depicts Mao Zedong as saying, " 'Chaos in Cambodia, in Chile, in Ireland . . .' Pooh." Mao "sneered: what sort of chaos could you get in those petty little countries no bigger than the palm of his hand? Genuine chaos could only occur in states of some size, and super-chaos only in China itself."[3]

◎   ◎   ◎

DAWN REVEALED A baked, yellow plateau with the Tien Shan mountains out of view. Then came irrigated fields of alfalfa and roads lined with young poplars. I thought of Marco Polo's story of how the Great Khan

[2]"Official Chinese publications state that all minority autonomous areas in the country . . . occupy more than 60 percent of the country's land area," according to A. Doak Barnett, in *China's Far West: Four Decades of Change*.
[3]See Ismail Kadare's *The Concert*, listed in the bibliography.

decreed that all roads in China "be planted with rows of great trees a few paces apart" to offer "solace to travelers." As the train approached Sinkiang's provincial capital of Urumqi from the west, I beheld miles of mudbrick squatters' settlements with honeycombed walls, one atop the other, as dirty, overcrowded, and wretchedly poor as any I had seen since West Africa. From the window of the slow-moving train I could see the narrow muddy spaces between the houses. They were cluttered with rickshaws and other vehicles. I saw raw meat hung on hooks amidst mounds of garbage. The settlements, I would later learn, were populated mainly by migrant laborers from the Chinese province of Sichuan to the southeast, who had come to take part in Urumqi's construction boom. Millions of peasants are on the move in China, where economic growth is as dramatic as it is uneven. City life was now accessible to these squatters, thanks to TV antennas atop many of their huts.

The train pulled into Urumqi at noon local time. I had left Alma Ata two days before at nine in the evening. I had traveled for thirty-six hours: The train was on time. Bicycles, taxis, and Russian-made Lada passenger cars filled the square in front of the station. The polluted streets were stacked with tall nondescript buildings in varying stages of construction. But after the super-ugliness of Soviet architecture, Urumqi was an aesthetic step up.

The street signs were in two scripts: Chinese and Arabic. China's Turkic Moslem population still used Arabic characters, as the Turks had done in the days of the Ottoman sultanate, before Ataturk reformed the language. When the communist Chinese invaded Sinkiang in 1949, only 6 percent of the local population of 4 million was Chinese. The rest were Turkic Moslems, mainly Uighurs (pronounced WE-goors), an ethnic subdivision of Turks who ruled Mongolia from 745 A.D. to 840 A.D., when the Kyrgyz drove them into East Turkestan. By the late 1980s, the Turkic Uighur population of Sinkiang had more than doubled to nearly 7 million, while Sinkiang's ethnic Kazakhs numbered over 1 million. In addition there were 126,000 Kyrgyz, 10,000 Uzbeks, and similar numbers of other Turkic groups, as well as 30,000 Persian Tajiks. But the real demographic story in Sinkiang was the Chinese, whose numbers had grown from 240,000 in 1948 to 5.4 million in 1986.[4] Mao had forcibly relocated

[4]These figures are cited by Barnett in *China's Far West*. A China expert who was born in China, he visited Sinkiang in the late 1940s prior to the communist takeover, and returned there in the late 1980s.

millions of them from central and coastal China to Sinkiang, in order to reclaim this vast region from the Turks—the feared enemy of China, against whose invasions the Great Wall may have been built. Though the Chinese now accounted for 40 percent of the population of Sinkiang, in terms of geographical area, their presence was mostly limited to cities like Urumqi and Korla (170 miles to the south).[5]

IN 1948, URUMQI had been a town of one-story shops and residences with a population of 80,000. Now it had grown into a densely packed metropolis of 1 million people, of whom 800,000 were Chinese and 200,000 Turkic Uighurs. Urumqi's Chinese majority had been force-marched over a thousand miles from central and coastal China and were now settled in Central Asia. Urumqi's concrete-block building materials and its construction workers had all been imported from the Chinese heartland. According to guidebooks, Urumqi's appearance and development are little different from those of coastal Chinese cities.

Taxi drivers in Urumqi used meters, unlike drivers in former-Soviet Central Asia, who haggled over flat fees. The currency was stable. The city lived on Beijing time. Dark fell near midnight in June. People ate late, and many offices didn't open until 10 A.M. The power of the state again!

The taxi from the station let me off at the side of a highway. To get to a hotel on the other side of the highway I had to walk through an underpass. Here, for the first time, I saw *China*.

As I walked down the steps toward the underpass, I saw a photographer with a rotted red wooden cart. With an old Polaroid, he was taking pictures of a family. Another cart was filled with sunglasses for sale. A woman with heavy makeup was trying some on and looked at herself in the mirror while her friend commented. At an ice cream stand, a woman and her two children relaxed on stools and ordered. Then I came upon three ancient men clustered together on tiny chairs, gazing ahead in silence. Beyond them was a luggage shop. All of this occupied only one side of the stairwell. At the bottom I turned under the highway. Rather

[5]Ross Munro writes in "China's Waxing Spheres of Influence" that Han Chinese constitute around half of the province's population. Munro believes that China will hold on to Sinkiang. But he intimates that this part of the world may revert to a "tributary states system," whereby outlying regions will pay tribute to Beijing, acknowledging its hegemony.

than a few vendors or panhandlers, I beheld a line of small trees; beneath them small groups of old men in straw hats were playing board games. There were rows of billiard tables, each the setting for its own drama, with comments from players and hangers-on. Bicycles went briskly by. At a restaurant under the highway, men and woman sat at long tables downing noodle soup. Leather belts, cigarette lighters, paper, glue, answering machines, cordless telephones, shortwave radios, rubber sink stoppers, fish tank accessories, circuit breakers, toiletry articles, and innumerable other items were being hawked from wooden carts. Many of the items had been locally produced for export. I saw a myriad of attractively bottled local soft drinks and mineral water, but hardly any alcohol. Everywhere business was brisk. People were in a rush: Nothing here reminded me of the sleepwalking quality of the Nile Valley and sub-Saharan Africa. This was a consumer economy, not an economy of desperate people selling their household goods whom I had seen in former-Soviet Central Asia. I sensed a deep cultural residue. There was a bookstand with many people around it, flipping through the volumes for sale. A cassette shop was playing a twangy old Chinese tune. I could smell lignite and urine. I mounted the stairs on the other side of the highway, where more wooden carts and their customers awaited.

I MET A young man named Wang Hsin-Long in the corridor of the Hongshan Hotel, which had dormitory beds for backpackers at a few dollars per night. In passable English, he tried to sell me a bus ticket in a comically aggressive manner that appealed to me. I told him that all I needed was a guide and translator. The next morning he came to my hotel with his fiancée, Monica. "It's a Western name," she explained. "And you can call me Alan instead of Wang Hsin-Long," he added. "It is easier for you, and these are the names that our English teacher has given us for use in the classroom." When I had met him in the Hongshan Hotel, Alan wore a T-shirt and jeans. Today he wore a suit and tie. Monica wore a dress, with a cheaply produced but stylish blazer, and some lipstick. They kept smiling at each other, looking into each other's eyes, holding hands.

Alan explained that his parents and Monica's had "answered the call to settle Sinkiang" in the 1950s. "Did they want to come out here?" I asked. His answer was noncommittal. He admitted, however, that with one or two exceptions, he has never met the members of his father's and mother's immediate families, who are all from Beijing and the adjacent Hebei province. Even more so than in Tashkent and the other cities in Central Asia, few inhabitants chose to come here.

Alan explicitly told me that he was a communist. He also said, just as explicitly, that his immediate goal was to raise enough money to open his own private travel agency, because the owner of the private firm selling bus and train tickets for which he currently worked always cheats him. I asked Alan whether, for him and many other Chinese, communism meant only the continuance of state control, in order to shepherd a peaceful transition to a more capitalistic economy with a higher living standard so that China will not have to experience the same criminal disorder as in the former Soviet Union. He nodded his head in agreement. Clearly, "communist China" was now less communist than "non-communist Kazakhstan," or most other parts of the ex-Soviet Union.

We said goodbye to Monica, who had to do an errand elsewhere. I accompanied Alan back to the ticket bureau in the Hongshan Hotel. On the way I tried to pay him for his services. But he said that his boss insisted on payment in the bureau itself, in his presence. The bureau was a cubby-hole: a bile-green godown with a metal-framed bunk bed in the corner, where the boss lay on a soiled bedroll. There were a few cheap tourist posters on the wall and a wooden desk with a telephone. As we entered, the sullen boss sat up and walked over to the desk. He took my money, counting it carefully. I hoped Alan would escort me into the hotel lobby so that I could tip him. But as I left, the door of the agency closed with Alan inside. It was the same China as before communism: a world of struggle, petty cruelty, and individual yearning. I knew that Alan was not going to stay long at that travel agency.

That day Alan had showed me a world of bustling department stores with crowded shelves, reminiscent of 1950s America, and hard-angled skyscrapers packed as closely together as the square wooden stands I had seen in the underpass beneath the highway. Everywhere I looked there was building, along with black fumes, loud drills, chain saws, and sky-cranes. Though North America, Europe, Japan, and South Korea were enjoying the computer age, clean suburbs, and quiet home offices, here on a baked-desert plateau in Chinese Turkestan, without enough ground water to sustain the growing population, was an antiquated paper-and-typewriter society—office buildings full of the clamor of clacking keys—in the making. I thought of turn-of-the-century Chicago as Theodore Dreiser describes it in *Sister Carrie*: "The sound of the hammer engaged upon the erection of new structures was everywhere heard. Great industries were moving in . . ." Urumqi was a maze of worker-bees with jackhammers. And there were many other, much bigger Urumqis in central and coastal China.

Though China obviously has computers and other high-tech gear—it even manufactures them—its economic boom is more that of a "NIC," a Newly Industrialized Country (like Thailand, Indonesia, and Mexico). It pollutes the atmosphere just as we did a hundred or so years ago, while we, too, were amassing wealth. When we berate the Chinese, Indonesians, and others for doing likewise, they naturally see a double standard, though as the world's population quadrupled since the nineteenth century and resource scarcities are thus more severe, the environmental costs of such unplanned and antiquated development are no longer as easily afforded. But my worries, as I stared out my hotel window at the black smoke and sky-cranes, were not primarily aesthetic or even health-related. They were political.

CHINA IS NOW a battleground for competing theories of the future. The optimists' scenario for China is well known. It rests on perceived cultural strength (a written language at least three thousand five hundred years old, an 80 percent adult literacy rate, and so on) and current economic activity. In 1992, the Chinese economy was highballing at an annual growth rate of 12.8 percent, with growth rates of as much as 14 percent reported by the mid-1990s. Per capita income has been increasing at 8 percent per year, at which rate it should more than double within a decade. The Chinese middle class has grown to 60 million, perhaps more, even under communist rule. In a specific reference to China and other NICs, Barton Biggs, the well-traveled chairman of Morgan Stanley Asset Management in New York, notes, "In almost any way you care to measure, life is getting better for people in developing nations." Conceding the problems of pollution and overcrowding, Biggs says, "But ask the people in these countries if they are willing to pay that price, and the answer is overwhelmingly positive."[6]

---

[6]Biggs's remarks are taken from a debate between him and me, which appeared in the context of an article written by Andrew E. Serwer, published in *Fortune* magazine. See Serwer, listed in the bibliography.

There is an alternative view, though. Thomas Homer-Dixon of the University of Toronto advises that "China's much-touted 14 percent growth rate may not mean it is going to be a world power. It means that coastal China, where much of this growth is occurring, is joining the rest of the Pacific Rim. The disparity with inland China is intensifying." Not only has this growth been lopsidedly in favor of the coast as opposed to the interior, but lopsidedly in favor of the cities as opposed to the countryside—leading to mass migrations to the cities, as in Iran in the period before its Islamic revolution. Not only have rural areas often been excluded from China's economic boom, but real income in many villages has actually fallen.[7]

Homer-Dixon's wary opinion of China does not rest on vague comparisons with Iran, but on more specific and more tantalizing factors. He explains that positive scenarios for China all are based on "social-social theory," which assumes only social causes for social and political phenomena, rather than a combination of social and natural causes. Social-social theory, Homer-Dixon explains, emerged with the Industrial Revolution, which separated many of us from nature. "But nature is coming back with a vengeance, tied to resource scarcity and population growth."

Understanding where China is actually headed requires "physical-social" theory.[8] To that end, Homer-Dixon has assembled a team that includes two China scholars who are also experts on environmental and population matters: Vaclav Smil, author of *China's Environmental Crisis: An Inquiry into the Limits of National Development*, and Jack Goldstone, author of *Revolution and Rebellion in the Early Modern World*. What follows is a synthesis of the research and ideas of these three men, particularly Smil's, whose book on the Chinese environment had a significant impact in intellectual circles, ranging from *The New York Review of Books* to the Central Intelligence Agency.[9]

It is a dangerous misconception that China has gotten its population growth rates under control. The huge cohorts of children produced in the 1960s and early 1970s, when Mao encouraged large families, are now reaching their prime child-bearing years. Even with China's repressive one-child policy in place, its population is due to increase by 25 percent,

[7]See Lena H. Sun's report on Chinese villages, listed in the bibliography.
[8]Homer-Dixon's ideas on "social-social" theory and "physical-social" theory have been heavily influenced by the work of another pioneering expert on the security aspects of the environment, Daniel Deudney.
[9]See Jonathan Spence's article about Smil's book, listed in the bibliography.

or 300 million people, over the next two decades. Given the regime's difficulty in enforcing the one-child policy in rural areas and in minority regions like Sinkiang, the increase could conceivably be 400 million. The most conservative estimate is for an increase of 200 million in three decades. In the 1990s, China will add the equivalent of another Japan to its population, and perhaps the equivalent of another United States between the early 1990s and 2020. But this assumes that the actual rate of population growth in percentage terms will begin *dropping* after 1995.

Among populous developing countries, only Egypt and Bangladesh have less arable land per person than China. In fact, 300 million Chinese in the interior—a fourth of the population—have less usable land per person than the Bangladeshis. This situation is about to become dramatically worse as the population grows, soil erodes, and urban settlements and transportation networks expand onto agricultural land: As much as a tenth of all China's good farmland could be destroyed within two decades. What will remain is rapidly deteriorating, because of declining organic content and salinization. Artificial fertilizers have already pushed crop yields to their attainable limit. Moreover, large-scale illegal logging to provide timber for everything from fuel and housing to mine-shaft supports is destroying Chinese woodlands by 10 percent every decade. Grasslands for cattle herds are being lost to desertification by as much as 3.7 percent a year. Smil warns that while air pollution is amenable to dramatic high-tech fixes, land degradation is largely irreversible, except in some instances and at extremely high costs.

By 1990, about 77 percent of all China's agricultural land was being irrigated. An increasing percentage of irrigation water is being polluted by industrial wastes. Because irrigation is depleting the underground water table, forty Chinese cities have been beset by drinking-water shortages. (In June 1994, while I was in China, *The China Daily* reported that "leaky toilets" were "causing a run on [drinking] water in China's 300 largest cities."[10]) Concomitantly, the extensive use of dams for irrigation has helped create a situation in which 10 percent of Chinese territory—inhabited by two thirds of the population producing 70 percent of China's economic output—is "below the flood level of major rivers," according to Smil.[11]

[10]See Xiao Li's article, listed in the bibliography.
[11]Also, as river beds silt up from erosion-induced silt, they get raised above the surrounding plain, increasing the risk of floods.

The loss of agricultural land, combined with an increasing concentration of wealth in the coastal cities, has put tens of millions of Chinese on the move. Since the 1980s, China has been experiencing the urbanization that Iran experienced from the 1950s through the 1970s.

Behind the collapse of the Ming dynasty in 1644, as well as the steep decline of the Qing dynasty in the mid-nineteenth century—culminating in armed revolts that killed tens of millions of Chinese—were similar imbalances between soaring populations and precipitous declines in arable land per capita.[12]

Meanwhile, relations between the central government and the twenty-two provinces are deteriorating fast, with wealthy coastal areas like Guangdong holding back large revenues from Beijing as they carve out their own geo-economic destinies. Regional warlord–business elite alliances could reshape China as they have in the past. At the same, the breakup of the Soviet Union has led to a massive influx of Kazakh, Kyrgyz, and Uzbek visitors to Sinkiang as the two parts of Turkestan begin to unify, de facto. "We will probably see the center challenged and fractured, and China will not remain the same on the map," Homer-Dixon says.

◎   ◎   ◎

WILL THIS BREAKUP—if it occurs—occur peacefully and gradually over years, and even decades, or will it be sudden and violent? The stakes are high. China, according to Lester Brown, president of the Worldwatch Institute, "is losing the capacity to feed itself. When that happens the food supply of the whole world will be affected . . ." China's huge population is growing while the amount of its farmland is decreasing. Perhaps agricultural technology will ultimately find solutions for this and many similar problems. But what of the medium term—the next few decades?

Good news about the environment in North America and Western Europe (along with news that the environment elsewhere can, over the long term, be replenished) should not blind us to the bad news just ahead for a *critical mass* of third world countries like China.

Optimists, like Wall Street strategist Barton Biggs, consider all of this "doom-and-gloom" stuff. Perhaps he's right. But what if he's wrong, even

---

[12]See Goldstone, listed in the bibliography.

partially wrong? Homer-Dixon, Smil, and others have offered a plausible and detailed analysis of China's problems. The consequences of ignoring them could be catastrophic.

THE LAST WORD on China may have appeared in a little-known monograph by a former U.S. diplomat, Jonathan Moore:

> China may be the most dramatically unreadable harbinger of the future of our species: a giant microcosm with mighty contradictions poised for collision . . . riding a tiger into the future at a gallop. China's rate of growth has been in double digits for the past three years, its free markets are running wild, its human rights abused. China faces massive internal displacement of people, its militarism is burgeoning . . . and a threat to its social stability exists in millions of unemployed generated by the closing of thousands of state-owned factories. With over one-fifth of the world's population in 1992 and practicing the most . . . coercive birth control in the world, China is assaulting the nexus head-on, trying to control the chaos it is generating. *The environment may be the final determinant.* (Italics mine)

20

Strategic Hippie Routes

THE BUS FROM Urumqi to Kashgar in Sinkiang—eight hundred miles and thirty-six hours to the southwest—was supposed to leave at 10 A.M. It didn't leave until 5:35 P.M. At the station I met Tom, a traveler in his early twenties from England, and together we wandered around Urumqi for seven hours until the bus left. Tom had studied math in college, and had just completed nine months of backpacking through the Indian subcontinent, Nepal, Tibet, and China. "It wasn't so interesting," he said. "I should have gone to Vietnam. In China everyone just wants your money."

We went first to a park with a pagoda, a lake with little boats, flower and rock gardens, and a willow-shaded square where groups of elderly Chinese practiced Tai Chi, slow-motion shadow boxing, and other synchronized exercises that, among other things, helped people get their minds off the pollution and traffic jams. The entrance fee was the equivalent of fifty cents in Chinese yuan. Tom showed the gatekeeper his student card and demanded he be let in for twenty-five cents. "It's a rip-off," he shouted. I offered to pay for him, but he said it was "the principle of the thing." The gatekeeper relented. I was embarrassed.

I had been traveling for six weeks on this leg of my journey. I needed a mental break and was content to waste the afternoon talking with Tom about nothing in particular. Later, the two of us wandered over to a café, where I treated him to stale cake and tea at a table with plastic flowers and a poster of a New England farmhouse on the wall. The café was frequented by up-and-coming young Chinese, like Alan and Monica. Tom began complaining about the price of the bus he had taken some weeks ago—which we were both planning to take in the other direction—from Kashgar over the mountains into northern Pakistan. "It will cost twenty-three dollars. That's a rip-off!" Then we talked about our stomach troubles. Tom mentioned that "everyone gets sick in Kathmandu. It's a good place to stop and have a stool test. There's a laboratory there that does it cheap." Our conversation drifted to the travails of Michael Jackson, to black holes in space, and to time travel. "Stephen Hawking is just another one of these ambitious people, just out for himself," Tom said. Tom asked me if there was anything worthwhile to see in Uzbekistan. It turned out that he had never heard of Bukhara or Samarkand before. Nor did he have a guidebook. "I just like the feeling of freedom, and I hate these credit-card places with stickers on their windows. They just rip you off." He confessed that "when I get to Pakistan, I may be at a dead-end."

Back at the station, Tom and I met another backpacker, a painter from New Haven who was en route back to Europe by land. He asked me if it was safe to sleep in the park in Alma Ata, since he had no money for even a youth hostel. There was also a young man from Switzerland who had been crisscrossing China for several months. "It's no good here, man. I can't wait to get to Pakistan." He added, "All the Chinese want is your money."

I had been encountering low-budget backpackers since Alma Ata, where the branch line from the Trans Siberian railway met the rail link into China. With the collapse of the Soviet Union and the loosening of travel restrictions inside China, backpackers could now go by land from St. Petersburg to Beijing. These neo-hippies of the 1990s did not always have long hair, they rarely used drugs, and they carried more gear than their counterparts of the 1960s and early 1970s. They looked more like mountaineers than flower children.

But in the 1990s there are few women. The former Soviet Union and China are difficult places. Crime is common. Food and accommodations compared to even European youth hostels are grim. And land travel is grueling, with longer distances to cover and none of the comforts of even second-class European train compartments. It was mainly a male's world (even if some of the best accounts of travel in this region have been written by women[1]). Without an interest in history and politics, and meeting only other males, many of these travelers find only a gritty succession of buses, trains, stomach troubles, and youth hostels. No wonder they were fixated on money: the journey becomes a matter of spending as little as you can.

THE BUS FOR Kashgar finally left. The heat was ferocious as we descended the southern slopes of the Tien Shan range into the Taklamakan Desert, whose Turkish name means "Go in and you won't come out." This was a "sleeper" bus, which meant that instead of seats there were metal bunks, with filthy khaki bedclothes and burlap blankets. The floor was concealed under metal canisters, oil and water tins, burlap sacks, and suitcases held together by rope. Whenever the driver slowed up, the brakes squealed like a dog being run over.

It was a rattling, jangling journey all the way to Kashgar, in which the driver's hand repeatedly pressed on the horn. We had set out through the netherworld of an industrial zone where the first Bactrian camels I had ever seen in the wild were grazing in the outer yard of a cement plant. Soon the snowy Tien Shan disappeared as we headed south into the crusty emptiness of the Taklamakan. The bus then headed westward for the remaining thirty hours of the journey, traveling along the desert's northern fringe. A greasy bath of fine sand and diesel fumes filtered through the open windows. I could feel the grit between my teeth. The other passengers had removed their shoes and socks and were smoking cigarettes. The driver's assistant snorted cocaine, which he would do intermittently till we reached Kashgar. He was with a young child, presumably his daughter.

When I climbed aboard the bus, I left China and entered a Turkic-Uighur world. The driver's cassette music was *gecekondu arabesk*, straight out of Istanbul. The language was Uighur. The women wore colorful kerchiefs. Though the Beijing time of our departure was 5:35 P.M., people's watches showed 3:35 P.M. Perhaps the state was not so strong here after all.

---

[1] I am thinking of Georgie Anne Geyer's book on Central Asia and Anne Applebaum's book on the western borderlands of the ex-Soviet Union.

Our bus had taken its place in a line of blue trucks, their axles sagging under the weight of huge logs, heavy loads of earth, metal piping, sand-bags, cement blocks, and oil drums. Everywhere there seemed a frantic need to build, build . . . Unlike the logs I had seen in Ghana, these were not for export to Europe in return for cash that would probably never find its way to Ghana's treasury. Here, timber was for local building. The pace of this activity, whatever the ethnic identity of the truck drivers, was pure Chinese. As the orange sun sank behind the gray gravel desert, around 9 P.M. Uighur time, I fell asleep on my steel bunk.

Just then the driver screeched to a halt. I beheld a line of mudbrick hovels in the desert where men were tossing yard-long noodles in the air over boiling vats of water. Long dining tables had been set for the passen-gers, who had lined up to refill their canteens with water trickling out of a rusty faucet by the roadside. Tom and I ate. The Swiss fellow became sick.

I fell asleep again around midnight and spent the entire next day on the bus, as well as most of the next night, until we arrived in Kashgar around 5 A.M. I was groggy. The trip had passed like one of those dreams before waking. The desert road stops were a succession of noodle stalls with old chairs and tables, wretched latrines blocked by knots of mangy dogs, and the occasional mosque or building facade, made of fantastic yel-low brick and crude blue-and-pink stucco, which the blinding sunlight revealed in all its psychedelic beauty. The inhabitants of these towns usu-ally wore drab workers' clothes, Mao-style. But every so often I came across a leathery oldster with a wispy beard and turban like those whom Marco Polo might have met along these same routes.

The driver stopped whenever he felt like it. The bus had broken down four times. Once the driver stopped at a village and a number of us, myself included, went outside to urinate, unaware that we could be seen by a Uighur peasant and his wife. The peasant ran after us, brandishing a stick, accusing us of insulting his wife. I got away in time. But another pas-senger, one of two Chinese on the bus, was not so lucky. The Uighur had got hold of him, and in an instant a crowd formed. Then the bus driver, also a Uighur, began shouting at his Chinese passengers, who shouted back at everyone on the bus for the next half hour. Then everyone seemed to tire of arguing and the bus continued on its way.

At sunset the second night of the journey, the bus climbed a series of knife-sharp, bald hills, bringing us back into the cool and tangy air of Central Asia after the burning desert. I could see yurts and nomads with their sheep. At last we rolled into Kashgar. It was nearly dawn when Tom, the Swiss fellow, and I banged at the gate of a hotel for a few minutes before someone let us in. It was a rambling hostelry with leafy courtyards, uncertain plumbing, mildewed walls, and a picture of Niagara Falls in the dining room. The hotel had been the Russian consulate at the end of the nineteenth century, when Russia and Great Britain were competing for these lands. Now owned by the Chinese government, the hotel operated on Beijing time, while the Uighur staff had their watches set to local Sinkiang time. I couldn't sleep, so I ate an early breakfast and went out to explore the town.

AROUND THE END of the first century A.D., the Chinese first established the Silk Route to the West, partly in response to the Roman appetite for silk, which, though rare in Europe, was common in China. Besides silk, the Chinese brought with them lacquerware, porcelain, gunpowder, rose and peony plants, paper, and so on to the Mediterranean. To China came wool and glass from Rome, lapis lazuli from Central Asia, and wine from Persia, among other wonders. Kashgar was, like Samarkand further to the west, an oasis town where various branches of the Silk Route converged. As early as two thousand years ago, the Han rulers of China, fearing Turkic nomads, established military garrisons here. The Uighurs started migrating to Kashgar from Mongolia in the ninth century A.D., long after the Chinese had been ejected from Central Asia by Arabs, who themselves had withdrawn not long afterward. (The Uighurs discovered Islam not from the Arabs but from the Karakhanids, a Turko-Persian dynasty that ruled from Bukhara in the tenth and eleventh centuries.)

The army of Genghis Khan captured Kashgar in the early thirteenth century. Later, Tamerlane (who, in 1370, claimed descent from Genghis) ruled here. Not until 1755 did the Chinese return. A Uighur rebellion broke out four years later and was savagely crushed by Manchu troops. Uighur-Chinese relations have been tense ever since. Uighur rebellions in Sinkiang in the nineteenth century helped weaken Chinese authority enough to permit Russian occupation and British interference. This imperial convergence—Russia expanding eastward from its base at Tashkent, China attempting to hold its western frontiers, and Great Britain expanding northward from the Indian subcontinent—allowed for Sir Halford Mackinder's otherwise incomprehensible description of Chinese Turkestan as the "geographical pivot of history." Kashgar, with its rebellions and diplomatic intrigue, tucked into a corner of what is today southwestern China—and near the frontiers of Kyrgyzstan, Tajikistan, Afghanistan, and Pakistan—has often been the pivot of this pivot.

In the 1990s, Turkic Moslem Uighurs accounted for 90 percent of Kashgar's population of three hundred thousand. "The Uighurs," writes Fergus Bordewich in *Cathay*, "look toward Mecca (and perhaps secretly to Ankara) for their identity, not to Beijing, and they regard the Chinese as interlopers; as recently as 1935, they [the Uighurs] massacred the city's [Kashgar's] entire population at a stroke." However, while the Uighurs see the Chinese as the enemy, beyond that they rarely think of themselves as a nation in their own right. Ask a Uighur who he is and he will reply, "I am a *Kashgarlik* [from the oasis of Kashgar]," or a *Turfanlik, Khotanlik*, etc.[2] Though the future of the Chinese in East Turkestan is uncertain, the indigenous Turkic inhabitants exhibit few signs of coalescing into a state. Marco Polo's description of Kashgar remains unnervingly appropriate, as I was soon to learn. "The inhabitants live by trade and handicrafts. . . . The natives are a wretched . . . set of people; they eat and drink in miserable fashion."

◎   ◎   ◎

A STEADY RAIN had stopped as I finished my breakfast. Kashgar was awash in grayish-brown mud splattered about by bicycles, motorized rickshaws, donkeys laden with fresh produce or firewood, and loud children: their faces covered in sores; their heads shaved against lice. Eating houses built of rotting wood were serving up fatty meat and mares' milk. Many more women were wearing *burkas* (opaque veils) than I saw in Iran. The dust of old carpets and the soot of coal fires blended with the fine grains of drying mud to thicken the air, as though I were seeing a nineteenth-century lithograph or daguerreotype of Kashgar. Most of the men wore flat caps and torn, mud-stained sports coats. Kashgar was populated by Turks who had never been refined by proximity to either the Mediterranean or Byzantium and whose culture had been ground down by Mao's awful threshing machine.

"Welcome to John's Café," the sign read. "Do you need information? See John. John can help with faxes, bike rentals, etc." Long tables

[2]See "The Ethnogenesis of the Uighur" by Dru C. Gladney, listed in the bibliography.

were set out on the street. The menu was Chinese. The clientele were hippie backpackers and similar Western travelers. It was like a Greek island in August. Though here, rather than a sex-and-beer get-together, small groups composed mainly of males kept apart, as if each group of travelers was determined to believe that it—and no one else—had discovered Kashgar. Kashgar was still a nexus, if not of the Silk Route then of this 1990s hippie route. The last time I had seen such a congregation of travelers was in the complex of cheap hotels along Chicken Street in Kabul in the 1970s, before the Soviet invasion of Afghanistan and the Islamic Revolution in Iran, when the hippie route to India was in full flourish.

Kashgar reminded me not only of Kabul in the 1970s but of late-1960s Marrakesh, Morocco, immortalized in a song by Crosby, Stills, Nash, & Young, a tourist trap where hippies came to "blow their minds" in a marketplace of preindustrial splendor. The Sunday market in Kashgar, held along the muddy banks of the Tuman River, was a scene out of Marco Polo's *Travels*, with congeries of ox-carts, horses, Bactrian camels, and old men holding scythes and pitchforks, testing such farm implements as horseshoes, saddles, whips, and so on. In addition were the carpets, spices, gold-plated dowry boxes, live poultry, parts of dead animals, and other "exotic" items typical of souks throughout the Near East. Men with long knives provided their clients with a weekly shave. But the single biggest crowd I saw was seated in front of a color television set, watching a commercial for Western sportswear. Kashgar, I felt, was at the beginning of a transition. And some of the signs were disturbing.

Not since sub-Saharan Africa had I seen so many packs of young men and boys with nothing useful to do, playing in the rough and swaggering manner propitious to crime and violence, given the right circumstances. These were authentic street urchins with hardened, miserly faces—faces that had been robbed by harsh circumstances of their childhood innocence. It is difficult to be optimistic about a place where ten-year-olds smoke cigarettes.

The Chinese one-child policy—a repressive means of population control—had already collapsed in the minority areas. Overcrowding, unemployment, and awful sanitation were endemic. In the absence of other comforts, a Moslem religious resurgence was widespread. So was the apparent lack of a burgeoning middle class or other signs of economic growth, unlike elsewhere in China. Without a middle class, I wondered, how could there be a meaningful nationalism to underpin a state after the Chinese left?

Leaving the market, I came upon the Chinese part of town: a cantonment that reminded me of the Russians in Tashkent and the British in Indian cities during the Raj. Chinese soldiers walked arm in arm with wives or girlfriends, dressed in out-of-date Western fashions that looked positively postmodern compared to what I had seen in the Uighur marketplace. A massive statue of Mao loomed from behind a building. Rather than the father of Asian communism, here he symbolized the conqueror from a more organized and technologically advanced civilization. How much longer would the Chinese last here? I asked myself. And what, if anything, would replace them? No doubt, the Chinese could control the international borders of Sinkiang and maintain a semblance of order here for the foreseeable future—but only if there were a strong central government in China itself, one that did not let China decompose into weakly linked regions.

◎　　　◎　　　◎

I TOOK THESE concerns to Abdul, a Uighur in his early twenties who had been educated in Beijing and spoke English well. Like so many youths whose educations had been paid for by a repressive regime trying to co-opt them—the students in the shah's Iran, for example—Abdul had turned against his Chinese benefactors. He wore a pressed white shirt, gray slacks, and brown shoes. His slick black hair had been neatly cut and combed. By the standards of Kashgar, he seemed to be part of an elite. Abdul's complexion was pale. His eyelids bore only vague traces of his Oriental origin. Abdul, like many in Kashgar, could easily have passed for an Anatolian Turk. What I remember best about him, though, is his cynical laugh. A slight cough, really, followed by a cruel flash in his dark eyes. "I'm the assistant manager of a factory. Of course, a Chinese guy is my boss." Laugh.

Abdul was one of four children. "This is a big province and we are a small people compared to the Chinese. We need to make many more children."

"But will there be jobs for these kids when they grow up?" I asked. "Many of them already look like delinquents."

"That is the fault of the Chinese," Abdul countered. "There is no investment in the Uighur areas of Sinkiang, only in the Chinese areas. You tourists and journalists believe Chinese lies. Sinkiang is the richest province, but the Uighurs get none of this wealth. The Chinese steal everything. Instead of Western businessmen in Kashgar, we see only these backpackers, who have nothing to spend. There is development all around us, but only high unemployment here. It must lead to something." I presumed he meant a revolt.

Abdul also told me about the influx of new ideas and information, brought by fellow Turkic ethnics visiting and migrating from Kyrgyzstan and Kazakhstan after the Soviet Union's collapse. Throughout their history, except for the communist period, Kyrgyz have had much closer ties with Sinkiang than with other parts of Central Asia.

"We Turks are one people," Abdul declared as we sipped tea a few feet from a steaming vat full of oily lamb, where some hungry boys had gathered. "Turks can all understand each other. Even the Hungarians are one of us."[3]

He continued: "After the collapse of communism [in the Soviet Union], the Chinese were frightened, so they sent troops here. See that building over there? It is closed. Do you know why? It housed the agricultural administration. Because the Chinese raised the tax on Uighur farmers, we set it on fire. This is Turkestan, not China. Chinese don't learn our language, and many of us don't learn theirs. Even on a personal level, relations are bad. After the communist old men die in Beijing, Guangdong [including Hong Kong] will leave China, then we will, too."

As we walked around town, Abdul kept introducing me to his friends, all about the same age. "Do they think like you do?" I asked. "Definitely," he said.

I argued with Abdul. Uighurs, I said, may have a high level of traditional culture, but how well could they govern themselves after the Chinese left? So poor, so isolated, their identity based so much on which oasis they inhabit—couldn't the order now being preserved by the Chinese give way to chaos, rather than to freedom? I was thinking of the mid-nineteenth-century Turkic liberator of "Kashgaria," Yakub Beg, who ejected the Chinese from Sinkiang, only to terrorize the Uighurs with his

---

[3]Hungarians, whose ancestors came to Europe from Central Asia, are a Finno-Ugric people, a subdivision of the Ural-Altaic peoples that include the various Turkic groups. Thus Hungarians are very distantly related to the Uighurs. In a graveyard east of Urumqi, Hungarian archaeologists have found objects similar to those found in Hungarian cemeteries of the ninth and tenth centuries. Inner Asian Studies are in vogue at Hungarian universities as the resurgence of nationalism following the Cold War has led to a search for ethnic roots.

rag-tag army, raping, stealing, and killing. Abdul responded with his cynical laugh.

◎　　　◎　　　◎

IN OTHER WORDS, hippie backpackers again seemed to have come right to where *it was happening*. The hippie route from Turkey through Iran, Afghanistan, and Pakistan to India was at its busiest just before the explosion of civil conflict in Turkey, the Islamic Revolution in Iran, and the Soviet invasion of Afghanistan that threatened Pakistan. If—*if*—Sinkiang was to be next, would this hippie presence be merely a coincidence, I wondered, or, like certain animals, did they sense a coming earthquake?

Backpackers went in droves to places that were moving too quickly from a medieval culture to a modern one; or, rather, they went to medieval locations that had been suddenly exposed to outside influences. Only places in such quick, uneven transition could satisfy two backpacker demands: that a place still be "wildly exotic" and that it also be reasonably accessible to Westerners. And places like this, moving from the fifteenth century into the twenty-first, were likely candidates for upheaval.

21

The Roof of the World

SEVEN HUNDRED YEARS ago, Marco Polo journeyed to the region south of Kashgar and wrote that

> . . . always among mountains, you get to such a height that it is said to be the highest place in the world! And when you have got to this height you find a great lake between two mountains. . . . There are great numbers of all kinds of wild beasts; among others, wild sheep of great size, whose horns are a good six palms in length. . . . The plain is called Pamier. . . . The region is so lofty and cold that you do not even see any birds flying.

It looked the same in 1994. The stormy sky was right out of Genesis. For three hours the Chinese bus, filled with Pakistani carpet traders, ached and groaned and jangled its way uphill over a potholed road strewn with boulders, gears grinding. Then an austere and solitary vastness opened up before me. Sawtoothed granite peaks disappeared behind gray cloud vapors, their snowy slopes the color of a shroud. Winds blasted against the bus windows as snow began to fall. It was mid-June. The occasional mudbrick hut punctuated the isolation.

At an altitude of ten thousand feet above sea level, Lake Kara-Kul (Black Sea) was a slate-blue void, as empty as the upper atmosphere. The lake was bordered by two mountains, Mustagh Ata (24,751 feet) and Kongur (25,318 feet), with no fewer than eleven glaciers descending from its summit. Herds of big-horned yaks littered the plain like slow-moving black boulders, driven by Kyrgyz cowboys in white felt hats. I saw not a single bird in the air. Three backpackers in the rear of the bus did not bother to look out the window, absorbed as they were in their paperback novels.

I was now in High Tartary—called the "Third Pole" in the eighteenth century, because it seemed as remote as the North and South poles.[1] Geographers refer to this mountain mass as the Pamir Knot, where the Pamirs converge with the Karakorams and the western Himalayas to form the true "Roof the World." Though the eastern Himalayas include Everest—the world's highest mountain, at 29,028-feet—the Karakorams alone, as the late Justice William O. Douglas wrote, contain no fewer than thirty-three peaks higher than 24,000 feet, including K-2, only 778 feet lower than Everest, and harder to climb.

In Kashgar that morning, it had taken two hours to load the bus, whose roof was now piled high with Central Asian carpets and Chinese-made bicycles, which traders from Lahore and Rawalpindi were going to sell in Pakistan and in markets farther west. The collapse of Soviet communism and the loosening of Chinese control in Sinkiang had combined with the 1978 completion of the Karakoram Highway to create a new Silk Route, which would ultimately connect Tashkent with Karachi on the Arabian Sea. The stretch known as the Karakoram Highway begins in Kashgar and ends just outside Rawalpindi, five days away by motorized transport over the mountains.

In *Roads and Rivals: The Political Uses of Access in the Borderlands of Asia*, Mahnaz Z. Ispahani uses the Karakoram Highway as a daring metaphor for how, in many parts of the world, the jet age is still irrelevant compared to the dirt roads and resurfaced highways, which are the real "instruments of history," defining borders and regions. For example, in 1960 the scholar Louis Dupree wondered how useful the new Soviet roads into Afghanistan were: "Logically . . . just how strategic is a road in the era of possible nuclear warfare . . . ?" In 1979, the Soviet overland invasion of Afghanistan gave the answer.

[1] See Rashid's *Resurgence of Central Asia*, listed in the bibliography.

Would the new Silk Route be like the old one, a narrow strip of civilization connecting a string of city-states in a borderless world, or, rather, as Ispahani implies, would this highway serve to strengthen at least one existing state, Pakistan, by allowing it to project its power into the remote mountain villages of its northern territories? The best way to answer this question, I felt, was to travel the Karakoram Highway myself.

The highway has been called an "engineering miracle" and the "eighth wonder of the world." It crosses twenty-four major bridges, and its construction involved the explosion of eight thousand tons of dynamite to move 30 million cubic yards of earth and rock. Eighty thousand tons of cement and one thousand trucks were needed. Fifteen thousand laborers at a time worked on the project. Four hundred Pakistani and Chinese construction workers lost their lives building the road, and an additional 314 were injured. From this description, you would imagine the Karakoram Highway to look something like the Pennsylvania Turnpike. It doesn't. The Karakoram Highway looks more like a badly maintained dirt track in West Virginia. But everything is relative. Just as the River Jordan is a frail trickle compared to the rivers of Europe and North America, by the standards of the water-poor Middle East, it is a great river. The same with the Karakoram Highway: It represents something where, before, there was simply nothing.

So, too, with accommodations along the way. I spent the first night of the journey in Tashkurgan, a small Tajik town just over the mountains from where Tajikistan, Afghanistan, and China meet. The Pamir Hotel was billed as a "modern" complex designed to service tourists traveling the new Silk Route. In Tashkurgan, which is at an altitude of 9,971 feet, the temperature dropped to near freezing at night. The room was unheated. The bed slumped. The sheets were dirty. So was the floor. The lavatory was flooded, and the toilet backed up. But it was something.

The Chinese-Pakistani border at the top of the Khunjerab Pass is, at 15,514 feet, the highest-altitude international border crossing in the world. But the actual Chinese and Pakistani border installations were seven hours apart. Chinese immigration procedures are carried out at a building outside Tashkurgan. The next morning, after everyone's passport was stamped, a group of five Chinese soldiers, ramrod-stiff, saluted the bus, opened the gate, and let us officially "out of China." That entire day we drove through what was essentially no-man's-land: a bleak and beautiful steppe populated by sheep, yak herds, Bactrian camels, and the lonely clusters of yurts where Tajik and Kyrgyz herdsmen lived. I was seeing Turkestan in its full glory, as Marco Polo had seen it, in the final days before I departed Central Asia.

The atmosphere in the bus was somewhat tense. The Karakoram Highway may have been an exercise in Chinese-Pakistani friendship, but there was no love lost between the Chinese driver and the Pakistani traders inside. The driver was driving as many Chinese do: slowly, and by the book. Even on the long, flat stretches, he never went faster than fifty miles per hour. The Pakistanis were enraged. In their culture, it is a sign of manliness to pass other vehicles on blind curves with only the horn as protection. This is why the Grand Trunk Road between Peshawar and Rawalpindi is one long, never-ending, bloody game of "chicken." The Pakistanis humiliated the driver, shouting epithets. The driver responded by going even more slowly, and stopping for a piss or a smoke in the middle of the road. "Sir," one of the Pakistanis explained to me, "this is why China is so backward and why Pakistan is going places. Because we are ambitious and dynamic, we need to get where we're going fast. But these Chinese—they have all the time in the world."

"But what about the highway deaths in Pakistan?" I countered.

"What to do?" He shrugged, as if such fatalities were a reasonable price to pay for what he claimed was Pakistan's social and economic dynamism.

◎　　　◎　　　◎

CHINA IS PART of the Asian continent; Pakistan, part of the Asian *sub*continent, which also includes India, Bangladesh, and part of Nepal. They are, literally, worlds—and at one time, an entire ocean—apart. The triangular continental plate we know as the subcontinent was once part of Antarctica. Some 70 million years ago it began drifting northward toward Asia.[2] Thirty million years ago it had reached what was the southern coast of Asia and began to slide beneath it, pushing it upward. This southern shore, once at sea level, took the full force of the collision and is now the Karakorams, the Black Gravel Range, home to many of the world's highest peaks. The shavings, curling up eastward from the collision, became the Himalayas. The collision never really ended. It is still happening, mil-

---

[2] See Giles Whittell's excellent and concise geological summary in *Central Asia*, listed in the bibliography.

limeter by millimeter, every second of every hour. Earthquakes are daily occurrences. Glaciers move the distance of more than six football fields in a twenty-four-hour period and have to be bombed by the Pakistani air force when they threaten roads and villages. The Karakorams—geologically perhaps the earth's most violent transition zone—are a lesson in the impermanence of everything and how the only really accurate map is one in constant motion.

After several hours of driving, the bus ascended a winding curve onto a bleak, flat mini-plateau. A ragged Chinese soldier ran out of his hut, his arm extended, as though he were begging. The driver stopped, reached under the seat for a package, and handed the lonely soldier a new pair of socks, still in its plastic wrapper. The soldier gave profuse thanks and didn't bother to check our passports. A few more miles and an equally lonely Pakistani soldier waved to us. We were now in Pakistan. The flat road over which we had traveled, streaked with snow in mid-June, was higher than the highest peak in the continental United States.

We descended into a canyon, from which I would not emerge until I arrived outside Rawalpindi four days later. Here the Karakorams were steeper and sharper than the Pamirs had been: black rock steeples coated with snow reached upward of twenty-four thousand feet, and downward deep into the canyon floor—right before my eyes—to only a few thousand feet above sea level. These were the most dizzying and frightening declivities on earth: majestic vertical landscapes descending from ice and granite to tropical greenery, the visible proof that continents had crashed. As the bus swung around one curve after another—no guardrails anywhere— I saw the landscape as a vertical line that met the clouds at a right angle.

Rocks fell onto the bus's roof and against the windows. Here and there the road was blocked by a small landslide, and we had to wait for Pakistani work crews to clear it. Just keeping the highway operable was a never-ending effort. I had never been to a place where geological effects were so palpable.

Some Pakistani buses began to appear: chrome-trimmed and garishly painted extravaganzas covered with evil-eyes, and uncomfortably bare on the inside—all show, bravura, and superstition. Like the daredevil driving, they seemed products of a naive culture.

A cluster of small cinder-block buildings, the Pakistani border installation, came into view near evening. The bus pulled into a dusty lot where, under a sheet-metal roof, there were a few rickety wooden tables. I walked up to the one labeled FOREIGNERS and had my passport stamped. The Pakistani customs inspection consisted of one question: "You have any booze, sir?" Upon my negative reply, the officer waved me away. Pakistan was officially an Islamic state. Unofficially, as in Iran, black market whiskey was everywhere, as I knew from previous visits.

I found a cold and bare cement room for the night in the border town of Sust. I satisfied my appetite with lentil soup, dal, vegetable curry, rice, and *nan* bread. Subcontinental cuisine was like a dietary homecoming after weeks of Central Asian food and greasy, badly prepared Chinese meals. After so much unrest, my stomach settled down. The only remnant of China on the table was the flat-bottomed soup spoon. In a world of artificial borders, I had crossed a real frontier that day, from one continental mass to another; from a bony and shaved steppe to narrow, gravelly canyons; from glum Chinese and reserved Kyrgyz to jabbering Pakistanis; and from one kind of food to another. The Chinese hold on Sinkiang may have been impermanent—and the Pakistani hold on these northern territories no more secure—but I was convinced that the Pamir Knot would always be a fault line between one civilization and another. As usual, the truth would turn out to be more complicated than I had supposed.

◎　　　◎　　　◎

"I AM TAJIK so I speak Tajik, sir," explained my waiter in the small hotel. "In Hunza, where you will go tomorrow, sir, they speak Burushaski. In Skardu, they speak Balti. In Gilgit, they speak Shina. In Chitral, they speak Khowar . . ." Pakistan's official tongue is Urdu, an Indic language with many borrowings from Persian and Arabic. Khowar and Shina are somewhat related to Urdu. Balti, however, is a Tibetan dialect. Tajik is more like Persian than any Indic language. And Burushaski is unconnected to any of these tongues, all of which are remnants of once-independent principalities. Marco Polo caught the flavor when he described the Karakorams as "noisy with kingdoms." It was a confusing landscape, but as critical as it was obscure. Historian John Keay calls the Karakorams "the hub, the crow's nest, the fulcrum of Asia." It is through here that most of the land routes from Central Asia to the Indian subcontinent pass. This very route system was the passage through which Central Asian and subcontinental peoples flowed back and forth and interbred, undermining the geological fault zone that I had assumed was so formidable.

Here was where the last and most critical chapter of the Great Game was played out. The activities of British and Russian secret agents, vying for allies among these hill tribesmen, determined the borders of czarist (later Soviet) Central Asia, Afghanistan, and British India, from which Pakistan later would be created. In Gilgit, a town south of here, I would soon visit the grave of one of these intrepid Englishmen.

In the morning, I bargained with a jeep driver to take me on the three-hour journey south to Karimabad, the principal town of the Hunza Valley, heart of Pakistan's "northern territories." I paid him twenty dollars. Like the Tajik waiter the night before, he was exceedingly polite and friendly. I felt as though I were back in Turkey and Iran—places where the inhabitants had developed a customer-service mentality, unlike communist-ravaged Central Asia. He pointed out to me the Passu Glacier, far off to the right, one of the largest in the Karakorams. In contrast to the dirty gray morainal glaciers, which to the untrained eye look no different from granite or slate rock, the Passu Glacier is pure white ice: a terrifying flowing mass that, nevertheless, appears deceptively motionless.

The Hunza Valley is a region abutting Kashmir and India. Technically, it is not part of Pakistan at all but merely "administered" by Pakistan. The lawyerly term exposes the fragility of this whole jigsaw border arrangement, which came into existence in the late 1940s, when the British left India and the new, warring states of mostly Hindu India and Moslem Pakistan could not agree on permanent borders.

Wars between giant states and civilizations could not have been further from my mind, however, as I entered the Hunza Valley and the town of Karimabad, with its dark-green terraced fields, abundant with fruit trees and trickling irrigation channels, the water cold and delicious, tripping down steep canyon walls on both sides of the Hunza River. I was engulfed by a splendid and peaceful isolation. Here could be the real Shangri-la, I thought, the setting for James Hilton's romantic novel *Lost Horizon*.

◎   ◎   ◎

I SAID GOODBYE to my driver and began walking along a poplar-lined road, my eyes nailed to the snowy rock face of Rakaposhi, another Karakoram giant, soaring 25,550 feet. I noticed a sign for the Mountainview Restaurant. I wanted a cold soda. So I climbed down the shaky wooden staircase onto a natural earth platform, at whose edge stood a wooden table offering a heart-stopping view of the descending black gorge and the ascending white slopes of Rakaposhi. Seated at the table was a strikingly handsome couple, blond and fair.

Dave, a New Zealander, shot his hand out and shook mine with a hearty hello. Lynn, his English wife, did likewise. I looked over her shoulder onto a stack of yellow legal paper covered with her beautiful handwriting. They were mountain trekkers who had been climbing and trekking in the remotest parts of Borneo, Tibet, Nepal, India, and now northern Pakistan. Both in their late thirties, they had sold their house and put their money in the bank, and had nothing with them except their backpacks and climbing equipment. They had calculated that they could live on the road forever on the income from Lynn's free-lance writing and their bank interest, provided they spend only twenty dollars per day between them. Though this might seem like very little, it was a fortune compared to what the other backpackers I had met were spending.

Lynn and Dave delighted me with stories of being awakened in the middle of the night by yaks outside their tent in Tibet, and of jumping over the cracks of groaning and creaking glaciers, concealed by soft snow. "Moving glaciers sound like a roaring train when you're on them. It's dangerous, but what the hell," Dave said. "I'd rather die on a glacier than be mugged in a Western city or be killed in a suburban car accident." Lynn added, "Of course, you get headaches when you're fifteen thousand feet up in Nepal, but you get used to them. Your system adjusts. The only hassle we've had has been the fleas at night."

Lynn told me that she sent her free-lance stories to England, New Zealand, and Australia by normal post. "It works. Here, look at these tearsheets," she said, showing me several of her published articles. "I write them all longhand. At home I would use a laptop, but to bring one to these places would be crazy. Where would I plug it in? Where would I find the electricity to charge the battery? Where we've been, even when you find a wall outlet the current fails or surges. Imagine the bribes at border posts in some places to import your computer. It would just be another thing to worry about."

I felt like hugging her. For years I had survived as a journalist using the same system. Here were two people who understood that there were large swaths of the earth at the end of the twentieth century that were not linked by the Internet. In the course of my journeys in Africa and Asia, I had gone into so many banks and hotels that had neither computers nor typewriters that I no longer even noticed. The vast disparities in the world following the collapse of communism and the end of the Cold War, symbolized by a computer revolution in some parts of the globe and the absence of reliable electric current in other parts, was something that I took for granted because I was constantly experiencing it. I had not brought a computer along on this trip, and rarely brought one anywhere. It was liberating, just like not having a fax or mailing address while I was on the road. My heroes in this regard were a Chicago ophthalmologist and his wife, whom I had met in eastern Turkey. Every year they went trekking in a remote part of the world where it was impossible for anyone to phone them. "Being able to cuddle up at night with a good book, knowing that no one back home can contact you even in case of an emergency, is the purest form of relaxation in an age where we're all tyrannized by messages," he told me.

Dave and Lynn were getting the equivalent of a classical education free-of-charge simply by traveling and studying the ancient spoken languages in these valleys. They were keen observers, too. "I'm no environmental purist," Lynn began, "but from the window of our hotel room in Kuala Lumpur, Dave and I counted a hundred sky-cranes. We were frequently reading newspapers stories about collapsing buildings. The slapdash construction is frightening in some of these countries. The pollution is worse. Dave and I made a long side trip to Agra from the Himalayas, because I had seen the Taj Mahal in the 1970s and wanted Dave to see it before it is ruined by smog. Well, whatever you read about pollution controls there, it's already being ruined. The Taj is no longer white but a grimy yellow. Local Indians are hacking away pieces off the facade and selling them. The guards do nothing. We splurged on a hotel room with a direct view of the Taj but could barely see it on some days through the haze. It's tragic." They then told sad tales of deforestation in Nepal.

But the Hunza Valley, they told me, was a happier story. It turned out that the stone irrigation canals zigzagging up and down the valley, along with much of the greenery, were products of the Aga Khan's irrigation and reforestation programs, which were regenerating the valley and making it self-sufficient without the help, or hindrance, of the Pakistani government. "The connectedness of the mountain people and the efficiency of these privately funded environmental projects are impressive," Lynn said. "The Pak government is superfluous up here. It might as well not exist."

"But all this would be impossible without the Karakoram Highway, which the government itself built, and which it now uses to spread its influence by building schools and a bigger military presence," I said.

"Yes," Lynn replied. "But the people here speak their own language. Much of the development and the social changes happen without the government. If Pakistan ever implodes, the Hunza Valley could do very nicely on its own."

◎   ◎   ◎

I CLIMBED INTO a crowded minibus, and for the next three hours followed the meandering Hunza River south, arriving finally in Gilgit, the largest town in the northern territories, where there was an airport with daily flights to Rawalpindi. But the flights, I soon learned, were canceled unless the sky was completely clear, since the pilots of the small planes had to fly between the mountains rather than above them. Gilgit, two days of hard, tortuous driving from the population centers of Pakistan, was largely cut off. Its dusty, Wild West streets, with step-up wooden sidewalks and one-story storefronts surrounded by sandstone mountains, was still more Central Asian than part of the Indian subcontinent. The woollen and fur headgear of the men were a mix of Kyrgyz, Afghan, and Russian styles. The electric mixers, ceramic tea services, and myriad other consumer goods on sale all came from China. The books in the bookstore were mostly about Central Asia. I spotted a cheap hotel called the Kashgar Inn. Pakistan was represented by the three truckloads of soldiers I saw patrolling the town, in armored personnel carriers with mounted machine guns, a reminder that a large crescent of territory, from Kashmir westward to the tribal areas near the Afghan border, constitute a region that the Indian and Pakistani governments control only at the point of a gun. The Karakoram Highway has done two things, it turns out: The highway gives the Pakistani military more maneuverability in the north, while at the same time it allows cultural and economic influences to filter in from Central Asia. Which function, over time, will prove more important?

◎   ◎   ◎

I STOPPED IN Gilgit because of a brave and crazy Englishman, one who had trekked from here to Chinese Turkestan, sleeping with neither tent nor fire in below-zero snows, and who had saved himself from starvation by eating a yak raw. Yet, over the earth's most difficult terrain, he neverthe-less managed thirty miles a day on foot. George J. Whitaker Hayward, an Irish-born loner and Indian Army veteran, with no close friends or family, certainly had a death wish. "I shall wander about the wilds of Central Asia possessed of an insane desire to try the effects of cold steel across my throat," he had confided in a letter. A photograph taken in 1870, just before his last expedition, shows Hayward in native dress, long swords attached to his waist, a spear in one hand and a shield in the other. His eyes are dead-set; his mouth clenched in grim determination.

In early summer, 1870, he and five native servants left Gilgit and dis-appeared into the mountains en route to the Pamirs, which Hayward hoped to map and explore for the sake of Great Britain's imperial inter-ests. On July 17, he set up camp in Darkot, about eighty miles northwest of Gilgit, on a hillside nine thousand feet above sea level. A bearer informed Hayward that a local tribal chief was out to do him harm. Hay-ward stayed awake the entire night, writing in his journal with one hand, a pistol in the other, and loaded firearms on a nearby table. Dawn came. Thinking himself out of danger, Hayward dozed off to sleep. That's when the tribal raiding party rushed in. Hayward had only one request of the execution squad: that he be allowed to walk to the edge of the cliff to watch the sun rise. The request was granted. He was thirty years old at the time of his murder. No clear motive for the deed was ever established.

An old man, squatting in the gloom of a dry-goods stall, wearing a soiled *shalwar kameez*,[3] had the key to the graveyard. He led me across a noisy street and unlocked the gate. Once inside, I no longer noticed the racket of Suzuki motorbikes and heard only birds chirping. In the midst of a grassy patch, shaded from the glaring sun by the trees, was an old, worn rock, at the foot of which an inscription was chiseled:

"Erected to the memory of G. W. Hayward, Gold Medalist of the Royal Geographical Society of London, who was cruelly murdered at Darkot July 18, 1870 on his journey to explore the Pamir Steppe. This monument is erected to a gallant officer and accomplished traveller . . ."

The rumble of an armored personnel carrier outside the gate inter-rupted my solitary thought. Could Gilgit again become politically critical to Asia, just as in Hayward's day? I asked myself.

[3]This is the traditional dress of much of the Indian subcontinent and Afghanistan, con-sisting of baggy cotton pants and a long, flowing shirt.

That, of course, depended on what happened in Pakistan, a state created in 1947 astride the fault lines between Central Asia and the Indian subcontinent. Pakistan's destiny could be discerned only in the teeming provinces of Punjab and Sind, south of here, where the overwhelming majority of Pakistan's 130 million people lived. As in China, if the central state apparatus held firm, outlying regions could probably be controlled; if the center did not hold, then such regions as Sinkiang and Pakistan's northern territories were imaginable under their own sovereignty, or that of someone else. Recall that throughout history, until the mid-twentieth century, Sinkiang traded far more with czarist and Soviet Turkestan than it did with China.

It is in Central Asia, I suggest, that the political eruptions emanating from Iran, China, and the Indian subcontinent will usually spill over.

ALL DAY LONG, my rented jeep tumbled downward loop after sweeping loop of the Karakoram Highway. I was driving along a rill that had become a stream that had become a river: a monumental curve of flowing brown silt; a wide gash through blistering canyons under the gaze of the white ramparts of Nanga Parbat (26,653 feet). This was the Indus River, the geographical border between the subcontinent and Central Asia before the British conquest of India.

A volcanic landscape now appeared—the remains of the ocean floor 30 million years ago, when an Antarctic fragment drifted northward to Asia, forming the subcontinent.

Sunlight beat upon my head. Nanga Parbat was the last of the mountain giants I would see ahead of me. Soon there were no more snowy summits. Beyond the volcanic landscape came soft scrubby hills and the pine scent of middle altitudes. Each bend gave way to a deeper green, with more birds, more color. The glare of hard surfaces was replaced by the shimmer of watery rice paddies. Instead of yaks there were water buffaloes. I stopped seven times during that day for soft drinks, in temperatures as high 117° Fahrenheit. At each stop, swarms of insects and beautiful brown children greeted me. In my nostrils I felt the kiss of loamy soil rather than mere dust. The hot and perspiring earth, damp and suffocating, closed around me.

Why couldn't I simply enjoy this earthly beauty, especially as I had seen it from the Pamirs and the Karakorams? Why, even amidst such spectacular landscapes, did I hanker after answers?

I thought of Keats's famous letter to his brothers, in which he praised the quality of "*Negative Capability*, that is, when a man is capable of being in uncertainties, mysteries, doubts, without any irritable reaching after fact and reason . . ." Keats wrote that what marks a "Man of Achievement" is his ability to be "content with half-knowledge," for "with a great poet the sense of Beauty overcomes every other consideration, or rather obliterates all consideration." I knew that I could never meet Keats's standard, even as I knew that all my "answers" might eventually be proven wrong. I took solace, once again, in Francis Bacon, who praised error, because only from wrong answers can the Truth emerge.

2 2

◎　　◎　　◎

The Last Map

I SPENT THE night in a guesthouse on the banks of the Indus. In the morning, I careened in my jeep down the last wave of hills, one being Aornos, the eastern limit of Alexander the Great's empire. I emerged on the smog-ridden plain of Punjab,[1] into such crowds and traffic jams that I had not seen since Cairo. The Grand Trunk Road on which I traveled—straight, flat, fully paved, with modern gas stations—was more hazardous than any-place I had been in Iran or Central Asia: a battleground of speeding trucks passing each other like motorcycles, inches away from head-on collisions. I avoided the turn-off for Rawalpindi and headed directly for nearby Islamabad, Pakistan's capital, constructed in 1961 along the rectangular lines of a military cantonment. Filthy and dehydrated, I arrived at the home of my friends Kathy and Pasha, in a wealthy suburb of the capital. They occupied a magnificent villa that Pasha, an architect, had designed himself. There was a problem, however. When I turned on the sink tap to wash, no water came out. The pipe made a hissing sound, followed by a

---

[1]*Punjab* is Sanskrit for "five rivers." The five are the Jhelum, the Chenab, the Ravi, the Sutlej, and the Beas—all part of the Indus water system.

death rattle. It was part of a long story, pivotal to the destiny of all the lands I had just passed through.

◎   ◎   ◎

THIS WAS NOT my first but my tenth trip to Pakistan. I had used it as a rear base to cover the Soviet-Afghan war in the 1980s, and had been almost everywhere in the country. Each time I returned I encountered the same trends: Some things were always getting better, and many others even worse.

I was perfectly aware what, for example, an upbeat Wall Street fund manager might see on his visits to Pakistan, ensconced in his luxury hotel with its own power generator and privately dug well. On each return trip, he would notice more personal-computer shops, telefaxes, and mobile phones; more Kodak stores with one-hour developing machines; more upscale restaurants and other conveniences to serve a growing middle class that increasingly has more in common with its American and European counterparts. He would notice a domestic airline, which kept to schedule and had an excellent safety record, connecting the major cities. As in India, he would smile upon a talented pool of humanity that had furnished the West with some of its finest physicians and research scientists. And, in Karachi, he would see a lively stock market. To him, Pakistan would mean ever more customers for Western consumer products and another shining success story of the global marketplace.

His optimistic assumptions would be accurate. Trouble is, they are only one element in a much larger picture, whose focal point is the dry sink tap.

◎   ◎   ◎

"PAKISTAN WAS . . . AN idea before it was a country, and whether it is a nation remains doubtful even today," wrote Edward Mortimer, the eminent British journalist, in 1982, in *Faith and Power: The Politics of Islam*. Mortimer noted then that Pakistan "is probably the only country in the world" whose official literature describes it as an "ideological state," based exclusively on Islam rather than on any shared history, ethnic identity, or geographical logic. Following the collapse of ideological states from Berlin to Vladivostok, plus the outbreak of civil war in Yugoslavia—an ideological state overwhelmed by disparate ethnic groups—one must think carefully about Pakistan, whose political establishment, supported largely by the sale of illicit drugs, is hell-bent on acquiring a nuclear arsenal.

The very word *Pakistan* is an acronym for Punjab, Afghania (the ethnic Pathan-inhabited Northwest Frontier province), Kashmir, Iran, Sind, "Tukharistan" (a reference to the Indo-European Tukharians who once inhabited Chinese Turkestan[2]), Afghanistan, and Baluchistan: all attesting to Pakistan's unwieldy and artificial nature. Pakistan also means "Land of the Pure." The word and concepts were invented by Moslem intellectuals from Bombay, living in exile in London. When the British left India, this intellectual elite demanded its own state and got it, though millions were killed in ensuing intercommunal bloodbaths. Because the new state contained several ethnic-geographical regions and twenty-two languages, Islam was proclaimed here "as nationality." A new capital was later built and called Islamabad. Iran may call itself, or even be, an "Islamic Republic," but it is its Persian ethnicity and language, not Islam, that gives Iran national cohesion. Nor is the United States a useful precedent for Pakistan, since its multiethnic nationalism is nonideological and emerged organically over two hundred years within an obvious geographical framework: It was not the result of shared religious will.

Moreover, millions of Moslems—the ones threatened by Hindus—whom Pakistan was supposed to have saved, still live in the heartland of India and have never migrated to the new state. Those who did migrate to Pakistan became known as *mohajirs* (foreigners). Because these *mohajirs* (which include the founding Bombay intellectuals) had no roots in their adopted land, they were unwilling to risk elections. So while India has been democratic for nearly half a century, Pakistan became a place where military dictatorship flourished in the name of Islam and where the creation of political parties merely institutionalized ethnic and regional divisions.

I had been in Pakistan under military dictatorship and also during various democratic interludes. I couldn't tell the difference. As British expert Christina Lamb painstakingly documents in *Waiting for Allah: Pakistan's Struggle for Democracy*, even under democratic rule "the army is the only force of stability and the Punjabis [the largest ethnic group, who dominate the army] are the colonizers of today." By the mid-1990s, this Punjabi-*mohajir* imperium was fast deteriorating.

[2]John R. Krueger, editor of Mongolia Society publications at Indiana University, provided me with information on Tukharistan. See the bibliography.

Unlike China, where social-social theory might yield an optimistic scenario and physical-social theory a negative one, Pakistan looks awful from either perspective.

◎   ◎   ◎

FIRST THE "SOCIAL":

Karachi, both Pakistan's and the province of Sind's biggest city, as well as the country's business center and source of 40 percent of federal revenues, is becoming a subcontinental version of Lagos. Its population has grown from 400,000 in 1947 to 9 million in the 1990s. This includes perhaps hundreds of thousands of heroin addicts and at least a million inhabitants of illegal squatter shanties.[3] Less than a quarter of Karachi's 1,300 tons of daily garbage is properly disposed of. Unemployment is at 25 percent, and the city's population is growing by 6 percent annually, twice Pakistan's national average, which itself suffers one of the highest population growth rates in the world. Each year, half a million more people are added to Karachi's population, more than the entire population of the city in 1947.

Karachi's streets are flooded for days at a time during the monsoon, its telephones silent, its homes without electricity or drinking water. Large areas are controlled by drug barons. Since the 1980s, gang warfare has been endemic and battles are fought along ethnic lines, between *moha-jirs* (foreigners who came from India), indigenous Sindhis, Pathans from the Northwest Frontier province, and others: all Moslems. The writer Ian Buruma describes Karachi and surrounding Sind province as "a kind of sandy Sicily."[4]

Just as the plight of sub-Saharan Africa is an extreme example of what is occurring less intensely elsewhere on the planet, Karachi is a somewhat extreme example of what is occurring throughout Pakistan. Highway gangs and religious riots made Pakistan's Northwest Frontier province bordering Afghanistan dangerous in the 1980s. I often needed special permission to travel in those areas. In the 1990s it was worse—a steady deterioration of effective government had become normal there. The Northwest Frontier province was now a haven for arms dealers and disillusioned *mujahidin* (holy warriors) from the Afghan war. Rising crime

---

[3] See Christina Lamb's *Waiting for Allah*, listed in the bibliography.
[4] Quoted in Steve Coll's *On the Grand Trunk Road*, listed in the bibliography.

throughout Pakistan led *The Muslim*, a respected nationwide daily, to write in its lead editorial on June 14, 1994, that "the country is fast moving towards anarchy."

Gang warfare extends in an emblematic fashion to the nation's politics. So far during the 1990s, Pakistan has been immobilized in complete political gridlock. The former prime minister, Nawaz Sharif, and his allies have, through parliamentary maneuvers, smear campaigns, collusion with local mullahs and some branches of the military, and attacks on other branches of the military, stalemated the reform program of the democratically elected prime minister, Benazir Bhutto. "No nation is more entangled in conspiratorial fantasy," writes *Washington Post* correspondent Steve Coll. "Pakistan is like an out-patient who refuses his lithium . . ."

All these fissures run along ethnic-regional lines. Sharif's allies are Punjabis; Bhutto's, Sindhis.

Pakistan has already become what the former Soviet Union is in danger of becoming: a decomposing polity based more on criminal activities than on effective government. By 1988, illicit drugs accounted for $4 billion annually in earnings—more foreign exchange than all of Pakistan's legal exports combined.[5] The Hundi banking system, an underground, off-the-books network of money changers in the bazaar, handles more capital than the official banks, and is a convenient means for laundering drug profits.

Mubashir Hassan, a former finance minister, said in 1990 that the legal "state structure in Pakistan has been rapidly collapsing. . . . The police are no longer the police. The magistracy is no longer the magistracy and the tax collector can no longer collect taxes. The collapse of the state has given rise to kidnappers, murderers, bank robbers, drug dealers. . . . The whole scene has become a bazaar."[6] The 1991 scandal involving the Bank of Commerce and Credit International, or BCCI, and its Pakistan-based founder, Agha Hasan Abedi, was a case of such *bazaari* business practices gone worldwide.

The United Nations reports that

illegal and criminal activities [in Pakistan] have been booming and while they have undoubtedly generated incomes and employment,

---

[5]This is according to the Pakistan Narcotics Control Board, as well as testimony by Melvyn Levitsky, U.S. Assistant Secretary of State for International Narcotics, given to Congress on January 8, 1989.

[6]See Steve Coll's *On the Grand Trunk Road*.

they have also eroded traditional values. . . . Their destructive effect
on the society must be a major cause for concern.

Meanwhile, the equivalent of another Karachi is added to the population of Pakistan every 2.3 years, while every two decades or so, the population doubles. Even were Pakistan's population growth rate to drop gradually to zero by the year 2040, its population will have increased from 130 million to several hundred million by then: perhaps more people than live in all of present-day Europe. Pakistan is one of the world's "most serious family planning failures," according to a report by Population Action International. While 22 percent of Iranian couples use contraceptives, only 9 percent of Pakistani couples use them.[7] The average Pakistani woman conceives almost seven times over her lifetime. The exponential increase in young people—the five-year-old to twenty-year-old age group will grow from 35 million to 55 million during the 1990s—will make a formal education system for everyone impossible. Already by 1991, half the Pakistani population was under fifteen.

Migration to urban shantytowns—not just in Karachi but in cities throughout Pakistan—is occurring at a faster rate than in Iran or Egypt, according to the UN and other organizations. Writes Lamb, in *Waiting for Allah*, about a typical day here:

"Twelve thousand more people will be born in Pakistan this day. . . . More of them will learn to use a gun than to speak the national language. . . . Only a third will have access to clean drinking water and only 15 percent will have sewerage. A quarter will go to school. Many will become heroin addicts."

THAT'S THE SOCIAL problem.

Now the "physical":

With 65 percent of Pakistan's land dependent on intensive irrigation, with massive deforestation, and 3 percent yearly population growth—which assures that the amount of cultivated land per rural inhabitant will be cut in half by 2010—governing Pakistan is becoming an increasingly desperate enterprise. Now add the fact that, according to the World Bank,

[7]See "Contraception and Smaller Families," by Boyce Rensberger, listed in the bibliography.

a quarter of all Pakistan's soil is deteriorating due to salinity and waterlogging, which in turn is caused by the madcap building of irrigation canals that lack proper drainage and are poorly maintained. "Dams here are silting up," explained a UN official I interviewed in Islamabad. "All local investment is in big bricks-and-mortar projects and not enough money is put into maintaining what has been built, and educating people to do the maintenance."

Thus, my dry faucet. Actually, having lived in Peshawar on the Northwest Frontier in the 1980s, I was used to water cutoffs. And Rawalpindi has been experiencing them for years. But no water in one of the wealthiest sections of the capital was "news," as it marked yet a further deterioration. *The Muslim* reported that an emergency committee had agreed to "draw another 20 feet of water from the already heavily depleted [Simly Dam] source" to alleviate the situation.[8] This is the environmental equivalent of using Social Security pension funds to reduce budget deficits.

The savior of Islamabad and the rest of Punjab is supposed to be the Kalabagh Dam, to be built on the Indus River in the Northwest Frontier Province. But the province's population of ethnic Pathans, as well as Sindhis in the south of the country near Karachi, vehemently oppose the project. They see it as a "water grab by Punjabis."

The UN official I interviewed explained:

"The water problem is symptomatic of the population problem, which is symptomatic of the political system breaking down, since that has affected the lack of good family planning programs. And the breakdown of the political system is symptomatic of ethnic problems. Everything is interrelated and feeds off each other in a downward spiral."

According to this analysis, Benazir Bhutto, rather than a symbol of female empowerment in the male-dominated Moslem world, is a symbol of helplessness: the head of a government who can no longer *cope*, because overpopulation and depleted resources have reached the point of saturation, thus destabilizing the state institutions. The crisis is so severe that democracy, with its necessary compromises and half-measures, cannot mount a credible counterattack against these destructive forces, while military rule leads to only more corruption and cynicism.

In its 1992 Summary Report, the United Nations Development Programme in Pakistan states categorically that "economic growth in Pak-

---

[8] See the article by Mobarik Virk listed in the bibliography.

istan"—which so excites that theoretical Wall Street fund manager—"is not sustainable," due to "the depletion of assets in general and, most importantly, the depletion of the natural environment which resulted from economic growth."

◎   ◎   ◎

MY BIRTHDAY OCCURRED a few days after my arrival. Pasha, my architect friend, threw a nighttime party for me. In the middle of the party, the electricity went off. No lights; no air-conditioning. Electric power in Pakistan is dependent upon hydropower. "What about raising taxes on water to conserve usage?" I asked. Everyone laughed. Pasha explained why Pakistan may collapse because of leaky toilets long before it joins a panIslamic Jihad:

"A lot of water is lost on leaky toilets, which are easy to fix. But if a government inspector went around issuing a one-hundred-rupee tax on each homeowner for his leaky toilet, do you know what would happen? The inspector, a poor man, would accept a twenty-rupee bribe in lieu of the one-hundred-rupee tax, which would then go into his pocket. The government would collect no revenue, and the toilets would still leak. This is a culture of corruption. How else do you think the upper classes manage to survive and even grow?"

Pasha was alluding to what I call the "bubble," a protective membrane inside which the Pakistani middle and upper classes survive and prosper, thus increasing the consumer lists of Western companies even as the state itself disintegrates. Clifton, a wealthy section of Karachi, where that Wall Street fund manager might be invited to dinner at the home of a rich local businessman, is such a bubble. The residents have their own electric power generators, their own water tanks, and their own security guards. Let's return, one last time, to my dry sink tap.

The badly maintained dams and a dwindling underground water table are the general causes. But the specific cause was this: Rural migrants had been drifting into Islamabad, as they were into all Pakistan's cities, escaping deforested and nutrient-poor hillsides. They erected a shantytown near Pasha's house, and built their own pipe network, which tapped into the local water supply, reducing the flow for the whole area. But a few hours later I got water and had my wash. Usually a water truck arrives in the neighborhood. Theoretically, it is for all the area's residents. But if you bribe the truck driver generously, he comes to your house first. By the time he delivers water to the homes of all those who could afford bribes, there is no water left for the poor. Still, the bubble isn't completely sealed. Contaminated water in February 1994 led to a hepatitis epidemic in Islamabad, affecting rich people, too.

"The seeds of destruction are writ large and clear if anyone would care to read them," Ahmed Rashid, one of Pakistan's leading journalists, told me at my birthday party. Ahmed, the Pakistan and Central Asia bureau chief for the *Far Eastern Economic Review*, had just returned from a visit to Jellalabad, a city in eastern Afghanistan near Pakistan. "It was over a hundred degrees Fahrenheit and humid," he told me. "There was no electricity in Jellalabad, so no air-conditioning. No water in the taps, and nothing safe to drink. Kids are dying steadily of disease. But no big fighting, so no news story. And no real economy except for the drug economy. Nor is there a central government in Kabul to turn to anymore. Give us five or ten years with the same trends, and we'll be like eastern Afghanistan."

WHAT IF AHMED is right?

What if Pakistan continues to deteriorate as the middle class expands and finds ingenious new ways to seal its bubble? What if the armored troop convoys disappear from Gilgit, even as the Chinese ones disappear from Kashgar? What if Pakistan metamorphosed into a loose regional confederation, without a strong, central state apparatus? What if China—with its own middle class in the process of building its own bubble—did the same? What might the future map of Central Asia look like then? What kind of world would it be?

After all, considering how the map of Central Asia has repeatedly—and radically—changed over the centuries, when even Persia disappeared completely during the high-water mark of Tamerlane's empire, is it so unreasonable to assume that the map will again be transformed, more radically perhaps, given the social and environmental upheavals now upon us?

For evidence, just look at Afghanistan. In the mid-eighteenth century the Pathans, a Moslem people of Indo-Iranian stock, established a buffer between the Safavid Persian empire and the Moghul empire in India. This buffer zone—Afghanistan—shifted as the czars extended their empire southward, while in India the Moghul empire gave way to a Sikh empire and then to a British one. Ultimately, Afghanistan became a fragile balance of Pathan, Turkic, and Tajik tribesmen surviving in the no-man's-land between the czarist-Soviet and the British empires. British rule in the Indian subcontinent ended in 1947. Soviet rule in Central Asia ended in 1991. The question arises: *With both empires gone and a buffer no longer required, who needs Afghanistan?*

The Turkic and Tajik tribesmen need it less and less, as they restore links with ethnic compatriots across Afghanistan's northern border in the former Soviet Union. Meanwhile, the flood of refugees to Pakistan during the Afghan war allowed Pathans on both sides of the southern border to strengthen ties.

As Afghanistan evaporates in the 1990s, emerging as a "Liberian mail-drop"[9] for drug smugglers and Islamic militants, the finely cut "map-maker" borders between the ex-Soviet Union, Afghanistan, Pakistan, and India are gradually being replaced by a Turkic world, a Persianized world, a Pathan world, and a Punjabi world meeting and shading into one other. Afghanistan is becoming a memory. And Pakistan could yet devolve into what the eleventh edition of the Encyclopaedia Britannica called the "lesser Frontier States."

In 1951, when Justice William O. Douglas traveled through the Afghan-Pakistani border area, he heard cries for "Pakhtunistan"—a homeland for the Pathans. A vaguely defined region, known as "Pakhtunistan," in place of a clean international border may well be a feature of future maps, especially as refugee migrations and smugglers finally erode the integrity of this border, which I have crossed six times without a passport in the company of *mujahidin*.

What we are increasingly seeing in Central Asia is the weakening of conventional states and the relative strengthening of what geographers and ethnographers call "ecoregions" or "bioregions":[10] specific landscapes—whether steppe-lands for Turkic tribesman, mountain ranges for Pathans, floodplains for Punjabis, and isolated river valleys for the "Hun-

---

[9] It used to be a common practice for major shipowners to register their cargo ships in Liberia, in order to avoid scrutiny by the tax authorities in their own countries. Their proof of residence in Liberia was sometimes just a post office box.

[10] In a study concerning Ethiopia, Jason Clay and Bonnie Holcomb note the association of politicized ethnic groups with "specific ecological niches." Bruce Byers elaborate on this theme worldwide in his monograph "Ecoregions, State Sovereignty and Conflict." See the bibliography.

zakots"—which for centuries have nurtured specific ethnic groups. Simply stated: Whatever can be managed at the local level will be.[11]

Throughout the 1980s, I personally have witnessed the transformation of one such ecoregion, Eritrea, into sub-Saharan Africa's best functioning state,[12] even though it took years for the world community to recognize it officially. Most ecoregions are not so lucky, though. Unlike Eritrea—enclosed by mountains and deserts and culturally unified by a thirty-year guerrilla war against Ethiopia—the majority of ecoregions tend to flow in and out of one another. Ecoregions where state power is weak and economic development is low are likely candidates to become what military strategist Steven Metz calls "ungovernables": the emerging "third tier," or bottom level of places in the world system. These ungovernables will, in turn, be divided between relatively civil locales and uncivil ones. Metz writes: "Regions with an organic substitute system of [codified, written] order such as Islam will tend to be more stable than regions where primalism [as exists in oral societies of sub-Saharan Africa] forms the only alternative to nationalism." Of course, other factors such as the rate of population growth and the availability of natural resources will further affect matters. An example is Pakistan, which, though Islamic, is more chaotic than some animist regions of sub-Saharan Africa, where population and urbanization are growing somewhat more slowly. In Kashmir, too, despite an entrenched Islamic value system, there is, in *Washington Post* correspondent Steve Coll's words, a *"Lord of the Flies* feel" to the youth culture after years of armed conflict.

Kashmir, perched like an unstable boulder in the western Himalayas, between Pakistan's northern territories and India—just beneath Sinkiang—is home to teenage insurgents backed by Pakistan and suppressed by India, whose government troops have committed vandalism, rape, and torture on a grand scale since 1991. Kashmir, simmering

---

[11]Geographer Bruce Byers makes this very point in his monograph on ecoregions. See the bibliography.

[12]Eritrea boasts Africa's best grass-roots famine relief and health care networks, an agricultural extension service, an education system, and a well-documented record of safeguarding human rights. Its guerrilla capital in the pre-state days of the 1980s featured a large underground hospital powered by wind and solar energy, producing its own aspirin and anti-malaria tablets, intravenous solutions, and sanitary napkins for women. As I saw for myself, Eritreans transformed the ideals of self-help and group cohesiveness into a new kind of ideology that resists classification. All this happened in sub-Saharan Africa, proving that no region is ever hopeless.

for half a century, is another weak link of this fragile Central Asian state system.

However, the years ahead in Central Asia will probably see neither widespread anarchy nor tidy cohesion—rather, a series of fractious experiments in free trade and the free movement of peoples, which may offer lessons in the virtues and drawbacks of national ambiguity.

Ambiguity and perpetual change are the key words. For even as old vertical state loyalties wither, new horizontal loyalties are forged. For example, the collapse of the Soviet Union is leading to better communications among the Turkic peoples of Central Asia, including the adoption of a common Latin script. The differences between the various Turkic languages are, therefore, starting to narrow. Another example of a strengthening lateral loyalty is the increasing display of common interests among the middle classes of both Western and Oriental societies. Clearly, I have more in common with my Pakistani friends than I have with poorer compatriots in my own country, just as my Pakistani friends have ever more in common with me than with their poorer compatriots. It is akin to the Middle Ages, when the aristocracies of various European kingdoms had more in common with one another than with the peasants of their own lands.

◎ ◎ ◎

IN *Geography and the Human Spirit*, Anne Buttimer, a professor at University College, Dublin, recalls the work of an early-nineteenth-century German geographer, Carl Ritter, whose work implied "a divine plan for humanity" based on regionalism and a constant, living flow of forms. If Central Asia is any indication, the map of the future may represent a perverse outcome of Ritter's vision. Imagine cartography in three dimensions, as in a hologram. In this hologram would be the overlapping sediments of various group identities such as those of language and economic class, atop the two-dimensional color distinctions among city-states and the remaining nations, themselves confused in places by shadows overhead, indicating the power of drug cartels, mafias, and private security agencies that guard the wealthy in failing states and hunt down terrorists. Instead of borders, there would be moving "centers" of power, as in the Middle Ages. These power centers would be both national and financial, reflecting the sovereignty of global corporations. Many of these holistic layers would be in motion. Replacing fixed and abrupt lines on a flat space would be a shifting pattern of ecoregions and buffer entities, like the Kurdish and Azeri buffer entities between Turkey and Iran, the Turkic Uighur buffer between Central Asia and inner China (itself distinct from coastal China), and the Turkic, Pathan, and Punjabi regions between Russia and the heartland of India. (Extrapolating further afield, a Latino buffer entity may replace a precise U.S.-Mexico border.) To this protean cartographic hologram one must add other factors, such as growing populations, refugee migrations, soil and water scarcities and—particularly in the case of Africa—vectors of disease. Henceforward the map of the world will never be static. This future map—in a sense, the "Last Map"—will be an ever-mutating representation of cartographic chaos: in some areas benign, or even productive, and in some areas violent. Because this map will always be changing, it may be updated, like weather reports, and transmitted daily over the Internet in those places that have reliable electricity or private generators.

On this map, the rules by which diplomats and other policymaking elites have ordered the world these past few hundred years will apply less and less. Solutions, in the main, will have to come from within the affected cultures themselves.

IT WAS TO south India, therefore, that I next headed: to witness a bold experiment in social and environmental regeneration begun by the indigenous inhabitants, without the help of Western or international aid agencies.

PART VI

◎   ◎   ◎

The Indian Subcontinent
and Indochina:

The Way of the Future

"The life of the future trembled behind all that silence. Mad humanity, which nothing could free from itself!"

—ANDRÉ MALRAUX
Man's Fate

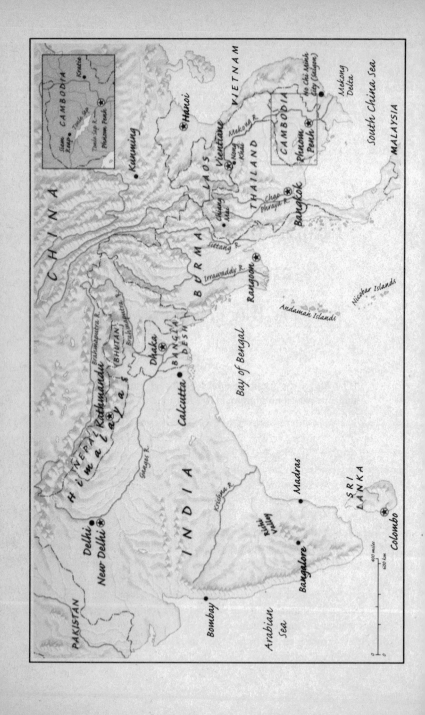

2 3

Journey in a Plague Year

I CAME TO India at a time of riots and plague. The riots were not unusual; the plague was.

In the 1990s there were often riots somewhere in India. On October 5, 1994, the day of my arrival, a mob killed five policemen in the northern Indian state of Uttar Pradesh, where nine towns were under curfew after arson and looting by lower, "scheduled"-caste Indians demanding an autonomous "reservation." In adjacent Bihar state, another set of riots killed two people. And several other Indian states, including Andhra Pradesh and Tamil Nadu, were in the midst of violent disturbances. The backdrop to these events was often land scarcity, tied to growing populations and predatory landlords, in parts of the country where the average woman was conceiving as many as five children over her lifetime.

But in the southern India city of Bangalore, the backdrop to riots that began three days after those in Uttar Pradesh was not poverty. It was relative prosperity. Bangalore is the site of India's leading technical university, as well as a booming technology center. It is the most Westernized and fastest growing city in India. The introduction of a ten-minute news bulletin on local television in Urdu, the language of the city's Moslems, caused Hindus in Bangalore to riot. Twenty-five people were stabbed to death; three hundred were wounded. In Bombay, another hive of prosperity, rush-hour gridlock sparked commuter violence in which thirty-four persons were hospitalized. The following week the riots were repeated. You had to wonder what India was going to be like in three or four decades, when the present population of 900 million will have reached at least 1.25 billion, if not much more.[1]

Outside India, however, all this violence was barely being reported. It was endemic. It was no longer news.

The plague was also a partial result of economic development. The city of Surat, north of Bombay on the Arabian Sea, where the plague first appeared, was an industrial boom town attracting migrant labor from surrounding villages. But as the Indian population grew and the effectiveness of state and municipal governments weakened, public health facilities became casualties. Only 13 percent of all Indians have access to public sewage systems and garbage collection. First had come bubonic plague—infecting rats, which were bitten by fleas and, in turn, bit human beings—then the plague became pneumonic and was spread by coughing.[2] In his account of the Great Plague in London of 1665, Daniel Defoe wrote:

> It must be confessed that though the plague was chiefly among the poor, yet were the poor the most venturous and fearless of it, and went about their employment with a sort of brutal courage . . .

In the whole of India, only several dozen persons actually died of the disease. Yet there was panic. This time the poor were afraid. Indians began wearing surgical masks to protect themselves against plague. That few people died mattered less than that the plague—an ancient disease—was a rare phenomenon in modern India.

---

[1]The figure of 1.25 billion is based on the most optimistic of recent projections, which indicate the possibility of India's population growth rate dropping to as low as 1.1 percent yearly.

[2]Another cause of the plague was the unusually hot summer of 1994 in the subcontinent, which killed animals, whose carcasses bred disease. The disease germs were spread by monsoons that had been intensified by the hot summer air. Paul Epstein of the Harvard School of Public Health and journalist Ross Gelbspan argued in *The Washington Post* (March 19, 1995) that India is an example of how global warming may spread disease. This is another reason why sub-Saharan Africa, with an even warmer climate than India, is at such a development disadvantage.

The plague made it necessary to create a "community." In the coastal city of Madras, in southern India, citizens' groups were setting wire-mesh rat traps. Bombay, meanwhile, "never looked so clean," according to a resident, as inhabitants began a massive garbage removal—something unique for a culture not known for public-spiritedness.

But the plague was having other effects, less salutary. It inflamed the conflict between Hindus and Moslems. Islamic countries were the only ones to embargo air flights to and from India during the outbreak, leading to harsh attacks in the Hindu press.

◎   ◎   ◎

MY ARRIVAL BY air at 1 A.M. in Madras, on the Bay of Bengal, was like my arrival in Abidjan on the Gulf of Guinea at a similar hour. The Indian subcontinent, like sub-Saharan Africa, constitutes its own environmental, climatic, and bacteriological field. I stepped out of a cool and antiseptic cabin, where I had been listening to Bach's Brandenburg Concertos from stereophonic headphones, and was hit by a dense, sticky molasses of damp heat and strange smells. There were the same squalid, fungal walls as in Africa, the same hacking coughs from airport personnel, and the same tickling of the ankles from mosquitoes and fleas. But there were also differences.

"It's extraordinary how we go through life with eyes half shut," writes Joseph Conrad in *Lord Jim*. Commenting on that phrase, Conrad scholar Cedric Watts declares how "habitual perception kills." The trick, suggests Watts, is to observe things fresh, in all their unfamiliarity. This is only possible during the first few moments and hours in a place, before familiarity sets in. And what I could not avoid noticing during my first moments in India were the sheer and stark differences from Africa.

At African airports I had often encountered a knot of local fixers holding passports aloft and shouting for the attention of a single, sullen-faced immigration officer. But here in Madras, visa requirements were published and strictly adhered to—they were not a matter of bribery and negotiation. It was the middle of the night in Madras and, unlike in many airports in Africa at such an hour, the airport bank was open: It cashed travelers' checks and supplied receipts. Unlike in Africa, not one of the arriving foreign passengers was met by a local fixer or an expediter at plane-side. In India, an airport fixer wasn't necessary because there was a codified procedure of entry into the country, not a series of intimidations and negotiations. In the Indian subcontinent, the unrest—as the violence demonstrated—was political and communal. In Africa, it was deeper and more random.

◎   ◎   ◎

IN THE BACKSEAT of a creaking and jangling taxi, transporting me out of Madras westward into the interior of southern India, I encountered a jarring new world. As the darkness of pre-dawn lifted, I saw billboards that advertised fax machines, personal computers, high-yield securities, and mutual funds. At street level were packs of water buffaloes, their horns covered in green paint and shiny brass rings, prodded along by men naked to the waist. The air from the open taxi window was a brew of dung, fresh sandalwood, and carbon monoxide. Buildings as contemporary as those in an American suburb were being constructed by armies of seminaked men and women, balancing buckets of mortar atop their heads. These buildings, with their polished-stone exteriors and with personal computers in many a flat, rise alongside clusters of thatched-roof huts. There will not be enough water to sustain the new inhabitants—Madras already faces a chronic water problem. The swarms of flies and mosquitoes I had seen in India in the early 1970s were still here. So were the old and soggy biscuits sold from corrugated-iron shacks, with broken glass counters and no toilet facilities.

The taxi went through a large village, a town really, with violent and garish movie billboards and restless swarms of young, bored men wearing tight polyester slacks and shirts: but with expressions that looked every bit as unsophisticated as those of the seminaked men driving the water buffaloes, only frustrated and filled with yearning. Did these young men go to school? Did they have jobs? Though the expanding economy was creating a small pool of high-salaried positions, most of the new jobs paid little. Seeing a link between rising crime in India and in the United States, Indian business columnist Kewal Varma notes that whereas crime in both countries used to be associated with unemployment, now it is linked with low-paid workers.

India—and to a lesser extent, Pakistan—has been growing economically at more than twice the rate of sub-Saharan Africa, according to the UN Human Development Report 1994: India and Pakistan have registered gross national product increases per capita of over 3 percent steadily since 1980, while many African countries have had negative or near-zero

GNP growth rates. Unlike much of sub-Saharan Africa, foreign business-men have been pouring into the Indian subcontinent.[3] Nevertheless, India's entry into the global marketplace has been destabilizing, for it changed a familiar landscape and inspired dreams that in many cases can never be realized.

India is putting more babies on the planet each year than any other country, yet it is a net exporter of food and one of the largest seafood exporters in the world. India has a burgeoning technology sector and a large middle class, numbering anywhere between 100 million and 250 million, depending upon how you define it. Its economic dynamism is a rebuke to the grim Malthusian certainties that seem to make sense in the Ivory Coast or in Rwanda, where the average woman gives birth to eight children over her lifetime, and where nothing is produced except rudi-mentary tools and subsistence crops, and where tribal fighting in 1994 claimed many hundreds of thousands of lives. And while democracy in Pakistan has been a series of unstable interregnums between military rule, India has been democratic for almost fifty years. Unlike Pakistan's bor-ders, India's borders are nearly geographically identical to those of the Indian subcontinent. India has territorial logic on its side. Even if the cen-tral government in New Delhi were to fall apart, it wouldn't matter much to mapmakers. India would go on being India, at least for Hindus.

Still, in India over 270 million people—more than the population of the United States—are "going continuously hungry."[4] And the signifi-cance of the much-acclaimed Indian middle class is exaggerated. Emma Duncan, *The Economist*'s Asia editor, writes:

> "India," chant the world's brokers and bankers like a mantra, "has a middle class of 250m people." If this is intended to convey some-thing about a decent house with a garden, a car, plenty of gadgets and a holiday a year, it is rubbish.

India, full of nuances and contradictions, enlivens the discussion of such issues as planetary overpopulation, environmental degradation, eth-

[3]While accounting for nearly 13 percent of the world's population, sub-Saharan Africa has garnered only about 6 percent of private capital flows in recent years. Though this figure might have improved slightly since the elections in South Africa, it is unlikely to change regarding West and East Africa.
[4]See Ross H. Munro's "The Loser: India in the Nineties," listed in the bibliography.

nic conflicts, and so on. Because Rishi Valley—the place where my taxi was headed—promised nothing less than a living theater in India in which to observe these epochal challenges, I should pause to explore them:

◎ ◎ ◎

SPEAKING IN 1991 at Los Alamos, New Mexico, where the world first entered the atomic age, the scholar Jessica Tuchman Mathews noted that "the latter half of the 1980s saw a fundamental new appreciation of the importance of the environment [and issues like demography] to the human condition. . . . The end of the Cold War released time and attention. As it did," these issues "catapulted from the quiet netherworld of what the diplomats call 'other' concerns to a place among international priorities."

As this happened, the ghost of an English clergyman, Thomas Robert Malthus, once again began to haunt the halls of foreign ministries and academe.

Malthus, like Freud, is a perennially unsettling figure, whose ideas continue to arouse bitter argument long after his death in 1834. "He is one of the few political thinkers whose arguments can be—and are—treated as if they had been written by a contemporary," writes Professor Mark T. Riley. In his *Essay on the Principle of Population*, published in 1798, Malthus propounded the thesis that population, when unchecked, increases in a geometric ratio, while the food supply increases only arithmetically. Thus, there is a constant check on population through war, disease, economic decline, or whatever. Charles Darwin, writing a half century later, saw how the struggle for existence "is the doctrine of Malthus applied . . . to the whole animal and vegetable kingdoms."

Malthus, who had actually worked among the poor in Surrey, England, had no illusions about them and was in constant conflict with utopian aristocrats, including the Marquis de Condorcet, who believed social evils were exclusively the fault of a coercive state. But Malthus failed to foresee the advances in agriculture generated by the Industrial Revolution that gathered force toward the end of his life, as well as the human migrations from Europe to virginal domains in North America and Australia, which would dramatically lower food prices. He proved too rigid in his emphasis on natural limits to population growth. Condorcet, the idealist, turned out to be right when he wrote, "New instruments, machines, and looms can add to man's strength. . . . A very small amount of ground will be able to produce a great quantity of supplies."

Nevertheless, while Condorcet is a name known mainly to specialists, it is Malthus and his fears that continue to haunt us. Take science journalist William K. Stevens, writing in *The New York Times*:

> Although birth rates are dropping, United Nations projections . . . show the world population reaching nearly 8.5 billion by 2025, with more than 7 billion living in what are now developing countries. The demographic momentum, even with slower growth, means the overall population will exceed 10 billion in 2050 and 11 billion in 2100, before stability finally sets in at 11.6 billion between 2150 and 2200.

Stevens says that third world populations will double in thirty years, will increase two and a half times before stabilizing, and in some places will grow three- or fourfold.

But is humankind once again about to overcome demographic growth, through a post-Industrial revolution in agriculture and urban planning? In which case, many of us will appear in hindsight as false Cassandras, like Malthus. Or was Malthus wrong only in his timing?[5]

Contesting this issue have been three groups:

- Neo-Malthusians, often biologists or ecologists, who claim that finite natural resources place strict limits on human populations, beyond which poverty and social breakdown result. Paul Erlich, who began warning of population doomsday a quarter century ago, is the best known proponent of this school.
- Neoclassical economists, such as Julian Simon, who claim there are few if any limits to human population growth or consumption since properly functioning economic markets will provide incentives for both conservation and the discovery of new agricultural technologies. Rather than a utopian like Condorcet, Simon is a conservative free-marketeer, like *The Wall Street Journal* editorial staff and the *Fortune* magazine crowd. If only governments will get out of the way, capitalism will solve future problems.

[5]At a November 1994 Washington conference on "Managing Chaos," Jessica Mathews said, "I think the jury is still out on Malthus. The question is, was he wrong in more than his timing?"

• Distributionists, who, while arguing for some limits to population growth, see the real problem as the maldistribution of natural resources and capital wealth. Africa is not to blame, in their view. The industrialized West is at fault, for exploiting the third world and devouring the planet's resources through unbridled consumption. Many distributionists are left-wing holdovers from the Cold War era, ideological opponents of corporate capitalism. But there are exceptions. Harvard University's Professor Amartya Sen, writing in *The New York Review of Books*, propounds a completely nonideological distributionism that perceptively attacks neo-Malthusian certitudes.[6]

Sen notes that despite rapid third world population growth, Africa's and Asia's share of world population (71.2 percent) is still less than what it was—78.4 percent—on the eve of Europe's Industrial Revolution. In other words, population growth in the third world may represent merely a historical correction, now that the machine age has spread beyond the West. However, though India and China are going through an industrial revolution, Africa is not. Africa's expanding population has little man-made industrial wealth to sustain it, while its food production—relative to population—has decreased.

There is a new, fourth, school of environmental-population strategists, one with which I felt increasingly comfortable as I traveled from Africa to Asia. This school, which includes Toronto University's Thomas Homer-Dixon and others, agrees with neo-Malthusians that there are limits to population growth beyond which poverty and social breakdown result. It also agrees with neoclassical economists that the products of human ingenuity can expand those limits to take people beyond mere subsistence level, as in the case of the Industrial Revolution. But this school believes that human ingenuity does not materialize automatically and that some societies and cultures are more ingenious than others. "By definition," writes Homer-Dixon, developing countries "do not have the financial, material, or intellectual resources of the developed world; furthermore, their social and political institutions tend to be fragile and riven with discord." Thus, in Sierra Leone and Rwanda, the Malthusian limit may already have been reached, with endemic ethnic strife the result. However, in the Indian sub-

[6]See Sen's "Population: Delusion and Reality," listed in the bibliography.

continent and China, more adaptable cultures are finding ways to expand their resource base. The key point to remember is that when a region becomes overpopulated, there is no open recognition of this fact. All we have to go on is how well, or how badly, that society functions. The establishment of democracy and a civil society may make the political system more flexible and responsive. On the other hand, a stable democracy will more easily emerge in places where a balance between population and resources already exists.

Demographic pressures may spur human ingenuity, but ingenuity is never evenly distributed. Moreover, technical ingenuity depends on social ingenuity—the ability to create a functioning society: What good are new Western vaccines in an anarchic African country where health clinics are constantly being vandalized or having their electricity cut?[7]

Deficient social ingenuity is, of course, partly the result of resource scarcity, which further aggravates rivalries within a society. Therefore, the ability of a policymaker—even one as gifted as Nelson Mandela—to be a good social engineer may decline in the face of South Africa's 2.63 percent annual population growth and diminishing soil and water resources. The same, obviously, goes for China and India and their leaders.

Homer-Dixon believes the world is headed for a split between "those societies that can maintain an adequate supply of ingenuity and those that cannot. . . . We will probably see, for example, falling grain prices and regional food surpluses in Western countries occurring simultaneously with scarcity-induced civil strife in parts of Africa and Asia." He concludes that

> the optimism of neoclassical economics . . . who have great faith in the potential of human ingenuity when spurred by need is deceptive and imprudent. We are taking a huge gamble if we follow the path they suggest, which is to wait till scarcities are critical and watch human ingenuity burst forth in response. Should it turn out, in the end, that this strategy was wrong, we will not be able to return to a world resembling anything like the one we have today . . . the soils,

---

[7]At a May 1995 conference at the University of Oklahoma, a disease specialist related the story of a Nigerian researcher for the World Health Organization. The cholera samples that the researcher had been studying were ruined when the laboratory refrigerator stopped working—on account of an electricity breakdown that, in turn, was caused by riots in Lagos.

waters, and forests will be irreversibly damaged, and our societies, especially the poorest ones, will be so riven with discord that even heroic efforts at social renovation will fail.

Homer-Dixon assumes, optimistically, that the West can respond, at least potentially. But can it, given its aging population and household incomes that have not risen for over a generation? Foreign aid from the West will likely decline.

◎   ◎   ◎

AND THUS INDIA, which is undergoing an industrial revolution and abounds in human ingenuity. Here a literature and a written language have existed for two thousand five hundred years and some of the earliest discoveries in algebra, geometry, and astronomy were made. But each year India adds 18 million people to its population, the equivalent of two New Delhis, or more than one and a half Calcuttas. In the mid-1990s India had 900 million people. Optimists think India's population will level off at 1.7 billion before the end of the next century; pessimists think 2 billion.

"As rising populations demand more services, but scarce resources provide fewer opportunities for government to increase its income, fiscal strain, debt, inflation, and corruption will rise. These trends undermine the effectiveness and legitimacy of the state which loses its ability to . . . maintain social order," writes University of California sociologist Jack Goldstone. Delhi, like Karachi, is an ominous example of these trends. At current rates, Delhi's population of 9 million will grow to 13.5 million by the end of the century.[8] Shantytowns have overrun many of the city's graceful gardens and avenues. Obtaining water, cooking gas, or electricity is impossible without a bribe. Delhi's air is the most polluted of any city in the world. Breathing it is as dangerous as smoking twenty cigarettes a day. Traffic policemen wear surgical masks. This pollution will worsen dramatically as hundreds of thousands of fuel-spouting automobiles are added to the roads of India each year. Given that between 1989 and mid-1991 alone, 2,025 Indians were, in *Washington Post* correspondent Steve Coll's words, "hacked, stabbed, burned, and shot to death in urban brawls" between Hindus and Moslems, it is apparent how surging populations, environmental degradation, and ethnic conflict appear to be related.

[8]See Edward Gargan's "New Delhi Journal," in the June 12, 1993, *New York Times.*

India is a world of both cellular phones and primitive public sanitation.[9] Not only is poverty destabilizing, but so is fast economic growth. The poor in India's cities are increasingly migrants from the villages, often fleeing land scarcity and erosion, uprooted from many of their traditions. Though they have insufficient food in their bellies, they often have transistor radios and are surrounded by Western billboard advertisements. Like the inhabitants of the Chinese and Egyptian shantytowns that I had seen, with television antennas rising above their mudhuts, these poor migrants know temptation. They are less fatalistic, perhaps more prone to revolt than before. And their numbers are growing as fast as those of the middle class.[10]

The new rich represent something just as frightening, according to *Time* magazine correspondent Ned Desmond:

> India's [Hindu] middle class was no longer an elite, Westernized group, as it was at partition, but a highly acquisitive, anxious class whose members only vaguely comprehended the point of secularism while very sharply feeling a grievance against any group with a supposed special status—especially Muslims.

Perhaps this is why Bombay, India's richest city, has seen the worst intercommunal violence. In a seminal article about India entitled "Modern Hate: How Ancient Animosities Get Invented," Susanne Hoeber Rudolph and Lloyd I. Rudolph point out that the Hindu hooligans who, in December 1992 tore down a sixteenth-century mosque in the northeastern Indian town of Ayodha "were wearing city clothes, shirts and trousers, not the *kurta* and *dhotis* of villagers or the urban poor. They looked like clerks, boys from urban lower-middle-class families. They are the educated unemployed, not the poor and illiterate. . . . They are victims of modernization, seeking to victimize others—like 'pampered' Muslims," since "their [the Hindus'] expectations have run well ahead of available opportunities."

In such circumstances, communications technology fosters hate more than unity. Instead of a diverse and localized Hinduism, Indian

[9]See Michael Specter's article on Siberia, listed in the bibliography, which examines these contradictions in another climatic milieu.
[10]For example, of Bombay's 12.5 million inhabitants, 5.5 million live in slums, according to Molly Moore, *The Washington Post*'s New Delhi bureau chief.

television has promoted a standardized Hinduism, from which an anti-Islamic power bloc has emerged, much like the manipulation of ancient hatreds by electronic media and videocassettes in Serbia after the Cold War. Cultural strife, as in the hotel nightclub in Samarkand, can be very modern.

The victim of these developments has been the Indian state. Atul Kohli, a Princeton University professor, writes in *Democracy and Discontent: India's Growing Crisis of Governability*:

> This state is omnipresent, but feeble; it is highly centralized . . . yet seems powerless. It has the responsibility to foster the "life-chances" of its many diverse social groups, but . . . appears capable neither of dealing with the concerns of diverse interest groups nor of directing planned development. Its dominant institutions are in disarray, and the search for new legitimacy formulas goes on. . . . Whenever a community's [or a state's] social and political fiber begins breaking down in this manner, the criminal elements in the society are never far away.

Of course, this sounds a lot like Russia and a little like the U.S., which, far as it is from the social chaos of India, is also subject to these trends.

As India's political parties are less able to deliver social spoils, they rely upon gangs to buy off, and intimidate, voters. As Hindu and Moslem groups, in addition to various Hindu castes, struggle for power outside the normal machinery of the state, they further invite the criminalization of politics, so India has become increasingly semianarchic. In Bihar, in the northeast, Kohli tells us that there are no longer elections without violence committed by "private caste armies" against other castes, whose votes the caste armies consider detrimental to their economic interests. "In addition, ordinary criminals, the *dacoits*, have entered the fray, further confusing the picture of who is killing whom and why." With the police impotent, "people's courts" have emerged, dispensing kangaroo justice that has ended with robbers dragged into forests to have their heads cut off.[11] Needless to say, in Bihar agricultural production has consistently lagged behind population growth.

[11] See John Ward Anderson's "Poor vs. Rich in Indian State," listed in the bibliography. His article details the operation of people's courts.

The Indian central government—like Pakistan's—is weakening. Rather than one bold line dividing the subcontinent into two main parts, the future will likely see many fainter lines and smaller enclaves. Again the dictum: whatever can be managed locally, will be. Thus, I come to Rishi Valley.

24

Rishi Valley and Human Ingenuity

I FELT AS though I were back on the road in West Africa, with its monotonous and intimidating greenery and red laterite underfoot, traversed by ant armies. The hollow and high-pitched bird calls were relaxing after the nighttime taxi ride. Butterflies completed the picture. There were fifty-five varieties of them here, I would later be told by Mr. S. Rangaswami, a local naturalist. The difference, though, between Rishi Valley and West Africa was total: Every tree in sight, in what looked much like a jungle, had been planted by a man's or a child's hand as part of a deliberate act of regeneration.

A few decades back, this valley had been deforested and became secondary growth scrub land, where farmers carved out a marginal existence in an area of chronic drought. The regeneration of the landscape had been achieved without the advice of a single Western aid expert, and with almost no outside funds. Indeed, Rishi Valley was a secret that the West knew very little about.

Friends at the University of Toronto had suggested I visit Rishi Valley. They said Rishi Valley was a place where the local inhabitants had found solutions to such ills as overpopulation and environmental degradation. No doubt, there are places in Africa I could have visited that would have given me as much hope as Rishi Valley, just as there are places in India that are as depressing as Sierra Leone. Rishi Valley may be less an Indian success story than it is a human success story. Rishi Valley shows that there is hope, that we as a species will not necessarily destroy ourselves. But it also taught me that if these hopes are to be realized, then solutions must emerge locally. Hope and solutions cannot be imported by big government or from international bureaucracies thousands of miles away.

◎　　　　◎　　　　◎

THE NATURALIST, MR. Rangaswami, binoculars dangling from his graceful, six-foot-plus frame, ambled out of the woods and began talking, sweeping me along with his commentary for a brief forty-five minutes: It was the overture to my valley experience.

"Birds are the litmus test," Mr. Rangaswami declared. "The return of the Yellowthroated Bulbul to Rishi Valley constitutes the official proof of ecological renewal here. Before we had heard that warble for the first time some years back, we just couldn't be sure of anything." Mr. Rangaswami led me through a rich undergrowth of vines, ferns, red sanders, sandalwood, custard apples, tamarinds, acacias, and lemon grass. "There has been a 300 percent biomass increase. Notice the red sanders. They are drought-resistant and grow absolutely vertically. We chose them because their roots anchor the soil without interfering with the other greenery. But Mr. Naidu will tell you all about that. He is the real worker of miracles, the real *presence* in the valley. You will meet him, I'm sure. Quiet! Hear that melodious cackle? That is the Pied Crested Cuckoo. We'll soon be entering Bulbul territory."

Mr. Rangaswami went on about solar panels, organic vegetable gardens, and replacing butane with the gas released by cow dung, while at the same time pointing out parakeets and a group of owlets. With his winglike arms constantly in motion, his plume of iron-gray hair, and lilting Indian voice, he seemed to be one of the "150 species of returned migratory birds" he so loved. Especially as he had never really introduced himself but, rather, had swept down into my presence. Suddenly, he stopped his lecture and put his finger over his lips, admonishing me to keep silent—as though I were the one who had been talking. "No, that's only a white egret," he said, somewhat disappointed. Then, hearing a high-pitched note through the bushes, he extended his arms against the blue ink-blot sky and dark monsoon clouds and exclaimed, "Ah, now the Pied King-fisher has come!"

◎　　　◎　　　◎

MR. RANGASWAMI, IN his seventies, had worked as an accountant and as a man-ager of a factory in Madras before he discovered his true vocation in Rishi Valley, where he took up bird-watching and became the "honorary chief warden" of the nature reserve. Eccentric he may be, but Mr. Rangaswami is not a super-romantic. Nor is he independently wealthy. He is part of a movement that believes ecological renewal is essential to cultural renewal.

The story begins in 1895 in the village of Madanapalle, a few miles from Rishi Valley, with the birth of Jiddu Krishnamurti. Krishnamurti, who died in 1986, was a modern philosopher—not a guru or a yogi. He created no hierarchies and collected no money. He discouraged disciples. "If you are very clear, if you are inwardly a light unto yourself, you will never follow anyone," he told admirers. Aldous Huxley, hearing Krishna-murti speak, said it was "amongst the most impressive things I have listen to—it was like listening to the discourse of the Buddha." Krishnamurti's beliefs are hard to pin down. He eschewed utopianism, and scoffed at a return to pastoral beatitude. He felt that such attitudes can be sustained only by closing one's eyes to the reality of "cruelty, competition, or pain that is so much a part of life on Earth." He was a skeptic who acknowl-edged a banal truth: "The Earth is ours, yours and mine, and we have to live on it together; we have to cherish it and grow things on its soil." Krishnamurti foresaw a historical phase in which people would identify with something like what environmental security expert Daniel Deudney calls "green culture" or "earth nationalism," which may emerge in tandem with a switch from "low" to "high" politics: the global management of many environmental problems by the mid-twenty-first century. Deudney describes this long-range trend as "the emergence of world domestic pol-itics." Krishnamurti's ideas may also be thought of as a precursor to "Gaia" theory, named after an ancient Greek earth goddess, which sees the Earth as a living system in which living and nonliving forms continu-ously interact. Jessica Mathews says this about Gaia:

> In the last few years Gaia has moved from fringe to mainstream sci-ence, opening up new areas of research and changing the way peo-

ple think—including those who think parts of the theory are wrong. The traditional view of life as something that passively adapts itself to an externally imposed physical environment is giving way to recognition that the living and nonliving realms are intricately entangled. . . . Ultimately, Gaia will, I think, demolish the prevailing view—which is deeply embedded in economics, law and political science—that human society exists largely separate from nature.

In the early 1930s, Krishnamurti and his friends established an elite boarding school on a completely barren patch of pebbled earth covering 240 acres, near his birthplace at the foot of Rishi Konda, an ancient rock where, two thousand years ago, *rishis*, or monks, went to do penance. This went against the prevailing Indian trend of locating boarding schools in picturesque hill stations. Because the Rishi Valley school attracted the sons and daughters of wealthy Brahmin families from throughout the linguistically diverse subcontinent, instruction was in English. Though this was not unique, the school's approach to education, and its evolving relationship with the surrounding villages, certainly was.

Indian education has often been criticized for being "rootless" and "abstract," for producing brainy prodigies disconnected from their own environment, exactly what one would expect to emerge from a caste system. Indians, thus, despite great achievements in the theoretical sciences, have often lacked a similarly strong engineering tradition. The Rishi Valley school sought to fill this gap by making environmental conservation a basic part of the curriculum and by forcing these wealthy students to work with their hands alongside local villagers. "Culture is renewed when people from the city, with intellectual resources, settle in the villages," explained Geetha Iyer, a teacher at Rishi Valley. That, of course, is the lesson that the shah of Iran and other third world despots never learned: that the village, not the city, is the key to modernity; that a nation cannot be modern while its villages are still medieval.

Geetha, a lithe and diminutive woman, with pink-framed glasses and eyes full of curiosity, drove me miles into the countryside, where two landscapes converged. One resembled a skull-and-bones vision of limestone hills, sculpted by wind and rain over millennia and topped by huge granite boulders, stripped of tree cover and topsoil from years of overgrazing and cutting trees for firewood. The other landscape was the regenerated forest of Rishi Valley, where, interspersed between the trees, were splashes of bougainvillea, hibiscus, marigolds, wild roses, and jasmine, with a bird symphony rising above it. The difference that a hundred yards made here was more palpable than many of the man-made borders I had crossed. In the reforested area, the breezes, rinsed clean of dust, and sunlight, reported into many colors by the canopy of leaves, gave a sense of well-being. I wondered if people who inhabit a regenerated landscape like this become less bellicose.

Geetha explained: "We say to the villagers, give us your worst land, your very worst. Not to own or keep, but as place for you and our students to work on." Her blue cotton sari trailing in the breeze, she led me to such a terrain.

Like a patch of blotched skin in the process of healing, to the nonexpert eye this piece of land didn't look like much. It was just ravine and hillside: not barren, not green, rather somewhere between. The middle represented the progress made by Geetha's students. "We select plants and trees that will yield good mulch, as well as anchor the soil." Noteworthy among these is the custard apple: a short, fruit-bearing tree of no particular beauty, yet a name I heard repeated like a mantra throughout Rishi Valley. The custard apple matures in just four years. It sinks deep and wide roots that anchor eroded soil. It is a hardy tree, requiring little rain and bearing leaves that goats won't eat. And in its shade other plant species emerge naturally. Mr. Rangaswami, the bird watcher, adored the custard apple.

The Rishi Valley schoolchildren plant twenty thousand trees and shrubs each year and distribute one hundred thousand seedlings throughout the valley. In his chronicle of the experience, *Birds of Rishi Valley: And Renewal of Their Habitat*, Mr. Rangaswami and his co-author, S. Sridhar, write:

> Armed with digging sticks and bags full of seeds, younger children climbed up a path to plant seeds into the hard soil. Older students dug pits for saplings. Large drums of water were transported by tractor from the well to the foothills. From there, the children filled buckets with water and relayed them up through a long line snaking over the hillside. . . .
>
> Nurseries with thousands of trees were developed. Students and workers joined hands in filling polythene bags with earth and watering the newly sown seeds until they were ready to be transplanted.

Geetha pointed out a series of "check dams," miniature dams, or breaks, fashioned from the soil itself, not much bigger than what a child would construct on a beach with wet sand. By stopping, or at least slowing, the flow of rivulets after a rain, these check dams help prevent erosion, and form deposits of nutrient-rich silt. "The silt is very fertile. It has much humus-matter. We transport the silt to dry areas that need regeneration," Geetha explained. Rishi Valley, I was beginning to learn, was like one big grafting operation, where healthy soil created in one area was shifted to another to spur the regenerative process. The students even produce their own organic compost by collecting all the school's garbage in cement-lined pits, where it is devoured by earth worms.

Grander than the check dams were the "contour bunds": sloping stone walls about six feet high and several hundred yards long, also constructed by the students in cooperation with the villagers, that channel the flood waters toward "percolation tanks." Percolation tanks, like the custard apples, was another name recited in a reverential tone. They were the invention of Mr. Naidu, the estate manager at Rishi Valley, whom Mr. Rangaswami had called the "real worker of miracles" here.

When I asked Geetha if these percolation tanks were for irrigation, she said, "Definitely not. We don't irrigate in Rishi Valley and we don't use chemical fertilizers. We replenish the underground water table and the soil."

The problem with India's Green Revolution, which yielded a manifold increase in food production, Geetha and others explained, is that it has dangerously depleted India's environmental base through overirrigation and overuse of artificial fertilizers. The custard apples, check dams, contour bunds, and percolation tanks are all elements in reversing that process. "Basically," Geetha said, "people have to like their place deep enough—that is, consciously enough—to work to preserve it."

If this were all, then Rishi Valley would constitute little more than an environmental theme park for wealthy children. But there is more.

ON THE DRIVE back to the campus Geetha and I passed through several villages: tight clusters of thatched-roof huts, bony cattle, and women, like petite mahogany sculptures, in flashy purple, red, and green saris drawing buckets of water from wells. But that eaten-from-within quality—the flies, the diseased gums, the smells—that I had always associated with India seemed missing. These villages were an air-brushed travel-magazine India. It took me a few days to learn why.

◎   ◎   ◎

RISHI VALLEY IS like a New England boarding school removed to Appalachia so that the students can work with the rural poor, like Peace Corps or Vista volunteers. Though outwardly its approach appears to be a model of Western liberal thought, the Rishi Valley staff—in Krishnamurti's own Indian way[1]—has internalized the conservative dictum that wealth creation is more a matter of culture than of politics.[2] And that while people are certainly born equal, environmental and human influences to which they are subjected from birth make them profoundly unequal by the time they reach school age.

Besides the English-speaking boarding school, there is a day school for one hundred village children where the language of instruction is Telugu, the local Dravidian language. The day school is the hub of an expanding network of "satellite" schools for the surrounding villages. I visited one of these village schools and was amazed.

It was a simple, one-room schoolhouse of lime-washed mudbrick with a corrugated-iron roof, surrounded by a garden of marigold and hibiscus. Inside the schoolhouse I saw four groups, of about five children each, sitting in circles on the floor and quietly working with instructional cards and small chalkboards. I heard no shouting and saw no bored or sleepy faces, just low, steady whispering as children tutored each other with minimal help from the teacher, who appeared almost superfluous. Paper cutouts of flowers and birds dangled from the ceiling a few feet above the children's heads. Shelves holding a neat arrangement of students' files and craft boxes were set against one wall. Against another wall were colorful charts that listed the number of people, plants, and animals in the village, each broken down into various categories. From the charts, I learned that this particular village has 271 inhabitants, of whom 106 are women, 97 men, and 68 children. An exhibition of the children's paintings hung from the third wall. Though only a year old, this school was already

---

[1] Krishnamurti was raised and greatly influenced by a British social reformer, Annie Besant, making his philosophy, perhaps, partly a Western product.
[2] In *The New Republic* of July 7, 1986, Daniel Patrick Moynihan writes: "The central conservative truth is that it is culture, not politics, that determines the success of a society. The central liberal truth is that politics can change a culture and save it from itself."

more than a hut—it was a "home," with a deeply personal touch both in the garden and in the classroom, which, with its wall charts, reflected an accumulation of knowledge and experience. I could not recall another classroom that seemed so calm and conducive to self-motivation. It was especially impressive when one considered the poverty of the students' background and the wide age-span within the class, in which children of various grade levels were working together.

I spent an hour in the classroom just watching the children. From time to time, for a minute or two they stared at me—an unfamiliar and foreign face that had sparked their curiosity. But then they returned to work. Not one child had an expression that seemed sullen or lost, the way many children appear in schools in poor neighborhoods in the United States. I observed closely from outside the door: Not one child was pestering the other. By American standards, the class was an anomaly—a room full of underprivileged kids of varying ages who were all well behaved. Because discipline was not even an issue, let alone a problem, everyone could concentrate on learning.

That classroom was not an accident. I was to visit several village schools in the area during various times of the day. The atmosphere was always the same. Just as the day school on the Rishi Valley campus was the hub for this satellite school network, each satellite school was the hub for a village, where courses in adult literacy, land reclamation, reforestation, hygiene, beekeeping, etc., are conducted in the evenings, and where students work with their parents to tend the school garden and plant nursery and to build contour bunds and check dams to stop erosion.

The oldest of these satellite schools is in Egavaboyapalle, a formerly deforested village of 250 families, all from a caste that has a reputation for "shiftlessness" and "highway robbery." Since 1986, when this school opened, literacy in Egavaboyapalle has climbed from near zero to 70 percent. The incidence of disease has dropped dramatically. The residents have adorned their thatched-roof huts with bougainvillea and hibiscus gardens. They have donated a gold clock, among other items, to the school, which is never locked at night. Trust among the villagers is growing. The student dropout rate here and in nearby villages has been falling to almost zero. Ninety-five percent of the students pass the entrance examination for advancement to upper grade levels.

I sat on the floor of a small office on the Rishi Valley campus, sipping milky tea with the young husband-and-wife team responsible for this achievement. Y. A. Padmanabha Rao, with his glasses, thick black hair, and mustache, resembles a younger clone of the Iraqi diplomatic hatchet-man Tariq Aziz. Whereas Aziz never fails to be nonsensical and insincere, Rao's intellect arises from homespun common sense. He and his stylish wife, Rama, dressed in a red-and-white sari, had moved to Rishi Valley from the city of Hyderabad, a few hours' drive to the north, to test out their revolutionary ideas about education outside the straitjacket of the Indian government school system. I was scribbling notes too fast to record who said what. Here is a summary in the couple's own words of how the Raos approach the problem of underachieving children from culturally impoverished backgrounds.

"Curriculum studies are increasingly abstract. Textbooks with pictures of airplanes and even cars aren't related to the daily experience of these kids. Textbooks the world over, let's admit, are boring anyway. Only bright kids with stable home environments and parental encouragement do well with textbooks. Moreover, the idea that a child from a broken and/or functionally illiterate home, without the requisite privacy, quiet, and electric lighting, will succeed at homework is absurd. To give such children homework is to program them for failure. And forget about good teachers. Most good teachers in India will use every stratagem to avoid a teaching job in a poor district. Those who get stuck in a poor district will be forever glancing at their watches, ready to run out of the classroom and catch the bus back to the city every day at noon. Nor, as a rule, should you expect good teachers to emerge locally. More often than not, local teachers will simply pass on their incompetence and prejudices to the students. Even if you find a good teacher in a poor area, he or she will be unable to deal with thirty youngsters with learning problems."

The Raos, thus, reinvented what a school is. A school need not be a classroom and a teacher. Nor is it a lecture by one big person to thirty little people, whereby teacher and textbook perform as if they were magicians and everybody else sits in rows and listens. A school is not about rote learning or memorizing. Oral cultures, the Raos asserted, already do too much of that. Only when children are taught to categorize and to analyze, rather than merely to memorize, can they achieve anything in the modern world. Intercommunal and tribal hatreds, the Raos explained, arise from too much faulty oral memory and too little self-motivated analysis.

According to the Raos, the ideal school in the developing world at the turn of the twenty-first century must be cheap, portable, easily replicable, and able to teach children to think as if they had been brought up in a literate home. It must also inculcate, "deep in the learning process," the values of family planning, concern for the physical environmental, and tolerance for other cultures. And all this can, literally, "fit in a box."

The Raos' "School in a Box" has spread beyond the fifteen satellite schools operated by Rishi Valley to two hundred more schools across southeastern India, where government-run education systems are breaking down and inhabitants are desperate for alternatives.

The "box" itself consists of five hundred illustrated instructional cards in mathematics, Telugu language, science, health, and environmental studies—and a manual for the teacher, who, for the most part, is a "facilitator," since the children end up teaching themselves.

The children start by playing with rubber circles and semicircles, also included in the box, which are similar to the shapes of the forty-five letters in the Telugu alphabet.[3] Then they move on to rubber letters, dividing them up into eight categories, according to how difficult they are to write and to pronounce. Following that, the children use game cards, where stones are placed atop the correct letter, pronounced out loud by the teacher. The next set of cards is for stenciling in the letters on paper. "The idea," explained Mrs. Rao, "is to begin by actually touching and feeling the rubber letters, and only afterward progress to writing them. Memory is not really required. You learn unconsciously by doing and playing more than by remembering."

There are also picture cards, in which the child writes the word for the picture, followed by puzzle cards, review cards, and so on. Children go on to the next level of cards only after completing the one before it. "The children are in the driver's seat, motivating themselves in groups," Mr. Rao said.

Story cards supply simplified versions of Indian epics. There are also stories modeled on Indian epics that promote ethnic harmony, sexual equality, and love of the environment. Children then write their own stories, which they take home to their parents, who must then learn to read in order to know what their children have written. This is what provides the incentive for the adult-literacy programs. "We use only what their own children have written in teaching the adults how to read," Mr. Rao

---

[3]The rubber is the kind used for shoe soles; the rough edge indicates which side is down.

explained. "This way you don't have a middle-aged peasant saying, 'What use is reading to me?' "

Yet another card series is used to teach measurement. "But not abstract measurement," Mr. Rao cautions, "such as one hundred centimeters equals one meter. We teach real measurement, such as your nose is so many centimeters long. And we teach time with an hourglass, so that students learn just *how* long an hour or a half hour is. The concept of time is urban. Villagers never learn it. That is why everyone is often late in India and in Africa. An urban idea of time must be instilled at an early age if a society is to produce material wealth."

The neat and well-organized classrooms that I saw were no accident. "The classroom," Mrs. Rao told me, "must be an extension of the ideal home: A functional household is an orderly one. The children must make activity files for themselves. The instructional cards implant the notion of categories and subcategories for everything. We make the children study their own village. They make statistical charts on the number of men, the number of women, the number of people who can read, the number who can't, the length of people's noses. . . . In short, the children learn to constantly compare. Thus, they develop objectivity, by finding out things for themselves, through research." To this end, the school organizes village fairs, where the children staff stalls, at which people get weighed and measured and guess the weight of that rock or the length of that leaf. The children then make written graphs of the results.

Just as the classroom is an extension of the ideal home, the garden outside is an extension of the classroom. Each satellite school has a flower, fruit, and vegetable nursery, which the students and their parents are responsible for. Like the Rishi Valley fruit fields whose incomes help subsidize the campus, the nurseries generate income so that each school is nearly self-sustaining. More important than the income—and the charts the children must maintain on plant growth—is the development of an aesthetic instinct. "The planting of bougainvillea in and around the school," Mrs. Rao said, "teaches the children to appreciate beauty. People who appreciate beauty are less likely to be violent."

WATCHING THE CHILDREN quietly go about their lessons amid the highly organized clutter of the schoolhouse, and listening to the Raos talk to the "teacher/facilitator"—a teenage girl in a red sari—it all seemed too impressive to be merely the result of an innovative learning technique. It occurred to me that South Asians just might enjoy cultural advantages that sub-Saharan Africans lack. Illiteracy here seems qualitatively different from illiteracy in Africa. The Raos pointed out that the oral stories and traditions that villagers in south India know are based on written epics that have been handed down in detail in Dravidian languages and scripts thousands of years old. Telugu, based on Sanskrit, has a larger alphabet than English. Illiterate villagers in Rishi Valley can tap into a well-developed, literate cultural environment, whereas in much of sub-Saharan Africa, local languages have been written down only in the last century or so.

The Indian population growth rate of under 2 percent is lower than that of practically every state in mainland sub-Saharan Africa. In nearby Kerala, in southwestern India, from where many Rishi Valley faculty come, the growth rate is lower still, and female literacy is an astounding 86 percent. Indians, like the Lebanese and Syrians, went to sub-Saharan Africa a century ago with little more than the shirts on their backs, and went on to form the middle class in a number of African cities. This couldn't have happened merely by accident, or through "exploitation," since even exploitation requires ingenuity. The Raos' "School in a Box" is, despite differences between South Asia and Africa, also applicable to Africa and other places where children don't learn as well as they might. Whether it can help close the ever-widening gap in material wealth between Africa and the Indian subcontinent, however, is another matter.

◎   ◎   ◎

MR. SRI NAIDU, the Rishi Valley estate manager of whom I had been hearing so much, did not greet me with a merry smile and explosion of chatter like the others. He was not an intellectual who had moved to Rishi Valley from the city. Born in a nearby village, Mr. Naidu was a shy, monosyllabic man, physically husky, with thinning gray hair, who worked with his hands. He was different from the other adults at Rishi Valley in the same way that an Israeli kibbutz farmer is different from urban Jews from Tel Aviv, or from New York. And that, I surmised, partly accounted for the awe in which the others held him.

"You are interested in farming?" he bluntly inquired.

"Yes," I replied.

"Follow me."

Mr. Naidu led me to an expanse of mango fields. "The whole valley was dry, so I went to Madras to find out about the cost of a drip irrigation system. It was too expensive. So I took these empty food tins, stuffed their opened ends with cotton, and filled them with water. Then I planted the cotton drums around the mango trees. Every four days I went around with a donkey cart to refill them with water and change the cotton. It worked. We saved a lot of money. Who needs a high-tech operation? There is too much technology in agriculture, and too many artificial fertilizers that are destroying our soil for the future. At Rishi Valley, I use only natural organic fertilizers like neem cake [a compost of decayed leaves from the neem tree]."

Mr. Naidu repeated what Geetha had said, that India's much-trumpeted Green Revolution has been achieved by overworking its crop-lands and depleting its watershed through overirrigation. (Norman Myers, a British development consultant, worries that Indians have "been feeding themselves today by borrowing against their children's food sources.")

We continued walking. Seeing me scribble in my notebook, Mr. Naidu warmed up a bit. He told me about the different kinds of soils and ferns. He led me to a rich undergrowth of ferns and said, "I want all of southern India to look like this."

I asked him about the percolation tanks.

"I got the idea watching the schoolboys take showers in the open air. All the shower water was running out into the field, wasted. So I had the students dig a trench around the shower area, to collect the runoff. With this waste water I grew beans and bananas. The percolation tanks are just bigger versions of the shower ditch."

Mr. Naidu explained how he had supervised the construction of con-tour bunds and check dams, which channeled water from the seasonal monsoon rains into a football-field-sized percolation tank: a ditchlike building foundation that took a year to fill up. Meanwhile, the flood catchment area formed by the long contour bunds was converted into a vast and productive rice paddy. "We got some money for the project from the local government [of the Indian state of Andhra Pradesh]. The gov-ernment bureaucrats were impossible to deal with, though. I will never go near the government again."

"What about the federal authorities in New Delhi?" I asked.

"They're even worse."

Mr. Naidu directed the Rishi Valley students and local villagers in the arduous task of transporting the enriched soil from around the percolation tank to drier parts of the valley in order to grow peanuts. "It takes twelve to fifteen inches of enriched tank silt to regenerate alkaline soil. It is a permanent and natural solution." He went on:

"We use the percolation tanks to replenish the underground water table, not for irrigation. Now it takes five or ten minutes of pumping to extract water from underground, instead of twenty minutes in the days before the percolation tanks. The water table in the valley has risen from forty feet below ground to as high as ten feet in places." Mr. Naidu kept repeating that "there is too much irrigation in the developing world," causing salinity, waterlogging, and depletion of underground water tables. Rising populations, he believed, will less and less be sustained by over-tilled, overfertilized, and overirrigated earth.

Rishi Valley under Mr. Naidu's direction is a big organic farm carrying out a "post–Green Revolution" revolution, by reinvesting money raised from the sale of its own produce. Indians in Rishi Valley have rediscovered, on their own, a two-thousand-year-old technique of channeling rainwater to make a dry area green, pioneered by the Nabateans, who lived in present-day Jordan around the time of Jesus and who built the famed "rose red" city of Petra. Mr. Naidu told me he had never heard of the Nabateans. He said:

"A society has to self-discover things, even if it is already known to outsiders. That way it will stick through experience and become ingrained in the local mentality."

Mr. Naidu and I climbed atop one of the contour bunds to survey the rich, green panorama of cultivation. "I haven't told you about my past, have I?" he said, tilting his head back and forth in the way Indians do as a means of emphasis, and punctuation. He told me how he and his family had lived in a large house on campus that he had, over the years, lovingly adorned with bougainvillea and hibiscus trellises, and with sweet jasmine. "But I can't bring myself to spend the nights there anymore. I sleep at my daughter's house in a nearby town. You see, I had three children," he began, as I noticed a mounting sadness in his voice.

"All of my children went to the Rishi Valley school. My daughter married a local lawyer. My eldest son works for IBM in Bahrain. My middle son was a champion of cricket and other sports. He took after me: I taught sports at Rishi Valley before I became interested in agriculture. My middle son was elected president of the YMCA in Madras. He was a real star. One day he went swimming and accidentally dived into a rainwater pit. He was sucked down through the silt and drowned. My wife later died of a heart attack. This is why, I think, I do what I do. To forget everything. I have lost myself in planting and regeneration. To give something back to Mother Earth."

Mr. Naidu, since the death of his son, had become a patriot of a future age: an age of Gaia. His success is being helped along by a propitious cultural context that includes the philosophy of Krishnamurti and the innovative teaching methods of the Raos.

◎   ◎   ◎

MR. NAIDU AND I ended our walk under a giant three-hundred-year-old banyan tree: the same tree, it is said, that inspired Krishnamurti. This tree has many aerial roots that grow downward from wide and sagging branches until they reach the ground and meld with the soil, thus forming natural pillars that support the branches and allow them to die peacefully without crashing to the ground. Some of these aerial roots grow into trees of their own. Looking at the aerial roots and branches of this great tree, I thought of old political and social systems dying and new ones being born, all in a gradual and nonviolent fashion. "But some of the branches crash," Mr. Naidu cautioned, "since not all of the aerial roots find a foothold in the ground to support what is overhead. That is why I have erected these granite supports: They keep the branches from breaking." I wondered if places like India and Africa would produce enough Mr. Naidus to support them against the crashes and cataclysms ahead, in the transition from old political forms to new ones.

2 5

◎　　◎　　◎

Bangkok: Environmental
and Sexual Limits

THAI DOCTORS EXAMINED all the Indian Airlines passengers arriving from Calcutta for symptoms of plague before letting us off the plane in Bangkok. Disease had helped erect an invisible, if penetrable, wall between sub-Saharan Africa and the rest of the world. Now, while the panic lingered, another wall stood between the Indian subcontinent and Indochina.[1]

The Calcutta airport had been a rambling godown of coughing and spitting porters with rusted and creaking luggage carts begging for tips when I landed there a few days before. Though it had been late at night and my plane from Madras was the only one arriving, we waited forty-five minutes for our bags. The cabdrivers, their skin further darkened by industrial soot, looked like chimney sweeps as they brewed tea on the filthy pavement outside the terminal building, waiting to ferry passengers to town in battered vehicles, some of which lacked headlights, and others

---

[1] Though the word *Indochina* is usually limited to the region of the former French colonies—Laos, Cambodia, and Vietnam—it is ethnographically and culturally accurate to apply the term to all of Southeast Asia.

doors. By the time I got to my Calcutta hotel I needed a bath to wash off the soot.

Bangkok, by contrast, had a modern airport, where my bag arrived off the conveyor belt even before I reached the claim area. Calcutta will probably have a modern airport too, one day. But it was at the airport parking lot in Bangkok where I first truly encountered Southeast Asia, where I came face-to-face with the vast development disparities in a world in which economic growth, even when accelerating, is lopsided—and destabilizing.

Bangkok's modern, air-conditioned airport gave me the illusion that I had arrived literally anywhere in the developed world. Then my driver led me through a glass door, beyond the air-conditioning, into the underground parking garage. As in Africa and India, suddenly the wet and steamy heat gripped me. Yet the garage was decorated with finely contoured chrome lines, without a trace of rust. The concrete was not stained. Rather than the battered and creaking automobile hulks and the occasional dark-windowed luxury Mercedes that I had seen, for instance, in Sierra Leone, now I gazed at a succession of late-model middle-class cars: Hondas, Toyotas, Nissans, and the like. The neatly uniformed parking attendant looked up from his paperback book and mechanically took a receipt from my driver. Instantly, we were driving beneath banana leaves and coconut palms, and then along sleek overpasses. Finally, we sat in motionless traffic under a thick and soupy gray sky. Bangkok's air pollution was different from Calcutta's: It was a pale and slate-colored grease of smog that refracted the watery tropical light, instead of blackened Coke-town soot. This was the kind of pollution I knew from Teheran and Athens.

Motorcyclists zipped between the lanes, wearing the latest aerodynamic polymer helmets. Bangkok was a sprawling construction site. The gleaming, tinted-glass skyscrapers here were different from the ones I had seen in Abidjan, Cairo, and Madras. In Bangkok, the buildings looked well maintained, and were not becoming instant slums. Though shacks lined the sludgy canals, I saw, as I had in Turkey, the architecture of the upwardly striving, with potted plants and ordered interiors glimpsed through the cracks in the cardboard and sheet iron.

I had arrived in Bangkok not from the West or from another Pacific Rim country but from Africa, the Near East, Central Asia, and the Indian subcontinent. Bangkok was my first encounter with the Asian economic miracle. I had come here deliberately. As with Rishi Valley, I came to Thailand to achieve some balance, to try to alleviate my gloomy picture of humanity. Even while I was concentrating on the parts of the world outside of Homer-Dixon's stretch limo,[2] I wanted to investigate at least one major third-world country that had succeeded in prying its way into the air-conditioned sanctum of the industrialized world. The point of my visit to the Ivory Coast was to see the glass half empty; the point of visiting Thailand was to see the glass half full. Of course, I might have visited another place in Africa besides Ghana that was showing some promise, such as Benin or South Africa. But I justified my choice with the knowledge that Africa, as a whole, was doing badly, while Asia, as a whole, was doing well. The places I visited were fairly representative of the two continents.

When I had reached my hotel in Madras after returning from Rishi Valley, the Indian cabdriver needed a wrench to open the trunk so as to retrieve my bags, which rested on a filthy spare tire and a heap of rags. In Bangkok, the driver silently released the trunk lid from where he was sitting, then jumped out, handed me my bags, and bowed. In Thailand, unlike in India, English is not an official language. Yet I had happened upon a civilization that knew intuitively what the client desired.

In the hotel lobby I skimmed several editions of *The Bangkok Post*. There were many stories about investment opportunities, bond issues, and cabinet reshuffles. There was nothing about the chronic riots and other civil disturbances in India or Pakistan I had been used to reading about. Barely ninety minutes' flying time away, the Indian subcontinent and its low-level chaos had simply disappeared.

I was staying in a small marble-and-glass "efficiency" hotel. I crowded into the elevator with several men in expensive lightweight suits. One held a Compaq Contura in his hand: the smallest of the new subnotebook computers at the time. It occurred to me that here, for one of the few times since Teheran, I could have a stable twenty-four-hour electrical current. With only my backpack and batch of blank notebooks and Bic pens, I suddenly felt antiquated. The poorer and more violent the

[2]Homer-Dixon likened the world to an air-conditioned stretch limo going through the potholed streets of New York City filled with homeless beggars. Inside the stretch limo are North America, Western Europe, the Pacific Rim, and a few isolated countries. Outside is much of the rest of the world. See Chapter 1 for the full quote. See also Kaplan's "The Coming Anarchy," listed in the bibliography.

country, the greater the social status enjoyed by a foreign correspondent. In Bangkok, a journalist was nothing compared to an investment banker.

◎　　　◎　　　◎

WHAT A DIFFERENCE geography makes! I thought. The Burmese jungles and the thickly forested massif of Yunnan-Szechuan had effectively cut Southeast Asia, or "Indochina," off from both the Indian subcontinent to its west and China to its north. Cultural influences have usually entered Thailand and the rest of Southeast Asia by sea from the south and east, traveling northward up the Mekong, Chao Phraya, and Irrawaddy river valleys. Because of its relatively small and compact land mass, its generally navigable rivers, and lengthy coastline with a profusion of good ports, Southeast Asia has been, throughout its history, more easily exposed to outside, cosmopolitan influences than either Africa or India. Sub-Saharan Africa, for example, despite its long coastline, has relatively few good deep-water ports or navigable rivers, given its immense size. Nevertheless, the riverine civilization that grew in Southeast Asia resulted in no major trade routes linking one upriver civilization to another. Just as mountains divided the Balkans into feuding tribes and ethnic groups, river valleys originally distinguished the peoples of Southeast Asia: Siamese (or Thais) from Laotians, Laotians from Khmers (Cambodians), and Khmers from Vietnamese. Southeast Asia, accessible to the outside world and at the same time divided and isolated internally, was to become as culturally dynamic as Western Europe, yet as war-torn as the Balkans. Like the Slavs, who migrated in the early Middle Ages from the great Asian land mass into the mountain valleys of the smaller Balkan peninsula (where they subdivided into ethnic groups), southern Chinese migrated, beginning in the thirteenth century, into what is now Thailand and Vietnam. As in the Balkans, each of these peoples—Thai, Khmer, Vietnamese, etc.—believes the regional map most accurate when its own kingdom was at its territorial zenith. In the words of Kishore Mahbubani, dean of Singapore's Civil Service College, the bloody "Balkan" phase of Southeast Asia's history appears to have wound down in 1989 with the end of superpower rivalry in the region, the opening of Vietnam and Laos to foreign investment, and the rise of economic growth in Thailand to 11 percent per annum. The Western European phase of the region's development now beckons.

The term *Indochina* is deceptive, since Southeast Asia in recent centuries has been increasingly less Indian and more Chinese. Tangible

Indian influence here is generally limited to alphabetic scripts, medieval architecture, curry-based cuisine, and various forms of Buddhism. Religion has an immeasurable influence on daily behavior. Still, as the scholar Philip Rawson writes, "By the sixteenth century the Sinized Buddhist Vietnamese had virtually obliterated all vestiges of the classical Indianized civilizations of Cambodia, Laos and Siam. Active coastwise settlement by Chinese colonists . . . was under way. And by the twentieth century people who were Chinese by race . . . had infiltrated into all the countries of Southeast Asia."

The geographical split between India and Southeast Asia that led to separate racial, historical, and economic patterns is reflected by the fact that there was no practical way for me to travel by land from one subcontinent to the other. I flew from Calcutta to Bangkok. The differences were stark. The economic and other advantages that India held over Africa were replicated by the advantages that Southeast Asia held over India.

◎   ◎   ◎

TAKING A WALK that first evening in Bangkok, I was struck by the noise: the grinding, piercing high-pitched racket of power drills and jackhammers, along with the churning ignitions of the three-wheeled *tuk-tuks.* As in Urumqi in Chinese Central Asia, building and road construction was a twenty-four-hour-a-day activity in Bangkok. In Urumqi, China's worker-bee activity signaled its emergence from the decades-long darkness of central planning. Here it represented the culmination of an economic and cultural process that made capitalism seem very much like religion. I had lived all my life in capitalist societies but had never thought of capitalism as a belief system until I came to Bangkok. By the time my stroll had taken me to the corner of Silom and Patpong roads in downtown Bangkok, I saw the result of many years of fast economic growth rates and correspondingly low birthrates that had worked to liberate Thailand from the horrors I had witnessed elsewhere in my travels. Thailand, among the poorest and most "third world" of the Pacific "tiger" economies, was still several long steps ahead of the economy and culture that had impressed me in Turkey.

As I walked, the night was brilliantly lit by lamps that reflected off glassy exteriors of marble, mirrored chrome, and other light alloys. Among the Westernized shopping malls that sold Gucci glasses, Lacoste shirts, soft-suede cowboy boots, Nikon telescopes, computers, fax machines, compact disks, cordless miniphones, condoms, contact lenses, and every manner of leather and gold designer "accessories," were wooden stalls offering T-shirts, mountains of luggage, souvenirs, and succulent fried fish. There was an abundance of fast food outlets and airline offices, and windows adorned with more credit card stickers than I had ever seen before. In the bars, girls in red satin undergarments danced atop platforms to electric Western "Rhinestone Cowboy" music. Other small-boned toy goddesses with erupting breasts and buttocks sat on black lacquered bar stools, calling you over in syrupy voices that reminded me of the carpet merchants I had met in Shiraz and Isfahan. "Girls Take Shower" Bar. "Lady & Boy Massage." "Big Boy: The Gent's Exclusive Bar." "Watch Lesbians Screw on Motorcycles." Sex here in the Patpong district was a commodity, like the Kodak film or expensive Scotch whisky that were also on display, separated from all moral prohibitions and, therefore, from its normal danger and mystery. Patpong was not the usual red light district, with hints of crime and danger and tattooed sailors. Go-go bars were sandwiched between paperback-book shops and Kodak one-hour development stores. Middle-class Thai families strolled about. The bars offered instant and mechanical gratification for those too timid to venture into such places in the West. Bangkok seemed to me a more soulless and efficient version of New York. Clean and well-lit public toilets are certainly easier to find in Bangkok than anywhere I had been in America.

In one shopping mall, I watched as a horde of teenage girls gathered around a mirror to adjust their makeup. I spotted several slightly older women and men speaking into tiny mobile phones in the midst of the nighttime crowd. I remember one woman in a gray pants suit, wearing designer glasses. Her finger played with a pocket calculator as she shouted into her phone—cupped between her chin and neck—above the squeals of a welder at a construction site. She might have walked to a quieter place less than fifty feet away. But, like so many men and women on the street, she preferred to reflect the style of glossy magazine advertisements, no matter how inconvenient the result.

The mall kids were a case in point. In fashionably baggy T-shirts and prewashed jeans, they were an Asian Generation X that on late Sunday mornings packed the Mah Boon Krong mall to buy compact discs and cordless miniphones—the latest "craze." For better or worse, this was clearly a more authentic, Westernized middle class than the one emerging in India, which, though able to afford such consumer items, often still dressed in polyester and maintained intercommunal grudges that Thais seemed to lack.

In 1973, Thai youth had rioted in the streets for democracy. Though Thailand's government twenty-one years later still had a noticeable military overlay, students in Bangkok in the mid-1990s are generally as politically apathetic as students in the West. Competitiveness for grades and for jobs, not political activism, is the priority.[3]

Thailand has been an identifiable nation since the thirteenth century, after the Siamese completed their migration from southern China into northern Thailand, where they established a kingdom. They henceforth referred to themselves as "Thais," or free people. Thailand has never been colonized, unlike the rest of Indochina—or sub-Saharan Africa, Egypt, Central Asia, or the Indian subcontinent for that matter. Nor have Thais been humiliated and meddled with by Europeans to the degree that Turks and Iranians have been; nor do the Thais have a minority problem to the degree that the Turks have with the Kurds. These are distinct advantages. The Thai royal family is so exalted that it is a criminal offense to insult any of its members. Thais write in a script that is some seven hundred years old. By the late Middle Ages, the Thai state had developed a highly intricate and organized bureaucracy. In the twentieth century, the Thais encouraged the immigration of a Chinese middleman minority to expand the labor supply.

Over 90 percent of Thais practice Theravada (also called Hinayana, or "Lesser") Buddhism: the earliest form of Buddhism, with a marked Indian influence. It emphasizes moderation, often called "the middle way," nonconfrontation, and compliance. Along with other Buddhist variants and Confucianism, it promotes precisely those personality attributes suited for a Western service economy.

Traditional dress in Thailand is relatively rare. Saris in Madras and Calcutta vastly outnumbered sarongs in Bangkok. As I walked along the streets, it occurred to me that Thailand is what Iranians—inhabitants of another ancient kingdom, age-old nation-state, and regional cultural magnet that has never been colonized—may secretly aspire to. The late shah traveled often to Thailand, openly admiring it. The mullahs who

[3]This is according to numerous observers, including Suvicha Pouaree, a faculty dean at Thailand's National Institute of Development Administration. A major student-led political protest a few years ago is the exception, not the rule, to student life.

succeeded him have maintained the tradition of good bilateral relations. The Thais' overt sensuality merely reflects the Iranians' own proclivities, however covert they have become since 1978. Prostitution once had an exalted status in Iranian society, and may well have again in the future.

A fellow journalist who has lived for years in the Far East disparaged my enthusiasm. Over a shellfish dinner at an outdoor restaurant amid the city's noisy traffic, he shouted: "This place is twenty years behind Japan. If you really want to see capitalism, don't waste your time in Bangkok, go to Hong Kong. In Hong Kong, and in Singapore too, you see cultures that have been specifically programmed for the acquisition of wealth, and even more specifically for the acquisition—and showing off—of fine clothes and expensive cars, since the lack of land in those places makes it very hard to acquire big houses. Bangkok is normal. Hong Kong, Singapore, and Japan are surreal."

With India and sub-Saharan Africa constantly in my mind, his remarks brought home to me once again how great were the regional economic disparities in the world. And these disparities were daily becoming greater. India, so far ahead of Africa, had a burgeoning consumer economy and a real economic growth rate of 4 percent in 1993,[4] while many economies in Africa had negative or near-zero net growth rates. Thailand, meanwhile, with yearly economic growth rates of between 8 and 11 percent since the mid-1980s, and a lower birthrate than India's, was moving ahead much faster than the Indian subcontinent. Yet Thailand was underdeveloped compared to other Pacific economies. In Thailand, according to *Asia Week*, there is a television set for every 8.9 persons. In India there is a television for every 31.7 persons. In many parts of sub-Saharan Africa televisions are meaningless because there is no stable electrical current.[5]

But instead of a division between haves and have-nots, there could be "an interaction between civilizations," writes Owen Harries, editor of *The National Interest*, a conservative journal of foreign policy. "A Darwinian process of selection will take place, with each culture borrowing from others in terms of what works best . . ." Such a process may work between cultures that have already achieved a high standard of know-how and prosperity, as when American firms employ Japanese management prac-

[4] See the C.I.A.'s *World Factbook*, listed in the bibliography.
[5] Electricity is generally far more reliable in India than in Africa, though even in India I found there was no guarantee that the current would always work, or be stable.

tices. But some cultures and regions may be so far behind, and so mired in intergroup struggle, that such borrowing is impractical.

◎ ◎ ◎

THERE MAY BE no better example of this borrowing than Thailand's long-standing willingness to welcome Chinese immigrants,[6] with their dynamic work ethic and sharp business acumen. "Thailand is Southeast Asia's only cultural melting pot, where the Chinese and their skills have been absorbed through generations of intermarriage. They haven't remained a separate, and suspected, community, as in Malaysia for example [with their own neighborhoods]," said Chalat Sripichorn, head of the Thailand office of the World Environment Center.

Of course, the greatest example of the no-nonsense business acumen of the overseas Chinese—so crucial to Thailand's cultural and economic development—has come in the person of the Singapore leader, Lee Kuan Yew. Two journalists, Stan Sesser, who writes for *The New Yorker*, and Robert Elegant, both point out that of all the post–World War II strongmen in the region—Mao Zedong in China, Jawaharlal Nehru in India, and Ho Chi Minh in Vietnam—only Mr. Lee has "ruled wisely." Ruled *successfully* would be more accurate. Mr. Lee's personal honesty, together with the meritocratic and relatively honest bureaucracy he built has—so far, at least—proved a blessing for Singaporeans. While the other Asian leaders left economic and political ruin, Mr. Lee forged booming prosperity out of abject poverty. While Western human rights advocates rightly detest Mr. Lee's obsession with order and cleanliness—he has placed sensors in public toilets to alert Singapore police if someone has failed to flush—many who are forced to live in lands beset by violent crime, stagnant economies, disease, and uncollected garbage see Mr. Lee's neoauthoritarianism as a credible challenge to Western democracy. In Cairo, a group of Egyptian businessmen told me that what their country needed, so as to extinguish the fires of Islamic extremism through economic growth, was not democracy but "someone like Lee Kuan Yew."

---

[6]Though the Chinese had a positive experience integrating into Thai life, the Vietnamese—traditional enemies of the Thais—had a tougher time when they began coming in the 1950s. Labeled fifth columnists, citizenship was often denied to their Thai-born children. But such discrimination generally no longer exists.

In Thailand, though, Mr. Lee is ridiculed for his repressive tactics, which even Thais, with their fiscally conservative governments that maintain trade and budget surpluses (but also their corrupt, drug-dealing military), find far too strict. That Mr. Lee's leadership style could suit an even more distant culture seems unlikely. Even in Indonesia under Suharto and in the Philippines under Ferdinand Marcos, for example, neoauthoritarianism (an alliance of military and business interests, a kind of corporate police state) has worked far less well. This is partly because Mr. Lee was both authoritarian *and* honest.

As for Thailand, it appeared in the 1990s that emerging democracy, with all its compromises, deals, and scandals, still worked better for the economy than direct military rule, which had been even more blatantly corrupt. Thailand provides evidence for Francis Fukuyama's "End of History" argument that democratic capitalism operating in the context of an economically developed, civil society is the best political system, and while it may not take hold everywhere, people will be happiest where it does. (But free and smoothly run elections in places like South Africa, Mozambique, and Cambodia will not be enough in the absence of sustained economic development.)

But even in Thailand, which has been moving beyond autocracy, there are unsettling trends, having to do with environmental degradation and disparities in regional development that are severely testing this democracy.

◎   ◎   ◎

TO LEARN ABOUT this challenge, I went to see Twatchai Yongkittikul, executive vice-president of the Thailand Development Research Institute (TDRI). TDRI is a Washington-style think tank, originally established with help from the United States Agency for International Development—Western know-how was welcomed, then improved upon by locals. Dr. Twatchai wasted little time with pleasantries. He delivered a thorough briefing about population growth, the environment, and the economy, then hustled me off to TDRI's publications department, where I could choose from over a hundred TDRI monographs on sale for a few dollars each. I didn't have to come to Bangkok for this information. I could have ordered the material by electronic mail through the Internet. This may seem inconsequential, but for someone emerging from Africa and Central Asia it was like finding mail at an American Express office after weeks in a third world village.

I spent about ninety minutes at TDRI. When I got back to my hotel room and excitedly went through the monographs spread all over my bed, I realized I had been given more data than I could have found in days of reporting in the Near East or the Indian subcontinent. In the case of Africa or Central Asia, much of this information is simply unavailable, except through a Western embassy or aid mission. The point is that information in Bangkok, which a few short decades ago was thought of as just another third world capital—like Lagos or Karachi—comes literally in byte surges.

When I entered my air-conditioned, metered taxi outside the TDRI office, it occurred to me that the rapid economic development in the Far East was, like Lee Kuan Yew himself, partly the outcome of a cultural pattern that could probably spread to adjacent countries like Laos and Vietnam, but was less likely to be exportable to India, Central Asia, the Near East, and Africa. Wealth, ultimately, cannot be donated or transferred as part of an aid budget, or even discovered under the earth like oil. To be sustainable, wealth has to be self-created.

IN BANGKOK, I experienced travel more through the reading of monographs than through conversations in the street or in buses—because here was one of the few places where accurate figures existed *on location*. (In the cases of West Africa and Central Asia, I got my figures in Washington.) In Thailand, moreover, the statistics told a very dramatic story—a story with important lessons for many of the other places I had passed through in the course of my wanderings.[7]

THAILAND ILLUSTRATES, FOR example, how important it is for a country to reduce its birthrate. In the 1960s, the average Thai woman gave birth six times over her adult lifetime. By the 1980s that number had dropped to two. Economic growth and literacy levels have risen in inverse proportion to declines in the birthrate. Since 1960, the average yearly growth of Thailand's gross domestic product (GDP) has surpassed 7 percent; and life expectancy has risen from fifty-two to sixty-six.[8] By the late 1980s and

[7]For the relevant monographs, look under Phantumvanit in the bibliography.
[8]The rise in life expectancy stemming, in part, from a declining birthrate challenges the view that sees "life" only in terms of more people—rather than in terms of more years of consciousness under better circumstances for the people already alive.

early 1990s, after the total fertility rate had been brought down to the replacement level of two children per family, GDP growth was 11 percent annually. Literacy in Thailand now stands at 93 percent.[9]

Thailand reduced its birthrate through women's literacy programs, as well as a clinically efficient, nonideological "cafeteria" approach to birth control—another triumph of Theravada Buddhist moderation. Everything, whether IUDs, diaphragms, condoms, the pill, family planning counseling, or abortions on some occasions, was available and publicized. There was no coercion as in communist China, where the birthrate is only slightly lower than in Thailand, despite the police state tactic of limiting each Chinese family to one child.

Nevertheless, as Dr. Twatchai told me, though Thailand's population of nearly 59 million is growing at only 1.5 percent or less each year, its rate of internal migration from rural areas to cities, particularly Bangkok, is twice that, or 3 percent per year. Thailand's economic growth has followed a pattern typical of the industrializing countries of the nineteenth century: People leave their villages and head for factory towns. In Thailand's case, this pattern has been exaggerated because economic growth began at such a low base and progressed so rapidly. "Our economy," said Dr. Twatchai, "is very much out of balance. Sixty-five percent of the population is producing 30 percent of the GDP. There is really no way to increase incomes in the agricultural sector. We need to move industrial jobs to rural areas in order to reverse the migration process." In other words, because Thai villages, particularly in the poor northeast of the country, are underdeveloped, Thailand is still not quite a modern country.

Greater Bangkok illustrates this problem. Founded in 1782, and with a population of only 500,000 in 1900, the Thai capital city now has 10 million inhabitants. Whereas in 1900, 6 percent of Thailand's people lived in Bangkok, now 17 percent do. Bangkok's population grows at 80 percent above the national average. The city contains 2 million registered automobiles, and every day on the average 480 new ones are registered. These figures omit motorcycles and all vehicles driven into Bangkok from the

[9]When, in the run-up to the 1994 World Population Conference in Cairo, a Vatican official pointed to high population densities in the Far East as evidence that big populations like Rwanda's did not impede economic growth, he failed to note that rises in GDP and literacy in places like Japan and Thailand did not occur until *after* their populations had stabilized. The average Japanese woman gives birth 1.5 times in her life; the average Rwandan woman gives birth 8 times.

surrounding countryside. The average speed of cars in Bangkok is 5 miles per hour. As I saw for myself, traffic in Bangkok does not crawl, it stops for minutes at a time, then crawls for a few seconds, before stopping again while exhaust fumes filter into your taxi through the air-conditioning. I heard of a portable toilet that had recently been produced locally, for use inside the car.[10]

In addition, over half of all the factories in Thailand are in Greater Bangkok. The amount of hazardous waste these ninety thousand industrial plants dump into rivers and landfills, or into on-site containers with little or no detoxification treatment, will double by the end of the century. Water, however, may be the city's greatest problem. Bangkok is built on alluvial deposits within a delta plain twenty miles from the Gulf of Siam. It was once a city of canals, a Far East Venice, many of which have now been filled in. The building and population boom means that Bangkok is both short of water and sinking at the same time.[11]

Floods, like the kind that ravaged Bangkok in 1982, are likely in the future, as water flows into the city from the eroded soil of the countryside, whose treeless wastes can no longer absorb moisture without creating new rivulets. Since the economic boom began in the 1960s, Thailand has lost 45 percent of its old growth forests to illegal logging and slash-and-burn agriculture. The Thai economic miracle has been achieved largely by devouring Thailand's environmental base.

India and China have been doing the same thing. Nevertheless, these countries and others may have the option of separating their economies

[10]Motor vehicles are the principal cause of air pollution in the city, responsible for 10,000 to 100,000 visits to the doctor annually, according to the World Bank. The situation will dramatically worsen as the percentage of lignite (coal fuel) used in primary energy generation here increases by nearly 300 percent by 2006, by which time Bangkok's air could be as black and sooty as Calcutta's. Sulphur emissions are set to rise several times by 2011, while carbon emissions from cars and other sources will more than double, even as blood tests show that the level of lead in Bangkok is already three times as great as those in the United States or Western Europe.

[11]From the mid-1980s to the mid-1990s, the demand for drinking water grew by almost 50 percent. From the mid-1990s to 2007 the demand will increase an additional 25 percent. But already by 1986, 11 million cubic meters of water in Greater Bangkok was being pumped from underground. This exceeds what experts consider the "estimated safe yield" by almost 40 percent. Underground aquifers are drying up, so that wells have to be sunk deeper and deeper. As aquifers dry up, the ground on which Bangkok rests sinks by as much as ten centimeters each year, increasing the city's exposure to dangerous floods. Meanwhile, only 2 percent of the city's population is linked to proper sewage treatment networks.

from their environments, by producing goods and services not dependent on local raw materials—like clothing, electronic items, or financial services—then exchanging the profits for the resources they no longer have at home, like food.[12] This demands a high degree of worker efficiency and labor skills, which these countries have been acquiring in the course of their industrialization. Sub-Saharan Africa, on the other hand, has been devouring its environmental base not through industrialization but merely through population growth and slash-and-burn agriculture. Much of Africa will be unable to produce anything not based on nearby natural resources because, in too many cases, Africa lacks the marketable labor skills of the other regions. The mere holding of elections cannot alleviate this problem.

Separating an economy from its environment will go only so far. Therefore, it is troubling that Thailand spends only a fraction of its GDP on environmental protection compared to North America and Western Europe. In 1996, though, the Thai government was to start a program to require, by the end of the century, that all new vehicles have catalytic fuel converters to alleviate air pollution. Also, a water pumping system similar to what has worked in New Orleans, another delta city, is planned for Bangkok. Environmental issues are increasingly a discussion topic in the Thai business community and in local newspapers. The hope is that a tradition of practicality and efficiency—evinced by the "cafeteria" approach to birth control—combined with the stability provided by an easily definable ethnic nation-state, will allow Thailand to neutralize environmental damage without having to succumb to Lee Kuan Yew–style authoritarianism.

Dr. Twatchai explained that to achieve this goal Thailand must lower its annual GDP growth from the 11 percent levels of the late 1980s to a steady 8 percent, which, in fact, it seems to be doing. More urgently, the Thai government has to decentralize its decision-making process. "Democracy," said Dr. Twatchai, "is not only elections, but transferring power to local authorities to allow for greater action and participation. Thais are willing to take hard decisions to improve their environment because they know how stressed they have become by the crowding and strain on resources. Stress has increased frustration and aggressiveness in urban areas. That is the real cultural change, not Westernization."

---

[12]See Homer-Dixon's "Environmental Scarcities and Violent Conflict," listed in the bibliography.

◎   ◎   ◎

OVER ONE HUNDRED THOUSAND PEOPLE live in the shantytown of Klong Toey in central Bangkok. One of these people, Buuboontham Somkuan-than, a fifty-four-year-old rice seller, was sitting on a wooden crate in an alley when I stopped to talk to her early one morning. A scrawny kitten played between her ankles. White coconut fiber used for animal feed lay strewn in the sticky mud. Electric wires dangled a few feet overhead. I was inert in the humid heat. But she smiled at me from behind her dark-framed glasses and told me about her life. I didn't have to ask her many questions.

"I came here twenty years ago from Prachinburi, a town near the Thai-Cambodian border. We were tenant farmers. We couldn't make in a year what we make now in a month. The first few years in Bangkok we suffered real hardship. I would rather have spent my life upcountry, but this place is destiny." She pointed to her house—a rusted structure, with rotted wood balconies, that overlooked a reeking landfill where schoolchildren with colorful backpacks were passing. "My husband makes six thousand bahts [$240] per month in a factory. My son also works there. My daughter is a salesperson at a Honda dealership, and is going to night classes for her bachelor's degree. I have only two children," she said, explaining that throughout much of her married life birth control devices have been available at a local government clinic. She then accompanied me and my translator to another part of the neighborhood, pausing for a moment to bow before a garlanded Buddha statue placed on an oilcloth between two wooden shacks and decorated with incense candles stuck into soda bottles.

I came to a row of corrugated-iron-and-plywood houses resting on oil drums over a dirty canal. Fat and cheerful Yom Meepoka invited me to her house, first asking me to take off my shoes. Inside, I noticed a fan, a bookcase, a bicycle, a sewing machine, potted plants, and a closet where shirts were neatly separated from trousers. Beneath my bare feet, I could see the canal water through the spotlessly clean floorboards. Yom Meepoka has lived in this shantytown for thirty years. She pays no rent, she told me, since she is still a squatter. She and her husband have four children (all secondary school graduates) and six grandchildren. At sixty-four, Yom Meepoka still works, sifting garbage for paper and bottles, earning eighty bahts ($3.20) a day.

"Education is the only tool," she said. "You can't get anywhere without studying. My children have not had the money for private schools, and the government schools give them an inferior education." I thought of the women in the Turkish shantytowns who had told me the same thing. Though differences between cultures are fundamental (as I had been learning), the ambitions of the subproletariat in industrializing nations like Turkey and Thailand are similar.

Crime is commoner in Buddhist Thailand than in Moslem Turkey, but random thuggery is rare. My translator, a twenty-year-old Thai woman, and I spent all day in the Klong Toey slum without a hint of danger.

A small, half-naked boy led my translator and me through another network of alleyways filled with garbage, creaking wooden planks, scampering rats, stray dogs, and hammered-metal Buddhas in makeshift plywood temples. We emerged beneath one of Bangkok's major freeways.

Shielded from the rain by the overpasses, a plywood-and-corrugated-iron squatter city flourished here. Children played on a rusted and squealing seesaw. Men and women slurped soybean milk and ate rice on long wooden benches. Nearby was a vast burnt-out ruin: pieces of black and charred wood stuck out of this sea of sludge and wreckage like grave markers in a cemetery. A few weeks earlier, a fire had destroyed over three hundred shantyhouses here. Now there was activity all around:

The "Lion's Club of Bangkok" was erecting temporary shelters. Inside a parked trailer van, a man with a loudspeaker read the names of those who had received mail that day, while a line of squatters stood waiting. A postal official explained to me, "It is hard for a mailman to find people in this area, especially after so many homes have been destroyed. We discovered that this is the most efficient way to deliver letters." Thai nurses in white uniforms were at makeshift counters, giving cursory medical examinations to local residents. There was not one Western aid worker in the crowd. The faces I saw were all smiling and purposeful, without a trace of languor or self-pity.

IT WAS "COWGIRL Night" at King's Castle I in the Patpong section of Bangkok. Lacquered female odalisques—ranging in age from their early teens to their mid-twenties—wore checkered shirts with sheriff's badges, high black-suede boots, and faded jeans cut off at crotch level, revealing sculpted, buttery-brown buttocks. The evening was sponsored by Pepsi

Max, whose red, white, and blue logo appeared on the girls' cowboy hats. Some of the "hostesses" had laminated ID cards, complete with numbers. A voice over the loudspeaker announced that all major credit cards were being accepted.

The girls ran their painted nails over the backs and arms and laps of Western oil riggers, stockbrokers, and tourists like me, men who would probably never set foot in a go-go bar in the United States. One girl with sculpted cheekbones, overdeveloped breasts, and large, idling eyes wore a red kerchief rather than a cowboy hat. "I'm Khmer Rouge, darling, Aren't they cool!" referring to Marxist guerrillas who murdered over a million people in Cambodia in the late-1970s, around the time she was born.

Instead of the ear-splitting punk rock of former-Soviet Central Asia, the music of Creedence Clearwater Revival played at a comfortable level over the speaker system. Girls gyrated atop the bar. Hostesses not busy with customers chatted among themselves, marveling at each other's sheriff's badges. I thought of high school girls comparing clothes at a dance. These weren't "whores," as Western tourists might conclude. You couldn't just take them to bed. Much flirting was required, and they didn't leave the bar with anyone they didn't like. Also, they were all looking for steadies—well-heeled foreign businessmen who could afford to set them up in apartments. Almost all of these girls glowed with good health. They lacked the hard mouths and cash-register eyes that I had seen among the prostitutes in the hotel restaurant in Samarkand.[13] This could almost have been a Long Island singles bar—and was, in fact, only one small step beyond. But here the girls put their palms together and bowed in Buddhist supplication before they mounted the bar table to gyrate, or left with a customer.

Bernard Trink, a *Bangkok Post* columnist specializing in the local sex industry, writes about a typical go-go dancer:

"She went back to her farm [upcountry] when her father died to help run it. Working the land for two years was hard work and she tired of it. Reasoning that she could earn more at the oasis [a go-go bar or massage parlor] and send money home to hire help, she made it back to the capital."

---

[13]This was a well-heeled establishment. Obviously, as women's groups note, there are places in Thailand where women prostitutes are terribly abused: witness the brothel in the south of Thailand that burned down, exposing the charred bodies of girls chained to their beds.

"These girls make thirty thousand bahts [$1,200] a month, a lot of money by Thai standards. They leverage jewelry and stocks to increase their wealth. They send the money back to their families in the country-side, many of whom have been impoverished by logging [often carried out by the Thai military, which exports the wood without government inter-ference].[14] They're not drug addicts, they insist on using condoms, and they don't have illegal kids. They're definitely not dysfunctional social types like prostitutes in the West. It's all very practical here," a local expert told me.

◎   ◎   ◎

THAI PROSTITUTION EXPOSES the link between family breakdown and the twin forces of industrialization and environmental devastation. That is the judgment of Sanitsuda Ekachai, a reporter for *The Bangkok Post*, whose graphic book *Behind the Smile: Voices of Thailand* focuses on Isan, the poor northeast of Thailand, where 85 percent of villagers earn less than they need to survive and 2 million people leave their homes and families each year in search of work, mainly in Bangkok.[15] Among young women from the deforested north, prostitution is a common occupation, writes the author. " 'I didn't sell my daughter,' " says one subsistence farmer apolo-getically. " 'She saw me suffer. She saw the family suffer. And she wanted to help.' "

Ekachai's book shows an important side of the global picture: Not only are income disparities increasing between some regions of the world and others; but even within relatively successful regions such as Southeast

---

[14]According to one study, 44.2 percent of Thai prostitutes worked in the agriculture sector before entering the sex industry. See Boonchalaksi and Guest in the bibliogra-phy.

[15]The situation is little better in Thailand's northwest. Ekachai writes of one village where "there are hardly any young people left." A landless farmer, Mae Tee Boonaree, tells the author: " 'My daughter does housework in Bangkok and my son works in a factory. . . . My husband and my eldest son have gone to the sugarcane fields, so I am left alone . . .' " A neighbor, Poh Nuan, adds: " 'It used to be thick forest here, and the rains were more regular. . . . Life seems to get worse . . .' " Pressure for farmland, writes the author, "has been exacerbated by the demands of Thai and foreign busi-nesses for large-scale eucalyptus tree plantations," which earn big profits due to the worldwide demand for paper pulp. But eucalyptus trees harden the soil and consume too much water, while their roots kill other trees and nearby plants. Yet many of the lands marked for reforestation will be planted with eucalyptus trees, which make wealthy Thais richer and poor farmers—like those mentioned above—poorer.

Asia, disparities are growing between some sections of the population and others.

For example, global optimists point out that worldwide aggregate statistics on social and economic development (such as literacy levels, birthrate falls, GDP growth, etc.) are improving. The optimists fail to note how uneven and poorly distributed (on all levels—local, regional, and continental) these rises are. "Thirty years ago," writes Jessica Mathews, "the world's richest 20 percent had 30 times the income of the poorest quintile. Today the ratio is 60 to 1."[16]

In many cases, it is precisely the unevenness of economic growth within societies that is inflaming violent conflict. Karl Magyar, professor of national security affairs at the U.S. military's Air Command and Staff College, told an officers' gathering in Boston in 1994 that much of the violence to unfold over the coming decades will be "fueled by rising expectations" rather than by mere poverty. In a sense, the world economy has become a larger version of prerevolutionary Iran's, where in the 1960s and 1970s per capita income rose from $200 to $1,000. But the rise was unevenly distributed, and a large subproletariat was created in the process. The result was upheaval.

◎   ◎   ◎

TONY BENNETT, AN American, is the senior program officer for the AIDS Control and Prevention Project and has lived in Bangkok for many years. Over dinner one night at a quiet Japanese restaurant in Patpong, sandwiched between two go-go bars, he told me about the spread of sexually transmitted disease.

"About 1 percent of Thai women in their teens and twenties—about 200,000—are prostitutes. The sex industry here is multitiered, with different kinds of establishments. It was well developed before the U.S. military arrived during the Vietnam War. You have go-go bars, massage parlors, cocktail lounges, escort services, etc. The chains-and-razor-blade scene and the pedophiles, despite the media attention, are statistically much less significant. We estimate between thirty and thirty-five thousand child prostitutes in Thailand. AIDS didn't begin in Thailand until the mid-1980s. But the disease here has registered one of the fastest increases in the world.

[16]Nor do these optimists note that an increasing proportion of the new wealth is because of socially corrosive drug and mafia-oriented activities.

"The prevalence of AIDS and HIV-positive cases is a trend that can change almost overnight. You can go for years with little increase, then in a matter of months see an upheaval on the graphs. In January 1988, 0 percent of intravenous drug users in Thailand were HIV-positive. In September 1988, 43 percent were. In mid-1988, 0 percent of the low-fee prostitutes in Chiang Mai [a city in northwestern Thailand] were HIV-positive. In mid-1989, 44 percent were. All it takes is a few new people in an area to change the picture. That's why the disease can be so unpredictable. Thai soldiers have their blood tested upon induction: 4 percent of military recruits here are HIV-positive. So are 1.5 percent of pregnant women. In Chiang Mai, a traditional center of the sex industry—local Chiang Mai girls are reputed to be even more submissive and more beautiful than elsewhere in Thailand—as many as one in five military recruits and one in twelve pregnant women are infected with HIV.[17] In 1988, 100 Thais were HIV-positive. In 1994, 700,000 were.

"HIV is causing a sexual revolution among Thai women. Because Thai men are now more scared of commercial sex, there has been a rapid breakdown of the cultural sanction against premarital sex. Virginity is less prized than it used to be among prospective brides. There has been a big condom push by the government and in the mass media. We're observing a real sea change in sexuality here. The high literacy rate, coupled with effective condom advertisements, the liberation of Thai women, and Asian efficiency and adaptability, gives Thailand defense mechanisms against AIDS that Africa lacks. The original prediction that 2 million Thais would contract HIV infections by the year 2000 has been scaled back to 1.5 million."[18]

This hardly means the picture is bright here. Thailand still had ten times more HIV infections in 1994 than it had in 1990. Between 85 and 95 percent of Thai prostitutes use condoms, but it is among those prostitutes who don't insist on condoms that the risk is greatest. Bennett explained: "Generally, the prostitutes don't get AIDS from Western tourists or from their occasional local customers. They get it from their regular customers or boyfriends—many of whom are married, with chil-

[17]These figures are corroborated by a World Health Organization report issued from Southeast Asia in 1994 and written by Dr. Michael H. Merson.
[18]Nevertheless, according to the U.S. Census Bureau's Center for International Research, Thailand's population by 2020 will be 21.8 percent smaller than it would normally have grown to, because of AIDS.

dren—men whom prostitutes are embarrassed to ask to use condoms. These guys can spread it to their wives and to other prostitutes. Then there is the link with tuberculosis. Thirty percent of TB patients in the north are HIV-positive. Another thing that can exaggerate the statistics is mutant strains of HIV, which we are watching for."

The biggest impediment to controlling AIDS here is that though Thailand is the region's most cohesive nation-state, it has too little control over its cross-border traffic. Fifteen percent of the sex workers in the Thai-Burmese border area are HIV-positive. Near the Cambodian border, the prevalence is 10 percent. AIDS is now set to explode in Cambodia, where 40 percent of the prostitutes in the Cambodian port city of Sihanoukville are HIV-positive. The World Health Organization reports that in 1994, Asia's share of global AIDS cases rose eightfold, with particular rises recorded in Burma and India. Bennett provides this frightening anecdote:

"Samastipur in the northeastern Indian state of Bihar is a junction point for the Nepal-India-Bangladesh trade route, connecting Kathmandu with Calcutta and Dacca. Around 1,400 truckers pass through each day. The sex workers there are mainly illiterate and have no familiarity with condoms. Because a clinic in Calcutta has found that at least 8 percent of these truckers are HIV-positive, we calculate that 36 percent of the prostitutes at Bihar truck stops are. Most HIV in the world is spread by land travel, by good roads. It is a disease of modernization that may slowly bring us to our knees."

2 6

◎　　◎　　◎

Laos, or Greater Siam?

ON THE MAP, the journey from Bangkok to Nong Khai, a town on the Mekong River near Thailand's northern border, seemed long, over four hundred miles away, a grueling distance in the developing world. But the overnight sleeper train, complete with a shower and an "American breakfast" of eggs and toast, got me there painlessly in eleven hours.

Alighting from the train in Nong Khai, I hired a three-wheeled *tuk-tuk* to take me to a hotel. Soon I saw the Mekong, a flowing, rust-red gash several hundred yards wide, separating Thailand from Laos. The Mekong (Mother Water), which rises in the snowy Plateau of Tibet, flows two thousand six hundred miles through southern China and the so-called "Golden Triangle"—where Burma, Thailand, and Laos meet and where most of the world's opium is harvested. The river continues its southeasterly journey through the Laotian highlands, then meanders along the Thai-Laotian border before dropping south through Cambodia and into southern Vietnam, where it fans out into a delta by the South China Sea. Historically, the Mekong has been a fulcrum of empire, along which the Siamese would gradually replace the great Khmer empire in the thirteenth century, leading to a rise in Thai fortunes and a decline in Cambodian ones: a trend that has yet to reverse itself.[1] In our era, the Mekong has been a "river of evil memory," synonymous with the postcolonial wars from the 1950s through the 1970s.

If Nong Khai is any indication, however, the Mekong at the turn of the twenty-first century may become a cornucopia. Along its banks were two new hotels, including a Holiday Inn. Joining Thailand with Laos was the Australian-built "Friendship Bridge," opened in April 1994. Nong Khai was immediately impressive, a boom town. The streets were swept clean, water flowed on demand from the sink taps, air pollution was minimal, the small, grayish satellite dishes were not ugly, and all the kids looked healthy. Whether it was the motorcycles, the pharmacies, the stores with running shoes, or the ATM machines, Nong Khai reminded me of a California suburb. The pickups were all late-model Nissans. Shops were run by women in designer jeans and pleasing makeup who might as well have been Asian immigrants in North America.

"We were the only ones here in 1981; we were practically out in the country. Now it's a busy street with motorcycles," said Suvan Boonthae, a local businessman. "The population of Nong Khai in 1984 was 26,000. Now it's 52,000. Property values have climbed 400 to 500 percent in a decade. Business is up 200 to 300 percent. Over 50 percent of the new jobs are in construction. Migrant laborers come from all over the surrounding provinces to work in Nong Khai. They live on the construction sites with their families. . . . I sell handicrafts and weavings produced by local women, so that they don't have to migrate to Bangkok to seek work. But I'm a drop in the ocean. So many people are migrating—from Nong Khai to Bangkok, from farming villages to Nong Khai."

I asked about crime.

"Not one violent crime. Not one. Only an occasional theft."

Much of the economic growth had been in the past two years, Mr. Suvan told me. That was when the Australians agreed to build the Friendship Bridge linking Thailand to Laos and, more important, linking Nong Khai to the Laotian capital city of Vientiane, less than fifteen miles away

[1]The Thais were called "Siamese" by the Khmers, which came perhaps from the Sanskrit term *shyama*, meaning "swarthy." This is a bit perplexing given that the modern Khmers are as dark-complexioned, if not more so, than the Thais. The Khmers, meanwhile, are synonymous with the Cambodians, both Cambodia and Kampuchea being corruptions of *Kambudja*, or the "empire of the Khmer."

on the opposite bank. The bridge itself is unimpressive: just a flat span across a river. But it is the first bridge ever built over the Mekong, and though it had opened only a few months prior to my visit, a thousand people were crossing it daily. "Ninety percent of Laos's industry and most of its population lies along the Mekong border with Thailand," Mr. Suvan explained, adding that the quickest way to get from Vientiane to Laos's second largest city, Savannakhet, is through Thailand.

◎   ◎   ◎

SIRIRATONA CHUKLIN, A thirtyish-looking businesswoman, is a Nong Khai parliamentarian, a member of the local chamber of commerce and of the management team at the Holiday Inn, and the executive director of the Royal Jommanee Hotel, the newest hotel in town, next door to the Holiday Inn. She handed me a business card with several phone, mobile phone, and fax numbers, then sat me down to tell me about the region's future. We were constantly interrupted by beeps from her mobile phone.

"We Thais are a big people. Burma, Laos, southern China, Cambodia were all originally part of Thailand. So we have been split up, but we will be coming together. The Friendship Bridge is part of a road network that will link Kumming [the main city of southern China's Yunnan province] with Bangkok. It's going to be a new Silk Route that will go all the way to Singapore through Laos, Thailand, and Malaysia. Thais will dominate it. Everyone will benefit. Forget the Cambodians, though: they're too busy killing each other. But Laos—it has everything. It has only 4 million people, but natural resources that you wouldn't believe— gold, silver, gems, timber. You dig thirty centimeters beneath the ground there and you know what?—you hit manganese," she said, her eyes opening wide in wonder. "We're going to develop it." She wasn't kidding. In Yunnan, the Chinese were planning up to seven new dams on the Upper Mekong and two thirds of the electricity generated in the future would be consumed by Thais, according to Chinese and Thai officials.

◎   ◎   ◎

A THOUSAND PEOPLE may have been crossing the Friendship Bridge into Laos daily, but almost all of them were local Thais or Laotians, in addition to a few foreigners stationed in the Laotian capital, who come over to

Nong Khai for the day to shop. In Bangkok, it would have taken the Laotian embassy almost a week to process a tourist visa. I despaired. But while strolling down a side street in Nong Khai, I happened upon a sign in English that read: "FAST — SAME DAY — VISA — VISA — LAOS."

I stepped inside. At the end of a dark and empty bar table, a little Thai girl was watching the TNT cartoon channel via cable television. There was a bulletin board covered with business calling cards. One read, "Nancy Rhodes, Tourist Thru Life." An office decorated with nude pin-ups beckoned. "Hello, mate," a voice called out in an off-key Australian accent.

Alan Patterson extended his hand and continued, "Aren't they just real beauts," pointing admiringly at the nude pinups. "What can I do for you, mate?"

"Can I get a visa to Laos?"

"Sure can. Takes two to four hours. No stuff-ups. I just send a fax and wait for the fax back. No photos or forms required. Just need your passport number and a hundred and thirteen dollars."

I gave him my passport number and a down payment. It was a good deal. In Bangkok, travel agents had wanted eighty dollars for a visa that would have taken at least four working days to get. "You see, mate, I work with a Laotian travel agency run by a former Laotian government official, with a contact in the Laotian Interior Ministry."

Patterson was the reverse of Conrad's Kurtz, in "Heart of Darkness," who escapes from Western civilization by journeying into the African interior. Patterson had come to Nong Khai not to escape but as an advance man:

"Why'd I come here, mate, you ask? Well, I just looked at the map and saw that here was this pretty little Thai town that just happened to be fifteen miles from the capital city of another country. Sooner or later the place would have to develop. I've got safe water, electricity, and they clean the garbage off the streets once, sometimes twice a day. Then they built this bridge." His eyes twinkled. "I could think of worse places to invest in real estate than Nong Khai. . . .

"Now, you want deviousness and skullduggery? Well, you've come to the right place. The Thais—the Thai military, that is," he said, lowering his voice, "are trying to buy up all the timber concessions in Laos. The Laotians are nice, quiet people. They're a bit hesitant to open up their country, not on account of their communist ideology. No, it's not ideology, mate, it's the Thais they're afraid of. That's why the Laotians want Aussies and Americans to invest, people like ourselves. Anyone who would be a buffer against the Thais and the Vietnamese."[2]

Alan hadn't exaggerated. Laos, a mountainous and landlocked country of 4.6 million, has always risked being swallowed up by Thailand, a wealthy regional superpower with a sea coast and a population of 58.7 million—almost thirteen times bigger than Laos's. Laos is descended from a medieval Thai warrior kingdom.[3] The languages and cultures of the two states are, from the Laotian point of view, dangerously close. During the Indochina wars, the two states were enemies. The Thai government was aiding the Central Intelligence Agency's effort to destabilize communist-leaning Laos. But the real threat to Laos has come in peacetime, as the powerful Thai economy threatens to overrun its neighbor. When the Thais finally banned logging in their own country, Thai entrepreneurs were in Laos the next day, trying to buy timber concession. One economist with whom I had spoken in Bangkok referred to Laos as "baht country," because in Laos you are just as likely to encounter Thai money, bahts, as you are Laotian kips.

Ross H. Munro, a former bureau chief in Asia for *Time* magazine and director of the Foreign Policy Research Institute's Asia program in Philadelphia, writes that Laotian provincial officials appear to have better relations with their Chinese and Thai neighbors than they do with Vientiane. That is about as practical a definition of "spheres of influence" as one can find, he says. China will dominate northern Laos, while Thai influence will predominate in most of the rest of the country.

Thai economic and cultural influence may be less of a threat to Laos if future governments in Bangkok cannot follow up with a strong foreign policy, partly because of troubles at home in Thailand, where a growing urban population becomes harder to satisfy. Thus, there would be a Greater Thailand in an economic and cultural sense and a Lesser Thailand in a political sense; and Greater China, along with Lesser China. These magnetic culture zones, freighted with strong state traditions and historical legitimacy, may expand their areas of economic attraction while at the same time weaken, or at least decentralize, internally. Their emerg-

---

[2] Vietnam also shares a long border with Laos.
[3] Philip Rawson writes in *The Art of Southeast Asia* that "The art of Laos is a provincial version of the art of Siam."

ing power, one hopes, will be benign. Iran and Turkey may also fit this category; as might Vietnam, a society that is pursuing economic growth with the same relentless acumen with which it once constructed tunnels underneath the Ho Chi Minh Trail.

Chai-Anan Samudavanija, director of a Bangkok think tank, also sees this "Greater-Lesser" pattern: He believes that "the Asia-Pacific region is more likely to see dynamic 'interactions over and under the state' . . ." Economic growth, in his opinion, will not be defined by "artificial state boundaries" but by "routes" of activity, like the Mekong River. "As this process develops, Asia needs new maps to replace the nineteenth-century-style nation-state map, which is becoming increasingly irrelevant."

◎   ◎   ◎

A FEW HOURS later, Alan said, "Here it is mate, your visa." He held aloft a piece of fax paper. I paid him the remainder of the $113. His Thai wife escorted me in a *tuk-tuk* to the Friendship Bridge, ten minutes away. At the foot of the bridge, I piled into an old bus along with crowds of Thais and Laotians for the ride over the bridge into Laos, where the border formalities involved no baggage checks, no bribes, and no surliness from officials. It was among the strangest communist border posts I had ever encountered. Communist states, even those that, like Laos, are slipping quietly away from ideology toward full-fledged capitalism, are often marked by icy officialdom. The friendly faces here reminded me of the border guards' in pre-1989 communist Bulgaria, which, like Laos, was characterized by a peasantry that had never really been urbanized and had, consequently, never lost its roots.

The *tuk-tuks* waiting to take people from the Friendship Bridge to Vientiane constituted the first material difference I noticed between Thailand and Laos. In Thailand the *tuk-tuks* were new, with fresh paint and relatively quiet engines. Here they were dilapidated, and their engines kept sputtering and stalling out. Then came the second, more significant, difference: the roads. In Laos they were seriously potholed. Suddenly, I was on a bone-jarring road where the *tuk-tuk* driver was forced to weave from side to side to avoid the deepest potholes. And this was in the most developed section of the country, between the new bridge on the Mekong River and the capital city. What were the roads like in the mountainous hinterlands, I wondered? Smooth paved roads, like those in Thailand, shrink distances and foster national unity and public order, as well as increase the flow of human vectors for sexually transmitted diseases. (Perhaps all that holds the Ivory Coast together is its modern road network, which also accounts for its high incidence of AIDS.) Laos, with less than half the land area of Thailand, nevertheless, loomed as a vast country in my mind.

It was near sunset as the wheezing *tuk-tuk* plied its way through the brick-colored dust toward Vientiane. In the course of the day I had seen the Mekong, in Nong Khai and here, change from rust-red to brownish-yellow to glassy blue, as if it were reflecting the region's development. I inhaled the sharp and sweet odor of burning wood and enjoyed the archetypal silhouettes of lumbering water buffaloes, as peasants with wide straw hats worked waist-deep in the rice paddies. The outskirts of Vientiane were marked by fly-bitten wooden stalls interspersed between banana leaves, lit by fluorescent lights and selling cheap dry goods, as well as other stalls with old tables and grills that offered barbecued chicken. Laos was a pictograph of classic Southeast Asia, a memory layered with dust. It is neither war-torn, as much of Southeast Asia was in the 1960s and 1970s, nor yet enjoying breakneck development, like Thailand and Vietnam in the 1980s and 1990s. For me, Laos had always stood for "foreignness" itself. My first exposure to foreign affairs had come in the third grade in 1960, when my teacher would lecture the class for fifteen minutes every morning about the "situation in Laos," where the U.S. was getting deeply involved in a power struggle between a weak right-wing regime in Vientiane, neutralist forces, and communist Pathet Lao insurgents. I remember no details of what my third grade teacher said, much less how she felt about all this. I remember only that it all sounded fascinating and "foreign": *Laos*. Though I was to have only a few days here, I was thrilled.

I fell asleep that night in a room in the old Lane-Xang Hotel, a communist-era pile on the Mekong. The furnishings were cozy and made of dark wood. There was a loud and struggling Russian air conditioner that coughed and wheezed throughout the night and finally conked out, yet I was thoroughly comfortable. The staff had welcomed me with a glass of fruit juice and hadn't even asked to see my passport. Had people not bothered to tell me that Laos in 1994 still had a communist government, I might have passed my entire stay here without finding out.

The first thing I noticed in the morning was the glossy poster inside the elevator, advertising a "Greater Mekong Sub-region," promoted by an association of Thai businessmen. It pictured a map with arrows pointing outward from Thailand in all directions over Southeast Asia. At breakfast I noticed that the crockery and silverware were all made in Thailand, as were most of the goods in the shops.

Vientiane is the French-language version of Viang Chan, "Citadel of the Moon." In the mid-nineteenth century, French expeditions trying to penetrate the markets of southern China made their way up the Mekong. Along the way, Cambodia and Laos enticed them. These kingdoms had raw materials, they were suitable for rubber and cotton agriculture, and they offered some recompense for France's loss of her Indian colonies to the British. In 1893, France united three Laotian kingdoms to form the protectorate of Laos. The relative weakness of Laos and Cambodia today, compared to Thailand's and Vietnam's surging power, is often explained by the fact that the Thais and Vietnamese are dynamic immigrant races from China, while the Cambodians and Laotians tend to be indigenous peoples who, while once expansive (especially in the case of Cambodia, with its medieval empire at Angkor), have in recent centuries declined. Had the French not reconstituted Laos and Cambodia, their native lands might have been absorbed by Thai and Vietnamese expansion. (Though the French also colonized Vietnam, they didn't have to reconstitute it.[4]) However, with the French, as well as the Americans, now gone and the postcolonial wars practically over, there are no Western powers left to "fix" the competition between peoples in Southeast Asia. So the map of the twenty-first century may bear some similarity to the map before France's arrival.

That morning as I walked through Vientiane I thought of Accra, in Ghana, another big, rustic village on the verge of a mini-boom after some troubled decades. The Laotian economy was cruising along at almost 8 percent annual growth, while its population was growing by under 3 percent. Those figures were marginally better than Ghana's, West Africa's "success story."[5] There were fresh credit card stickers in the storefronts, the latest photocopy and fax machines, and new restaurants, hotels, and shops sprouting along dusty, weedy roads clogged with motorbikes, *tuk-tuks*, and rusted bicycle rickshaws. The number of

---

[4] See David P. Chandler's *The Tragedy of Cambodian History*, listed in the bibliography.
[5] The UN Human Development Index of 1994 bore out the similar standings of Laos and Ghana. Of 173 nations, Laos ranked 133 in human development; Ghana, 134.

motorized vehicles on Vientiane's streets had doubled between 1992 and 1994. A bustling market offered Thai fruit juices, Amstel beer, and Pepsi amid the stacks of Laotian silk. The public toilets were flooded and full of spiders, but ice cubes made from boiled and filtered water were readily available. The new store signs were in English (and Laotian), the old signs in French. Laos's advantage over Ghana, I thought, was its location. While Ghana was surrounded on all sides by stagnant or declining states, Laos sat amid newly prosperous ones, whose escalating economies were spreading beyond their borders. Whatever its sovereignty, Vientiane was a provincial outpost of the advancing Thai economy, which somewhere in the mountains to the north was cross-hatching with a Chinese economy spreading south (though, in Southeast Asia, you heard much less about "China" per se than about the increasingly autonomous southern Chinese provinces of Yunnan and Szechuan[6]).

Vientiane has only 120,000 inhabitants. The smallness of Laos and its capital struck me, when on a side street I encountered a sign that said, in English, MINISTRY OF EDUCATION. Behind the sign was a single, one-story building with a corrugated-iron roof. Hidden amid some trees was a second such building. These two buildings were the Ministry of Education for all of Laos. It was at this moment that I understood, once and for all, the utter stupidity of America's bloody adventure in Indochina in the 1960s and 1970s. The United States dropped more bomb tonnage on Laos than on Nazi Germany, or three times as much as the U.S. dropped during the entire Korean War, in order to cut off the Pathet Lao and disrupt activity on the Ho Chi Minh Trail in the Laotian-Vietnamese border area. The bombing of Laos cost U.S. taxpayers $7.2 billion, or $2 million every day from 1964 through 1973—or, as one writer puts it, "one planeload of bombs every eight minutes around the clock for nine years."[7] The goal: subjugate a country so small that its national education ministry is only slightly larger than a suburban house. But the goal was not achieved. The communist Pathet Lao won

---

[6]Yunnan, according to Thai and other local experts, is indeed carving out its own identity independent of China. Yunnan has twenty-two minority nationalities who share ethnic and linguistic ties with the inhabitants of Laos, Thailand, Vietnam, and Myanmar (Burma). Much of Yunnan is closer to the port cites of Thailand and Myanmar than to Chinese ports like Shanghai.

[7]See Stan Sesser's *The Lands of Charm and Cruelty*, listed in the bibliography.

anyway. By now it didn't seem to matter. The Pathet Lao government was encouraging American interest in Laos, in order to counter the Thais.

◎   ◎   ◎

MY SCHEDULE DID not permit me to travel into the Laotian mountains beyond the Mekong River valley. In Vientiane, though, I met a United Nations aid official who had traveled extensively in rural Laos. Over dinner he told me, "The borders are breaking down: Thailand-Laos, Laos-China, Laos-Vietnam. You're always seeing these trucks taking giant logs out of the forest toward Thailand or China. These are magnificent hardwoods. The logs go for as much as twenty-five thousand dollars apiece—it's very high quality wood, and there's a lot more building and furniture material in each hardwood than meets the eye. The building boom is not just in Thailand but in Yunnan too. . . . The forests are getting further and further away. In addition, there's no way for the Laotian economy to grow in the uplands, since it's stony and mountainous and the usable farmland is limited. So people have no choice but to migrate to the cities, which are in the Mekong Valley, along the Thai border, under Thai economic domination. The Laotians in the hills watch Thai TV—rock videos and wrestling matches—on television sets that they're running off car batteries . . ."

The figures bear out his testimony. Already, almost eight out of ten Laotians live near the Mekong River, even as migration to the urban centers in the Mekong Valley proceeds by 6 percent each year. That is one of the world's highest rates of urbanization—as high as sub-Saharan Africa's in the 1980s. Meanwhile, the Laotian population as a whole is growing at between 2.6 and 3 percent annually—a rate at which it will double in twenty-five years. This does not mean, necessarily, that Laos will be over-populated. With nineteen persons per square kilometer in Laos compared to 115 in Thailand, and a rich natural resource base, Laos has a lot of growing room, unlike many places in Africa.[8] It does mean, however, that Laos will become a river valley civilization, akin to Egypt's, where almost all Laotians will live in crowded conditions along the border with Thailand, and be dominated by it.

[8]Though Laos is about the same size as Ghana and has about the same percentage of arable land, its population is less than a third that of Ghana's.

Already, Thailand uses 70 to 75 percent of Laos's hydropower. And Thailand will use almost all of the water generated by the new dams and power stations to be built here.[9] Laos is on the verge of becoming a true extension of Thailand, with its forests (boasting the highest percentage of woodland in Asia) prone to rape by Thai entrepreneurs. Or, looked at another way, the Mekong River valley—both Laotian and Thai—will be a powerful economic region, more real and viable than many states on the map.

[9]The statistics in this and the preceding paragraph come from Laotian government publications, Oxford Analytica, the C.I.A.'s *World Factbook*, and other sources.

27

Cambodia: Back to Sierra Leone?

IN THE PICTURE gallery of twentieth-century horrors, Cambodia is a consumate icon: its towering sugar palms, green paddy fields, and dark monsoon clouds racked by the violent forces of communist ideology and class warfare, colonialism and anticolonialism, and the utopian ideals of the French intellectual left, stretched out of all proportion by a peculiarly Asian tendency for literalness and chilling abstraction. Between 1975 and 1979, the result of these forces was one of history's great holocausts. Under the communist regime of "Democratic Kampuchea," between 1 and 1.5 million Cambodians out of a population of 8 million were shot, bludgeoned, starved, or worked to death, or died of disease, in the most intense and awful attempt at social transformation history has ever recorded.

It was also the mass murder that will prove hardest to explain to future generations. In 1959, a Cambodian exchange student at the Sorbonne in Paris, Khieu Samphan, argued in a doctoral thesis that cities and towns were inhabited by "parasites" and should, therefore, be emptied out by "mass transfer" in order to stimulate agricultural growth, since the "parasites" could be used for farm labor. Crackpot doctoral dissertations are nothing unusual, especially those by third world peasants who go directly from their villages to the Left Bank of the Seine and, without any intellectual underpinnings, begin imbibing Marxist economic theory. But who would expect that such a thesis would actually be carried out?

Samphan was part of a coterie of Cambodians, born in the 1920s and 1930s, who studied at the Sorbonne. Their leader was one Saloth Sar, born in 1928, the son of a well-off landowner. He would later call himself Pol Pot. These students converted to Marxism-Leninism, went back to the rural countryside of Cambodia in the early 1960s, and began a movement to be known as the Khmer Rouge, or Red Khmers. According to one version, it was King Norodom Sihanouk, the dilettantish Cambodian leader, who first used the term Khmer Rouge, almost as a term of endearment.

◎   ◎   ◎

THE CAMBODIAN COUNTRYSIDE to which these French-educated radicals returned was different from the rest of Indochina. Ever since 1431, when the Thais captured the medieval Khmer capital of Angkor in northwestern Cambodia, Khmer fortunes have been in gradual decline. Angkor's great sandstone temples, or "wats," had been reclaimed by the jungle: rediscovered by French colonialists only in the nineteenth century. For hundreds of years, Cambodia was a weak and enticing chunk of real estate wedged between the stronger states of Thailand and Vietnam: sparsely populated yet easily accessible, and *rich*, with alluvial soil and the Tonle Sap, or "Great Lake," the richest freshwater fishing zone in the world. In the nineteenth century, Thailand and Vietnam fought for influence in Cambodia, and had the French not established their protectorate in 1863, Cambodia east of the Mekong River may well have become part of Vietnam, just as Cambodia west of the Mekong may have become part of Thailand. Rather than fortify Cambodian nationhood, however, the French added to Khmer feelings of inferiority by favoring the Vietnamese. The French strengthened Vietnamese bureaucratic institutions rather than build Cambodian ones, and shipped Cambodian raw materials to Vietnam. When the French departed in 1954, Thailand and South Vietnam, now aligned with the United States, renewed their historic ambitions against Cambodia for which their anticommunist ideology was mere pretext. Prince Sihanouk's response was neutralism, which would earn only the disdain of the West and its allies, and of the Khmer Rouge as well.

Once in the forest, the Khmer Rouge were prone to several extremely powerful psychological undercurrents that rather than soften their ideological certainties only intensified them. For one thing, there was the Khmer warrior tradition, evinced by the hideous violence of the battle scenes carved in relief upon the hundreds of temples at Angkor. The Khmer Rouge mentality did not emerge from a vacuum. Barbarity had been a constant in Cambodia. During the 1970–75 civil war that had preceded the Khmer Rouge takeover, two members of the legislature were killed and their livers publicly eaten by an angry crowd. During the five years of fighting before the Khmer Rouge victory, a half million Cambodians, mainly civilians, were killed. Abetting this violent streak was a deliberate Khmer Rouge policy of recruiting young teenagers and children as young as ten or twelve as fighters and cadres. Khmer Rouge leaders thus created an army whose troops had yet to be fully "socialized." It was an army of children without a trace of compassion. These heavily armed youngsters rarely left the forest. They knew nothing of an outside world except what their leaders told them: a world that had exploited the countryside and was synonymous with foreign imperialists. Truly, nowhere else in Indochina has there been such a divide between town and country as in Cambodia, where forests are dense and towns, especially the capital city of Phnom Penh, are laid out in a grid pattern of streets marked by colonial-style European architecture.

In Khmer Rouge minds, these towns and cities were populated not by fellow Cambodians but by "parasites" and "enemies," like the Vietnamese immigrant community, members of a group that throughout history had exploited Cambodia. Helping the southern Vietnamese were the French colonialists and the urban parasites, and in recent years the American imperialists.

While the kids with the AK-47 assault rifles were learning how to hate and kill such enemies, the top echelon of Khmer Rouge leadership was also ensconced in the jungle, developing models of abstract purity for the revolution to come. These models derived from several sources, including the terror regime of the French Revolution, the collectivization of agriculture as practiced under Stalin, the "total mobilization" of the population as it was carried out in 1950s China during the Great Leap Forward, the unrestrained class warfare of Mao's Great Cultural Revolution, and the self-reliance of communist North Korea. Former U.S. diplomat and Cambodian specialist David P. Chandler writes in *The Tragedy of Cambodian History: Politics, War and Revolution since 1945* that "the literalness and speed with which these models were" later to be "followed made them especially destructive." Just as the encroaching forest had engulfed the great monuments of civilization at Angkor, the armed teenagers from the forest—foot soldiers of Sorbonne ideologues—were to trample down the civilization of Cambodian cities.

The top leadership of the Khmer Rouge didn't even use noms de guerre. They sometimes referred to themselves as "Brother Number One" or "Brother Ninety-nine." Actual names were considered bourgeois extravagances. But such realizations about the Khmer Rouge are mainly after-the-fact wisdom. As the Khmer Rouge capture of Phnom Penh approached in 1975, these details either weren't known in the West or were ignored. Author William Shawcross contends that in Washington, the Khmer Rouge were assumed to be merely another band of communists, like those in Vietnam, and that such idiosyncracies as the ethnic hatred with which the Khmer Rouge looked toward the North Vietnamese communists was discounted.[1] The clumsiness of Nixon's policy was evinced by its secret bombing of Cambodia in 1969, followed by more bombing in 1973. As the B-52s wasted the Cambodian countryside, they only drove more and more furious peasants into the arms of the Khmer Rouge, while the Khmer Rouge itself intensified its hatred of the West and urban Cambodians. Nixon and Kissinger's apparent ignorance of Cambodia and the Khmer Rouge was a foreign policy disaster with few parallels in modern history.

The weeks preceding the collapse of the pro-American regime of Marshal Lon Nol in Phnom Penh in 1975 were to be burned not only into historical memory, but into literary memory as well: a result of the enormity of what happened immediately after the Khmer Rouge arrived in the capital, and of the Westerners who happened to witness it, including the British poet James Fenton and Sidney Schanberg of *The New York Times*, whose reports of the horror have become classics.

◎   ◎   ◎

APRIL 17, 1975, Day One of the Year Zero by Khmer Rouge reckoning, was the day that the Khmer Rouge occupied Phnom Penh and a Khmer Rouge government spokesman proudly announced that "more than two

[1] See Shawcross's *Sideshow: Kissinger, Nixon and the Destruction of Cambodia*, listed in the bibliography.

thousand years" of Cambodian history had come to an end. In a matter of hours, prodded by heavily armed Khmer Rouge soldiers, often in black pajamas and red-checkered kerchiefs, many of them hardly more than children, the inhabitants of Cambodia's capital were marched out of the city in a broad river of humanity. Not Stalingrad, not Hiroshima, never before had a city been so completely emptied of its inhabitants.[2] Within two weeks, Phnom Penh and several other major cities were empty: several million Cambodians had been forcibly evicted to the countryside. Concerning a second evacuation later that year, from the rural southwest of Cambodia to the northwest, diplomat Chandler says:

"The image of tens of thousands of people jammed upright into trucks and slow-moving freight cars, making their way through an empty landscape toward an uncertain but ominous future, hauntingly echoes the Jewish experience in World War II. There was an important difference, however: in Cambodia the oppressors had the same nationality and (until shortly before the evacuations) the same religion as the oppressed."

This, after all, is the point where all explanations become inadequate, where the madness of twentieth-century ideology takes over. By Cambodian standards, even Rwanda, where one ethnic group, the Hutus, killed hundreds of thousands of members of another ethnic group, the Tutsis, seemed almost comprehensible, for in many instances the opposing sides had at least some distinct physical characteristics. But in Cambodia, "base people" killed "April 17 people": base people being those Cambodians who were rural, and April 17 people being those Cambodians who moved from the cities to the countryside only on April 17, 1975, when the mass transfers began. The base people showed no mercy, for in the minds of the Khmer Rouge leadership, the April 17 people—women, children, and babies, too—were simply the slag of history.

History, according to the plan of the Khmer Rouge, now had to be propelled forward. Besides the evacuation of cities and towns, money was abolished. So were mail delivery and all forms of formal education, such as public schools and universities. All newspapers were shut down. The Buddhist religion was prohibited. Everyone was made to wear a peasant costume, and all meals, henceforth, had to be eaten in "collective" groups. "As in Thomas More's Utopia, strict rules for behavior [clothing, haircuts, vocabulary . . .] were laid down," writes Chandler. Anyone with post-

[2] See *Phnom Penh: Then & Now* by Michel Igout, listed in the bibliography.

secondary school education was marked for execution. Because the Khmer Rouge forest children thought that all people who wore glasses were intellectuals, glasses were as deadly as the yellow star in Nazi Germany. Ninety percent of the country's medical doctors were murdered between 1975 and 1979. Babies were bashed to death against trees.

Chandler writes that under the Khmer Rouge, "Cambodia soon became a gigantic prison farm." Many thousands, perhaps more, of the 1 to 1.5 million casualties of the Khmer Rouge regime were executed by having their heads smashed in with hoes and shovels, since ammunition had to be hoarded for fighting fellow communists across the border, whose crime was that they were Vietnamese. (The murder of an estimated two hundred thousand Vietnamese civilians, who had lived peacefully in Cambodia for generations—but who represented in Khmer Rouge minds a potential fifth column—was at least one Khmer Rouge atrocity that made some "sense," since it had racial connotations and thus is no more inexplicable than what would later occur in Rwanda.)

Regarding the Cambodian deaths, though, the most extraordinary thing was that the top echelon of the Khmer Rouge—isolated within their Marxist abstractions—never intended them to happen. Pol Pot, Khieu Samphan, and the others actually thought that their plan of rapid social transformation would provide a better material life for most Cambodians without the need for killing anyone. "When their program failed," writes Chandler, "the leaders were confused . . ." The brutality had gotten out of hand. Perhaps the problem was a flaw in Khieu Samphan's doctoral thesis?

◎   ◎   ◎

FIGHTING BETWEEN CAMBODIAN and Vietnamese communists in the late 1970s flared into open war that ended in January 1979, when the Vietnamese marched into Phnom Penh and the Khmer Rouge fled into the forests. Next came famine in Cambodia, which led to an international relief effort. However, because the Vietnamese communists were allied with the Soviet Union, throughout the 1980s the United States and its ally Thailand backed—of all groups—the Khmer Rouge, who were armed by China and were now fighting the Vietnamese occupation authorities.

With the end of the Cold War, the United Nations organized a national reconciliation process, which involved twenty-two thousand UN troops and cost $2 billion, the biggest UN operation in history. The reconciliation process was capped by elections held in May 1993, which the UN, with much fanfare, declared a success. What happens in Cambodia hereafter will say much about the long-term value of such UN operations. Cambodia's future will be crucial to any historical reckoning of the UN.

◎   ◎   ◎

LESS THAN AN hour after leaving Bangkok's modern airport, I saw through the plane window a succession of red laterite roads, corrugated-iron roofs glinting in the sunlight, and intense tropical greenery. From the air Thailand had looked like a manicured lawn. Cambodia was a weedy garden. The ragged landscape indicated a poor country, as did the absence of both paving and traffic on the country roads. The fact that I had to fly into Cambodia was another bad sign. Phnom Penh is no further from Bangkok than Nong Khai, which is easily reached by train or bus. Phnom Penh isn't, since the Khmer Rouge still controlled the border areas on the Cambodian side.

From the vantage point of Thailand, everything that I had recently heard about Cambodia seemed unreal. Thailand was booming economically, Laos was full of promise, and Vietnam was about to emerge as a dynamic oil-producing power of the early twenty-first century. Yet Cambodia was said to be back-breakingly poor, politically unstable, and dangerous, not unlike the West African countries I had visited. But wasn't I in prosperity-bound Southeast Asia?

On July 26, 1994, a few months before my trip, three Western backpackers—a Briton, a Frenchman, and an Australian—were kidnapped by Khmer Rouge guerrillas only about seventy miles south of the capital of Phnom Penh, where the Khmer Rouge ambushed the train the three were traveling in. In November 1994, while I was in Cambodia, I would read a Reuters dispatch describing the eventual murder of the backpackers by the Khmer Rouge, the recovery of the victims' bodies, and the autopsies that followed. The dispatch said:

> They were bound. The three died from massive head injuries. . . .
> The method of execution bore all the hallmarks of a classic "Killing Fields"-style murder—a blow from a hoe to the back of the head.

In addition, *The Cambodia Daily* of November 4–6, 1994, reported that the Khmer Rouge had murdered forty villagers in western Cambodia.

Some were "bludgeoned and axed to death with hoes." Others were bound together in pairs and shot.

In 1994, the very existence of the Khmer Rouge seemed, like much else about Cambodia, absurd. The Cold War had ended. Vietnam was on the road to becoming a new vacation destination for Americans. Yet in Cambodia, the Khmer Rouge were still in the forest: It was as if the SS were still roaming through Germany.

The landscape outside my plane window helped explain why. I had seen such landscapes before, when I flew into Guinea and Sierra Leone. Show me a poor country with bad, potholed roads and, often enough, I'll show you a country with bandit soldiers or a guerrilla insurgency. Thailand was fifty minutes and a million miles away.

Graham Miller, the Cambodia office director of CARE, greeted me with a bear hug at plane-side. Graham and I were friends from the days of the 1984–85 Ethiopian famine and hadn't seen each other for years. A tall and bluff South Africa–born Australian, Graham had lived in eleven troubled third world countries and had worked in forty-three. A veteran geologist, his specialty was digging water wells in rural areas. He could just look at a landscape and tell you how far down the water table was. Graham is what foreign affairs sophisticates call an "expat" working for an "NGO (non-governmental organization)." In other words, he is an expatriate employed by a private Western relief agency—in this case, CARE. As human disasters multiply on account of ethnic wars, famines, the collapse of states, and refugee migrations, NGOs have filled the gap left vacant by Western governments and their militaries. Diplomats and journalists often rely on NGOs for their information as to what is going on *in-country*—that is, away from the capital city. Indeed, while the American public appears increasingly unwilling to put its soldiers at risk, it apparently thinks little of putting its relief volunteers—American "expats"—in extremely dangerous situations. Cambodia in 1994 had as many as ninety NGOs operating around the country, staffed by as many as one thousand expats, including Americans. With a population of under 10 million,[3] Cambodia may have had more resident expats and NGOs per capita than any other third world country. Cambodia is, thus, at the cutting edge of this little-mentioned but pivotal foreign policy evolution.

[3] Despite the mass murder of the 1970s, Cambodia's population has risen because of a high birthrate in recent years.

"Cambodia, mate, well, it's a bloody mess. But you never know. Here at the airport, for instance, they seem to be getting their act together." Without Graham's help, I stood quietly on line, purchased a visa for twenty dollars, and got my immigration stamp. There was a system, in other words. We jumped into Graham's four-wheel-drive vehicle for the twenty-minute drive to his house. Along the way, I stuck my head out the window while listening to Graham's briefing. This is what I saw and heard:

◎   ◎   ◎

THE AIR HAD that dense and dirty fish-tank quality of the poor and crowded tropics: garbage, stray dogs, and crying babies. I saw relatively few cars but encountered many motorbikes and rickety, rusted bicycle-rickshaws driven by men wearing wraparound sunglasses and baseball hats. Other men were rebuilding auto parts in stalls along the dusty streets. Yet it was "charming," in the heartbreaking sense in which that word is often applied to the underdeveloped world—with the usual banana groves, flame trees, and those old and scabby lemon-colored colonial buildings with rotting balconies. There were the water lilies floating in urban swamps, and little boys selling jasmine blossoms stuck into the ends of sugarcane sticks. Phnom Penh had something else besides, something particularly Cambodian, which I would learn to appreciate at Angkor: those mottled, weather-stained Buddhist temple buildings of autumnal stone, with fungus growing on the red tiles, which only seemed to increase their preciousness. The somber facades, more evocative of medieval cloisters in Europe than of the sun-splashed tropics, help give Cambodia a visual texture that other third world countries lack. It was my first intimation of Cambodia's specialness. I thought of what a relief worker had told author William Shawcross about Cambodia: "It had everything—temples, starving brown babies and an Asian Hitler figure [Pol Pot]—it was like sex on a tiger skin."[4]

Phnom Penh is named after a hill, or *phnom* in Cambodian, topped by a Buddhist temple built by a woman named Penh. It had been a ghost town between 1975 and 1979. Then it came under Vietnamese occupation, and now was still coming back to life. The city's mood and character had yet to be buried beneath the high-rises that dominated Bangkok. The

[4]See Shawcross's *The Quality of Mercy*, listed in the bibliography.

population had risen to 1.3 million because of recent migration from the countryside, but Phnom Penh is small compared to other Asia capitals, and has relatively little industry, a more crowded and sprawling version of Vientiane.

It was the people that gripped my throat: those buttery, cocoa-brown faces blending Melanesian, Indian, and Oriental features, and bearing an archetypal forest-spirit quality, enhanced by eyes of such smiling brightness that each face was like a charity poster.

I also noticed many beggars and amputees in the streets.

"Ten million land mines, my friend," Graham informed me, "one for every person in the country. Cambodia has one of the highest per capita ratio of amputees in the world, maybe the highest. There are two hundred to three hundred injuries per month from mines. Legacy of the civil war and the Khmer Rouge war with the Vietnamese. The Western community here is operating some interesting de-mining programs you may want to look at. But the Khmer Rouge now re-mine in days what it takes us two to three months to de-mine. It costs the Khmer Rouge an average of one to four dollars to lay a mine. De-mining costs thousands . . .

"The city looks beautiful now, doesn't it?" Graham went on cheerily. "Last summer many of the streets were flooded. No drainage. By the way, I hope you brought lots of U.S. dollars in small denominations. The dollar's more or less the currency here. Credit cards are pretty useless. Not much of a financial or tax system in Cambodia. There's probably a lot of dirty drug money around, too. Army's a mess: 2,004 generals for an army of only 80,000. I've observed the soldiers quite a bit—they're drunk, bored, and underpaid. The government roadblocks outside Phnom Penh can be lethal. Peasants are as fearful of the soldiers as they are of the Khmer Rouge. That's the heart of the problem: the Khmer Rouge are weak and corrupt, but so is the government."

"What about disease?" I asked Graham.

"Cerebral malaria. But it's not like Africa, it only exists in isolated pockets deep in the bush. Though in Phnom Penh there's quite a bit of dengue fever, which is also carried by mosquitoes."

"What about river blindness—onchocerciasis, like in West Africa?"

"None here. But there's quite a bit of schistosomiasis—bilharzia—in the irrigation canals."

Graham pulled to a stop. My heart sank as he reached his hand down and retrieved a Club to lock onto his steering wheel. The Club is an anticar theft device familiar to those in American cities and crime-plagued suburbs. Seeing my questioning eyes, Graham explained, "No choice, mate. We've already had some vehicles stolen." He continued:

"Crime's high here. Lots of robberies, carjackings even. Our French neighbors were robbed at gunpoint; the six-year-old was shot. The thing about this place is, with a bandit, drunken army, too many people around here have guns." Two slightly menacing street urchins with baseball hats appeared out of nowhere. "I'll pay these boys to watch the car," Graham explained.

My melancholy intensified, and I could feel it in my belly. I was light-headed. It was not the fear of crime that I felt or the fear of disease, but the deeper writer's fear of having oversimplified something—in this case, the idea of culture, which now seemed like a greater mystery to me than it had at the beginning of my journey in West Africa. I had assumed that the random crime and other social chaos of West Africa were the result of an already-fragile cultural base, the lack in most places of a written language until this century, and geographical isolation from other major civilizations: It was now coming further undone as a consequence of high birthrates and urbanization. But here I was, in the heart of Buddhist-Confucian Southeast Asia, in a land where the written script was one thousand two hundred years old and every surrounding country was in some stage of impressive economic growth. Yet Cambodia was eerily similar to Sierra Leone: with random crime, mosquito-borne disease, a government army that was more like a mob, and a countryside that was ungovernable because of guerrilla insurgents. True, Cambodia's literacy rate was higher than Sierra Leone's: 35 percent compared to 21 percent. But so was the population growth rate: a shocking 4.4 percent, higher than anywhere in West Africa.

I know, I know. Nixon, Kissinger, and especially the Khmer Rouge had inflicted destruction upon Cambodia. It was in the crosshairs of twentieth-century ideological and superpower politics, while West Africa was an ideological and strategic backwater. Cambodia's plight could be blamed on outside forces to a degree that Sierra Leone's plight could not. Moreover, Cambodia might simply be the exception that proves the rule about Asian cultural vitality. But I doubted this.

After all, it was Cambodians who had killed 1.5 million other Cambodians, and they were still killing them: The murderers weren't Americans or Martians. To absolve Cambodian culture of responsibility is as illogical as to heap all the blame for what had happened on Henry Kissinger. Culture, I suspected, was still crucial to the question of why some states like Cambodia and Sierra Leone failed. Perhaps, to paraphrase Leo Tolstoy's remark about families—while all successful cultures share similar traits, unsuccessful ones fail in their own highly complex ways.[5]

Perhaps indigenous people like the Khmers are simply less dynamic than groups whose history has been marked by large-scale migration, like the Thais and Vietnamese. Perhaps the special problems of Cambodia had something to do with its dense forests, which, like Liberia's, engendered isolation and suspicion. I didn't know. All I could do was poke around and use my intuition. But to avoid the subject of culture as a determinant would be to avoid a principal cause for the difference in development patterns.

The issue of development is even more complex than I can describe, since the most extraneous event of the briefest duration in a country's history might have the most fundamental and long-term repercussions. For example:

Between 1948 and 1968, Cambodia's population more than doubled, from 3 million to 6.6 million; and by 1968 the Cambodian economy was a shambles. Agricultural production was stagnant and the annual deficit amounted to an eighth of the entire budget. Sihanouk's solution was to open government casinos in Phnom Penh and the port city of Sihanoukville, so that money spent on illegal gambling would be diverted to the national treasury. The casinos opened in early 1969 and operated twenty-four hours a day. Students, peasants, cyclo-drivers, soldiers, and officials lost their savings at the casinos as gambling fever gripped Phnom Penh and Sihanoukville. Still worse, Sihanouk's relatives were stealing most of the casino profits. The casinos closed in January 1970, shortly before Marshal Lon Nol toppled Sihanouk. Many Cambodians to this day believe that had Sihanouk not decided to open the casinos, he would not have been overthrown and the trajectory of Cambodian history, including the Khmer Rouge holocaust, would have been different. Who can say for sure?

Moreover, in early 1971 Lon Nol suffered a stroke. It was mild and he recovered quickly. But coming as it did after a Vietnamese communist

---

[5]In *Anna Karenina*, Tolstoy wrote that while happy families are alike, unhappy ones are each unhappy in their own way.

commando attack on the airport that destroyed the Cambodian air force, news of the illness seriously convinced Cambodians that his rule was doomed. What if Lon Nol had not taken ill and what if the casinos never opened—would the Khmer Rouge still have come to power and wrought the havoc that so damaged the local culture? No one knows.

I'm not suggesting, for instance, that the distress of a whole continent, like Africa, can be the result of a series of unlucky accidents like those mentioned above. On the other hand, the idea that the source of national success or failure can be discovered by scientific study, as many political scientists hope, struck me as absurd by the time I reached Cambodia.

For example, "controlled case comparisons" are the basis for much political science analysis. A researcher might select several cases of conflict around the world that are identical except for the one variable under study—scarcity of farmland, let's say. The political scientist could then, perhaps, draw conclusions about whether land scarcity causes upheaval. But this is nonsense! How can there be such a thing as "controlled case comparisons" when every single conflict around the world is different from every other one for a plethora of complex cultural and accidental reasons, such as Sihanouk's flirtation with casinos? Human cultures aren't bacteriological ones—so many microbes of this kind and so many microbes of that kind. A political scientist can do little more than what a journalist does: go to places where there appear to be interesting linkages between, say, land scarcity and violence, and see if causal relationships exist. From this, some useful ideas or theories might emerge. To call it science, though, is an overstatement.

◎　　　◎　　　◎

"MANNY, I WANT you to meet Robert, an old friend of mine from Africa," Graham announced.

"I'll stand you a beer, Robert," Manny replied. Manny was an ethnic Greek former Australian diplomat who had *stayed on* in Phnom Penh and opened a bar-restaurant. Manny's bar was the unofficial information clearinghouse for the expat and NGO community in Cambodia, the place where expats returning from the countryside fortified themselves with steaks and beer while trading war stories. Given that foreign diplomats in Phnom Penh got much of their information from relief workers, who had told their stories first to Manny, I figured Manny, who wore shorts and a loud Hawaiian-print shirt, was worth talking to.

"There's a lot of banditry and too many firearms," Manny said. "Many Cambodian generals have their own private militias in the countryside—like warlords, actually. In the government, everyone is trying to steal what they can, in case this whole UN-engineered democracy collapses. Gold's the thing, mate. Everybody who can is hoarding gold. The Vietnamese, Thais, Singaporeans are all in Phnom Penh buying up pieces of Cambodia. The place is ripe for plunder. Of course, much of what everybody will tell you—including what I'm telling you—has to be regarded as hearsay, conjecture. Outside of Phnom Penh, for instance, it's difficult to know what is happening."

One unassailable truth emerged from Manny's monologue: the fact that, like little Sierra Leone, Cambodia was "big." The smallest country in Southeast Asia in square mileage, Cambodia was the largest country in Southeast Asia in the danger and difficulty of land travel, and it was hard to know in advance what lurked in the countryside. Kampot was only eighty-eight miles south of Phnom Penh, on the Gulf of Siam, but trains to Kampot were periodically held up by both bandits and Khmer Rouge. The last Westerners to ride the train—the three backpackers—had been kidnapped and murdered. Kratie, upriver on the Mekong, was only one hundred miles to the northeast, but the "slow boat" there took more than a day and was sometimes shot at by Khmer Rouge hiding in the forested banks or was boarded and robbed by government soldiers. A "fast boat," however, took five and a half hours and was considered safe. The fast boat, privately operated by Singaporeans, was the only reliable link to the town from Phnom Penh. Nong Khai, by contrast, was three hundred miles north of Bangkok—or three times the distance between Phnom Penh and Kratie—but could be comfortably reached by train or bus, or by airplane and air-conditioned coach in a journey that took under two hours. Information about Nong Khai, complete with fax numbers of hotels and businesses there, was readily available in Bangkok, whereas news of Kampot and Kratie in Phnom Penh was sparse and laced with rumor.

Officially, Cambodian and Western observers in Phnom Penh said that the elected government controlled 80 percent of Cambodian territory, while the Khmer Rouge held the rest—mainly in the mountainous and heavily forested areas in the south near the Gulf of Siam, and in the west near the Thai border. But in 1994, the situation on the ground was less clear-cut. Of the area that the government controlled, only about half, or 40 percent of Cambodia's total land area, was assumed to be safe. The other half was safe during the day but overrun by Khmer Rouge patrols at night. Or it was safe during the dry season but was deserted by government troops when the rains started. John Holloway, Australia's former ambassador to Cambodia, reported that "during the . . . wet season, while the government forces are marooned in their barracks playing cards, the Khmer Rouge will send out cadres on foot through the mud into remote villages to sit and talk with villagers and ascertain their needs. Sometimes these needs are for protection from government troops, in which case the Khmer Rouge cadre will return with weapons and mines . . ." Later, when I visited the northeast of the country, a German expat showed me a map of Cambodia and said, "Basically, wherever you see large tracts of thick forests, that's Khmer Rouge territory."

Three to 4 percent of Cambodia's old growth forests were being lost yearly to illegal hardwood logging.[6] With the Cold War ended, the Khmer Rouge had begun to lose allies in the disintegrating Asian communist bloc. But they were gaining them among Thai, Malaysian, and Singaporean businessmen willing to pay in U.S. dollars for hardwood timber, which Khmer Rouge patrols escorted on heavy trucks out of the forest. The alliance between the Khmer Rouge and Thai generals and businessmen involved the transfer of lumber, gems, and even children for Bangkok sex markets: worth tens of millions of dollars per year. Hardwood logging in the Thai-Cambodian border region had led to massive soil erosion in the upper reaches of Cambodia's Tonle Sap, or Great Lake, and silted up parts of the lake where fish spawn. Not only was this critical freshwater fish reserve dying out, but as the Great Lake silted up, it closed off an exit valve for the lower reaches of the Mekong River. This increased the frequency of flooding in eastern Cambodia and in Vietnam's Mekong Delta. Cambodia's Great Lake region, which dominated the center of the country, was becoming a smaller version of the Amazon: a lawless netherworld of illegal logging and similar environmental devastation. Meanwhile, the Khmer Rouge were gradually transforming themselves from ideological warriors of the twentieth century to nihilistic road warriors of

[6]Topographical surveys indicate that Cambodia has lost about a third of its forest cover since 1969. Forests still cover 49 percent of the country, about half of which is primary growth forest. Severe droughts and flash floods are thought to be linked to the loss of forests. This and other information about the Cambodian environment comes from the International Development Research Centre in Ottawa, Canada.

the twenty-first. "Just as it makes no sense to ask why people eat or what they sleep for," writes Martin van Creveld, an Israel-based military historian, "so fighting in many ways is not a means but an end." However elusive, that was one of the best explanations I could find for why the Khmer Rouge kept fighting.

In the middle of the last decade of the twentieth century, Cambodia was, like some other third world countries including Angola and Afghanistan, a land of internal exiles, land mines, disorder, and disease. According to Dr. Tea Phalla, a Cambodian government health expert, "2 million" of the country's 10 million inhabitants could die "directly or indirectly" from HIV infections in the future.[7] The World Health Organization reports that "trends among blood donors suggest that Phnom Penh may experience an even larger HIV epidemic than has occurred in northern Thailand."

Perhaps the most telling and frightening aspect of recent Cambodian history, one that might be a harbinger for other places in the twenty-first century, is its very lack of theme. Chandler refers to the successive collapse of "one-reign dynasties." There was the monarchial rule of King Sihanouk, then the military regime of Lon Nol, then the Marxist-Leninist "central committee" structure of the Khmer Rouge, then Vietnamese occupation, and since 1993 a democratically elected coalition of royalists linked to Sihanouk and communists linked formerly to both the Vietnamese and the Khmer Rouge. The king, Lon Nol's military, and the Khmer Rouge all advertised a new and stable phase of Cambodian history. Would democracy fare any better than they had?

◎   ◎   ◎

GRAHAM HAD TO stop at the market to run errands. As I looked around, I saw things that did not track with the negative image of Cambodia I had been developing. In the rickety shops made of scrap wood, corrugated iron, and cement were electric lights, air-conditioning units, photocopy machines, some computers and fax machines, and photographic development equipment. Electronic appliances everywhere looked clean and well maintained. Furthermore, as I learned, public electricity and water systems were fairly reliable. Many of these appliances were not being run off private generators as in West Africa and even Pakistan. Graham, who

[7]See the article by Moeun Chhean Nariddh listed in bibliography.

had run office operations in Sudan, Kenya, and Angola, told me that "people here maintain equipment better than in Africa." I checked this with other expats who had lived in both Southeast Asia and sub-Saharan Africa, and they agreed. In fact, the clean and well-lit shops in Phnom Penh were familiar to me: They looked like the shops run by the Lebanese and Syrian merchants in Freetown, Sierra Leone, and those of Indian merchants I had seen in East African cities during my visits in the 1980s. Then I recalled how much more orderly the immigration procedure had been at Phnom Penh airport compared to airports in West Africa. Was Cambodia an unusual combination of efficiency and chaos? Was the ability to organize death camps and to repair a photocopy machine the result of a common cultural trait? Or was I now too protective of Africa? Were these well-functioning shops proof that even violent, chaotic Cambodia was about to pull steeply ahead of most places in sub-Saharan Africa?

Probably the biggest difference, though, between Cambodia and Sierra Leone was that whereas Sierra Leone was engulfed by the failed and semi-failed states of Liberia and Guinea, Cambodia adjoined the two powerboat economies of Thailand and Vietnam, with tigers such as Malaysia and Singapore close by. As a result, Cambodian cities were being modernized even as Cambodia's natural resources were being plundered.

Inflation had fallen from 100 to 30 percent between 1992 and 1994. And every day that the unwieldy coalition between royalists and communists (who weren't really communists) survived was a victory for the UN process and a defeat for the Khmer Rouge. A provincial governor in the northeast would tell me: "In people's minds, there are only two parties, that of the government and that of Pol Pot. The differences between royalists and communists may seem big to us, but to the peasants they are increasingly seen as the same party."

There were two views about the UN in Cambodia. The first held that the much-trumpeted elections were "an expensive stunt" that got rave reviews while it happened but, like many attempts to "force history" in the third world, was gradually looking less worthwhile. It seemed futile to impose an American-style election system on a country that had never known individual freedom and where a communications infrastructure barely existed. Democracy for Cambodia seemed an effort that should begin with economic development and the establishment of schools.

Instead, Cambodians, many of them illiterate, were exposed cold turkey to a Western election campaign.[8]

I listened to stories about how the UN had moved in with an army of expensive vehicles and high-tech communications gear, and sent the Cambodian economy, especially the real estate market, into overdrive to meet the need for Western-style villas and restaurants. After the elections were over, the UN deserted and monthly rental rates for villas dropped from $3,700 back to $1,200. "It was an event, not a process," said one expat. "Had the UN spent $2 billion for roads, schools, and rural development rather than on an election, the Khmer Rouge would be weaker in rural Cambodia than they are now," said a second expat. A third said, "Elections should have come last, not first, in the process of regeneration." A number of Cambodians told me, "The UN, it came, now it's gone."

The other view held that as long as the democratic government survived, the UN elections would constitute a pivotal turn in Cambodian history, in which for the first time Cambodians experienced the dignity of voting in secrecy in a closed booth. And in the course of my journey beyond Phnom Penh, I would meet Cambodians who volunteered praise for the UN reconciliation process.

◎   ◎   ◎

GRAHAM PICKED UP his wife, Elizabeth, and the three of us went for a meal at the Phnom Penh Foreign Correspondents' Club. It was the most alluring foreign journalists' club I had ever seen: a Somerset Maugham cliché-in-waiting for a glossy magazine feature, composed of dark, varnished wood and bamboo, with wicker chairs, mustard-yellow walls, and Corinthian pilasters—and, of course, the obligatory slow-moving fans. The club had an open-air bar, from which I could look out over the confluence of the Mekong River and an egress of the Great Lake. With no glass to separate us from the street below, I could enjoy Campari and soda with steak and eggs while watching Cambodian children sift through the garbage a few feet away.

It occurred to me that rather than dissolve into poverty and chaos or be lifted into prosperity, Cambodia was moving in both directions simultaneously—with its powerful neighbors taking economic advantage of the chaos while helping to generate the prosperity. Either way, the region was

[8]See Stan Sesser's *The Lands of Charm and Cruelty*, listed in the bibliography.

looking more and more like a late-seventeenth-century French map of Indochina that I had purchased in Thailand, with the Mekong River valley as both an informal dividing line between Thai-dominated Cambodian lands and Vietnamese-dominated areas, as well as a major zone of settlement in its own right. In *The Warrior Heritage*, Seanglim Bit writes that until the arrival of the French in 1863, "the concept of nationhood was embodied in a cultural version of political geography. Cambodia was where Cambodian was spoken in the villages . . ." In an age of open borders, whether the UN process succeeded or failed, nationhood would probably return to something like that.

GRAHAM TOOK ME to Tuol Sleng, a school in the heart of Phnom Penh that the Khmer Rouge had converted into a prison and torture facility after they emptied out the city. Experts estimate that between sixteen and twenty thousand persons passed through Tuol Sleng between 1976 and early 1979. Except for six known cases, none came out alive. After the Vietnamese liberated Phnom Penh and opened the prison to the public, comparisons between Tuol Sleng and Auschwitz and Dachau were inescapable. Actually, as both Shawcross and Chandler are careful to note, the better comparison is between Tuol Sleng and Stalin's Lubyanka prison during the purges of the 1930s. Almost all the victims of Tuol Sleng were themselves Khmer Rouge, or relatives of Khmer Rouge, who fell afoul of party doctrine at a time when that doctrine, in addition to changing almost daily, was actually known only to a select and increasingly paranoiac inner circle that included Pol Pot and Khieu Samphan.

But Tuol Sleng was different from Auschwitz and Dachau in a more important way. Auschwitz and Dachau had been converted into museums. They had been sanitized by Western curators with heating and air-conditioning, polished-glass display cases, stage lighting, museum shops, and modern toilets for the visiting public. Tuol Sleng had gone through no such sterilization process. The display cases were crude. It was miserably hot. Rats scavenged in the hallways and wretched toilets. I saw dust balls, spiderwebs, and dried blood splattered on the peeling walls. For all I knew, the Khmer Rouge might have left yesterday. The building, with a wire net stretched over the balconies so that torture victims could not commit suicide, had literally been left as it was. The smells of human feces, human sweat, and dead flesh had been erased—that was the only difference. In such a setting, the sight of chains, fingernail and nipple pliers, and photographs of young women with swollen and blackened eyes achieve an effect that you do not find in Europe's particular hells.

In the courtyard, the gallows were next to a child's swing. I noticed a pile of split coconuts that reminded me of the pile of smashed skulls I had seen as I entered the building. I recalled reading about how a Bosnian Serb militia leader had taken a poor and illiterate farm boy and converted him into a genocidal monster by having the youth slaughter pigs over and over again. The difference between killing hogs and people had become, with practice, trivial.

Nine miles south of Phnom Penh was Choeng Ek, a Khmer Rouge extermination site where 129 mass graves holding 8,985 corpses of men, women, children, and infants had been unearthed.[9] Choeng Ek was the original killing field from which the film got its name. The drive from Phnom Penh through flat paddy fields graced by swaying sugar palms was reminiscent of the film footage. Water buffaloes meandered over the grave pits. White water-lilies dotted nearby wetlands.

Two tomato-colored tour buses pulled up. One unloaded a group of Thais and the another a group of Greek tourists. The groups looked alike: prosperously middle-class, with expensive cameras, sunglasses, and "casual" clothes. Each group contained the usual one or two shouters, fifty-year-old men who acted like teenage boys. The shouters insisted on being photographed while holding one of the bleached human limbs lying about. Some of the Thais and Greeks appeared uncomfortable about this, and remained quiet. But by the time both tour buses departed, everyone was back in good cheer. This year Cambodia, next year Hawaii.

[9]There is apparent confusion over whether many of these victims had first passed through Tuol Sleng, meaning the figures cited for each facility may be a result of counting the same people.

28

Jungle Temples and the "Milk of Chaos"

AS I FLEW at low altitude over central Cambodia at the end of the rainy season, the land looked like a sheet of translucent and veiny green silk, a fragile fiber of earth whose watery rice panels reflected the plane as it moved across the sky. The forty-five-minute journey from Phnom Penh in the southeast to Siem Reap in the northwest revealed Cambodia as one vast floodplain of recession agriculture, where, as in ancient Egypt, the withdrawal of the waters allowed for the tilling of newly deposited alluvium. The utter flatness of this water-logged landscape made it impossible to tell where the Great Lake began and ended. There was no real shoreline: The checkerboard of paddy fields simply retreated deeper and deeper into the water until it disappeared. Thus, as a layman, I had no way of measuring the silting up of the Great Lake that I had heard so much about.[1] The trip by land from Phnom Penh should take about eight hours. But no Westerners were attempting it. The danger was caused not

[1]Siltation rates in the Great Lake are thought to have doubled in recent years, according to the Cambodian Department of Fisheries. As a result, the northwest corner of the Great Lake, over which my plane flew, has narrowed by 5 kilometers, from 40 kilometers to 35.

so much by the Khmer Rouge as by the government soldiers manning the roadblocks.

The town of Siem Reap, situated at the northwest extremity of the Great Lake, lay a few miles south of the old Khmer capital of Angkor.[2] Angkor had been the hub of a medieval kingdom that included present-day Cambodia and parts of Thailand, Laos, and Vietnam. At its zenith, the Angkorian empire boasted a population of 30 million, supported by a highly sophisticated network of reservoirs and irrigation canals. The empire was founded by a Javanese prince, Jayavarman II, in 790 A.D. Java was strongly influenced by the culture of Indian seafarers. And India's artistic precepts, in addition to its god-king mythology, which was woven into Hinduism, held great sway over early Khmer culture. Hinduism was supplanted by Buddhism in Angkor, perhaps late in the twelfth century, after an invasion by people from what is today central Vietnam. Angkor recovered, and the empire lasted until 1431, when it was sacked by Siamese. Thailand's artistic roots are, in fact, Cambodian.

From the ground, the landscape looked like a copper engraving as sunlight met the yellow dust kicked up by bicycles, water buffaloes, and armed military convoys. Here in rural Cambodia, the faces seemed more stoical than in Phnom Penh: Rather than smiling forest-spirits, I saw a succession of what looked like bronze Buddha statues riding by me on bicycles. During the 1970–75 civil war, government forces were holed up in Siem Reap while the Khmer Rouge lived in the ruins of the great medieval temples a few miles away. In 1975, the Khmer Rouge evacuated Siem Reap's inhabitants. After the Vietnamese drove the Khmer Rouge back into the forests in 1979, the surrounding area became the scene of periodic fighting. Siem Reap, as a consequence, was a traveler's paradise from the days before mass tourism. The wanton destruction and suffering had precluded several decades of development. In the 1950s, a British writer described Siem Reap as "a pleasant, sun-baked, sleepy cluster of buildings nestling beside a rivulet."[3] It was the same in the mid-1990s, with a primitive airport, dirt roads, no computers, intermittent electricity, and a grand hotel whose seedy rattan interior was decorated with out-of-focus tourist posters. All it lacked was Frenchmen with pith helmets on the porch swatting away flies. The quaintness of Siem Reap was part of the Cambodian tragedy.

---

[2]*Angkor* means "great" or "the capital."
[3]See Malcolm MacDonald in the bibliography.

LY SARITH DISPELLED this impression of timelessness. "Much has changed here since 1992. Since the UN came, there have been more visitors and better security. The UN did a lot for us." Ly's voice was squeaky and breathless: a high-pitched cackle. He looked and talked like someone who had, only seconds before, seen a ghost. Fright and pain were etched permanently on his stiffened face. Ly was tall for a Cambodian, with a sad and gawky Lincolnesque appearance, and a mole on his right cheek. He was born in Siem Reap in 1960. His foster father was a police officer. In 1975 the Khmer Rouge evacuated him and his foster father, along with everyone else in town, to a work camp about forty miles east of here. "I saw my father killed there."

I was silent, then I asked awkwardly, without thinking really, "What did you do in the camp?"

Tears slowly began to roll down Ly's face. His body shook uncontrollably in a few shivers. I had only met Ly an hour earlier and he was crying before my eyes. It was at that moment that the reality of what had happened between 1975 and 1979 in Cambodia sank in.

Trauma was the ghost haunting everyday Cambodian life. A significant sector of the population suffered from some level of war- and torture-related psychological illness. But unlike AIDS or illiteracy or deforestation, it couldn't be quantified, so it was often overlooked.

More of Ly's story would slip out over the coming days. For now, though, he was silent.

IN THE HOTEL, in the airline office, on the street, in the dingy restaurants with greasy food and no air-conditioning, people always bowed and smiled. If they so much as touched me, they bowed and smiled again. They seemed so shy and embarrassed. There was an abstract, antiphysical aspect to East Asia that struck me as the cultural flip side of West Africa. Yet Cambodian history was certainly filled with as much violence as West African history. As I said, the effect of culture was more a mystery to me near the end of my planetary journey than at the beginning.

Ly drove north through a potholed road, pointing out the dividing line between government-controlled territory and Khmer Rouge territory during the 1970–75 civil war. Until 1970, he told me, the area was old growth forest populated by gibbons. The fighting had destroyed it all.

The entire complex of medieval ruins in the Angkor region constitutes, arguably, the greatest surviving wonder of the old world: more remote than the Pyramids, the Acropolis, or the Taj Mahal, and equally spectacular.

It was early, so we bypassed the great temple of Angkor Wat itself, preferring to see it in the late afternoon, when the sunlight reflected on its grand entranceway. Instead, Ly headed for Angkor Thom, or the "Great City." After driving for several minutes through dense, secondary growth forest we reached a jungly vista of tall gum trees and clouds of dragonflies. Water buffaloes browsed through the bushes. An old Cambodian woman with a straw hat slept in a hammock. A girl, the woman's daughter or granddaughter perhaps, sold fuzzy postcards from a wooden table. The sounds of crickets and parakeets filled the sky. Before us, though, dwarfing human beings out of all proportion, were seventy sandstone colossi, about thirty-five demons lining one side of a bridge leading to the entrance of the medieval city, and thirty-five gods on the other side. These turbaned sandstone giants, each blotched with lichen, were pulling on the elongated body of the "cosmic serpent," or Naga, which serves as a kind of butter churn—separating out the solid world and its social structures from the mythical "milk of chaos."[4]

Each colossus was slightly different from the others and this gave the impression of constant movement, or pulling, on the cosmic serpent. They had been built in the eleventh century by King Udayadityavarman II, and may have been renovated in the late twelfth and early thirteenth century by Jayavarman VII. Some of the giants were without heads. Others had had their heads replaced with cement replicas. "Thais and Khmer Rouge come at night," Ly told me. "They take the heads to antique dealers." To prevent more thefts, the archaeological site is now sown with antipersonnel mines in the evening and de-mined in the morning. We crossed the bridge and climbed the earthen ramparts on the opposite bank, looking out over the moat filled with white water-lilies, where ancient Khmer warriors had aimed their crossbows at invaders. In my mind, I confused the ancient warriors with the Khmer Rouge, who had also occupied these temples and dressed similarly, with kerchiefs around their heads.

---

[4]The imagery is based on a Hindu myth popular among Khmer kings. See Rawson's *The Art of Southeast Asia*, listed in the bibliography.

Beyond the Street of Giants that served as the entrance to Angkor Thom came another one thousand meters of forest road before the three-tiered pyramid of the Bayon temple rose before me. Bayon, like almost all of the major monuments in the Angkor region, is a product of the twelfth-century golden age of Khmer art and architecture. This gigantic dried-lava bubble of dense sandstone and basalt, seething with unreal fungal growths, was like a mad finger-drip castle made by a child at the beach and worn away by the tides. I thought also of a worm-eaten tower of charred bodies piled up to the sky. *Elaboration*, *concavity*, and *compression* were the words that came to mind: a baroque squeeze of artistic endeavor. Through massive, shaded corridors of black basalt Ly and I walked amid slick and shiny walls with finely cut relief carvings, a Grand Guignol of conquest and atrocity, including buffalo sacrifices and crocodiles eating their victims. How sharp and neat these ancient Khmer carvings were, as precise as the modern Thai countryside, even as the Cambodia of today was seedy, indistinct, and overgrown! At the end of one hallway, submerged in darkness, was an antechamber dominated by a coal-black sacral Buddha, draped in a bright orange silk robe with a burning candle stuck in its stone lap. Sharp incense overpowered the room. We passed through more ranked galleries. We were alone amid the fifty-four towers of Bayon.

Novemberish stone, dark tropical greenery, and bruise-gray cloud formations—the Cambodian landscape was a palette of caked oils. What would Gauguin have done with Angkor had he come here instead of Tahiti?

◉　　◉　　◉

ALONGSIDE THE TEMPLE were a few plywood drink stands. Sipping a Coca-Cola, Ly talked:

"They woke us every morning at four. Every dawn, loudspeakers screamed in our ears: '*Angka* calls. *Angka* calls to educate you.' *Angka* was 'the Organization.' That's what the Khmer Rouge called themselves. They were so secret, they didn't even use the word *communist*. When they called 'to educate you,' they meant that some of us were going to be killed in order to educate the others. Every morning they killed some people. It was the normal thing. They made you dig your grave, tied your hands, and beat you over the head with a hoe. All the killing was done by boys, thirteen to fifteen years old. These boys knew nothing except that Pol Pot told them we were the people who had bombed them in the forest. Every day I'm thinking I don't see the sunrise of the next day.

"After the education session we worked in the field until eleven-thirty. Then they allowed us to eat rice and water—standing up. Then more work."

◎   ◎   ◎

PRIOR TO ASSUMING power, the Khmer Rouge lived in these temples. They hunted gibbons for food with their AK-47s, contracted malaria among other illnesses, and survived. It was similar to what they were doing again in the mid-1990s, though further back in the forest. Sleeping at night amid these fantastic stones, which to educated and uneducated minds alike summon up vague notions of lost glory, and then going on to conquer Phnom Penh and the other Cambodian cities, must have infused the Khmer Rouge with a feeling of destiny, which helps explain their certainty that history could be forced, that the victims of their cruelty were mere details in a generally happy story. It could not be accidental that the three principal towers of Angkor Wat make up the Khmer Rouge emblem.

The era of Khmer Rouge domination and instability that followed in northwestern Cambodia enshrouded the temples of Angkor—and Angkor Wat, in particular—in mystery, similar to the shadow thrown by the Iranian revolution over the Gumbad-i-Qabus in northeastern Iran. Angkor Wat is not a lonely tower, though. It is the single largest religious building in the world, built by the Khmer king Suriyavarman II between 1113 and 1150 A.D. The compound comprising Angkor Wat is 960 meters—or over ten football fields—long and 800 meters wide. It is completely surrounded by a rectangular moat, nearly a mile long from west to east, and three quarters of a mile from north to south: the moat's entire length of almost four miles is lined with stone steps. King Suriyavarman ordered construction started on Angkor Wat from all four sides at once, so that this complex and galleried structure—almost four times the ground space of the Great Pyramid of Cheops and with almost as much stone, though here the stone is carefully dressed and ornamented—was completed in only thirty-seven years.

Angkor Wat is surrounded by a forest of sugar palms and some hardwoods. Naked children bathe in its giant moat, a vestige of the ancient water system that looks like a curdled skin of floating oil with white waterlilies poking out. There are a few beggars and humble eating houses made of unpainted plywood with benches, offering soft drinks and noodle dishes in crude bowls. All are dwarfed by the 220-meter stone causeway that merely gets one across the moat to Angkor Wat's half-mile-long black basalt retaining walls. There may be no horizontal vision of architectural grandeur to compare with what one sees while walking over this causeway, with the multitiered lotus towers of the pyramidal temple in the distance and the forest to one's back.

The retaining walls enclose long colonnades scented with incense and filled with statues of the Hindu pantheon. Here, I saw two saffron-robed Buddhist monks listening quietly to a flute player.[5] Carved deeply into these walls were bas-reliefs of *apsaras*: voluptuous female water spirits of Indian mythology, with large breasts and jewelry around their necks. On the other side of the retaining wall loomed the Wat and its towers, separated from me by several hundred meters of windy grassland, where dozens of cows and water buffaloes grazed near a lily pond. Angkor Wat appeared twice to my eyes, once in the distance and once reflected in the pond.

There are so many tiers, colonnades, interior hallways, carvings, and steep, monumental staircases—all as compressed and detailed as the miles of relief carvings that chronicle the countless wars—that after enough time, the architectural and historical facts dissolve into a welter of meaninglessness. The murder of 1 to 1.5 million people between 1975 and 1979 could be covered in just one stretch of stone, on one of the many long walls: ultimately forgotten except to analysts. And the process had already begun. I thought of the unknowing and insensitive Greek and Thai tourists at the killing field outside Phnom Penh. Perhaps *chaos* has a secondary meaning— as another word for history that can no longer be remembered and is no longer part of a pattern. *History*, after all, comes from a Greek word implying a "narrative": a sequence of events that fit into a thematic order. So when people say they "live in a historical age," what they really mean is that they live at a time when events occur in a comprehensible pattern.

Is ours a historical age? Or are we beyond history, because too much has happened and there is no longer a theme? Or is the theme hidden, and we are at the beginning of a passage to a new phase of history, when much of what now seems like mere chaos will become clear?

◎   ◎   ◎

LY DROVE OFF the road into a field where a few wooden houses stood on stilts in the traditional Cambodian style. Cattle used to sleep under the

[5]Angkor Wat was completed almost eight hundred fifty years ago, while Hinduism still held sway here, but eventually it became a Buddhist temple.

house, now Ly put his car there. He and his wife had five children. A sixth had fallen into a well and drowned. That was the tragedy that now burdened their lives. "Because of the UN, more Westerners feel it's all right to come here. So I am much in demand, because I speak English. I can save money for my family."

Next, Ly took me to a drab and modern cement wat on a lonely plain. The wat had an unpainted plywood door, which Ly pried open. A pile of crushed skulls and limbs lay inside. Some tumbled onto my feet. We carefully put them back inside. I noticed that the wire used to tie up the victims prior to their execution was still on the wristbones. I did my duty as a journalist and snapped a picture of Ly holding the door open with the skulls inside. On the picture, though, Ly's eyes are closed. (The sunlight was strong, I remember.) But that is how Ly's eyes appeared to me even when they were wide open: as if a veil had been drawn over them, on which the blackest of memories had been imprinted. There were no signs or tourist buses announcing this killing field, so it had not yet been desecrated.

2 9

◎   ◎   ◎

One Death at the Edge
of the Earth

NORTHEAST FROM PHNOM PENH, Kratie (pronounced KRAT-cheh) is the last navigable upriver port on the Mekong. Beyond Kratie a series of rapids makes the river impassable. A town of perhaps fifteen thousand inhabitants, it has been considered "insecure" ever since the first days of the Khmer Rouge insurgency in the early 1960s. Only sixty-five miles from the Vietnamese border, the area around Kratie was a western terminus for a feeder route of the Ho Chi Minh Trail system, making Kratie a victim of Nixon's undisclosed bombing campaign inside Cambodian territory in 1969. In 1972, Kratie became the first province taken by the Khmer Rouge during the Cambodian civil war. In 1973, the Americans invaded the area, looking for Vietnamese communist sanctuaries. At one time or another, the Kratie region—or at least a part of it—was held either by Sihanouk, Lon Nol, the Khmer Rouge, the Americans, the Viet Cong, or the South Vietnamese army. Because so many males were involved in the decades-long fighting, 60 percent of the two hundred thousand inhabitants of Kratie province are now women. In the mid-1990s, a significant number of villages in the area were still being held by the Khmer Rouge. Malaria, tuberculosis, diarrhea, dysentery, dengue fever, and schistosomiasis (bilharzia) are prevalent. So is illegal logging.

Ten young expats employed by four Western relief agencies, or NGOs, were living and working in Kratie in 1994. So the day after I returned to Phnom Penh from Angkor, I boarded a "fast boat" for the five-and-a-half-hour journey upriver.

Kratie's port area was just a stretch of dirt reaching out into the wide and muddy Mekong, where about two dozen wooden boats, similar to sampans, were moored. A series of rickety old planks led up the steep mud embankment. At the top was a French-designed provincial outpost composed of a gridwork of streets, fungal red tiles, peeling mustard-colored walls, and rusted metal siding. The roads were crowded with bicycles and old, backfiring motorbikes. I looked back at the brown river and saw barges laden with logs riding low in the water. Before the UN-sponsored election, all of the timber chopped down in the Kratie region had been taken to Vietnam; now, after the election, with more international business confidence in Cambodia, Malaysian and Singaporean businessmen had also come upriver to make deals, presumably with Khmer Rouge elements, to cut timber for export.

"Our biggest problem is rising crime and security," Pao Ham Phan, a deputy governor of the province told me. "The Khmer Rouge recently destroyed a school and a bridge. They come in at night through the forest. They can destroy any place, but they can't hold it for long. Because of the bad roads, it is difficult for the government and foreign relief agencies to operate beyond the town. There is not even a road to Phnom Penh yet. It takes six hours of dangerous driving just to travel eighty-three kilometers [fifty-two miles] to Snuol, southeast of here. So Snuol has better relations with Vietnam than with Kratie or any other town in Cambodia."

The deputy governor explained that the economic growth since the UN elections, coupled with the continued lack of paved roads in the countryside, has contributed to an increasing disparity in wealth between the town of Kratie and the surrounding villages. "But with rural development—roads, schools, potable water—we can gradually dry up the Khmer Rouge while at the same time increasing trade with both Phnom Penh and Vietnam." In other words, rather than being at the end of the line of communication with Phnom Penh, Kratie could henceforth be in the midst of a borderless prosperity sphere. And the key to this, the deputy governor insisted, "are the NGOs. They can make a big difference in drying up the Khmer Rouge."

CARE and the three other NGO organizations in Kratie had, at the moment, modest programs whose centerpiece was digging water wells. So far, the relief agencies had built 130 cement-covered "pump wells" in nearby and outlying villages. The wells cost only about one thousand dollars each. Yet their construction improved village life dramatically by supplying safe drinking water and reducing disease. The wells also made it unnecessary for villagers to walk long distances for river water. In Kratie, the wells were the first artillery bombardment in the NGOs' war against the Khmer Rouge.

The second bombardment was to be a schistosomiasis-vaccination program. The Khmer Rouge knew that this late-twentieth-century army of relief workers posed a greater challenge to its influence in the rural interior than did the Cambodian military. The more the expats accomplished, the more popular they became among the villagers. And in local political terms, that meant greater popularity for the democratically elected government, which was sponsoring the NGOs in the country. The expats, therefore, were a potential target of the Khmer Rouge, which, as the torture-murder of the three Western backpackers had made clear (not to mention the periodic kidnapping and murder of scores of Cambodian villagers), had an undiminished appetite for cruelty.

◎　　　◎　　　◎

"I'M NOW CONFINED to town because of the Khmer Rouge threats against me. They've told the villagers that they're interested in kidnapping a foreign relief worker. And now that we're entering the dry season, there will be more fighting," Jeannie lamented. An American, she was used to working twelve-hour days in the outlying villages, counseling and providing health care for rural women. Jeannie was a vegetarian who didn't believe in reading newspapers, watching television, or listening to the radio. She was in Cambodia taking such physical risks because she genuinely liked it. Her motives, actually, were no better or worse than those of many individuals who join a Western military service, then volunteer for combat duty. Rick, another young American in Kratie, was a geologist who came to Cambodia after three years of Peace Corps experience in a village in Mali, one of the hardest and loneliest countries in West Africa for expats to work in. He and Jeannie, while they took great risks, were not foolish or irresponsible. They told me the story of two British tourists who were.

"These two Brits told us they wanted to hitchhike from Kratie north to the Laotian border. I told them they were crazy," Jeannie said. "Well, they didn't listen and tried it anyway. They actually made it to the border, then were turned back, and hitched back to Kratie. When we saw them again, they had visibly aged. The whole trip had been a series of government roadblocks interspersed with Khmer Rouge blocks. The soldiers were often drunk and demanded money. In these types of situations, you're sometimes lucky if all they do is shoot you."

I had met Rick and Jeannie, along with a few other expats, in Kratie's best restaurant one Saturday night. The restaurant had fluorescent lights, peeling blue walls spotted with crawling lizards, flying cockroaches, and greasy food. But Kratie did have one luxury: an ice-making factory—so all the ice that local restaurants put in their soft drinks was made of purified water. The ice factory also distributed electricity at a reasonable price to nearby houses, where some of the expats lived.

Dinner discussion among the expats centered around what video they were going to watch later. The videos were all pirated copies, often of extremely low technical quality, but as Gustl Stich, an expat from Germany, told me, "We get very excited over the Saturday night video because it's one of the little things that make life here tolerable."

Gustl, like Rick, had also worked in Africa. "Cambodia is different," Gustl said. "Here you have an old writing system and a rich, highly complex, and ancient culture, Buddhism, that can compete with Christianity, Judaism, and Islam head-on. But it is still so dangerous, even more than Africa. I had to send my wife and son back to Phnom Penh for a while because we had been threatened by the Khmer Rouge. The threats have stopped for the time being, so my family is back with me. But my son now has dysentery. I am a medical doctor, so I know how to treat my son and I know exactly how sick he is. But this doesn't make me more secure about him. You know, when it's your kid you want the best facilities available."

As I drank Coke with filtered ice cubes, it occurred to me that these people around the table were the international army of the future. They put up with far worse conditions, and in many cases more physical danger, than do increasingly pampered Western troops, whom the Western public and politicians are more and more reluctant to expose to real physical risk.

And, as Western militaries look for hot spots that offer the possibility of easy victory with few casualties, relief workers are filling the vacuum.

◎　　　◎　　　◎

GUSTL, THE GERMAN expat, ran the local hospital in Kratie on behalf of the Swiss and Dutch branches of the French organization *Médecins Sans Frontieres* (Doctors Without Borders): The whole arrangement showed the increasingly multinational quality of the foreign relief community, in which one's own national identity is coming to mean less and less. Gustl lived with his wife and toddler—the one with dysentery—in a traditional Cambodian wood-frame house on stilts along the Mekong River. As I sat on Gustl's porch in the late afternoon, the river passed by like a stick of grease. Living here had its difficulties. The roaches gave no relief, so that even tightly capped condiments like sugar, salt, and instant coffee had to be kept in the refrigerator rather than on the counter. Loaves of bread had to stand in the refrigerator, too, or hang from somewhere; they could never be left on a flat surface, not even inside a bag.

At dusk I put on mosquito repellent against the "malaria vectors" from a nearby swamp. Then Gustl and I set out for the hospital he ran. Pao Ham Phan, the deputy governor, had been enthusiastic about the hospital: "Before the NGOs came, nobody wanted to stay in the hospital. It was like a jail. Now three hundred people per month use it." But Gustl was hesitant about showing it to me.

"Have you ever seen a third world hospital?" he asked.

"Yes, of course," I replied.

"Then you know what to expect, what to compare it to?"

"Yes," I replied again.

I understood perfectly what he meant. Even a well-maintained third world hospital would be a shock to most Westerners. For example, in Snuol, the town near the Vietnamese border that took six hours of dangerous driving to reach, the hospital consisted of a one-room shack made out of rusted iron and mildewed walls. The bed frames were also rusted and lacked mattresses. There was no electricity or running water. Water was fetched for the patients from an open oil drum surrounded by mosquitoes.

By those standards—standards that I had gotten used to in almost two decades of reporting from the third world—Gustl's hospital was a dramatic improvement in local conditions. Rather than bare bed frames, there were reed mats and coarse burlap blankets, though no mattresses. Nurses were always on duty—a rarity in the third world. Intravenous quinine solutions were available to fight cerebral malaria. There was running water for the patients, and the floors were mopped regularly. Most significantly, there was a Western physician, Gustl, in charge, overseeing a Cambodian staff trained in Western medical techniques. As a result of these improvements, the hospital's occupancy rate had risen by 1,000 percent.

Of course, the hospital had no regular electric current, and no X-ray machine yet. At night, a generator provided enough power for necessary surgical procedures, and for one lightbulb per ward from 6 to 10 P.M. Theft of equipment was a problem. The staff of three doctors was down from seven, since the bad security situation involving the Khmer Rouge made it difficult to attract Cambodian doctors. There was no air-conditioning, which meant that in the year-round tropical heat, mosquitoes, cockroaches, and awful smells abounded. Pigs and water buffaloes grazed and townspeople made cooking fires only a few feet from the intensive care ward, whose door had to be left open to allow breezes inside. In the rainy season, flood water approaches the hospital doors. The intensive care ward was distinguished from the rest of the hospital by a lone and rusted oxygen tank. As night descended and dragonflies entered the wards, it was the very averageness of this hospital that was so shocking: For the majority of the people on this planet—and for the vast majority of Africans—this is what they come to when they are seriously ill, if they are lucky. Thirty percent of the earth's inhabitants have no access to any health care whatsoever; 50 percent have no toilet to use.[1]

Those percentages are growing: The industrialized countries, which accounted for 40 percent of the world's population after World War II, now account for only 20 percent, though they earn 85 percent of the world's income. In coming decades, the industrialized world is expected to make up only 12 to 15 percent of the planetary population,[2] as 90 to 95 percent of all births take place in the poorest countries. The fact that this is happening at a time when income and life expectancy rates worldwide

[1] These figures, from the World Bank and other sources, were provided by Professor Joel Cohen of Rockefeller University in New York City, an expert on third world development and demographic problems.
[2] See Jessica Mathews's "Immigration and the Press of the Poor," listed in the bibliography.

are moving up illustrates just how uneven this material growth has been, and how what is really growing is the disparity between rich and poor.[3]

Never before—not at the time of various democratic revolutions in Central Europe in 1848 or at the conclusion of World War I—has wealth disparity been so great as after the Cold War. And never before, because of the global communications revolution, has this disparity been so visible. The human race is like an awkward adolescent whose political and social mechanisms are not keeping up with his physical growth.

◎   ◎   ◎

AS NIGHT FELL in the intensive care ward, I could hear deep, struggling breaths. I could see big and beautiful dark eyes shining through the shafts of dust in the half light of declining dusk as mosquitoes whined in my ears. I saw the alert eyes of a young girl about ten years old. She was covered by coarse burlap. Her darting eyes showed how desperately she was trying to follow the conversation between Gustl and me, though English was unintelligible to her. "In this case," Gustl was saying, "the TB is too far advanced. This child will probably die within a few days. There is little we can do except keep her as comfortable as we can, under the circumstances." Again, it was the squalid normalcy of the situation that hurt. For too much of humanity, this was a typical child dying of a typical disease—tuberculosis—in a typical hospital ward, in a typical provincial outpost with guerrilla insurgents in a forest not very far away.[4]

◎   ◎   ◎

FORTY-EIGHT HOURS later, after taking the fast boat back to Phnom Penh and then a plane to Bangkok, I was inside Bangkok's international airport, en route to North America, amid shops selling luxury apparel. Television monitors in the departure lounge were broadcasting the November 1994 U.S. election results on CNN.

On the plane, I wondered about what it all proved—that girl, my journey from Sierra Leone to Cambodia? I could have watched a homeless person die of TB a few blocks from a pricy restaurant in Manhattan. I didn't have to come to Southeast Asia to see suffering and disparity.

---

[3]The rich nations of the industrialized world consume 70 percent of the planet's energy, 75 percent of its metals, and 85 percent of its wood, according to the UN.
[4]One out of five people in the world are infected with the tuberculosis bacterium, even if they do not have the disease.

That girl is, of course, far more typical of Cambodia than a homeless person is of America: Cambodia is a world leader in the prevalence of TB, whereas the U.S., despite a resurgence of the disease, barely rates on the charts. And while there is only one physician for every 18,518 Cambodians, in the U.S. the figure is one for every 389.[5]

Nevertheless, many of the problems I saw around the world—poverty, the collapse of cities, porous borders, cultural and racial strife, growing economic disparities, weakening nation-states—are problems for Americans to think about. I thought of America everywhere I looked. We cannot escape from a more populous, interconnected world of crumbling borders.

We woke up late to the European disorder that erupted in 1914 and again in the 1930s. The Cold War, a tailpiece of World War II, kept us involved overseas. But many tens of thousands of people or more were murdered, and a million or more forced out of their homes, a few hours' drive from Vienna in the early 1990s and we have done little until recently. When we awake it won't only be Europe that we'll have to confront, but a wider world, bearing, perhaps, a more amorphous terror than what we confronted in the two world wars: disease pandemics like AIDS, environmental catastrophes, organized crime that will have advanced its borders to, for instance, the failed states of West Africa, where government security structures are collapsing, and so on. Or, the threat might be more insidious: future crises beyond our borders—in South Africa and Mexico, for instance—that sharpen ethnic and economic fissures at home. The boozy soldiers in Sierra Leone and the girl dying of tuberculosis in Cambodia are closer than we think.

But I would be unfaithful to my experience if I thought we had a general solution to these problems. *We are not in control.* As societies grow more populous and complex, the idea that a global elite like the UN can engineer reality from above is just as absurd as the idea that political "scientists" can reduce any of this to a *science*. And as the tax base of the West stagnates and populations climb (though more slowly) in the third world, foreign aid will make even less of a difference in coming decades. Besides, in an age of localized *mini*-holocausts, decisive action in one sphere will not necessarily help the victims in another. People will either solve or alleviate their problems at the local level, as in Rishi Valley, or they won't.

[5]These figures are available in the *Britannica Book of the Year 1995.*

The many factors at work in Rishi Valley will replicate themselves only rarely. And only in a few cases will an organization like the UN make a truly pivotal difference.

On the plane, I was overwhelmed by the complexity and apparent hopelessness of what I had seen. But isn't this the way the world has always been? The great ages of virtue are few and far between. Athens's Golden Age barely exceeded a lifetime. In *The Decline and Fall of the Roman Empire*, Edward Gibbon wrote that for the empire's inhabitants, a "happy period" lasted only from the ascension, in 98 A.D., of Trajan, a talented civic administrator, to the death of the socially progressive emperor Marcus Aurelius eighty-two years later. Then—as before that happy interlude—came many wearisome centuries of violence and chaos.[6] The Cold War years may have been such an interlude for Europe, even as it clouded our view of the themeless violence occurring elsewhere in the world that we now focus on.

Of course, all analysts, including myself, are eventually proven wrong. Solutions to specific problems I encountered in my journey will someday arise: population growth, even in West Africa, will flatten out; ingenious ways to restore the soil will be found; and so on. But if the past is any guide, in too many places there will be a time lag between extreme social deterioration and strategies which might have prevented it. The long-range future may be bright, but the next few decades will be tumultuous. Keep in mind that the collapse of just a few small countries scattered around the globe has overwhelmed policymakers in the West. Were a major regional power to dissolve somewhere, we would have no answers. Americans, because of our own history, tend to see optimistic scenarios in places where endings have rarely been happy. But the banal truth is that economic and social development is generally cruel, painful, violent, and uneven—and humanity is developing more dramatically than ever before.

As a species, we can imagine justice and harmony. But how can justice and harmony be possible for much of humanity, given the evidence of history, plus the inflamatory potential of a fourfold increase in population since the nineteenth century, with antennas rising from mudhuts that allow the poor to see how the rich live? To escape the world is folly—we tried that before each world war. As AIDS shows, Africa's climate and

[6]Another exception may be the relatively peaceful rule of Caesar Augustus, from 31 B.C., to 14 A.D.

poverty beget disease that finds its ways to the wealthiest suburbs. We are the world and the world is us.

THE MORE I saw of the world, the less I felt I could fit it into a pattern. No one can foresee the precise direction of history, and no nation or people is safe from its wrath. Earlier in my journey, upon descending the Karakoram Highway, Keats had urged me to be "content with half-knowledge." Now, at the end of my journey, drifting asleep in the plane, I heard the poet again:

> And other spirits . . . are standing apart
> Upon the forehead of the age to come;
> These, these will give the world another heart,
> And other pulses. Hear ye not the hum
> Of mighty workings?—
> Listen awhile ye nations, and be dumb.[7]

---

[7]From the poem "Addressed to Haydon." Benjamin Robert Haydon was a painter and writer whom Keats greatly admired.

ACKNOWLEDGEMENTS

As with my previous books, this one began as a project for *The Atlantic Monthly*. Cullen Murphy and Bill Whitworth at *The Atlantic* nursed me along, from one idea to another. Then Jason Epstein at Random House brought me back to ground level, providing the kind of painstaking criticism and line editing that is less common in the book industry than it used to be.

Dr. Richard Shain, an assistant professor of African history at the Philadelphia College of Textiles and Science—who taught for several years in the Nigerian university system—corrected the West African section of the book. Large parts of the Egypt section were checked by the staff of *The Atlantic Monthly*. Bulent Ali Reza of the Center for Strategic and International Studies in Washington checked the Turkey and Azerbaijan sections. Edward Shirley, the pseudonym of a Persian-speaking analyst, formerly at the Central Intelligence Agency, checked the chapters on Iran. Martha Brill Olcott, a professor at Colgate University, went over the chapters on Central Asia. Barbara Crossette, a *New York Times* correspondent in South and Southeast Asia, went over the chapters related to those areas. For further research assistance, I am indebted to Joy de Menil at Random House, Peter Gizewski, Val Percival, and Jane Willms at the University of Toronto, to Craig Johnson at the International Development Research Centre in Ottawa, and to Amy Meeker and Eric Haas at *The Atlantic Monthly*. Mistakes that remain, along with all the interpretations expressed in the text, are mine alone.

My literary agent, Carl Brandt, worked from the beginning to garner support for this work. I thank Klaus Schwab, Maria Livanos Cattaui, and Elizabeth Haefner of the World Economic Forum in Davos, Switzerland, for putting me in touch with scholars and diplomats who stimulated my thinking and helped me in my travels. More stimulation came from the School of Advanced Military Studies at Fort Leavenworth, Kansas: I thank the Chief of the United States Army, General Gordon Sullivan, and Professor Robert Berlin. Michael Vlahos of the Center for Naval Analysis in Washington was also helpful. A seminar organized by the World Policy Institute in New York provided me with constructive criticism of my ideas as they emerged.

This book could not have been completed without financial assistance from the United States Institute of Peace in Washington, administered through the Foreign Policy Research Institute in Philadelphia. For this, I especially thank Ken Jensen, Alan Luxenberg, and Harvey Sicherman. The Olin Institute for Strategic Studies at Harvard University administered another grant and arranged seminars where, thanks to Professor Samuel P. Huntington, scholars could offer me sound criticism.

In West Africa, Ambassador and Mrs. Hume Horan supplied insights and hospitality. I am also indebted to Chuck Cecil and Fidel Blay-Mackey. On Egyptian matters, I thank Mohammed El Dakhakhny, Barbara Epstein, Shafik M. Gabr, Michael Georgi, Chris Hedges, Philip Eagleton, Judith Miller, and Tim Sullivan. Regarding Turkey, I thank Gunay Evinch, Yucel Guldag, Ayse Hersek, Reza Deghati, Bob Poole, and Erla Zwingle. Regarding Iran, I thank Zorz Crmaric, John Fox, Steve Grummon, Edward Shirley, and Hashi Syedain.

Kathy Gannon appeared in Pakistan to help me once again, as she did for my book on Afghanistan seven years back. The best thing about researching books is the friends you make along the way. Others who helped me in my Central Asian travels include Doug Bakshian, Naeem Pasha, Ahmed Rashid, Alexei Shlykov, and Anna Terterian.

Concerning India, I thank Radhika Herzberger, A. Kumaraswamy, Patabi Ram, and M. S. Sailendran. For Thai, Laotian, and Cambodian matters, I thank Peter Gajewesky, Judith Gilmore, Bruce Hills, Sally and Frank Light, Nuth Ly, Robert J. Muscat, Glenis Rutledge, Parachai Satasuk, Eric Seldin, Pichayaporn Utumporn, James E. Vermillion, Tony Zola, and particularly Dan Robinson, an old friend from Ethiopia.

For encouragement of a more general kind, I thank Yehuda Mirsky at the Washington Institute for Near East Policy and Matthew Rees of *The Wall Street Journal Europe* for sending me relevant clippings, and my wife, Maria Cabral, for providing a wonderful home environment in which to work. Thanks also to Avril Cornel, Debi Hoffenberg, Amy Levine, Lucie Prinz, Yvonne Rolzhausen, Jack Beatty, and the rest of *The Atlantic Monthly* staff in Boston. More thanks go to Alison Humes at *Condé Nast Traveler*, and to Veronica Windholtz at Random House for copy editing the entire manuscript.

Ambassadors Jane Coon and Carleton Coon, Jr. provided advice of the kind that comes from years of living experience in some of the most troubled regions of the planet. Ambassador Herbert S. Okun made me aware of Laurence Sterne's *A Sentimental Journey*. Indeed, I need to pay homage to the officers of the United States Foreign Service. Wherever I went, without exception, American diplomats provided me with assistance, despite the fact that my published writings have sometimes made their lives more difficult.

BIBLIOGRAPHY

Articles and Books

Abramowitz, Morton. "Pol Pot's Best Pal: Thailand." *The Washington Post*, May 29, 1994.

Ajami, Fouad. *The Arab Predicament: Arab Political Thought and Practice Since 1967*. New York: Cambridge University Press, 1981.

Allworth, Edward A. *The Modern Uzbeks*. Stanford, Calif.: Hoover Institution Press, 1990.

Anderson, Benedict. *Imagined Communities: Reflections on the Origin and Spread of Nationalism*. New York: Verso, 1983.

Anderson, John Ward. "Poor vs. Rich in Indian State." *The Washington Post*, February 2, 1994.

Anderson, John Ward, and Khan, Kamran. "Heroin Plan by Top Pakistanis Alleged." *The Washington Post*, September 12, 1994.

Applebaum, Anne. *Between East and West: Across the Borderlands of Europe*. New York: Pantheon Books, 1994.

Ash, John. *A Byzantine Journey*. New York: Random House, 1995.

Asiyo, Phoebe. "What We Want: Voices from the South." Presented at the National Council on International Health Conference. Arlington, Va., June 23–26, 1991.

Ayittey, George B. N. "Whose God Will Save Nigeria?" *International Strategies*, February/March 1993.

Ayliffe, Rosie; Dubin, Marc; and Gawthrop, John. *The Real Guide: Turkey.* New York: Prentice Hall Press, 1991.

Babur Padshah, Zahirud-din Muhammad. *Babur-nama*, trans. Annette S. Beveridge. Lahore, Pakistan: Sange Meel Publications, 1987.

Bacon, Francis. *The Works of Francis Bacon*, ed. J. Spedding, R. L. Ellis, and D. D. Heath. New York: 1869.

Bagis, Ali Ihsan. *GAP Southeastern Anatolia Project: The Cradle of Civilisation Regenerated.* Istanbul: Interbank, 1989.

Bakhash, Shaul. "Prisoners of the Ayatollah." *The New York Review of Books*, April 11, 1994.

Baoxia, Zhu. "Polluters Warned of Criminal Penalties." *China Daily*, June 6, 1994.

Barnett, A. Doak. *China's Far West: Four Decades of Change.* Boulder, Colo.: Westview Press, 1993.

Barq, Sultan Ali. "Kalabagh Dam." *The Nation*, December 14, 1990.

Benjamin, Walter. *Illuminations.* London: Fontana, 1973.

Berkeley, Bill. "Liberia: Between Repression and Slaughter." *The Atlantic Monthly*, December 1992.

Bernier, Nichole. "Do You Need That Shot?" *Condé Nast Traveler*, January 1994.

Bit, Seanglim. *The Warrior Heritage: A Psychological Perspective of Cambodian Trauma.* El Cerrito, Calif.: 1991.

The Book of Dede Korkut, trans. Geoffrey Lewis. New York: Penguin, 1974.

Bonner, Raymond. "Why All Eyes Are on a Place Called Tajikistan." *The New York Times*, November 7, 1993.

Boonchalaksi, Wathinee, and Guest, Philip. *Prostitution in Thailand.* Bangkok: Institute for Population and Social Research, 1994.

Bordewich, Fergus M. *Cathay: A Journey in Search of Old China.* New York: Prentice Hall Press, 1991.

Bradnock, Robert. *South Asian Handbook.* New York: Prentice Hall, 1992.

Bremmer, Ian. "Minority Rules." *The New Republic*, April 11, 1994.

Brown, Janet Welsh. *In the U.S. Interest: Resources, Growth, and Security in the*

Developing World. See chapter "Dimensions of National Security: The Case of Egypt," by Nazli Choucri, Janet Welsh Brown, and Peter M. Haas. Boulder, Colo.: Westview Press, 1990.

Brown, Lester R. *State of the World 1993.* New York: Norton and Worldwatch Institute, 1993.

———. "How China Could Starve the World." *The Washington Post*, August 28, 1994.

Buck, Pearl S. *The Good Earth.* New York: John Day, 1931.

Burton, Richard Francis. *Wanderings in West Africa.* London: Tinsley Brothers, 1863 (Mineola, N.Y.: Dover, 1991).

Butterfield, Fox. *China: Alive in the Bitter Sea.* New York: Random House, 1982.

Buttimer, Anne. *Geography and the Human Spirit.* Baltimore: Johns Hopkins University Press, 1993.

Byers, Bruce. "Ecoregions, State Sovereignty and Conflict." *Bulletin of Peace Proposals.* London: Sage Publications, 1991.

Byron, Robert. *The Road to Oxiana.* The Estate of Robert Byron, London: Picador, 1937 (reprinted 1981).

Cambodia/Laos. Munich: Nelles Verlag, 1994.

Canetti, Elias. *Crowds and Power*, trans. Carol Stewart. London: Victor Gollancz Ltd., 1962.

Carol, Jacqueline. *Cocktails and Camels.* New York: Appleton-Century-Crofts, 1960.

Carothers, J. C. *The Mind of Man in Africa.* London: Tom Stacey, Ltd., 1972.

Carson, Rachel. *Silent Spring.* Boston: Houghton Mifflin, 1962.

Cavafy, C. P. *Collected Poems*, trans. Edmund Keeley and Philip Sherrard; ed. George Savidis. Princeton, N.J.: Princeton University Press, 1975.

Céline, Louis-Ferdinand. *Journey to the End of the Night*, trans. Ralph Manheim. New York: New Directions (1934) 1983.

Chamier, Captain. *Life of a Sailor.* No other information is available; mentioned in Burton's *Wanderings in West Africa*, listed above.

Chandler, David P. *The Tragedy of Cambodian History: Politics, War and Revolution Since 1945.* New Haven, Conn.: Yale University Press, 1991.

Chatwin, Bruce. Introduction to Robert Byron's *The Road to Oxiana*. London: Picador, 1981.

Chitty, Derwas. *The Desert a City*. Oxford, England: Oxford University Press, 1966.

Clay, Jason W., and Holcomb, Bonnie K. *Politics and the Ethiopian Famine 1984–1985*. Cambridge, Mass.: Cultural Survival, 1986.

Coll, Steve. "Environment Going Down 'Big Drain': Africa in the 1990s." *The Washington Post*, August 15, 1994.

———. *On the Grand Trunk Road*. New York: Times Books, 1994.

———. "Turkey's Dire Strait." *The Washington Post*, June 14, 1993.

Condorcet, Marquis de. *Sketch for a Historical Picture of the Progress of the Human Mind*. 1795.

Connelly, Matthew, and Kennedy, Paul. "Must It Be the Rest Against the West?" *The Atlantic Monthly*, December 1994.

Conquest, Robert. *The Harvest of Sorrow: Soviet Collectivization and the Terror-Famine*. New York: Oxford University Press, 1986.

Conrad, Joseph. *The Nigger of the "Narcissus."* 1897. Introduction by Cedric Watts. London: Penguin, 1963.

———. *Lord Jim*. 1900. Edited by Robert Hampson; introduction by Cedric Watts. Middlesex, England: Penguin Classics, 1986.

Cooley, John K. "The War Over Water." *Foreign Policy*, Spring 1984.

Coon, Carleton Stevens, Sr. *Caravan: The Story of the Middle East*. New York: Henry Holt and Company, 1951.

Critchlow, James. "Land of the Great Silk Road." *The Wilson Quarterly*, Summer 1992.

———. *Nationalism in Uzbekistan*. Boulder, Colo.: Westview Press, 1991.

Crossette, Barbara. *India Facing the Twentieth Century*. Bloomington, Ind.: University of Indiana Press, 1993.

Cummings, Joe; Storey, Robert; Strauss, Robert; Buckley, Michael; and Samagalski, Alan. *China: A Travel Survival Kit*. Berkeley, Calif.: Lonely Planet Publications, 1991.

Curtin, Philip D. *The Image of Africa*. Madison, Wis.: University of Wisconsin Press, 1964.

Curzon, George Nathaniel. *Curzon's Persia*, ed., with introduction, Peter King. London: Sidgwick & Jackson (1892) 1986.

Danner, Mark. "The Truth of El Mozote." *The New Yorker*, December 6, 1993.

Dantzig, Albert van. *Forts and Castles of Ghana*. Accra, Ghana: Sedco Publishing Limited, 1980.

Davidson, Basil. *Africa: History of a Continent*. London: Spring Books, 1966.

Davie, Michael. *In the Future Now*. London: Hamish Hamilton, 1972.

Defoe, Daniel. *A Journal of the Plague Year*. 1722. Introduction by Anthony Burgess. London: Penguin Books, 1966.

Desowitz, Robert S. *The Malaria Capers: Tales of Parasites and People*. New York: W. W. Norton, 1991, 1993.

Deudney, Daniel. "Global Environmental Rescue and the Emergence of World Domestic Politics." Chapter-Monograph. Unpublished.

———. "Bringing Nature Back In: Concepts, Problems, and Trends in Physiopolitical Theory from the Greeks to the Greenhouse." A University of Pennsylvania monograph presented at the Annual Convention of the American Political Science Association, Washington, D.C., 1993.

Douglas, William O. *Beyond the High Himalayas*. New York: Doubleday, 1952.

Drakulic, Slavenka. "Lav Story: Romania's Dirty Little Secret." *The New Republic*, April 25, 1994.

Dreiser, Theodore. *Sister Carrie*. New York: Doubleday, Page, 1900.

Duncan, Emma. "India: Hello, World." *The Economist*, January 21, 1995.

Dupree, Lous. *Afghanistan's Big Gamble, Part II: The Economic and Strategic Aspects of Soviet Aid*. N.H.: American Universities Field Staff Reports, Hanover, 1960.

The Economist. "China's Communists: The road from Tiananmen," June 4, 1994.

———. "Requiem for Karachi," August 13, 1994.

———. "Growing and Growing," October 3, 1992.

Ekachai, Sanitsuda. *Behind the Smile: Voices of Thailand*. Bangkok: Thai Development Support Committee, 1990.

Encyclopaedia Britannica, Eleventh Edition. New York: Encyclopaedia Britannica, Inc., 1910.

————. Chicago: William Benton, Publisher, 1963 edition.

Eren, Nuri. "Gengis Khan's Mercenaries?" *Turkish Daily News.*

Evans, Ruth. "Tanzania: Pride and Prejudice." *Focus on Africa* (London), July–September, 1993.

Faksh, Mahmud A. "Withered Arab Nationalism." *Orbis* (Philadelphia), Summer 1993.

Faulkner, William. *Go Down, Moses.* New York: Random House, 1940, 1942.

Fenton, James. *Children in Exile: Poems 1968–1984.* New York: Farrar Straus Giroux, 1994.

Feshbach, Murray, and Friendly, Alfred Jr. *Ecocide in the USSR: Health and Nature Under Siege.* New York: Basic Books, 1992.

Firdausi. *The Shah Nameh,* trans. James Atkinson. Teheran: Sahab Geographic & Drafting Institute, 1990.

Frater, Alexander. *Chasing the Monsoon.* New York: Henry Holt, 1990.

Frazer, James. *The Golden Bough: A Study in Magic and Religion.* New York: Macmillan, 1922.

Fukuyama, Francis. *The End of History and the Last Man.* New York: The Free Press, 1992.

Fussell, Paul. *Abroad: British Literary Traveling Between the Wars.* New York: Oxford University Press, 1980.

Gee, Marcus. "Apocalypse Deferred." *The Globe and Mail* (Toronto), April 9, 1994.

Geyer, Georgie Anne. "Our Disintegrating World: The Menace of Global Anarchy." *1985 Britannica Book of the Year.* Chicago: Encyclopedia Britannica, 1985.

————. *Waiting for Winter to End: An Extraordinary Journey Through Soviet Central Asia.* Washington, D.C.: Brassey's, 1994.

Gibbon, Edward. *The Decline and Fall of the Roman Empire*; introduction by Hugh Trevor-Roper. New York: Knopf, 1993.

Gizewski, Peter. "Rapid Urbanization and Violence: Will the Future Resemble the Past?" Pew Global Stewardship Initiative. Washington, D.C., 1994.

Gladney, Dru C. "The Ethnogenesis of the Uighur." Central Asian Survey, London, 1990.

Goldstone, Jack A. *Revolution and Rebellion in the Early Modern World.* Berkeley: University of California Press, 1991.

———. "Imminent Political Conflicts Arising from China's Population Crisis." Working Paper for the Pew Global Stewardship Initiative. Washington, D.C., 1994.

———. "Population Growth and Political Crisis in the Developing World." Working Paper for the Pew Global Stewardship Initiative. Washington, D.C., 1994.

Gore, Al. *Earth in the Balance: Ecology and the Human Spirit.* Boston: Houghton Mifflin, 1992.

Gourou, Pierre. *The Tropical World.* London: Longman, 1953.

Gramsci, Antonio. *Selections from the Prison Notebooks.* New York: International Publishers, 1971.

Greene, Graham. *The Heart of the Matter.* New York: Viking, 1948.

———. *The Comedians.* London: The Bodley Head, 1966.

———. *Journey Without Maps.* London: Heinemann, 1936.

Greenwald, John. "Black Gold Rush." *Time,* June 20, 1994.

Hafiz. *Teachings of Hafiz,* trans. Gertrude Lowthian Bell. London: The Sufi Trust and the Octagon Press, 1979.

Hall, Stephen S. *Mapping the Next Millennium.* New York: Random House, 1992.

Hansen, Carol Rae. *The New World Order: Rethinking America's Global Role.* Flagstaff, Ariz.: Arizona Honors Academy Press, 1992.

Harden, Blaine. *Africa: Dispatches from a Fragile Continent.* New York: W. W. Norton, 1990.

Harries, Owen. "Power and Civilization." *The National Interest* (Washington) Spring 1994.

Harrison, Lawrence E. *Who Prospers? How Cultural Values Shape Economic and Political Success.* New York: Basic Books, 1992.

Heinl, Robert Debs, and Heinl, Nancy Gordon. *Written in Blood: The Story of the Haitian People 1492–1971.* Boston: Houghton Mifflin, 1978.

Helms, Christine M. *Arabism and Islam: Stateless Nations and Nationless States.* Washington, D.C.: The Institute For Strategic Studies, July 1990.

Henze, Paul B. "Turks and Turkish." *The Wilson Quarterly* (Washington) Summer 1992.

Herzberger, Radhika. "Education and the Landscape at Rishi Valley." Unpublished paper.

Hiestand, Emily. *The Very Rich Hours: Travels in Orkney, Belize, the Everglades, and Greece.* Boston: Beacon Press, 1992.

Hogarth, D. G. Section on Turkey in *The Balkans: A History of Bulgaria, Serbia, Greece, Rumania, Turkey.* Oxford, England: Clarendon Press, 1915.

Holloway, John. "Aust[ralian] Diplomat's Cambodia Analysis." *Phnom Penh Post,* November 4–17, 1994.

Holmes, Peter. *Turkey: A Timeless Bridge.* London: The Stork Press, 1988.

Homer-Dixon, Thomas F. "On the Threshold: Environmental Changes as Causes of Acute Conflict." *International Security* (Harvard College and the Massachusetts Institute of Technology, Boston), Fall 1991.

———. "Environmental Scarcities and Violent Conflict: Evidence from Cases." *International Security* (Boston), Summer 1994.

———. "The Ingenuity Gap: Can Poor Countries Adapt to Resource Scarcity?" *Population and Development Review* (New York), September 1995.

Homer-Dixon, Thomas; Boutwell, Jeffrey; and Rathjens, George. "Environmental Scarcity and Violent Conflict." *Scientific American,* February 1993.

Hopkirk, Peter. *The Great Game: The Struggle for Empire in Central Asia.* New York: Kodansha America, Inc., 1990.

Horowitz, Michael. "Victims of Development." *Development Anthropology Network, Bulletin of the Institute for Development Anthropology,* Fall 1989.

———. "Victims Upstream and Down." *Journal of Refugee Studies,* 1991.

Hotham, David. *The Turks.* London: John Murray, 1972.

Huntington, Samuel P. "The Clash of Civilizations?" *Foreign Affairs,* Summer 1993. (See also reactions to this article and Huntington's response, in the September–October 1993 issue of *Foreign Affairs.*)

———. *Political Order in Changing Societies.* New Haven: Yale University Press, 1968.

Ibn Khaldun. *The Muqaddimah: An Introduction to History,* trans. Franz Rosenthal; ed. N. J. Dawood. Princeton, N.J.: Princeton University Press, 1967.

Igout, Michel. *Phnom Penh: Then & Now.* Bangkok: White Lotus Company, 1993.

Ispahani, Mahnaz Z. *Roads and Rivals: The Political Uses of Access in the Borderlands of Asia*. Ithaca, N.Y.: Cornell University Press, 1989.

Jahn, Janheinz. *Through African Doors*, trans. Oliver Coburn. London: Faber and Faber, 1960, 1962.

Jhabvala, Ruth Prawer. *Travelers*. New York: Harper & Row, 1973.

Kadare, Ismail. *The Concert*, written in Albanian and translated from the French of Jusuf Vrioni by Barbara Bray. New York: Morrow, 1994.

Kamarck, Andrew M. *The Tropics and Economic Development: A Provocative Inquiry into the Poverty of Nations*. Baltimore: Johns Hopkins University Press, 1976.

Kamil, Jill. *Coptic Egypt: History and Guide*. Cairo: The American University in Cairo Press, 1987.

Kaplan, Robert D. "The Coming Anarchy." *The Atlantic Monthly*, February 1994.

———. "Shatter Zone: Central Asia." *The Atlantic Monthly*, April 1992.

Kapuscinski, Ryszard. *Shah of Shahs*, trans. William R. Brand and Katarzyna Mroczkowska-Brand. New York: Harcourt Brace Jovanovich, 1982.

———. *The Soccer War*, trans. William R. Brand. New York: Knopf (1986, 1990), 1991.

Kazantzakis, Nikos. *Journeying: Travels in Italy, Egypt, Sinai, Jerusalem and Cyprus*, trans. Themi Vasils and Theodora Vasils. Boston: Little, Brown, 1975.

Keats, John. *Keats: Poems*. New York: Knopf, 1994.

Keay, John. *The Gilgit Game*. Oxford, England: Oxford University Press, 1979.

Keddie, Nikki R. (and Richard, Yann). *Roots of Revolution: An Interpretive History of Modern Iran*. New Haven: Yale University Press, 1981.

Keegan, John. *A History of Warfare*. New York: Knopf, 1993.

Kennedy, Paul. *Preparing for the Twenty-First Century*. New York: Random House, 1993.

Khalid, Mansour. *Nimeiri and the Revolution of Dis-May*. London: KPI Limited, 1985.

Kinross, Lord. *The Ottoman Centuries*. New York: Morrow, 1979 (1977 original copyright).

Kohli, Atul. *Democracy and Discontent: India's Growing Crisis of Governability*. New York: Cambridge University Press, 1990.

Kolars, John. "The Middle East's Growing Water Crisis." *Research & Exploration* (National Geographic Society, Washington, D.C.), November 1993.

Kortepeter, Carl Max. *The Ottoman Turks: Nomad Kingdom to World Empire.* Istanbul: The Isis Press, 1991.

Krishnamurti, Jiddu. *Krishnamurti at Rajghat.* Madras: Krishnamurti Foundation, 1993.

Krueger, John R. Letter to the author. March 25, 1992.

Kuhn, Thomas S. *The Structure of Scientific Revolutions.* Chicago: The University of Chicago Press, 1962.

Lamb, Christina. *Waiting for Allah: Pakistan's Struggle for Democracy.* London: Viking, 1991.

Lamb, David. *The Africans.* New York: Random House, 1983.

Law, Robin C. C. *The Oyo Empire c. 1600–1836.* Oxford, England: Oxford University Press, 1977.

Lemonick, Michael D. "How Man Began." *Time*, March 14, 1994.

Lewis, Bernard. *The Shaping of the Modern Middle East.* New York: Oxford University Press, 1994.

Lewis, I. M. *Islam in Tropical Africa.* London: Oxford University Press, 1966.

Linden, Eugene. "Megacities." *Time*, January 11, 1993.

London, Jack. *Martin Eden.* New York: Macmillan, 1909.

The London Observer. Article on page 24 that covered drug smuggling in Africa. September 26, 1993.

Lopez, Barry. *Arctic Dreams: Imagination and Desire in a Northern Landscape.* New York: Scribner's, 1986.

Lorch, Donatella. "In Nairobi, Car-Jacking Is a Bitter Fact of Life." *The New York Times*, December 19, 1993.

Lubin, Nancy. "Pollution and Politics in the USSR: Public Opinion and Pressure for Change." Chapter appearing in *The New World Order*, ed. Carol Rae Hansen. See entry under Hansen.

Macaulay, Rose. *The Towers of Trebizond.* New York: Farrar, Straus & Giroux, 1956.

MacDonald, Malcolm. *Angkor.* London: Jonathan Cape, 1958.

Maclean, Fitzroy. *Eastern Approaches.* Boston: Little, Brown, 1949.

————. *A Person from England: and other Travellers to Turkestan.* New York: Harper & Brothers, 1958.

Majd, M. J. "On the Relationship between Land Reform and Rural-Urban Migration in Iran, 1966–1976." *The Middle East Journal* (Washington, D.C.) Spring 1992.

Malcomson, Scott L. *Borderlands: Nation and Empire.* Boston: Faber and Faber, 1994.

Malraux, André. *Man's Fate*, trans. Haakon M. Chevalier. New York: Vintage (1934) 1990.

Malthus, Thomas Robert. *The Works of Robert Malthus*, ed. E. A. Wrigley and D. Souden. London: Pickering and Chatto, 1986.

Mann, Thomas. *The Magic Mountain*, trans. H. T. Lowe-Porter. New York: Vintage (1927) 1992.

Mathews, Jessica. "The Greater Threat to Democracy." *The Washington Post*, March 13, 1992.

————. "Nations and Nature: A New Look at Global Security." Twenty-First J. Robert Oppenheimer Memorial Lecture. Los Alamos, New Mexico, August 12, 1991.

————. "The Abortion Distraction: The true subject at Cairo is population—it's a lot more urgent than some think." *The Washington Post*, September 12, 1994.

————. "Immigration and the Press of the Poor." *The Washington Post*, November 21, 1994.

Mbembe, Achille, and Roitman, Janet. "Figures of the Subject in Times of Crisis." *Public Culture* (University of Chicago, Chicago), 1995.

McGreal, Ian P., ed. *Great Thinkers of the Western World.* New York: Harper-Collins, 1992.

McPhee, John. *Basin and Range.* New York: Farrar, Straus and Giroux, 1980.

Metz, Steven. *America in the Third World: Strategic Alternatives and Military Implications.* Carlisle Barracks, Pennsylvania: U.S. Army War College, 1994.

Michaels, Marguerite. "Retreat from Africa." *Foreign Affairs*, March 1993.

Minc, Alain. *Le Nouveau Moyen Age.* Paris: Gallimard, 1993.

Mische, Patricia M. "Ecological Security in an Interdependent World." *Breakthrough*, Summer/Fall 1989.

Moore, Barrington, Jr. *Social Origins of Dictatorship and Democracy: Lord and Peasant in the Making of the Modern World.* Boston: Beacon Press, 1966.

Moore, Gerald. *Seven African Writers.* London: Oxford University Press, 1962.

Moore, Jonathan. *Morality and Interdependence.* Hanover, N.H.: The Nelson A. Rockefeller Center for the Social Sciences at Dartmouth College, 1994.

Morgan, Vivien. "Kyrgyzia Town Rebuilds After Untold Massacres." *The Independent* (London), July 19, 1990.

Morier, James. *The Adventures of Hajji Baba of Ispahan*, Introduction by Richard Jennings. London: The Cresset Press, 1949.

Mortimer, Edward. *Faith and Power: The Politics of Islam.* London: Faber and Faber, 1982.

Munro, Ross H. "China's New Silk Road in Central Asia." *Foreign Policy Research Institute Wire* (Philadelphia), November 1, 1993.

———. "The Loser: India in the Nineties." *The National Interest* (Washington), Summer 1993.

———. "China's Waxing Spheres of Influence." *Orbis* (Philadelphia), Fall 1994.

Muscat, Robert J. *The Fifth Tiger: A Study of Thai Development Policy.* Armonk, N.Y.: M. E. Sharpe, 1994.

The Muslim (Islamabad). "Curbing Hooliganism." June 14, 1994.

Myers, Norman. "Environmental Security: The Case of South Asia." *International Environmental Affairs*, Spring 1989.

Naff, Thomas. "Water: 'That Peculiar Substance.'" *Research & Exploration* (National Geographic Society, Washington, D.C.) November 1993.

Nahaylo, B., and Swohboda, V. *Soviet Disunion: A History of the Nationalities Problem in the USSR.* London: Hamish Hamilton, 1990.

Naipaul, V. S. *Among the Believers: An Islamic Journey.* London: Andre Deutsch, 1981.

———. *An Area of Darkness.* London: Andre Deutsch, 1964.

———. *India: A Wounded Civilization.* New York: Random House, 1976.

Nariddh, Moeun Chhean. "Aids Threat to Two Million." *Phnom Penh Post*, October 21–November 3, 1994.

Newton, Alex. *West Africa: A Travel Survival Kit.* Berkeley: Lonely Planet Publications, 1992.

O'Donnell, Terence. *Garden of the Brave in War: Recollections of Iran*. Chicago: The University of Chicago Press, 1980.

Okie, Susan. "AIDS Devouring Africa Even as Awareness Grows." *The Washington Post*, August 18, 1994.

Okri, Ben. *An African Elegy: Poems*. London: Jonathan Cape, 1992.

Olcott, Martha Brill. "Central Asia's Catapult to Independence." *Foreign Affairs*, Summer 1992.

Oliver, Roland. *The African Experience*. New York: HarperCollins, 1991.

O'Neill, Thomas. "The Mekong." *National Geographic*, February 1993.

Ophuls, William. *Ecology and the Politics of Scarcity: A Prologue to a Political Theory of the Steady State*. San Francisco: Freeman, 1977.

Otabil, Mensa. *Beyond the Rivers of Ethiopia: A Biblical Revelation on God's Purpose for the Black Race*. Accra, Ghana: Altar International, 1992.

Ouologuem, Yambo. *Bound to Violence*, trans. Ralph Manheim. London: Secker & Warburg, 1971.

Ozturk, Yasar Nuri. *The Eye of the Heart: An Introduction to Sufism and the Tariqats of Anatolia and the Balkans*. Istanbul: Redhouse Press, 1988.

Parker, Ian. "Auden's Heir." *The New Yorker*, July 25, 1994.

Pearce, Fred. "Africa at a Watershed." *New Scientist* (London), March 23, 1991.

Pfaltzgraff, Robert L., Jr., and Shultz, Richard H., Jr. *Ethnic Conflict and Regional Instability*. Leavenworth, Kans.: U.S. Army War College, 1994.

Phantumvanit, Dhira, and Liengcharernsit, Winai. *Coming to Terms with Bangkok's Environmental Problems. Environment and Urbanization*. Reprinted by Thailand Development Research Institute Foundation, Bangkok, 1989 and 1994.

Phantumvanit, Dhira, and Panayotou, Theodore. *Industrialization and Environmental Quality: Paying the Price*. Bangkok: Thailand Development Research Institute, 1990.

Phantumvanit, Dhira, and Sathirathai, Khunying Suthawan. "Thailand: Degradation and Development in a Resource-Rich Land." *Environment*. Washington, D.C.: Heldref Publications, 1988.

Pinchin, Jane Lagoudis. *Alexandria Still: Forster, Durrell, and Cavafy*. Princeton, N.J.: Princeton University Press, 1977.

Pinstrup-Andersen, Per. "Prospects for Meeting Future Food Demands." International Food Policy Research Institute, March 1993.

Pipes, Daniel. *Greater Syria: The History of an Ambition*. New York: Oxford University Press, 1990.

"Editorial comment: Politics in maps, maps in politics: A tribute to Brian Harley." *Political Geography*, March 1992.

Polo, Marco. *The Travels of Marco Polo*. New York: Library Publications, no date.

Population Reference Bureau. *World Population Data Sheet*. Washington, D.C., 1992.

Pouaree, Suvicha. "21 Years Later [Thai] Democracy Has Barely Developed." *Bangkok Post*, October 16, 1994.

Prussin, Labelle. *Hatumere: Islamic Design in West Africa*. Berkeley: University of California Press, 1986.

Ptolemy, Claudius. *The Geography*, trans. and ed. Edward Luther Stevenson. New York: Dover, 1991.

Rangaswami, S., and Sridhar, S. *Birds of Rishi Valley: And Renewal of Their Habitat*. Bangalore, India: Rishi Valley Education Centre, 1993.

Rashid, Ahmed. *The Resurgence of Central Asia*. Atlantic Highlands, N.J.: Zed Books, 1994.

———. "On Again, Off Again: Islamabad grapples with worsening power shortages." *Far Eastern Economic Review*, May 12, 1994.

Raven, Peter H.; Berg, Linda R.; and Johnson, George B. *Environment*. Orlando, Fla.: Saunders College Publishing and Harcourt Brace & Company, 1993.

Rawson, Philip. *The Art of Southeast Asia*. London: Thames and Hudson, 1967.

Reclus, Élisée. *La terre et les hommes*. Paris: 1877.

Reid, Walter V., and Miller, Kenton R. "Keeping Options Alive: The Scientific Basis for Conserving Biodiversity." World Resources Institute, Washington, D.C., 1989.

Rensberger, Boyce. "Contraception and Smaller Families." *The Washington Post*, September 4, 1994.

Rice, Edward. *Captain Sir Richard Francis Burton*. New York: Scribner's, 1990.

Richburg, Keith B. "Continental Divide." *The Washington Post Magazine*, March 26, 1995.

Riley, Mark T. Essay on Thomas Robert Malthus, in *Great Thinkers of the Western World*. New York: HarperCollins, 1992.

Ritter, Karl. *Allgemeine Erdkunde* ("Comparative Geography"). Edinburgh: W. Blackwood, 1817.

Roosevelt, Archie. *For Lust of Knowing: Memoirs of an Intelligence Officer.* Boston: Little, Brown, 1988.

Rudolph, Susanne Hoeber, and Rudolph, Lloyd I. "Modern Hate." *The New Republic*, March 22, 1993.

Rumer, Boris Z. "The Gathering Storm in Central Asia." *Orbis* (Philadelphia), Winter 1993.

Sai, Fred T. "The Population Factor in Africa's Development Dilemma." *Science*, November 16, 1984.

Salimanov, Emile, and Chenciner, Robert. *Architecture of Baku: Fabled Capital of the Caspian.* London: UNESCO and the Royal Asiatic Society, 1985.

Samudavanija, Chai-Anan. "Bypassing the State in Asia." *New Perspectives Quarterly* (Los Angeles), Winter 1995.

Schuyler, Eugene. *Turkistan: Notes of a Journey in Russian Turkistan, Khokand, Bukhara, and Kuldja.* New York: Scribner's, 1885.

Seale, Patrick. *The Struggle for Syria.* Oxford: Oxford University Press, 1965.

Sen, Amartya. "The Threats to Secular India." *The New York Review of Books*, April 8, 1993.

———. "Population: Delusion and Reality." *The New York Review of Books*, September 22, 1994.

Serwer, Andrew E. "The End of the World is Nigh—Or Is It?" *Fortune*, May 2, 1994.

Sesser, Stan. *The Lands of Charm and Cruelty: Travels in Southeast Asia.* New York: Knopf, 1993.

Seth, Vikram. *From Heaven Lake: Travels Through Sinkiang and Tibet.* London: Chatto & Windus, 1983.

Settle, Mary Lee. *Turkish Reflections: A Biography of a Place.* New York: Touchstone, 1991.

Shaban, Hussein, and Johnston, Robert. *The Fall of Theocracy in Iran.* Hamilton, Ontario: McMaster University, 1994.

Shawcross, William. *Sideshow: Kissinger, Nixon and the Destruction of Cambodia.* New York: Simon and Schuster, 1979.

———. *The Quality of Mercy: Cambodia, Holocaust and Modern Conscience.* London: Andre Deutsch, 1984.

Shipman, Pat. *The Evolution of Racism.* New York: Simon and Schuster, 1994.

Shirley, Edward G. "Not Fanatics, and Not Friends." *The Atlantic Monthly,* December 1993.

Shlapentokh, Vladimir. "The American Vision of the World: The Tendency to Find Nice Things." *The American Association for the Advancement of Slavic Studies Newsletter* (Stanford, Calif.), May 1993.

Silver, Cheryl Simon, with DeFries, Ruth S. *One Earth One Future.* Washington, D.C.: National Academy of Sciences Press, 1990.

Simon, Julian. *The Ultimate Resource.* Princeton, N.J.: Princeton University Press, 1981.

Sloane, Wendy. "Uzbekistan Cracks Down on Human Rights Activists." *The Christian Science Monitor,* May 25, 1994.

Smil, Vaclav. *China's Environmental Crisis: An Inquiry into the Limits of National Development.* Armonk, N.Y.: M. E. Sharpe, Inc., 1993.

Smith, Anthony D. *National Identity.* Reno, Nev.: University of Nevada Press, 1991.

Sowell, Thomas. "Middleman Minorities." *The American Enterprise* (Washington, D.C.), May/June, 1993. (Included in his book *Race and Culture: A World View.* New York: Basic Books, 1994.)

Specter, Michael. Siberia: "5 Million Miles of Frozen Dreams." *The New York Times,* August 21, 1994.

Spence, Jonathan. "The Chinese Miracle?" *The New York Review of Books,* September 23, 1993.

Stark, Freya. *Alexander's Path.* London: John Murray, 1958.

Starr, Joyce R. "Water Wars." *Foreign Policy,* Spring 1991.

Stein, Susan R. *The Worlds of Thomas Jefferson at Monticello.* New York: Harry N. Abrams/Thomas Jefferson Memorial Foundation, 1993.

Sterne, Laurence. *A Sentimental Journey: Through France and Italy.* New York: Three Sirens Press (Williams, Belasco & Meyers), (1768) 1930.

Stevens, William K. "Feeding a Booming Population Without Destroying the Planet." *The New York Times,* April 5, 1994.

Strohmeyer, Virgil B. Letter to the author about Turkic Uighurs in China, 1992.

St Vincent, David. *Iran: a Travel Survival Kit.* Berkeley: Lonely Planet Publications, 1992.

Sulzberger, C. L. *A Long Row of Candles: Memoirs and Diaries, 1934–1954.* New York: Macmillan, 1969.

Sun, Lena H. "China's Villagers Vent Hatred at Leaders They Say Are Corrupt." *The Washington Post*, April 28, 1994.

Swaggart, Jimmy. *The Christian and Demon Spirits.* 1980.

Tekin, Latife. *Berji Kristin: Tales from the Garbage Hills*, trans. Ruth Christie and Saliha Paker. New York: Marion Boyars Publishers, 1993.

Toops, Stanley. "Recent Uygur Leaders in Xinjiang." *Central Asian Survey* (London), 1992.

Tostevin, Matthew. "Sinking to the Depths: Sierra Leone." *Focus on Africa* (London), July–September, 1993.

Tucker, Robert C., ed. *The Marx-Engels Reader.* New York: W. W. Norton, 1972.

Turkmen, Erkan. *The Essence of Rumi's Masnevi.* Konya, Turkey: Misket Ltd., 1992.

Ungar, Sanford J. *Africa: The People and Politics of an Emerging Continent.* New York: Simon and Schuster, 1978.

United Nations Development Programme. *Human Development Report, 1994.* Delhi: Oxford University Press, 1994.

———. *Balanced Development: An Approach to Social Action in Pakistan.* Islamabad, Pakistan, 1992.

United Nations Secretariat. Executive Summary. "The Carter Camp Massacre (near Harbel, Liberia)." Panel Members: S. Amos Wako, Robert Gersony, Mahmoud Kassem. New York, 1993.

Van Creveld, Martin. *The Transformation of War.* New York: Free Press, 1991.

Varma, Kewal. "Jobs Grow, But Problem Ones." *Business Standard* (Calcutta), October 14, 1994.

Vlahos, Michael. "The Next Competition." Unpublished essay, 1993.

Vesilind, Priit J. "The Middle East's Water: Critical Resource." *National Geographic*, May 1993.

Virk, Mobarik. "Work starts at Simly dam to improve water supply to capital." *The Muslim* (Islamabad), June 12, 1994.

Waldman, Peter. "As Economy of Iran Worsens, Government Reverts to Hard Line." *The Wall Street Journal*, June 28, 1994.

Walsh, James. "China: The World's Next. . . . Superpower." *Time*, May 10, 1993.

Waterbury, John. *Hydropolitics of the Nile Valley*. Syracuse, N.Y.: Syracuse University Press, 1979.

Wayne, Scott. *Egypt & the Sudan: A Travel Survival Kit*. Berkeley: Lonely Planet Publications, 1990.

West, Richard. *Back to Africa*.

Whitley, Andrew. "Minorities and the Stateless in Persian Gulf Politics." *Survival*, Winter 1993.

Whittell, Giles. *Central Asia: The Practical Handbook*. Old Saybrook, Conn.: The Globe Pequot Press, 1993.

Wirth, Timothy E. "Sustainable Development: A Progress Report." Address Before the National Press Club. Washington, D.C., July 12, 1994.

Wittfogel, Karl A. *Oriental Despotism: A Comparative Study of Total Power*. New Haven: Yale University Press, 1964.

The World Factbook 1993. Washington, D.C.: Central Intelligence Agency, 1993.

World Resources Institute. *World Resources 1992–93: A Guide to the Global Environment*. New York: Oxford University Press, 1992.

Wurm, Stefan. *Turkic Peoples of the USSR*. Oxford: St. Anthony's College, Oxford University, 1954.

Xenophon. *The Persian Expedition*, trans. Rex Warner. Middlesex, England: Penguin Books, 1949.

Xiao Li. "Toilet Leaks Send Cities Scrambling for Water." *China Daily* (Beijing), June 7, 1994.

Zelichenko, Alexander. "Tien Shan Columbia." *Kyrgyzstan Chronicle*, May 31, 1994.

INDEX